Rethinking History and Myth

Rethinking History and Myth

Indigenous South American
Perspectives on the Past

Edited by Jonathan D. Hill

University of Illinois Press
Urbana and Chicago

© 1988 by the Board of Trustees of the University of Illinois
Manufactured in the United States of America
1   2   3   4   5   C   P   5   4   3   2   1

This book is printed on acid-free paper.

Rethinking history and myth : indigenous South American perspectives
  on the past/edited by Jonathan D. Hill.
        p. cm.
     Bibliography: p.
     Includes index.
     ISBN 0-252-01543-6 (cloth: alk. paper). ISBN 0-252-06028-8 (paper: alk.
paper)
        1. Indians of South America—Religion and mythology—Congresses.
2. Indians of South America—History—Congresses.   I. Hill,
Jonathan David, 1954– .   II. American Anthropological Association.
Meeting. (83rd : 1984 : Denver, Colo.)
F2230.1.R3R47   1988
980'.004'98—dc19   88-4408
                                                              CIP

Contents

Introduction

Myth and History

Jonathan D. Hill

This volume aims at rethinking the analytic distinction between myth and history by exploring indigenous South American narrative, ritual, and oratory as ways of formulating and interpreting the history of Indian-white contact. We hope to transcend the artificial separation of scholars into highland and lowland specialists by giving roughly equal coverage to indigenous societies of the Andes, Amazonia, and the transitional upland forest (*montaña*) areas, thus cultivating an appreciation for the substantial cultural and historical diversity of indigenous South American peoples not only within the Amazonian and Andean "super-regions" but across them as well.[1]

Rethinking History and Myth appears at a time when even Claude Lévi-Strauss, the acknowledged founder of the structural theory of myth (e.g., 1955, 1963a, 1964, 1966a, 1966b, 1968, 1971), has spoken in highly positive terms of the recent rapprochement between anthropologists and historians (see Bucher 1985). The coming together of these two disciplines has been imminent for several years, especially among scholars working in Africa (Comaroff 1985; Miller 1976, 1980; Feely-Harnik 1978), Afro-America (Bastide 1960; Price 1983a, 1983b), Oceania (Rosaldo 1980; Sahlins 1981; Harwood 1976), the circum-Mediterranean (Herzfeld 1982, 1985), and South Asia (Appadurai 1981). In addition, the theoretical groundwork for a rapprochement of anthropologists and historians has been cleared in a special volume of the *Journal of Interdisciplinary History* (1981). The indigenous societies of South America, some of which formed the main focus of Lévi-Strauss's earlier works on structural theory of myth (e.g., 1955, 1964, 1966a), are only now beginning to be heard from in this growing dialogue between historians and anthropologists. This volume on Amazonian and Andean social histories is the first major attempt to bring together the results of a generation of anthropologists who have all done fieldwork in indigenous South American societies and who all went to the field with both historical and ethnological research interests.

The anthropological concept of history that has begun to emerge in the 1980s is taking shape through a weaving together of poststructuralist approaches to symbolic action (T. Turner 1969, 1977; R. Wagner 1972, 1975) and political-economic approaches to historical process (Schneider 1978; Wallerstein 1976; Wolf 1982). Among anthropologists, the renewal of interest in history is concerned with studying how specific cultural and linguistic traditions shape social consciousness in any given set of political-economic conditions. It is not a return to the excessively "capitalist" worldview of world systems theory (Frank 1967) and an exclusive focus on the political-economic structures of domination the expanding market economies of the West have thrust upon indigenous societies of South America and other regions. As Ortner (1984:143) has warned, political-economic theory in 1970s' anthropology largely ignores the importance of local and regional histories, as analysts have built their interpretations almost entirely from the vantage point of "the ship" of Western social science rather than "on the shore" of diverse social "others."

The contributors to this volume would go a step beyond Ortner's critique of political-economic approaches to history by asserting that the exaggerated importance some anthropological historians have attributed to extralocal structural domination has tended to preempt an understanding of the sociohistorical agency of the subjects of anthropological research. Whether intentional or not, the effect of narrow political-economic approaches in anthropological theory is that of reproducing rather than critiquing the cultural and political hegemony of Western industrialized societies.

The view of history taken here is consistent with the political economists' insistence on examining each particular social history in the context of national and global situations of contact (Cardoso de Oliveira 1974). At the same time, all the essays are equally as concerned with exploring indigenous ways of interpreting history as they are with contextualizing indigenous historical interpretations within situations of contact. Rethinking History and Myth takes us back to the problem of the relationship between structure and agency (Giddens 1979) and questions about the construction, reproduction, and transformation of the shared experiential and interpretive frameworks that shape the historical consciousness of individuals and groups of individuals in changing objective conditions (Cohn 1981). In sum, history is not reducible to the "what really happened" of past events nor to global situations of contact but always includes the totality of processes whereby individuals experience, interpret, and create changes within social orders and both individuals and groups change over time as they actively participate in changing objective conditions.

This volume thus challenges anthropologists, historians, and scholars in related disciplines to part with a number of comforting myths that have prevented the emergence of a truly critical, hermeneutic consciousness of social history. The first myth to fall by the wayside is that of objectivity in social and/or historical research as a product of "bracketing out" the individual researcher, a sort of "nonparticipatory," detached observation of cultural or historical "others" in which the researcher acts as a mirror reflecting spatially and temporally remote events (Fabian 1983; Karp and Kendall 1981). The purpose of deconstructing this theoretical myth of the observer-observed dichotomy is not to dissolve sociohistorical research into a purely subjective, or even intersubjective, phenomenon but to assert the need for a critical, reflexive awareness of social and historical research as a personally mediated and historically situated activity to produce knowledge.

Another theoretical myth that comes unraveled in rethinking history and myth is the view that historical interpretations based upon written documents are necessarily more "objective" (i.e., reliable and accurate) than those embodied in oral narratives or nonverbal genres of activity. The indigenous South American formulations of history explored in this volume demonstrate that historical "accuracy" is not separable from the specific sociocultural and linguistic traditions that both limit the range of acceptable renderings of historical processes and serve as the resources in terms of which such interpretations are created (Rosaldo 1980). Although oral and nonverbal formulations cannot be literally read as direct accounts of historical processes, they can show how indigenous societies have experienced history and the ongoing means by which they struggle to make sense out of complex, contradictory historical processes. Combining these indigenous formulations with reconstructions of the global political-economic structures of contact and colonization, the researcher is then able to identify the criteria of historical accuracy and the range of acceptable renderings of the past in terms of the local or regional understandings of what constitutes historical process and its interpretation (Price 1983a, 1983b).

The Myth of "Cold" Societies

This collection of essays contributes to the growing number of historical and anthropological works (e.g., Rosaldo 1980; Fabian 1981) that have criticized Lévi-Strauss's (1966b:234) distinction between "cold," mythic societies that resist historical changes and the "hot" societies that thrive upon irreversible, cumulative changes. Like the history and myth issue in general, the theoretical myth of "cold" societies has been most directly treated by scholars working in Africa, the Mediterranean, Oceania, and Afro-America. Here we add fresh support to the global shadow of doubt that recent research has cast upon the theoretical myth that there are, or were, such things as "cold" societies without history or "hot" ones that have "progressed" beyond myth. By showing how native South Americans in a number of widely different sociocultural traditions have used narrative and nonverbal genres of activity in the interpretation of historical processes, the contributors to *Rethinking History and Myth* empirically demonstrate that the Lévi-Straussian notion of "cold" society does not fare at all well in the Amazonian societies (which were supposed to have most clearly illustrated the concept) or in Andean societies.

For the Waurá, an Arawak-speaking society of the Upper Xingu region in Brazil, myths do not form a closed, symbolic system in opposition to historical narratives (see Ireland, this volume). Instead, the Waurá classify both mythic and historical narratives as complementary subgenres of a single narrative genre, called *aunaki*, or collectively owned stories. Mythic narratives (*aunaki yaji*, or "real story") are generally distinguished from stories about "mere facts" (*kamalajita*), or events witnessed by human beings at some firmly fixed point in the past. Most interesting is how the Waurá override this distinction in classifying a narrative about the extinction of the Kustenau during a measles epidemic around the turn of the century. Even though the narrative refers to events that took place at a fixed point in the past, it is considered a myth, or "true story." Waurá narratives doubly refute the Lévi-Straussian notion of "cold" society by showing that myth is only one of several narrative genres that can be used for understanding historical processes and that the genre of myths, or "true stories," can itself be creatively expanded to formulate new collective understandings of historical processes.

In their analysis of narrative and ritual among the Aymara pastoralists of K'ulta, Dillon and Abercrombie show how myth becomes a part of history by embodying a reflexive awareness of the principal metaphors of social reproduction. Through a total synthesis of Andean solar and sky deities with Christian deities and saints, the Aymara myth of origin has become a vehicle for understanding the hegemonic relationship between Christian and indigenous traditions in terms of specifically Andean metaphors for hierarchical control. Thus, far from being a "cold" structure of symbolic relations, closed and opposed to historical processes, Aymara myth draws upon a richly polysemous, metaphoric imagery that comments upon historical processes through references to such varied domains of social experience as modes of economic production and exchange, food processing and cooking, the ecology of local flora and fauna, and relations between the living and the dead. In addition to commenting upon history through integrating images of social hierarchy into a total artistic structure, the Aymara myth of origin forms part of history through the parallel structuring of moiety-level rituals, which also model the hierarchical relations between the colonizing, Christian state and indigenous society.

What we find when we explore Amazonian and Andean formulations of the past is not "cold," ahistorical structure but a range of more-to-less dynamic ways of interpreting historical processes of change. Indigenous peoples in both areas are equally capable of creating dynamic interpretations that delineate historical processes of change. Within indigenous South American societies, there is great variation in levels and types of historical consciousness, just as there is in the modern urban industrial societies of the West or any other ethnographic area. A truly open dialogue between the "West and the Rest" (Sahlins 1976) can only arise when the multiplicity of levels and types of historical consciousness within and between non-Western societies is given serious consideration on its own terms. The more we read into the essays in this volume, the more apparent it becomes that the structuralist concept of "cold," mythic societies is a historically and culturally specific construct of our own society, one that neither comprehends nor does justice to the colorings of the past embodied in indigenous South American oral narrative, ritual practice, and oratory.

Myth and History as Modes of Social Consciousness

The structuralist approach to myth and history was based upon an uncritical distinction between myth as atemporal order and history as chronological sequence of events. Furthermore, the disengagement of mythic "structure" from historical "event" in structuralist theory resulted in a view of myth as fiction as opposed to history as fact, a dichotomy that disappears as soon as it is recognized that neither myth nor history is reducible to a text, thing, fact, or event. Both history and myth are modes of social consciousness through which people construct shared interpretive frameworks. Like myth, the socially constructed concept of history "still retains that combination of formal arbitrariness and ideological motivation that characterizes the entire phenomenon of social semiosis" (Herzfeld 1985:206).[2] The problem of distinguishing between myth and history is thus not that of classifying the order of things at the phenomenal level but of rethinking the relationship between structure and agency from a point of view that considers agency as the social creation of meaning. Structure, in this sense, is not a timeless, abstract entity but a flexible, negotiated, concrete set of relations that is embodied in the social activity of constructing shared understandings and that serves as a program for orienting social action. Agency is the social process of creating, re-creating, and altering collectively shared interpretive frameworks and of participating in other social activities informed by such frameworks (Giddens 1979; Bourdieu 1977).

Although not phenomenally separable, myth and history can be analytically distinguished as modes of social consciousness according to the different weightings each gives to the relations between structure and agency. Mythic consciousness gives priority to structure and over-riding, transformational principles that can crosscut, contradict, and even negate the sets of relations established through social classifications (T. Turner 1977). In doing so, mythic consciousness and its embodiment in genres of narrative and non-narrative activity ensure that relations of contrast and difference of major social importance will not be forgotten or become mere objects that can be subjected to instrumental manipulation. If human actors are perceived as having any power to change their conditions, it is because they possess some form of controlled access to the hierarchical structuring of the mythic power of liminal, neither-here-nor-there beings. When focused upon temporal relations, mythic consciousness does not establish a timeless order but a temporal one in which the past differs from the present. The essays in this volume contain numerous examples to illustrate how mythic consciousness serves to construct and reproduce the difference between humans living in the present and the powerful beings of past times: the Kayapó jaguar-people (see Turner), the Southern Andean ancestor-people and solar deity (see Rasnake, and Dillon and Abercrombie), the Wakuénai social animals and primordial human beings (see Hill and Wright), the Arapaço anaconda-grandfather (see Chernela), the Canelos Quichua *supai* (see Reeve), the Waurá Atujuá spirits (see Ireland), and the Central Andean lightning-ancestors (see Silverblatt).

Historical consciousness gives greater weighting to agency and social action in the present which is informed by knowledge of past times that are qualitatively the same as the present. Like the present, the historical past is seen as inhabited by fully human, cultural beings who, although perhaps living in different conditions from those of the present time, had essentially the same powers for making changes as do people living in the present. Historical consciousness thus implies a reflexive awareness on the part of social actors of their abilities to make situational and more lasting adjustments to social orderings that are "temporary, incomplete, and contain elements of inconsistency, ambiguity, discontinuity, contradiction, paradox, and conflict" (Moore 1976:232). Historical consciousness includes a sense of the indeterminate and processual nature of one's own social order and an ability to understand that ordering as it is situated in larger, more encompassing spatiotemporal orders that include others who are socially different.

Historical consciousness is a selective rather than an objective rendering of "facts." The mere choice of which events, persons, and details to include is already an interpretive activity. The historical consciousness of indigenous South American societies discussed in the essays that follow often reveals itself as radically selective. History is understood in relation to a few "peaks," or critical periods of rapid change, rather than a smoothly flowing progression. In Amazonian societies, the periods most frequently selected are the rubber boom (see Chernela, Hill and Wright, Reeve, and Roe) and times of abrupt, violent change forced upon indigenous peoples from outside and above (e.g., the epidemics of exogenous diseases that have devasted the Waurá and other lowlands societies; see Ireland and Turner). In this sense, Amazonian historical consciousness resembles that found in other small-scale societies that have struggled through narrow historical passages and violent social changes (Rosaldo 1980; Price 1983a; Taussig 1980a). The rubber boom, which lasted from approximately 1860 to 1920 in lowland South America, most seriously affected riverine societies in accessible headwater regions (Cardoso de Oliveira 1974; Murphy 1960; Murphy and Murphy 1974) rather than interfluvial hunting societies, such as the Gê-speaking societies of Central Brazil, or fishing and gardening societies in remote headwaters inaccessible to river travel, such as the Upper Xingu region. This empirical, historical difference is important for understanding why the historical situations of contact are so different among the Kayapó and Waurá (see Turner and Ireland) from the other Amazonian societies discussed in this volume. In Andean societies, the Spanish conquest is often singled out as a period of greatest importance in indigenous oral histories (see Dillon and Abercrombie, and Rasnake).

The distinction between mythic and historical modes of social consciousness is a relative contrast between complementary ways of interpreting social processes. Mythic consciousness can become the basis for a reflexive understanding of temporal processes within a social order and the principal metaphors through which society reproduces itself:

the life cycle of individuals, the developmental cycle of domestic groups, and the core relations that must somehow be re-created in each generation for society to retain a sense of identity and autonomy. Often, the collective reflexivity of mythic consciousness is either directly or implicitly evoked as a parallel frame of reference in narrative expressions of historical consciousness.

The complementarity of mythic and historical modes of social consciousness is very clearly illustrated in the way Canelos Quichua narrators weave back and forth between *callari uras,* or "beginning times," and *unai,* or "mythic time-space" (see Reeve). Shared origin in *unai* is a defining attribute of fully human (*runapura*) social identity and distinguishes the *runapura* from other *runa* who have become *runa*-like through intermarriage and adoption of *runa* language and culture. *Unai* is temporally prior to the cultural separateness of human beings and animals, and it is spatially outside the realm of human social action or control. In contrast to narratives about mythic time-space, narratives set in *callari uras* are about human, social processes of trade, intermarriage, and warfare that brought about a specifically *runa* identity in relation to non-*runa* indigenous peoples and Europeans. In their accounts of these historical processes, narrators evoke a parallel narrative frame set in mythic time-space, shifting back and forth between historical consciousness of social otherness and mythic consciousness of spatiotemporal heterogeneity.[3]

Narrative traditions of the Arawakan Wakuénai of Venezuela and Brazil illustrate how a mythic mode of consciousness can be implicitly evoked in accounts about historical processes (see Hill and Wright). Wakuénai narratives about Venancio Camico, the leader of a nineteenth-century millenarian movement, portray him as a great shaman whose powers resembled those of the creator-transformer (Iñápirríkuli) of the undifferentiated time-space of mythic origins and also those of the monstrous, world-transforming, primordial human beings (Kuwái and Amáru). The narratives refer equally to the historical processes through which the Wakuénai and other indigenous peoples of the upper Río Negro basin struggled to free themselves from political and economic domination by non-native peoples during the rubber boom and to the mythic processes through which social and natural worlds came into being. Again, mythic and historical modes of consciousness complement, rather than oppose, one another.

Among the Shipibo-Conibo of the Ucayali basin in Peru, the overlapping, complementary interrelations between mythic and historical modes of consciousness are given clear expression in the genre of "Inca tales" (see Roe). These stories are set in an intermediate time-space between primordial, mythic origins and the recent past, which is described in personal reminiscence stories. The Inca tales refer to historical processes in the period immediately prior to white contact and show a concern for understanding the social inequalities both within the Inca state and between the Inca and the Shipibo-Conibo. Through an implicit parallel between polarized "Good" and "Bad" Incas with the mythic figures of Sun and Moon, respectively, and by means of such explicit symbolism as the world-transforming flood, the Inca tales articulate mythic and historical pasts into a dynamic interpretive framework that becomes both a means of understanding the history of white-Indian contact and, in revitalization movements, a mode of political consciousness enabling collective indigenous action against external domination by whites.

Mythic-Historical Consciousness

Once it is recognized that historical and mythic consciousness can simultaneously develop within a single society or even within a single speech (Turner and Ramos), narrative cycle (Chernela, Rasnake, and Hill and Wright), narrative genre (Ireland and Reeve), or ritual act (Dillon and Abercrombie, and Silverblatt), it becomes possible to examine the interrelations between the two: how these types of social consciousness are differentiated into genres of narrative and non-narrative activity and how they are articulated into mythic-historical genres wherein the two types of consciousness are merged. Genre differences are not a reflection of an abstract, conceptual structure but of social action situated in the time and space of local group organization, relations between indigenous societies, and situations of contact with non-native, colonizing societies (see Turner). Through careful study of the full range of genres that give expression to mythic and historical (or mythic-historical) consciousness, researchers can begin to study how indigenous peoples have constructed shared interpretive frameworks for understanding the social situations of contact and the historical process of coping with a dominant, external society. Genre analysis of this sort can show how indigenous formulations of the past are multivocal, iconic embodiments of social-historical processes and, as such, can serve as a resource for social action in the present. Also, by casting their nets widely to study the full range of genres in a society, researchers may become aware of expressions of historical consciousness that would not even have been perceived using traditional anthropological methods of studying and recording myths and other stories (Rosaldo 1980; Turner and Ramos, this volume).

The essays in *Rethinking History and Myth* discuss a number of genres in which mythic and historical modes of consciousness are brought together. These mythic histories are the integrating genres through which indigenous South American peoples coordinate the relations between, on the one hand, mythic consciousness focused on liminality and reflexive reproduction through temporal processes unfolding primarily within social orders and, on the other hand, historical consciousness of social otherness and changing relations with other societies. South American mythic histories attempt to reconcile a view of "what really happened" with an understanding of "what ought to have happened." The mythic consciousness that organizes the past acts as a vehicle for expressing interpretations of historical process. Mythic-historical consciousness thus becomes the locus for generating various symbolic tropes of historical consciousness and often uses multivocal, linking metaphors to imbue historical consciousness with meanings from a number of different domains of social experience. Mythic histories are about human past times in which events and persons are integrated into the interpretive framework of the coming-into-being of social formations and the liminal, powerful beings of mythic consciousness.

Expressions of mythic-historical consciousness are a key to understanding indigenous South American modes of interpreting history, since they are not "layered onto" indigenous genres of expressing historical and mythic consciousness from above as a completely new set of genres. Instead, formulations of historical process unfold through mythic consciousness as transformations of indigenous genres of narrative and non-narrative activity. These transformations may be based on metaphor or on any of the other master tropes, including metonymy, synecdoche, and irony (Sapir and Crocker 1977). Symbolic transformations generally develop along three dimensions of social process: the creation of novel semantic categories; the organization of thought so as to color an approach to subjects and shape social action; and the struggle to cope with actual situations (Colby, Fernandez, and Kronenfeld 1981; Sapir and Crocker 1977). The South American mythic histories discussed in the essays that follow provide many illustrations of the three-dimensional social use of metaphor.

Chernela's analysis of Arapaço narratives, for example, shows how a novel semantic category encompassing non-native technology of whites is generated from the indigenous metaphor of sexual intercourse between an anaconda-ancestor and a human woman and their socially charged relation to the betrayed husband, who kills the anaconda with a blowgun. In the second part of the narrative cycle, the snake-human child of this illicit sexual union is shot and blinded in one eye by a bullet fired from a white man's rifle. Thus, the indigenous relation "wronged husband kills wife's lover with blowgun/dart" is transformed into the novel relation "anonymous white man shoots snake-child with rifle/bullet." Part three of the narrative cycle continues the creation of a novel semantic category that makes sense out of the whiteman's more powerful technology by replacing the anaconda, considered the mythic ancestor of the Arapaço and other Eastern Tukano-speaking societies, with a twentieth-century technological contraption of the whiteman, a submarine laden with steel tools and other trade goods. This substitution of submarines for anacondas in Arapaço narrative illustrates a complex interpretive process of transforming indigenous metaphors into metonymy, a trope that depends upon contiguity and the conveyance of a wholeness within which two terms are related as members of a single category (Sapir and Crocker 1977:21).[4] Both anacondas and submarines share in the domain of "large, elongated, mobile, underwater creatures," the one as an ancestral snake-canoe that brought human society into being and the other as a container that brought the powerful technology of the whiteman under indigenous control.

In addition to showing how the Arapaço have successfully created a novel semantic category from an indigenous social metaphor, Chernela's analysis of the narrative cycle demonstrates that the linkage of anaconda-ancestor to snake-child to anaconda-submarine serves as a symbolic strategy for coping with historical and political-economic realities that have very nearly finished off the Arapaço as an autonomous society. The key to understanding the narrative cycle as a genre of mythic history is to be found in Chernela's method of contextualizing the spatial movements of the snake-child downstream in the second part of the story and the complementary, reverse movement of the anaconda-submarine upstream in the third part. The movement downstream reproduces, or iconically embodies, the historical relocation of the Arapaço and other native peoples of the Northwest Amazon region (see Wright 1981; Hill and Wright, this volume) under the Brazilian policy of *descimentos* ("descents") during the early nineteenth century. The second part of the Arapaço narrative cycle, as Chernela points out, is transitional between a mythic understanding of the indigenous society as an autonomous order and a historical consciousness of the restoration of partial autonomy, or a "righting of history." The transitional imagery explores the technological power of the whiteman (i.e., rifles and bullets) as the basis of a brutal form of coercive authority that has betrayed the Arapaço (i.e., blinded them in one eye) but has not totally destroyed them. In the end, the Arapaço assert control over the whiteman's technology by bringing it back upstream in the anaconda-submarine, away from the dangerous, unsocialized political authority of the whiteman and his urban centers.

In his study of three stories from the Quechua-speaking Yura of highland Bolivia, Rasnake focuses on the use of mythic and historical consciousness as a symbolic strategy for coping with social complexity resulting from the historical meeting of two stratified social systems, one Andean and the other European. Yura stories about the period of the Spanish conquest aim at expressing the indigenous society's paradoxical situation within the Bolivian national power structure. The Yura are at one and the same time a powerless, marginalized ethnic minority and, through all the centuries of forced labor and extreme economic exploitation by outside forces, a society that has retained a limited sense of its autonomy and independence. Rasnake explores the conflicting imagery of subordination versus autonomy in three related Yura narratives. As with the second part of the Arapaço narrative cycle discussed by Chernela, the second Yura story analyzed in Rasnake's essay is loaded with transitional, mythic-historical imagery. The story begins with Tyusninchis, the creator-transformer of Yura religion, running away from a group of men on horseback (yawlis). This initial setting evokes the historical period of the conquest and the terrifying power of the invading Spanish horsemen. While giving expression to this outside power, the narrative goes on to show that the indigenous society is able to retain a certain "distance" from the yawlis (i.e., the successful escape of Tyusninchis), not through direct confrontation, but through selectively imparting information to the yawlis in such a way that they are fooled into misinterpreting the situation of contact. Thus, the Yura narrative expresses a limited ability to control the historical process of external domination through framing it in a mythic idiom that makes sense to the indigenous society but remains intentionally opaque, or even misleading, to the representatives of external force.

The symbolic process at work in Yura narrative is a complex one of converting indigenous social metaphors and mythic consciousness into the symbolic trope of irony or the juxtaposition of concepts that are felt to contradict each other. Sapir and Crocker (1977) note that irony is the most complex trope because its interpretation is highly situational and contextual rather than purely formal. Similarly, White (1973:37) sees irony as "metatropological," or a self-conscious use of figurative language to call into question its own capacity for distorting reality. As a symbolic trope of historical consciousness, irony is perhaps the most well suited of the master tropes for expressing the indeterminacy of social orderings and the paradoxes that arise in historical processes where widely different societies come into contact and negotiate "working disagreements" among themselves. Ironic mythic histories are powerful symbolic strategies for coping with historical situations because they are based on "felt" contradictions within and among societies. Like the metonymic-symbolic strategy embodied in Arapaço narratives (see Chernela), the interpretive power of ironic mythic history derives from a creative capacity to reformulate the underlying social metaphors of indigenous mythic consciousness into a different trope of historical consciousness, which can then be used in the social genesis of new interpretations.

Perhaps the most ironic expressions of historical consciousness contained in the essays that follow are the Central Andeans' adoption of beliefs in Santiago, the same mythic figure to whom the Spanish conquerors attributed their victories over both the Moors and the Inca state (see Silverblatt). In this case the irony is compounded by the highly ambivalent feelings local Andean peoples held toward lineage–father spirits, or Illapa, in preconquest times. This ambivalence reflected a basic contradiction within Andean social organization: the Illapa, or thunder spirits, were formally associated with the great emperor of Cuzco and thus also with the imposition of political rank and hierarchy on local social groups primarily governed by kinship. When the Spanish arrived, Santiago did not merely replace Illapa in Andean belief systems; rather, these two religious symbols became totally synthesized in such a way that Santiago came to represent a power capable of defeating, or at least resisting, the Spanish. In what almost amounted to a historical parody of the Spanish conquest, Andean peoples invoked native deities through naming Santiago and asked their gods' forgiveness prior to worshiping Catholic saints. During the early colonial period the Andeans' adoption of Santiago beliefs served as a symbolic strategy for resisting their own situation of powerlessness under Spanish rule. In later periods, however, this same constellation of religious beliefs and practices became a means of accommodation to externally imposed domination.

Context and Consciousness

No essay in this volume better expresses the deeply contextual and situational nature of "felt" mythic reformulations of historical process than Turner's study of narrative genres among the Northern Kayapó of Central Brazil. Turner shows us how the same social process of village fission, dating from approximately 1850, is alternatively interpreted in mythic and historical genres. The outsider-enemies of the Gorotire interpret the nineteenth-century social fission as a result of mythic-sexual intercourse between a snake and a woman,[5] whereas the Gorotire, who are direct descendants of the group that split apart in the last century, interpret the process in fully historical terms. Turner observes that the historical narrative "survives because it formulates a major tension in Kayapó society," the ritualized relations between bachelors' and mature men's age sets. Turner's discovery of the importance of ritual relations as a means of giving cultural form to historical consciousness among the Northern Kayapó is a particular case of a more general feature of the indigenous South American expressions of historical consciousness discussed in this volume: verbal accounts of ritual activities are often a cornerstone of oral histories and other narratives about the historical past.

In the conclusion of his essay on Northern Kayapó genres of expressing mythic, historical, and mythic-historical consciousness, Turner focuses on a bilingual, now mythic–then historical–then mythic speech made by a Kayapó headman who was addressing his own people at a 1976 meeting with representatives of the Brazilian government. Also present at the meeting was a camera crew that was filming the event for the BBC. The Kayapó mythic reformulations of historical process consist mainly of "anti-myths," which interpret the Brazilians as a simple negation of the indigenous society, rather than the more elaborated metonymic and ironic tropes of historical consciousness found in other indigenous South American societies. Nevertheless, the Kayapó headman's speech, as transcribed by Turner, is without doubt the clearest expression of why, from the indigenous perspective, mythic and historical consciousness must be integrated into coherent symbolic strategies for understanding and coping with situations of Indian-white contact. The headman's speech deploys " 'myth' and 'history' side by side in a dialogically sophisticated performance in which different modes and levels of consciousness are synthesized into an effective rhetorical unity." The Kayapó headman is telling the outside world that no understanding of indigenous societies is possible if we fail to recognize that the past differs from the present. Indigenous societies cannot survive as even partially autonomous orderings if they are not given an opportunity to bring historical consciousness into a controlled relation with a reflexive mythic consciousness of social reproduction. When historical processes violate the processes by which societies symbolically reformulate themselves over time, the results can be tragic, as in the 1981 clubbing deaths of eleven Brazilian ranch-hands by Kayapó warriors. Rethinking history and myth is, like the Kayapó headman's speech, no mere exercise in empty rhetoric but a necessary activity whereby people in all societies become reflexively aware of their own modes of mythic and historical consciousness and how these modes differ from those that have developed in other societies.

In her analysis of political speeches made by indigenous leaders of the pan-Indian movement in Brazil, Ramos explores the symbolism of an emergent political order of confrontation between indigenous minorities and the national society. What distinguishes this symbolism from the symbolism of myth and history is not so much its content as the uses made of symbols: political symbolism is mainly directed toward the national society, whereas mythic and historical symbolism are aimed at the members of the indigenous society. As the leaders of the pan-Indian movement become more conscious of their own historical agency, they "often evoke the past, when their cultures were different from now, before being affected by contact." A heightened awareness of white society and a national political arena characterized by domination and coercion has reinforced rather than undermined the importance of ethnic differences: "They are not just 'Indians,' they are Shavante, Terena, Kaingang, Makushi, Guarani." At the same time, indigenous leaders have appropriated the term "Indian" as a mark of social otherness vis-à-vis the nationals, and in doing so they have begun to convert "Indian" from a discriminatory label into a legitimate player in the national political arena.

Comparison of geographically dispersed societies is an inherently difficult procedure and can all too easily become another anthropological device for juxtaposing isolated things, events, texts, and structures. The type of comparative perspective that emerges in this volume is not merely one of certain essays addressing the same empirical topic(s) in a variety of different cases; nor, most emphatically, is it one of several detached, omniscient observers vicariously detailing the historical plight of indigenous South American peoples. It is, rather, more like a chorus of voices being listened to, contextualized, and understood as the historical consciousness of a continent of peoples who are confronting similar external pressures in their dealings with South American nation-states. The voices of the Waurá Atujuá spirits, the Wakuénai millenarian shaman-Christ, the Arapaço snake-grandfather, the Kayapó shamanic loner, the Quechua ancestor-people, the Yura creator-transformer—all are listened to in the present through indigenous storytellers, ritual specialists, and political leaders. An age set of historically oriented ethnologists is starting to make this multivocal, multilingual, Amazonian and Andean narrative intelligible as a coherent whole through exploring a number of distinct sociocultural orderings of historical, mythic, and mythic-historical consciousness.

NOTES

I would like to thank Michael Herzfeld, Terence Turner, Michael Olien, and Norman E. Whitten, Jr., for reading and commenting upon earlier drafts of this essay.

1. The volume results from a year-long process of reviewing one another's papers and ideas, begun after earlier versions of the papers were read in 1984 at the 83rd Annual Meetings of the American Anthropological Association in Denver, Colorado. The session, entitled "From History to Myth in South America," was organized by Pierre-Yves Jacopin and Joanne Rappaport and brought together smaller circles of scholars, many of whom had already been actively collaborating at a regional level of comparison for several years. Turner's paper on Northern Kayapó myth and history is the only one that did not form part of the 1984 session. However, in discussions by Turner and others after the session, it became evident that a substantive paper on Gê myth and history would fill a major gap in the ethnographic coverage.

2. In a general critique of realist approaches to philosophy of history, Goldstein (1976) argues against a view of historical events as things that are somehow "out there," waiting for the historian to describe them. Instead, the events of the past are constituted by the community of historians (1976:57–58). Thus, another dimension of the ongoing rapprochement of historians and anthropologists is a reflexive awareness of the process by which researchers constitute social knowledge as they study it. Factuality, whether historical or ethnological or both, is rooted in inquiry and is not reducible to mere things or events that are "out there" to be discovered and described.

3. For analyses of how parallel mythic frameworks are evoked in historically situated ritual action of the Canelos Quichua, see N. Whitten (1976, 1978, 1985) on the *dominario*, or *ayllu*, ceremony. For the Canelos Quichua, the anaconda is one of three master-images that together encode relations between human social processes and the native understanding of natural ecosystemic processes. N. Whitten's (1978) analysis shows how the anaconda has become a metaphor for organizing Canelos Quichua actions toward the expanding nation-state of Ecuador, which threatens the indigenous society with cataclysmic social and ecological changes. In dramatizations that give cultural form to a consciousness at once fully historical and mythic, the Canelos Quichua men dance and sing into being the world-transforming powers of the anaconda by crashing through the walls of the local Catholic mission, calling for a great flood to free the *runa* ("people") from the alien oppression of the priests (N. Whitten 1976, 1978, 1985).

4. To give credit where credit is due, the transformation of metaphor into metonymy is, of course, none other than the Lévi-Straussian "law of mythic thought" (1966b). In Arapaço narrative, however, the transformation of metaphor into metonymy is not the manifestation of an abstract, universal "law of thought" but of a mythic-historical consciousness situated in a specific social and historical time-space.

5. The theme of sexual intercourse between snakes and humans is found in the narratives of many Amazonian societies (see Chernela, and Hill and Wright), and the anaconda is a symbol of both life-giving rain and world-destroying floods in Central Andean societies (Urton 1981) as well as among the Canelos Quichua of lowland Ecuador (N. Whitten 1978). Contrary to the ethnocentric, Western interpretation of anacondas and other snakes as symbols of "evil" or "darkness," the anaconda is a symbol of rejuvenation and self-generativity (Drummond 1981) in many societies of South America, in part because of its ability to shed its skin and replace it with a new one.

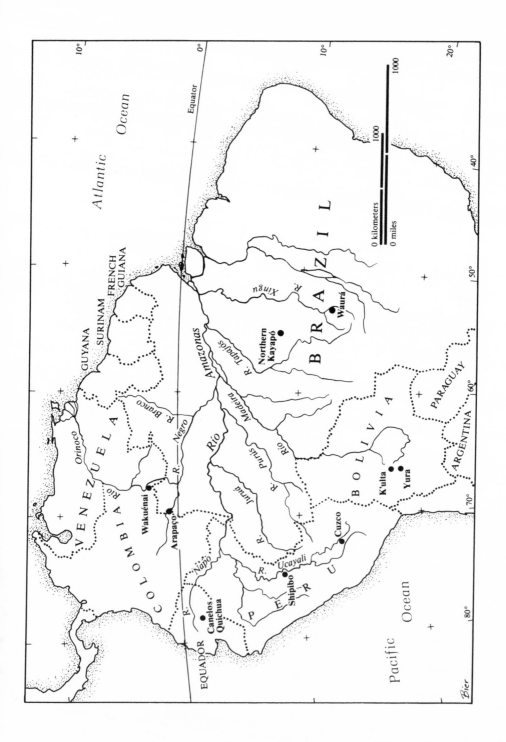

1

Cauchu Uras: Lowland Quichua Histories of the Amazon Rubber Boom

Mary-Elizabeth Reeve

The Curaray Runa group of Canelos Quichua occupy an extensive territory along the meandering, silt-laden Curaray and lower Villano rivers in Amazonian Ecuador. The Canelos Quichua are a multiethnic Upper Amazonian people constituted historically of intermarrying Zaparoan, Canelos Quichua, Achuar, and Quijos Quichua peoples who have adopted the Quichua language and identify themselves as Runa or *runapura* (Quichua speakers among ourselves). Canelos Quichua territory extends eastward from the base of the Andean cordillera into Peru and is bounded on the north by the Villano-Curaray and on the south by the Pastaza-Bobonaza river systems (Reeve 1985; N. Whitten 1976, 1985).

During the late nineteenth and early twentieth centuries, the Upper Amazon teamed with rubber merchants (*caucheros*), who came to this ungoverned territory from the Peruvian and Ecuadorian highlands and various European countries with the hope of extracting vast riches from the jungle and its native peoples. In the Curaray region the majority of these rubber merchants failed miserably to realize their dream. Curaray Runa maintain an oral tradition about these times, referred to in Quichua as *cauchu uras* (rubber times). Narratives set in rubber times are part of a corpus of accounts dealing with beginning times, referred to as *callari uras,* which in turn is contrasted to *unai* (mythic time-space), the undifferentiated state of primordial beginnings.[1]

Curaray Runa narrative forms deal with themes of differentiation among classes of beings. Texts set in mythic time-space contain Runa knowledge of the first differentiation between humans and nonhumans, a time when animals were Runa—or consorted with Runa—by disguising themselves as humans. Mythic time-space also exists alongside of and interpenetrates present times. Texts set in beginning times, which is the frame of reference for rubber times, focus on interethnic relations between Runa and non-Runa peoples or between those peoples who historically became Runa. The texts are part of what Runa refer to as *ñucanchij yachana* (our cultural knowledge), which is contrasted to knowledge possessed by foreign peoples. This essay is about the nature of Runa historical thought, particularly accounts of Runa experience of the Amazon rubber boom, or *cauchu uras.*

In the narratives of European/Runa contact and interaction set in rubber times, Curaray Runa portray Europeans[2] as *huiragucha* (from the Andean *viracocha*),[3] wealthy and wealth-seeking yet ignorant beings whose not quite human status is symbolized in terms of the asymmetrical exchange, and therefore great social distance, between Europeans and Runa. Contemporary Curaray Runa contrast the concept of *runapura* with that of "non-forest-dwelling foreigner." When referring to beginning times, foreigner is glossed as *huiragucha;* in a present-time frame of reference, the foreigner is *ahuallacta.* The concept of "Quichua speakers among ourselves" is equally contrasted with "those animal-like tropical forest peoples who have killed or captured our relatives," or *auca.* These concepts of the foreigner together form a class of beings with whom Runa interact with a great deal of caution, beings who because of their questionable humanity are considered inferior but who nevertheless appear to possess great power alien to Runa control. Foreigners are considered potentially marriageable but only if the non-Runa individual is capable of becoming Runa through adoption of the Quichua language and Runa culture. The concept of *runapura,* by contrast, includes kin and potential kin—those believed to share a common origin in mythic time-space. Runa use stipulated shared descent as a symbolic statement of commonality that unites the several historically intermarrying ethnic groups as one people. This indigenous theory of identity is at the core of Runa historical thought, a theory transmitted and reinforced through the telling of events from mythic time-space and beginning times.

Knowledge from mythic time-space and beginning times serves as a guiding construct for the creation of meaning, reflects and gives coherence to worldview, and provides metaphors for understanding present reality. History—not the simple recounting of events—is created by actors, in dialogue with listeners, with reference to a present shared reality. It is continually retold, re-created, as part of the ongoing process of social reproduction.

Events in the past shape the present as well as make sense of it, giving mythic time-space, beginning times, and present times the characteristic of interpenetrability. This characteristic sets up a problem for our understanding of indigenous exegesis: in both Amazonian and Andean societies, the distinction between a corpus of accounts that could be called "myth" and others that we might label "history" appears to be of little value; fragments of myth break into narratives that look to us like history. Furthermore, in both Amazonian and Andean societies history is often told not in narrative form but by commentary and allusion interspersed in conversation or encoded in art, in ritual, in geography, in genealogies, in rights to territory, and so forth (see Allen 1984; Price 1983a; D. Whitten 1981; N. Whitten 1978, 1985).

For Curaray Runa, mythic time-space and beginning times are seen to exist also in the present, as interpenetrating present times and a source of knowledge. Narrative texts reflect this interpenetrability. For example, the speaker may interject an accounting of a personal visionary experience when recalling past events or important places, the account referring to the same places or similar events. Genealogical information concerning the speaker's ethnic origins may serve as a personal validator of knowledge of past peoples. Additionally, a general accounting may include mythlike episodes, as nonhuman agents affected beginning-times peoples just as they affect Runa living today.

To understand Curaray Runa historical thought we must begin with a cautionary note: for Runa, time and space appear to be similar qualities. There is no word in Quichua for "time," per se. The words *timpu* (time) and *uras* (hours) are derived from Spanish to refer to a historical period, yet Curaray Runa, when they wish to express the idea that they "have time" (e.g., to do something), use the Spanish word *lugar* (space): *Lugar mana charinichu,* "I don't have time." It is the nature of time-space that we must grasp before we can really comprehend indigenous "mythic" or "historical" narrative. We must also recognize historical thought as knowledge and knowledge as a kind of power. Runa recognize powerful individuals within their communities as repositories of knowledge about mythic time-space and beginning times. They consider the corpus of this knowledge as the source of collective identity, as *runapura.* This knowledge is also a source of autochthonous power, forming a counterdiscourse through which a system of political and economic domination by foreigners is apprehended (see Taussig 1984a:497; 1987; N. Whitten 1985). Here I focus on a particular application of this knowledge: the Runa interpretation of the rubber boom and interaction with Europeans during that period.

The narrative subject of the rubber boom is examined from several different perspectives: a Runa who worked as a rubber gatherer; the descendants of rubber merchants who married Runa and became Runa;

and documentation left by European visitors, missionaries, and a rubber merchant who witnessed the rubber boom era in the Villano-Curaray and Pastaza-Bobonaza river regions. This plurality of perspectives reveals the various meanings given by distinct peoples to a subject significant for Runa today; and it reveals as well those contradictions in Runa social life in the present that are seen to derive from rubber times. Such contradictions pivot around the problem of the questionable human-ness of Europeans who both claimed Runa territory and left Runa descendants.

The Rubber Boom Era

The rubber boom meant enslavement and dislocation for the indige-nous populations of the Villano-Curaray and Pastaza-Bobonaza river regions. Entire populations were carried off to work rubber in remote areas or were subjected to merchants who established landed estates in their territory. Ethnohistorical sources mention distinct groups of Záparo, Gaye, Semigaye, Caninche, and Canelos peoples in the Villano-Curaray and Pastaza-Bobonaza regions (see Chantre y Herrera 1901; Grohs 1974; Jouanen 1941, 1943). By the end of the rubber boom era in these regions (ca. 1935), all references to the distinct groups disappear. While not comparable in its impact to that felt in the Putumayo and other areas where indigenous populations suffered near extermination (Casement 1912; Collier 1968; Taussig 1984a, 1987), the rubber boom era in this area was nevertheless significant as a period of ethnocide as well as transculturation. Distinct peoples came into contact with each other at mission sites, rubber estates, and camps. In so doing they intermarried and became *runapura* at those foreign-dominated sites (see N. Whitten 1976 and Reeve 1985 for a full discussion of this process).

A number of estates were established on the Curaray River to which Zaparoans, Canelos, and Quijos were brought to work as peons. No civil authority yet existed in the region (Bravo 1907:58), and rubber merchants vied with missionaries for control over indigenous popu-lations. While indigenous peoples occasionally sought refuge in mis-sion settlements, they also sometimes allied with merchants against the missionaries (Magalli 1890:69–70). Details of the effect of rubber extraction on indigenous peoples in this region have in part been preserved in various documents written by European visitors to the region (Bravo 1907; Simson 1886) and by missionaries (Magalli 1890; Valladares 1912); in a manuscript produced by a rubber merchant on the Curaray (Porras 1979); and also in oral accounts by the Runa descendants of estate owners and Runa who worked at rubber extraction.

During the height of the rubber boom the Curaray River was a major area for rubber exploitation. Indigenous people were enticed to serve as laborers or were brought there by force. The Dominican priest Magalli noted in 1889 that one hour by river from the mouth of the Villano on the Curaray was the estate San Antonio, which had twenty-nine Záparo laborers attached to it. Downriver from San Antonio was an estate owned by an Italian merchant with twenty-six Záparo laborers. Two days' travel further downriver Magalli encountered the establishments of French, English, Italians, and Peruvians, all exploiting rubber, with some forty Záparo laborers each, as well as a number of peons from various European countries. These peons carried out armed excursions up the tributaries of the Curaray, encountering indigenous peoples whom they often attacked and tried to capture (Magalli 1890:28, 29).

Bravo (1907) described the prosperous estate San Antonio as consisting of three main buildings and eleven indigenous residences. Both banks of the river were under cultivation, the produce including sugarcane, rice, tobacco, and the local subsistence crops, in addition to cattle. The white population totaled 58 men, women, and children, while the resident indigenous population totaled 118 men, women, and children. Bravo estimated a migrant population of some 300 white and indigenous rubber workers in the immediate area, as well as traders and their peons who traveled the river (1907:62). In 1916 San Antonio maintained an indigenous population primarily of Záparo but also of Canelos and Achuar from the Bobonaza and Quijos from the Napo region. The marriages and baptisms recorded by a visiting Dominican priest during this year give evidence of intermarriage between Achuar and Canelos, and Záparo and Quijos. Also recorded are numerous instances of ritual co-parent ties between indigenous and European families, as well as the baptism of children of mixed European and indigenous descent.

Curaray Runa recall that on arriving at a rubber estate they were immediately subjected to a system of debt peonage: they were often given clothing and a few tools and would then attempt to work off the debt thus incurred. Runa established residences near the estate but traveled to headwater areas to collect rubber, subsisting on toasted, dried plantain and manioc. These excursions were fraught with danger, as Runa sometimes encountered hostile peoples (auca) in these areas. Runa descendants of the rubber merchants recount that all produce from the estate was carried to Iquitos by Peruvian merchants, who plied the Curaray in launches laden with durable dry goods. These goods were then purchased with rubber by the rubber merchants and exchanged with the Runa laborers through the system of debt peonage. In addition, the rubber merchants produced and sold cattle, pigs, coffee, and cotton. They also manufactured cane alcohol from sugarcane, which they sold to other merchants as well as to the Runa when they returned from the forest to deliver the rubber.

Not only the Záparo of the Curaray River region but the Canelos, Achuar, and Zaparoan peoples resident in mission settlements on the Pastaza and Bobonaza rivers were subject to predation by rubber merchants. In 1890 the mission settlement of Andoas, on the Pastaza, was found completely deserted and destroyed, having been abandoned two years earlier when rubber merchants had forcibly carried off all the residents who had not fled into the forest. The unfortunate ones were put to work in rubber camps along the Tigre and Ucayali rivers or were taken off to be sold as slaves in Iquitos or Pará (Magalli 1890:28–30). Magalli estimated that close to a thousand rubber merchants had set up camps on the banks of the Tigre River in the 1890s and made armed excursions up the tributaries of the Tigre and to the missions in search of labor. The Dominican priest Valladares, in his 1912 visit to the mission of Juanjiri (Montalvo) on the Bobonaza River, noted that it was completely abandoned, the population having been carried off to work for a rubber merchant. Juanjiri had been founded by indigenous people from the missions of Andoas on the Pastaza and Sarayacu on the Bobonaza who were themselves fleeing the tyranny of Peruvian rubber merchants (Valladares 1912:42).

In addition to indigenous labor, the economic base of the rubber estates depended upon river transport of rubber and other agricultural products from the region to the port of Iquitos. With the advent of the Peruvian-Ecuadorian war of 1941, however, all access to markets from the region was cut off. A few merchants established new estates on the Napo River, with its upriver access to the port of Napo, but the war, the collapse of the market for rubber, and the severe epidemics that had raged through the region in the 1930s combined to topple most rubber merchants, who eventually abandoned the region.

A few of the sons and daughters of these rubber merchants who had established estates on the Curaray remained and married Runa, becoming Runa themselves through the adoption of the Quichua language and Runa culture. Some of their descendants have continued to operate in the region as merchants, exchanging clothing, dry goods, and cane alcohol with indigenous people for forest products such as the palm fiber used in the manufacture of brooms. Their social and economic position is not unlike that of Peruvian, Colombian, and Ecuadorian traders who intermarried with Runa and became Runa while simultaneously gaining control over important sectors of indigenous trade. Some of the grandsons and inmarried indigenous relatives of merchants have in turn become important political leaders, representing the interests of Runa at the national and international level.

Curaray Runa Concepts of Time-Space

Out of the turbulent and destructive indigenous experience of the rubber boom era has come an oral tradition that focuses on European/Runa relationships. To discuss these accounts, it is necessary first to examine in some detail Runa concepts of time-space, which relate directly to the types of knowledge exemplified in these accounts.

The Curaray Runa differentiate three concepts of time-space: mythic time-space, beginning times, and present times, all of which are recognized as following from the beginnings of life to the present in the sense that knowledge gained in mythic time-space and beginning times is transmitted down through present times. The three are also seen as existing simultaneously in the present, as nonlinear, as living on in Runa experience today, each referring to a specific type of knowledge. There are many present times because there are many different peoples, each with their own system of knowledge. No present time exists that is not a continuation from the past—those who are elderly live in old present time because they possess knowledge of what is, for most Runa, part of the past. By contrast, ancestors of contemporary peoples lived in beginning times. They were more knowledgeable than present time Runa, but with the arrival of Europeans they died out and much of their knowledge is said to have been lost (N. Whitten 1976:46–47).

For Curaray Runa beginning times includes the experience of their Runa ancestors through the rubber boom era, which had a profound impact on peoples of the Curaray. At that point beginning times is transformed into present times, an indigenous interpretation that is paralleled in ethnohistorical documentation by the disappearance of references to distinct non-Quichua-speaking peoples in the area now controlled by the Canelos Quichua. By contrast to beginning times, which incorporates a specific referent to past time and past peoples, mythic time-space refers to an undifferentiated state of the universe, a period before the earth had its present form and before humankind and animals were separate beings; it is any space thought to be controlled by supernatural beings and possibly any space outside the realm of culturally appropriate social action or control.

The knowledge from mythic time-space is part of "our cultural

knowledge" that is shared just among Runa, including intermarried
Achuar, Canelos Quichua, Quijos Quichua, and Zaparoan peoples, but
excluding whites, mestizos, blacks, and indigenous peoples such as the
Waorani (Lluchu Auca), all of whom are seen as having a different
origin in mythic time-space. Additionally, each group of Runa main-
tains a slightly different version of the knowledge from mythic time-
space, such that internal variation within "our cultural knowledge" is
preserved according to ethnic group of origin. Stories set in mythic
time-space describe events taking place in an undifferentiated domain
in which human/animal transformations occur as the protagonists of
each episode discover their true identity through their actions. The
principle of differentiation and identification extends into beginning
times. Narratives set in beginning times deal not with human/animal
transformability per se but with relationships between peoples. These
texts serve to establish a model of Runa distinctiveness based upon
relationships of trade and intermarriage or warfare and exploitation
with other groups, both indigenous and nonindigenous.

The accounts set in beginning times record inter- and intraethnic
warfare, migration, the harsh conditions of the rubber boom, and the
disappearance, through extermination and transculturation, of two
Zaparoan groups, the Gaye and the Záparo. Curaray Runa define and
reinforce their identity in relation to non-Runa through the telling of
encounters between these peoples in narrative texts. Accounts told in
this discourse style are always set within the frame of beginning times
but contain a parallel reference frame of mythic time-space in which
human/animal transformability and the role of nonhuman agents in
guiding and informing human action are paramount. Mythic time-space
existed alongside of and occasionally infused beginning times, just as it
does today, in present times.

The interpenetration of mythic time-space, beginning times, and
present times is evident in the knowledge-seeking, knowledge-building
formulations of individual Runa. Runa interpret mythic time-space as
accessible through night dreams, through vision states induced by
datura or *ayahuasca,* through artistic means such as song or the playing
of musical instruments, and collectively through ritual. In these performances and experiences, human/animal transformability becomes
part of present-day experience. For example, in both dream and vision
states, and occasionally while walking deep in the forest, Runa may
encounter nonhuman spirit-beings (*supai*). Such encounters signify a
crossing into the domain of mythic time-space. This domain may also
be called up or into the mundane through song—for example, a woman
sings of herself as a dove, flying to bring back her husband, and then

depicts her dove-self in an anthropomorphic ceramic vessel for drinking festival *asua* (manioc brew); or a man playing the drum may sound
the call of an animal, such as the golondrina bird; or men in a ritual
setting may be instructed to play loudly "so that Amasanga [the forest
spirit-master of animals] will hear." (See Brown 1985 for similar Aguaruna
Shuar materials and N. Whitten 1985 for a complete discussion of the
knowledge and vision-seeking process among the Canelos Quichua.)

   The capacity to interpret and manipulate experience and knowledge
from mythic time-space is associated with beginning times people.
Knowledgeable Runa today may speak of living simultaneously in "two
times," in beginning times and present times, and they are called upon
to speak about beginning times. In these accounts, the narrator moves
back and forth between mythic time-space, beginning times, and present
times within a single text. For example, a story about *cauchu uras*
(rubber times) was recounted by a knowledgeable Runa during a visit
to his house by his ritual co-parents, his wife's brother, and me. The text
reproduced here is part of a much longer narrative dealing with beginning times and is illustrative of the way in which a narrator shifts back
and forth from beginning times to personal validation in present times,
making reference also to mythic time-space in recounting visionary
experiences of beginning times Runa, of non-Runa, and, as validation,
of the speaker.

   The speaker began with a recounting of the names of Europeans who
came to the Curaray and where they settled in rubber times. He validated this by identifying the rubber estate where he lived as a small boy
and which members of his family lived there. He then affirmed the
existence of rubber in the region today as a validator for the narrative
setting. Then, shifting to rubber times, he described how rubber was
worked and how Runa traveled to the headwaters to obtain it, commenting
that he has "traveled everywhere" (i.e., is knowledgeable). Returning to
beginning times, the speaker described how rubber was loaded onto
launches on the Curaray to be carried to Peru and then asked, "How
much was that rubber worth . . . ?" He identified which areas produced
what type of rubber and validated this by stating that he had traveled
there and found rubber, shifting to mythic time-space in recounting an
encounter with a spirit-being.

Callari Cauchu Uras

   How much was that rubber worth in *callari uras?* How much were those
balls of rubber worth? Remembering as if it were now, how much was it
worth? For no good reason we Runa came into debt, we exchanged five or
six balls of rubber for two lengths of cloth. Because we were in debt, they

only paid us half and we remained in debt, the old debt was never paid off, they never cancelled it. Without provocation they stole from us. That was how we worked rubber in *callari uras*. From the rubber they became wealthy.... They say that Gonzalez[4] had a large gold sack, a sack of pure gold. The sack was filled with Peruvian gold coins and bank notes. They say that he made all this money with rubber, then before he died, buried it near his estate. His sons, wishing to know where it was buried, took datura [a powerful hallucinogen] so that the spirit-owner of datura would show them, as in a dream, the place where the sack of gold was buried. The two sons took the datura, but not being Runa, they were unable to see anything. They did not dream with the datura. For what reason did they do it? It did not cause them to see. But the datura did show them a burning flame. They looked everywhere, but without success. Why did they take the datura? Not for the reasons that we Runa do.... That sack was worth 500 million *sucres* [Ecuadorian currency]. We Runa worked in vain. The rubber merchant obtained everything with the rubber and the Runa obtained only a few things, always on credit. Then the Runa would go again to steal, without reason, the rubber from the forest. Now there are only the very young rubber trees left.

From the narrative, three central statements emerge about Europeans as *huiragucha*. The merchant is portrayed as wealthy but greedy or stingy, hoarding his wealth; he is powerful yet profoundly asocial. The merchant buries his wealth rather than share it even with his sons, behavior that is antithetical to norms of reciprocity among Runa and at once establishes him as not-quite-human. This status is further amplified in the image of the rubber merchant's interaction with Runa, in which he is described as a thief, taking the valuable rubber and exchanging it for cloth (which the European priests required Runa to use). The Runa are portrayed as powerless to escape their plight, ensnared in a web of indebtedness to the rubber merchant, who grows wealthy. Here, again, the European emerges as not-quite-human. Further, the Runa are trapped into behaving like non-Runa, stealing from the forest and killing all but the immature rubber trees in the process of draining their sap.

The entire narrative turns on the point at which the sons of the rubber merchant foolishly take datura in an attempt to discover where their father's wealth is buried. Here the narrator uses datura as symbolic of Runa knowledge from mythic time-space. Europeans, who are powerful and not-quite-human, are profoundly ignorant of Runa knowledge and incapable of seeing with datura as Runa do. This point is further elaborated in the narrator's description of what the sons do see. The burning flame is a specific reference to a highland Andean belief that the area where treasure is buried becomes a swamp; when the earth opens up (in August), the gold—associated with the wealth of Jesuits (Zuidema, personal communication, December 1984)—is visible as a flame. Using the symbol of the burning flame, the narrator appears to clarify the rubber merchant's sons' status as non-Runa; just like their greedy, stingy father, they have a foreign system of knowledge associated with the highlands and the Catholic church. This is an ironic commentary on the nature of non-Runa wealth, lost forever due to excessive stinginess and lack of vision.

Such themes are not unique to narratives dealing with rubber times but are employed throughout the accounts from beginning times that describe interaction between Runa and Europeans. In these accounts the European is portrayed as powerful, in the sense of wealthy, yet as not-quite-human in establishing extreme social distance through asymmetrical exchange, and as ignorant or powerless to apprehend the Runa system of knowledge from mythic time-space.

What of the European version of this reality? Two travelers in the region (Bravo 1907; Simson 1886) recorded their view of the indigenous people who worked the rubber, a view based on a dichotomy between "civilized" and "savage." Bravo conjured up an image of the semicivilized Indian, stating that indigenous peoples of the Curaray are

> ... generally heathens (*infieles*) who nevertheless live alongside Europeans and adopt European customs, the men wearing shirts, pants ... the children with clothing. In every house there is an axe, machete, rifle, ammunition, washbasins, towels, pots, plates. ... They eat besides their own food the rice, chickens and so forth eaten by Europeans. They fish, hunt and travel without anyone molesting them and all are voluntarily subordinate to their *patron*. ... Their obedience is such that no force or punishment is necessary. They work contentedly and when wishing to hold a celebration, ask permission of their patron. (1907:62–63)

This dichotomy between civilized and savage also forms the core of Simson's statements. He used "Indian" to refer only to the Quichua-speaking "semi-Christianized" peoples, the others being savages, or *aucas* (1886:153). These terms reflect both Andean and European concepts of the distinction between fierce or uncontrolled, animal-like beings and the civilized, subjugated members of a body politic (see also Salomon 1981; Taussig 1984a, 1987; N. Whitten 1976). Contemporary Curaray Runa may employ this distinction when talking about their Záparo ancestors, saying that they were fierce (*piñashca*) while the Runa of today are tame (*mansa,* Spanish). Bravo and Simson, both visitors to the region, saw this dichotomy clearly and simply; for them there was no ambiguity in the relationship between civilized Europeans, semicivilized "Indians," and savages.

When we turn to the accounts of rubber merchants and their descendants, for whom reality included the undeniable fact of intermarriage with indigenous peoples of the region, a different and certainly more ambiguous view of this dichotomy emerges. Porras (1979) has published portions of a manuscript alleged to have been written by Sr. Llory in 1913, during the time he resided at his rubber estate, La Mascota, on the Curaray. Other documentation suggests that Llory was married to a woman of Záparo descent and may have been a black man.[5] Llory debunked the dichotomy between savage and civilized when he noted that the indigenous people of the region " . . . profess the Catholic religion . . . on the surface only. . . . The affinity in the beliefs of the Indians and those of the Záparos binds the two groups closely together. I have been able to observe the same superstitions, the same beliefs, with slight variations" (quoted in Porras 1979:20–21). Where Europeans lived among indigenous peoples, he claimed, they became like them: "The [European] enthusiasts of manioc brew prove that instead of civilizing the Indians by their company, they are making savages of themselves by learning the Indians' customs" (quoted in Porras 1979:18).

Both the Runa narrative and the rubber merchant's manuscript treat the question of whether or not, from the indigenous view, Europeans are even human and, from the European view, whether indigenous peoples are wholly human. Llory noted that the indigenous person "hates even the language we speak, his favorite word for it being *supai-shimi* [language of nonhuman spirit-beings]" (quoted in Porras 1979:43). He also doubted the humanity of the indigenous people, even though there is evidence that he married a woman of Záparo descent. Llory reflected that "perhaps they are insensitive to deeper feelings and moral considerations. Perhaps they have only a material being" (quoted in Porras 1979:21).

Those descendants of rubber merchants and Runa who live today in Runa communities evince ambiguity with respect to their own position. When recounting the rubber boom era they are quick to give genealogical information that clearly traces their own European/Runa ancestry. Yet in other contexts I have elicited quite different responses. Several of these individuals, at the time of major ritual celebrations in Runa communities, vehemently insisted that they are "from here" (e.g., are Runa). Elsewhere, on the streets of the provincial capital, reference to intermarriage becomes a slur, eliciting the response that descendants of rubber merchants who speak about intermarriage are "speaking as ignorant savages." Clearly, correspondences persist among the European dichotomy of civilized and savage, the Andean concepts of Runa and *auca,* and the Curaray Runa distinction between fierce and tame. These correspondences form critical points around which dominant/subordinate relationships might be established or else debated and challenged—as they are by the Curaray Runa when *huiragucha* is included with the savage classes of not-quite-humans.

Another aspect of the relationship between Europeans and indigenous peoples that was/is treated by the Runa, by European travelers, by rubber merchants, and by descendants of Runa and merchants alike is that of the debt peonage system. Taussig (1984a:481, 495) argues that this system served as a pretext for the appropriation of indigenous labor; indeed, these people were forced to accept goods for which they had no need. This is vividly communicated by the Runa narrator who says that Runa traded rubber for cloth to make the clothing Europeans demanded they wear—a trade of what for the Runa was one useless commodity for another; thus the Europeans stole indigenous labor. Exchange relationships between distinct peoples are a key factor in the maintenance of regional social systems in Amazonia. Not-quite-humans, by definition, do not exchange but steal, capture, and kill.

The Runa observation that they were never given goods equivalent to the value of the rubber is confirmed by the European travelers who nevertheless rationalized it, not in terms of the not-quite-human nature of the "other," as do Runa, but as the operation of pure market principles. Bravo explained that the launches had no secure business on the Curaray and came up from Iquitos only when paid in advance for the voyage. Only one proprietor could afford this, according to Bravo, and "it is therefore reasonable that he [had] to resell his merchandise at very high prices" (1907:64).

Again, it is only when we look at statements of the rubber merchant Llory and Runa descendants of such merchants that another factor emerges to lend ambiguity to exchange relations—that is, the role alcohol played in the outcome of exchanges. One Runa remembered that her father, a rubber merchant, had produced a lot of cane alcohol. She said, "When Runa brought in rubber, they sold it to the rubber merchant for goods, and they would drink *trago* [cane alcohol] as well." Llory's commentary was even more to the point: "As for the white inhabitants of these places, they achieve everything by means of alcohol and this never runs out" (quoted in Porras 1979:20).

Frustration and a sense of failed vision characterize these accounts of the rubber boom, yet church records of marriages and baptisms at rubber estates on the Curaray concur with indigenous testimony that intermarriage was at least fairly common and ritual co-parent ties the norm in European/Runa interaction at these sites. Runa descended from both European and Runa parentage, living in Runa communities, insist that they are Runa, and they are most often sought out by other Runa and Ecuadorian nationals alike to serve as intermediaries to the dominant Ecuadorian society. They are found among the indigenous traders, schoolteachers, and political leaders who occupy powerful positions in Runa communities, positions that parallel, but do not supplant, those of the powerful shaman and woman master potter who stand as intermediaries between Runa society and the domains of mythic knowledge and killing/curing power and who serve as transmitters of "our cultural knowledge" from generation to generation of Runa.

Discussion

"Mythic" narratives attempt to resolve contradictions that exist between social-structural principles within a society (Rasnake, this volume). The ambiguous position within Runa society of descendants of rubber merchants and Runa is one such contradiction. On the one hand, Runa stress transformability of Runa and non-Runa statuses such that a non-Runa who learns to speak Quichua and live as a Runa, raising children who are Runa, becomes Runa. They may go to great lengths to stress how a particular individual is "now Runa." On the other hand, in a different context they may refer to the same individual as non-Runa, a negative statement that is often substantiated by citing behavior antithetical to Runa norms or by reference to the common origin in mythic time-space that Runa share and that separates them conceptually from persons with distinct heritage. Negative commentary is generally stimulated by non-Runa behavior or by attempts to become too powerful or too influential in community affairs.

Narrative texts set in beginning times deal specifically with this paradox, by recounting the events that brought various peoples together, depicting the nature of exchanges between groups according to the social-structural principles particular to Runa society (and where Europeans treat the same subject, principles of European society). The narratives set in beginning times engage with these contradictions, exposing them according to a particular sense of order, so that present realities, in which the same events can reoccur, are understandable according to patterns revealed through knowledge from mythic time-space and beginning times.

The interpenetrability of time-space frames, in which the past and what lies in mythic "beyond time" reference are separated from the present yet punctuate it with significance, seems to be characteristic of both Andean and Amazonian historical thought, making it a form of social reproduction. Historical thought gives meaning to a present reality; it is a source of power from which that reality can be interpreted, a source from which an autonomous indigenous sense of being is maintained with knowledge, as power, at its source. Within Amazonian and Andean societies it seems that European power (as a type of foreign power) is ambiguous and is either subverted by relegating Europeans to a class of not-quite-humans, in the same sense that *auca* is not fully human (i.e., Runa), or is transformed into an indigenous form of power. Historical thought creates a counterdiscourse to domination by foreign cultural values, while at the same time it addresses real paradoxes within Andean and Amazonian societies, paradoxes that continue to inspire debate among indigenous peoples.

NOTES

An earlier draft of this essay was read at the 83rd Annual Meetings of the American Anthropological Association, in the symposium "From History to Myth in South America." The research was carried out in Amazonian Ecuador between December 1980 and May 1982. I gratefully acknowledge support through doctoral fellowships from Fulbright-Hays, the Social Science Research Council, and the Organization of American States.

1. See N. Whitten 1985, 1976:46–56 for a detailed discussion of the Canelos Quichua concept of mythic time-space.

2. I use the term "European" to refer to European culture bearers, whether they are racially white, mestizo, or black. This may be closer to the Runa meaning of *huiragucha,* which appears to be a cultural rather than a biological distinction. It is important to keep in mind that whites, blacks, and mestizos operated in Amazonian Ecuador as merchants.

3. *Huiragucha* is the lowland Quichua form of *viracocha,* the Incaic myth-being. In Andean thought *viracocha* is associated with the outside, with uninhabited areas, with night, and with the floods of the rainy season (Zuidema 1982). Curaray Runa explain that *huiragucha* is an old term used for Europeans, who are now more commonly referred to as *ahuallacta* (literally, "highland town or residence group"). One implication of such terminology is that *ahuallacta* is a class of people who do not possess the necessary knowledge for survival in the tropical forest environment. *Nucanchij yachana* includes such knowledge.

4. I use a pseudonym here to maintain anonymity of living Runa. Names referred to by the narrator are those of persons who have descendants in Runa communities today.

5. This individual may be the Llore (*sic*) Simson met at Ahuano on the Napo

River. Simson described this man as a New Granadian who hailed from Esmeraldas (on the Ecuadorian coast) and had a Záparo mother-in-law. He stated that Llore knew the entire Napo River well, having spent two or three years roving its course in search of rubber. Llore was said to be conversant with the ways of the Záparo, with their language, and also with Quichua (Simson 1886:128, 140, 165, 180).

2

Righting History in the Northwest Amazon: Myth, Structure, and History in an Arapaço Narrative

Janet M. Chernela

To counter the reading of myth as codified history, students of myth have meticulously separated historical from mythic text. However, in doing so they have created false distinctions and resulting analytic problems. Lévi-Strauss's (1979:40) comparison of myth and history is one example: "Mythology is static, we find the same mythical elements combined over and over again, but they are in a closed system, let us say, in contradistinction with history, which is, of course, an open system." The severe shortcoming inherent in this approach is that it neglects the relationship of myth and history. This essay takes a different point of view. Using a myth complex collected among the Arapaço of the Northwest Amazon, I argue that history is important to structural-symbolic methods of analyzing narratives, for history makes sense of structural play. Furthermore, as the example will show, myth is not static: it consumes history and may be consumed by it.

In the myth presented here, an Arapaço culture hero moves into and out of white society. The circumstances of his birth as the offspring of an illegitimate union between a supernatural snake and a human are recounted in part 1. In part 2 the hero emigrates downriver, out of the native area, and into a city where he is shot by a white man. The hero returns to the Arapaço in part 3, bringing goods and knowledge obtained in the whiteman's world.

Variations of parts 1 and 2 have wide distribution, but part 3 appears to be a uniquely Arapaço innovation. This last elaboration, and its particular meaning to the Arapaço, make a study of this myth significant.

Moreover, the three parts, combined, constitute an exceptional example of mythic discourse with political impact, rich in historical reflection and reaction. The material provides a means for addressing questions about the way in which historical experience is incorporated into language, particularly into mythic discourse. The complex myth is of special interest because in it the traditional symbols introduced at the beginning are transformed into modern ones at the end.

Ethnographic Background

Located on the lower Vaupés River (spelled Uaupés in Brazil) in Brazil, the Arapaço are one of approximately fifteen named, exogamous groups of the Eastern Tukanoan family in the Northwest Amazon. The language groups of the Vaupés form a single, integrated network united by kin ties and marriage. Although the Tukanoan groups of the Vaupés basin share many common features, the Arapaço depart from the pattern in significant ways.

The Arapaço are one of the few exogamous descent groups that do not speak a distinct, identifying language. Among Eastern Tukanoan peoples language is an important source of social identity, marking membership in a major descent group and finding expression in common brotherhood. On this basis, researchers working with Eastern Tukanoan peoples have referred to the "tribes" or nations of the Vaupés as "language groups" (Jackson 1974), a convention that will be followed here. The Arapaço are exceptional among Eastern Tukanoan peoples, however, in that they no longer speak their own language, known as both Arapaço and Konea.[1] Instead, the Arapaço now speak Tukano or Portuguese, yet they continue to identify themselves as one descent group.

The founding ancestor of a language group in the Vaupés basin is called both "grandfather" and "the people's oldest brother" (Chernela 1983, 1984). He is also called "head," a term that refers not only to his leadership role but to the anatomical head that leads and "speaks for" the body; the term also refers to the head of the ancestral anaconda, from which the descendants of the earliest (called "first"), most senior ancestors originated. Members of each language group conceptualize their relation to one another by virtue of the founding ancestor.

Such heads or leaders are perceived by the Arapaço as necessary to the continuity and integrity of the tribe. It is thought that a group's vitality, its life force (yeheripona), depends upon the ongoing "rebirth" of the first ancestors. Only then, and through proper "sitting" (continuity over generations in the same locality), breathing, and speaking in the place where the ancestors first emerged, can the group persist. Settlement relocation disrupts the correspondence between descent and locality, dividing residents into "those in place" and "those who wander" or "mix with others."

The language groups of the Vaupés recount many of the same myths. For example, according to a sacred myth shared by all the Vaupés groups, the first people emerged from a primordial anaconda who swam up the Río Negro to the Vaupés with the rising waters. Arriving at the headwaters, the primordial "canoe," as the anaconda is called, reversed its direction and from its body emerged the first ancestors of each language group. The place where each ancestor emerged is considered sacred.

In another variation the snake-canoe contains the patrilineal descent groups, or sibs, that comprise a single language group. The anaconda represents the body of the brotherhood and each sib a constituent segment of that body. The Arapaço recall fourteen member sibs, although only one of these survives today. The names and ranks of the missing groups are remembered and kept alive through sib litanies and legends recounting their demise. The one surviving Arapaço sib is said to have subdivided, producing ten subsibs.[2]

Such losses characterize Arapaço history. Located on the lower Vaupés, the Arapaço were in the path of an expanding colonial frontier that proceeded upriver from the Río Negro. From 1730 on, slaving, forced labor, and disease ravaged the Arapaço region.[3] Only five Arapaço villages have survived. Former sites are today occupied by members of other language groups, such as Tariana, Piratapuya, and Tukano.

History

Amazonian drugs, gold,[4] and diamonds made the Vaupés area highly desirable to competing European powers in the seventeenth and eighteenth centuries (Burns 1980:72), and with the Spanish as a major threat, Portugal made efforts to secure its Amazon holdings. To prevent a Spanish presence, reconnaissance expeditions were sent up the Vaupés River and its tributaries in 1740, and troops were dispatched as far as Ipanorê, near the mouth of the Vaupés. It is likely that the Arapaço were the first Vaupés tribe encountered by such expeditions. The first documented slaving in the area is attributed to official expeditions of soldiers, known as *tropas de resgate,* who were sent into the interior to expel "foreign invaders." These soldiers are reported to have taken large numbers of Indian slaves. Indeed, one chronicler estimated that in the single decade between 1740 and 1750, some 20,000 Indians from the upper Río Negro were enslaved (Szentmartonyi, quoted in Wright 1981:600–610).

The threat of Spanish incursion into the region in the 1750s further inspired the Portuguese to fortify their presence, and in the following decade a number of military outposts were built on the upper Río Negro. One of these, São Gabriel da Cachoeira, established in 1761, was situated below the confluence of the Vaupés on the Río Negro, adjacent to the area occupied by the Arapaço. By 1779, Indians were recruited by force to work for colonists in the newly established posts, where they produced cloth, indigo, and brick; they also worked on the large plantations where indigo, coffee, and cotton were grown (Lopes de Sousa 1959:204). During the especially brutal period between 1780 and 1820 the Indians were ravaged, enslaved, and dispersed by such recruiting campaigns, known as *descimentos* (descents), and by 1820 the indigenous population of the Río Negro had been reduced dramatically (Lopes de Sousa 1959:205).

Ipanorê as a Center of Resettlement

During this period of recruitment the Portuguese also instituted campaigns of relocation, whereby Indians of dispersed villages were consolidated into large settlements within indigenous areas. These people were to be schooled in Portuguese language and culture, trained and encouraged in techniques of intensive agriculture, policed, and generally educated in the ways of the whites. The government guaranteed freedom to Indians who would speak Portuguese and take Portuguese surnames (Burns 1980:48). The Arapaço were moved into such a controlled settlement in 1790, when Andre Fernandes de Sousa, the parish priest of São Gabriel, gathered them and other tribal inhabitants from the lower Vaupés into a single large settlement on an island at Ipanorê (Figueiredo 1907). Ipanorê, a former Arapaço center, was to become the focus of mission and trade activities for the next two centuries.

Ipanorê offered several strategic advantages to administrators, missionaries, and traders. First, its turbulent waterfall was a barrier to heavy-bodied riverboats, such that cargos of construction equipment or agricultural supplies could reach Ipanorê but proceed no further. This allowed for the development of a large settlement area to which Indians could be enticed with trade goods or brought by force. Ipanorê was also a desirable mission center, for it was considered the site where the ancestral anaconda first emerged and thus regarded as sacred. Missionaries could take advantage of existing sentiment, overlaying one set of symbolic meanings onto another. One writer called the Ipanorê of 1883 "the capital of all Uaupés and Papori villages" (Coudreau, quoted in Figueiredo 1907:33) and described it this way: "Ipanore . . . was the village that possessed the largest number of houses and inhabitants. Besides the church, that was, in architecture and proportion the largest and best of any on this river, it also had a cemetery, school, missionary residence, and a jail." (Coudreau, in Figueiredo 1907:58, my translation)

The attempt to consolidate Indians into such large settlements, in order to expand export production and facilitate policing and education, resulted in sibs of diverse language groups inhabiting the same settlement. For example, the mission-created settlement at São Jeronymo at Ipanorê contained the Arawakan-speaking Tariano and members of several language groups of the Eastern Tukanoan family: Tukano, Piratapuia, and Arapaço. The schools taught Portuguese to the Indians and official incentives were offered to those who would speak that language. The Arapaço eventually abandoned their own language for the lingua franca of Tukano and for the official Portuguese tongue. The populations of Ipanorê and other lower Vaupés villages eventually became commercial and cultural middlemen between downriver whites and upriver Indians.

Rubber

From 1853 on, rubber surpassed all other Río Negro forest products, monopolizing all extractive labor for the next ninety years. The rubber camps on the middle Río Negro were particularly lucrative, and São Gabriel functioned as one of the bases from which patrons recruited indigenous labor for temporary service. Once outside the indigenous area, many Arapaço settled in cities. Some became itinerant workers, alternating between temporary residence in the rubber camps and home villages. Still others found that they could not return to their home villages.

The rubber years brought several forms of forced labor, documented in Serviço de Proteção aos Indios (SPI) reports written between 1925 and 1951. One practice was to retain laborers by manipulating them into an indebtedness from which they could not free themselves, a system of forced labor observed in many parts of the world. A second, widespread practice was the illegal removal of Indians to the more undesirable flooded or malaria-ridden rubber collection areas, as rubber continued to be the principal export from the Río Negro valley until 1950.

Following a pattern now two centuries old, such practices took many people from the Vaupés region but brought in few long-term outsiders. After the decline in demand for Amazonian rubber, São Gabriel continued to function as the base of white commerce and bureaucracy. There was little motivation for white settlement in the Vaupés itself, however, and except for missionaries and itinerant traders, whites rarely ventured into the area.

Population

According to the Arapaço and some authors (e.g., Bruzzi 1977; Giacone 1949; Azevedo 1933), the Arapaço were the earliest inhabitants of the Vaupés, occupying its margins from the mouth of the river to the Japura, before other Tukanoan- and Arawakan-speaking peoples. Bruzzi (1977), Lopes de Sousa (1959), and Coudreau (1887) all report a once thriving population; yet when Koch-Gruenberg (1909:20) encountered the Arapaço in 1904, he found two desolate longhouses with only 100 persons in residence.

Statistics compiled in 1958 from the parishes at Taraqua and Iauareté show 283 Arapaço (Bruzzi 1977:84). My own census from 1979 reveals an Arapaço population of 202, representing a decline of 29 percent in just twenty years. The five settlements I encountered in 1979 ranged in size from 11 to 83 inhabitants, with a mean population of 40 persons per village. Bruzzi's list includes two additional villages, which were abandoned in the twenty years between our surveys.

The Myth of Unurato

Text Translation and Organization

The text related here may constitute a single speech performance or it may be enacted in three segments. Part 1 is recounted as a totality by all of the tribes in the Vaupés basin.[5] The Arapaço, who are alone in considering the prominent culture hero their grandfather, continue the myth (part 2) so that it contains several unusual episodes that take the hero out of the Vaupés and bring him into contact with whites. Variants of part 2 are reported from the Amazon River region, but apart from the Arapaço version I have not encountered the myth in the Vaupés. Part 3 appears to be exclusively Arapaço.

This particular text was recounted by Crispiniano Carvalho [6] in Portuguese in the Arapaço village of Dia Phosa Yu?uro[7] (Parana Jucá), where I taped the narrative; the translation is mine. For this presentation I have eliminated some repetition and detail, inserted proper names where they are not found in the original, and bracketed explanatory material so that the myth can be easily followed by an audience not already familiar with it.

Part 1

This water snake [anaconda], Dia Pino, our grandfather, lived under the water in the stream across from Loiro—a place called Dia Wekuwi— the House of the Capyvara. Every day when the sun was high he would swim downriver from Loiro, above São Luis. There he would go into a passageway—it was a kind of corridor for him, for us it was a stream. He would arrive at the edge of the river and there transform himself.

We are grandchildren of the Anacondas, we are the Arapaço snake-children. He was our grandfather. Unurato is our oldest and most cherished brother. He will come back to us; we are waiting for him.

It happened this way. When he crossed the river he saw a woman [Iapo's wife] bathing. On arriving at the river's edge, he transformed himself into a human being, and lay with her. She was struck with his startling beauty and his shimmering gold ear ornaments. She was bewitched and thought of nothing else. So he lived this way, having contact with her, each time returning to his underwater house as an enchanted snake. Every day when she came back from the garden, she carried her calabash to the river's edge and beat it to make the sound "coro, coro, coro." He would hear it and come to meet her. This happened every day.

Her husband [Iapo] became distrustful. He put a companion of his, a bird, in a termite nest high in a tree. Then he hid and waited with a blow-gun and poisoned darts.

When it was nearly midday, the woman was returning from the garden, and, as was her custom, she carried the calabash to the river. She made the sound and our grandfather heard it and went to her. When he got to the edge, he changed into a human. He lay with her; and just as he was at that moment, as he lay on top of her, the husband blew into his blowgun and sent flying a poison dart which hit the snake in the buttocks. The snake felt almost nothing and thought it was a horsefly. When a third dart hit him, the termites on which the woodpecker[8] was feeding fell and landed on the woman. She looked up, and there she saw her husband. Terrified, she shook her lover to tell him her husband was watching them. But it was too late. Our grandfather, the snake, had been poisoned. We are the family of that snake; he is the grandfather of the Arapaço.

He fell into the water, and as he did he changed into a snake and went rolling downriver. There is an island called Tununi Nuku, and he rolled there. He went rolling until he arrived at Numiani Nuku and there he surfaced. He floated one day, then two days. On the second day while the wife was making manioc flour, the husband went there to fish. He caught many small fishes. [Wrapping them in manioc bread,] he made a bundle for himself and another for his wife. Then, he cut off the penis of the snake. He mixed the penis into one of the bundles and took them home. When he arrived home, he gave the bundles to his wife to roast. They ate together: he ate his bundle and she ate hers. When he finished eating, he picked up his flute, lay in his hammock, and played. He played "toro, toro, toro." It was enough for her to understand. The melody meant this: "A woman who liked her husband wanted to love. She ended up eating that which she most loved." Understanding the meaning of the music, she took her calabash and ran to the river's edge. She dipped it and drank many times. A kind of fish, like a snake, came out of her mouth. She returned home, thinking that the penis had left her body.

I will tell only a part of how our beloved Unurato, our oldest brother, reappeared and is here today. Well, the husband left the woman. He went away and she remained here, alone. She was pregnant. When she was about to give birth, she went to a stream above São Luiz, looking for shrimp to eat. In the leaf debris in the water, she found a little fruit—bacaba—which she wanted to eat. A voice within her womb called out: "Mother, I'll climb the tree and get the fruit for you." She said: "Don't speak: you are not people. You cannot speak as a human." He was the son of the enchanted snake. But, in truth, he had the spirit of a human. He answered: "I am a person. I am a man and I can do it. I will get you [the fruit]." He slipped out of her mouth, and slithered up the tree. He climbed very high until he was able to reach the fruit. Each time he dropped a fruit, the mother responded, "uh, uh." She couldn't escape because his tail was still inside her mouth. She was frightened: he was a human child but he was also a snake.

When she saw the snake, the mother was frightened (we know well that he was really a man). She folded a leaf of the duhpiapiuli tree into a funnel shape and spit saliva into it. She put a frog called ditaro near the funnel to call out "uh, uh."

Then she ran to the port and escaped in a canoe, leaving the stream, crossing the river, and entering another stream [Diya, the Stream of Blood] where she bathed [cleaning the birth]. From there she set out paddling home.

Our grandfather, high in the tree, saw her leaving when a beam of light—a reflection—hit her paddle. He shouted to her. He was a spirit. He flew to the house and lay on top. It was really a hill of earth, but for them a house called Ditabua in Wituriro. She hid in a large ceramic beer vessel as he remained on top of the house shouting. When she was thrown out by her family, she threw herself into the water and was transformed into the fish pirarara.

Part 2

Unurato entered the water and there he grew very big. Soon, there wasn't enough water to contain him, so he moved downriver to deeper water. First he went to the Río Negro, then to the Amazon. In the Amazon he found fishes even bigger than he. So he went to Manaus. He arrived in Manaus at night. As he came on land he transformed into his human form and spent the night drinking and dancing. At dawn he returned to the water and assumed his snake form. After some time, he went to one of the whites with whom he was drinking and asked him to meet him at midnight on a beach. The white had whiskey, a rifle, and a hen's egg. He was to throw the egg at Unurato. The white went to the river's edge and waited. Suddenly the waters rose and Unurato appeared as an enormous snake. In fear, the white shot him with the bullet instead of throwing the egg. With the blow, his snake skin fell into the water and his human body remained on the beach. The blow destroyed his supernatural qualities. He remained a simple man, on the beach, blinded in one eye. He began to live as any man.

We are his descendants. That's why we are called Pino Masa, People of the Snake.

Part 3

Unurato went to Brasilia and there he worked constructing large buildings. He came to know every kind of thing: houses, furniture, taxis—things we don't have here. And he moved among many people.

Last year, the waters rose very high. That was Unurato coming back. He swam upriver. He was a gigantic submarine, but since he is a supernatural snake he passed the rapids. The submarine is here, across from Loiro. It appears at midnight. It is so full of goods, it is impossible to count the number of boxes on that ship. The ship has electric lights. With the machines the snake-beings [*wai masa*] are building an enormous city under the river. You can hear the noise of these submerged machines when you go near there. Every kind of *wai masa* [underwater, supernatural beings] is at work on that ship. Now we are few, but he will give us back our prosperity, and our numbers.

Discussion

Part 1 of this narrative would appear to be concerned with the supernatural, yet it is at least as concerned with humans and human relations. Unurato is the prominent symbol. The unwanted offspring of an illicit union between a human woman (who is known as Iapo's wife)[9] and a snake-being (Dia Pino), Unurato is both human and snake. Thus a set of problems related to classification and boundary definition is introduced at the outset: insider versus outsider; divine versus human; self versus other.

In the opening of the narrative we are told that Dia Pino (River Snake) transforms himself into a man and cohabits with Iapo's wife. Dia Pino's union with Iapo's wife is illicit on two grounds: the parties are not proper in-laws; and the union usurps Iapo's paternity over his wife's offspring. Dia Pino is Arapaço, an "other," since he is neither of Iapo's own nor Iapo's wife's group. By rules of patrilineal reckoning, Dia Pino's children will also be "other" in relation to Iapo. Partial resolution is accomplished when Iapo counters the sorcery (usually accomplished through breath, i.e., smoke) and kills Dia Pino with a blowgun dart as he lies with Iapo's wife. Dia Pino's corpse falls into the river and returns to snake form.

The problem is a moral one, and the cuckolded husband takes revenge by tricking his wife into ingesting her lover's penis. Iapo compounds his wife's contamination through a dramatic, inverted reenactment: as he fishes, Dia Pino is fished and eaten. Thus the sexual organ of the progenitor enters the woman's body through an improper orifice. Although partial resolution to the contamination is accomplished when the wife vomits, she is not purged, for she has conceived. Her residence is now changed from her husband's conjugal household to her premarital household.

The problem is that within her womb she carries a snake-being, not a human. "Don't speak," she tells him, "you are not people." Mother and son are reciprocally defined: he is a snake; she is not. He is enchanted; she is worldly. He is of the water; she is of her earthen house and earthenware beer container. What she is, he is not. Most important, she speaks, but he may not.

Whereas husband and wife were once adversaries, now mother and son are adversaries and she plots to rid herself of him. Birth occurs through an improper orifice as the enchanted snake offspring emerges by way of the mother's mouth (where entered her lover's penis). The son is careful to leave his tail there, so as not to separate himself entirely from his mother. She tricks him, however, as the realms of the actors reverse: he climbs to the treetops and she takes to the water in her canoe. A beam of light—a reflection—hits the snake offspring, as the dart had the snake father and as the bullet would later strike the city snake. Each blow marks a betrayal and a critical transformation in the dialectical process.

The son flies through the sky in pursuit of his mother and rests above the hillock that is her house. He lies above her house in repetition of the juxtaposition of his father and mother in coitus. She tries to hide in an earthen vessel in her terrestrial house, but her family expels her. Resolution is accomplished when she enters the water and becomes a fish. No more is heard of her. Both mother and son swim away from their place of origin, the traditional center of the world.

In part 2 of the narrative, an "other" who is now called Unurato, deprived of his heritage, journeys downriver to the white city of Manaus. Human by night, he socializes in white company; a snake by day, he returns to the river. Unurato chooses to sacrifice his divinity, associated with his snake form, to become fully human. He asks a white acquaintance to meet him that night at the river with a hen's egg, whiskey, and a gun. Again, Unurato's being is defined negatively: that which he is, is not white. The whiteman's products are the requisite instruments for his becoming human: the whiteman's alcohol, not manioc beer; domestic, not feral animals; firearms, not blowguns. The white man is to throw the egg at Unurato to make him human. But Unurato, arriving as a snake in a large wave, overwhelms the man and is shot with a bullet rather than the egg.

This part of the narrative is pivotal: in it, the traditional symbols from part 1 are transformed into the modern symbols of part 3. Earlier, Unurato's father was killed by a blowgun dart from his lover's husband. Now, a white man who has promised to help Unurato instead betrays him and blinds him with a bullet. The blow, a moral response in part 1, is an act of betrayal in part 2. The fall of the destroyed snake form into the water recalls the fall of the murdered father, whose dead snake body falls into the river in part 1. The blow from a blowgun, which sent Unurato's father from human form into snake form in part 1, is inverted in part 2 when the blow from a bullet sends Unurato from snake form into human form. The whiteman's bullet strips Unurato of his ancestral qualities and breaks continuity with his Arapaço kin. Exile is now complete.

A transaction has occurred as divinity is exchanged for the whiteman's goods. Whereas the egg (of a domestic animal) and the whiskey may be transformations of meat and manioc beer, the proper mediating products between different groups, the bullet is an improper mediator between different groups of nonkin. Betrayal by the whiteman reiterates betrayal by a woman. The wife, always of another language group by virtue of linguistic exogamy, is one form of an outsider who betrays; the whiteman is another. Relations of violence, not affinity, obtain between white and Indian.

In part 3, Unurato, whose divinity has been sacrificed, becomes a laborer in the whiteman's world. He journeys to Brasilia, the nation's capital, represented as the center of commerce and political power. Here, the whiteman is the owner of drink, animals, and weapons, while Unurato is maimed and impotent. As his mother closed her eyes and then opened them, Unurato now has one eye closed and the other open.

Events in part 2 are overturned in part 3 when, in the form of a submarine laden with machinery, Unurato returns to the Vaupés with the rising water. Traditionally associated with the abundance of fish runs, rising waters now carry an abundance of manufactured products. Under the water Unurato builds a great city for the Arapaço nation. The wealth is immersed in the river—the supernatural realm—and is attended by supernatural *wai masa*, snake-fish-beings. The wealth, or cargo, remains potential, but signs of it can be heard and seen.[10]

Unurato retrieves his supernatural power in two ways: by returning the ancestral line to its proper birthplace; and by appropriating the whiteman's technology. The two are combined as the supernatural snake-being builds a large industrialized city at the sacred birthplace of the Arapaço nation. Spatially and socially Unurato moves from liminal to central, and with him go the Arapaço; the political and supernatural center of the world returns to the Arapaço.

Both snake and man, supernatural and natural, Unurato is a go-between with significant synthetic and mediating powers. As a mediator between earth and water, Unurato is human on land and a snake in water. Likewise, he crosses the boundaries between the rural (Arapaço) and urban (white) worlds. Unurato first moves from the rural realm to the urban, where rural = Arapaço/ancestors, and urban = white/technology. Drinking whiskey and dancing, he becomes "as a white."

The culture hero creates the boundaries over which he passes and defines the world by his passage. As the ancestral "head" moves from the rural realm to the urban, the center moves with him so that the rural, formerly central, becomes peripheral and the urban, formerly distant, becomes central. As the culture hero returns to the rural realm, he brings technology from the urban setting to the rural and with his presence restores the center to the Arapaço.

In the historical events summarized earlier, the Indian moves to the commercial center. In this narrative account, the commercial center and technological nexus move to the Indian. With the coming of the whiteman, the Arapaço area became peripheral. Thus the myth reworks that history, reframing the world to include new locations and peoples and reauthorizing the rural and the Arapaço as center. Just as Unurato is hybrid (simultaneously snake and human) and mediating, so too are the Arapaço. Eastern Tukanoans who do not speak their own language, the Arapaço are "other" to neighboring in-law groups as well as to whites. They are mediators in a historic encounter.

Myth and History

Part 1 of the narrative poses a problem unique to the Arapaço that is only resolved in part 3. The first part is apparently sufficient for other Vaupés groups, as only the Arapaço recount the extended, three-part myth. As the first ancestor of the Arapaço, Unurato is necessary to the group's coherence and vitality. In the absence of a distinct, identifying language, the Arapaço have only a "first ancestor" through which to define and negotiate "groupness." Only with ancestral authority may they "speak." The mythic return of the ancestor renders the Arapaço whole and viable.

Part 3, for all its modern appearance, might have been overlooked in a conventional selection of myths, but it raises questions about that which distinguishes myth from other types of discourse. For example, a number of structural and stylistic features of the final episode set it apart from the rest of the cycle. In the earlier sections incompatible relationships are juxtaposed and resolved. By contrast, the final episode consists of a series of resolutions, a feature consistent with millennial types of discourse. Also, the ideas in part 3 come very close to experience. One can "listen" to the machinery beneath the river. The reference to "last year" throws the episode into contemporaneity; although "last year" is not to be taken literally, that the myth is not reported in the literature suggests that the later section may indeed be a recent addition.

The modern symbols of part 3 veil traditional concepts and relations. For example, the symbolic import of Unurato's upriver journey as a regenerative motif is best understood in light of the Vaupés origin myth which describes the peopling of the world. In it a snake-canoe swims upriver and from its procreative body emerge the original ancestors of each of the tribes. Now the ancestral snake is a submarine (laden with goods, not people), and with its return Unurato's divinity, associated with his snake form, is restored.

In the myth recounted here, an ancestral anaconda swims downriver to labor in white commercial centers. His descent, an exile, recalls the forced *descimentos* of two centuries of colonial domination. But a dilemma posed by history finds mythic resolution. The descent is countered by its reverse: the ascent. While the descent recalls enforced labor and tribal death, the ascent recalls the Vaupés creation myth. Whereas the descent represents disintegration and group dismemberment —the (historic) loss of the remembered, extinct senior sibs and (mythic) separation of the ancestral head from the brotherhood body—the ascent brings regeneration and integration.

White elite authorities or "heads" would manipulate symbols to their own ends: to pacify or to mobilize a population to labor for the reward of manufactured goods. Indians were moved to centers where manufactured goods and technologies never before available to them were used as enticement to increase production. In Unurato this process is reversed: goods, historically manipulated to draw the Indian into the whiteman's world, are shown here to be the vehicle of independence. The ideological formulation expressed does not reinforce white control; rather, it makes symbolic moves to usurp it. The myth does not express a subservience to this ideology but frees itself from the polity associated with such value and differentiates an autonomous polity.

History and myth come together here and turn on one another. The sequence of events reads as historical metaphor: proceeding from a traditional time in which the opposing relations were kin- or sex-based; moving to the colonial encounter; and finally arriving at the appropriation of white technology and the establishment of a separate moral and social order. A historical dilemma is mythically resolved as moral and physical defeat by the whiteman's weaponry and technology are overturned with divine ancestral restoration. Unurato's divinity is restored when the tools of white power are brought under Arapaço ancestral control and the source of power and generation is returned to the ancestors. The sacred and profane are thus synthesized as the past is restored to the future. History is "righted."

Whereas myth may take its impetus from history, it does not take its dictate. As the myth described here shows, history does not determine myth, though it may compel it, provoke it, and inspire it. The result is not a replica but a counterimage, a reformulation, a reworking of time and events to meet needs other than accuracy of reproduction. Through myth, history is appropriated and transformed by culture.

NOTES

An earlier version of this essay was read during the symposium "From History to Myth in South America" at the 83rd Annual Meetings of the American Anthropological Association, in Denver, Colorado, November 1984. The author thanks Crispiniano Carvalho, Miguel Carvalho, and Joao Bosco for their invaluable assistance in recording and translating the myth; and Eric Leed, Robin Wright, Steve Fjellman, Brian Petersen, Leonardo Figoli, Sheila Dauer, and Nancy Fried, all of whom read and commented upon earlier versions of this essay. The research was carried out between 1978 and 1981, and 1983 and 1985, with funds provided by the Fulbright-Hays program of the U.S. Department of Education; the Social Science Research Council; the Instituto Nacional de Pesquisas da Amazonia; the McKnight Foundation; and the Joint Committee on Latin American Studies of the American Council, funded by the National Endowment for the Humanities, the Ford Foundation, and the Andrew W. Mellon Foundation. I also wish to thank the members of Cultural Survival and the Department of Anthropology at Harvard University, where, as a resident fellow and visiting scholar, I was provided the excellent facilities in which portions of this essay were written.

1. Konea, or Korea, is the Tukanoan name of the group and language; Arapaço, or Arapasso, is the *lingua geral* name and that by which the group is known in the literature on the Northwest Amazon.

2. My informant reports ten sibs, Bruzzi (1977) reports four, and Beksta (n.d.) reports seven.

3. Bruzzi (1977:84) reports in detail several factors in Arapaço population decline and places the Tariana in the lower Vaupés after the Arapaço:

Padre João Marchesi, on arriving in 1925 among them, learned from the elder Arapaço, that they had been the "nobles" and leaders of the Uaupes, [occupying settlements] from São Jose to the mouth. For having been more sociable and agreeable than the other Indians, many women became wives of whites and many men were carried off to work. Many remained in the lower Río Negro and others disappeared entirely. From constant cross-breeding with Arapaço, a large population of mixed-bloods evolved in that region. The tribe was greatly reduced. There had been a large group at Pinu-Pinu, on the Uaupes, who emigrated to the lower Río Negro. On return, they found the Taryana in their place. Not wishing to cede the land, the Taryana adduced that they were many, whereas the Arapaço were few. (my translation from Portuguese)

4. The earliest entry into the Vaupés was motivated by a search for precious metals and for Indian slaves, as in the 1730s when official Portuguese ransom troops entered the Vaupés area in search of a "Lake of Gold" (Sweet 1974; Wright 1981:60, 125–28).

5. See, for example, a Wakuénai version in Wright (1981:571–74) and Uanano versions in Chernela (1988).

6. Crispiniano Carvalho has provided invaluable assistance to me since 1978. He and his wife were my hosts when I visited their village, Dia Phosa Yu?uro.

7. The orthographic symbol ? is used here to indicate a glottal stop.

8. Both Konea, the Eastern Tukanoan name, and Arapaço, in *lingua geral*, gloss as "woodpecker."

9. The actor known to the Arapaço as Iapo's wife is referred to in the original narrative as "the wife" or "she."

10. Imminent, unrealized wealth is an earmark of the phenomenon that has come to be called "cargo." Part 3 establishes the myth complex within that genre.

3

The Destroying Christ:
An Aymara Myth of Conquest

Mary Dillon and Thomas Abercrombie

To explore the role of myth in South American societies, in trans-
mitting and transforming the experienced past, scholars often focus
on the uptake by these peoples of what were to them events of momentous, world- and society-transforming consequence: the arrival and
actions of Western outsiders (conquerors, explorers, missionaries, etc.).
One might suppose that, given the lack of writing in the indigenous
Andes, such events would be "remembered" in oral traditions such
as myth. Indeed, our first impression of the myth we present here
was of an oral "syncretic" form, casting a memory of the conquest as
cosmogony.

The myth we discuss, titled "Jesus Christ and the Supay-Chullpas,"
is told by present-day Aymara-speaking llama herders of Ayllu K'ulta,
Bolivia. Essentially, it is an account of the creation of the present world
order through the destruction of a previous one. As such, the Christian
myth of death and resurrection is incorporated into the framework of an
Aymara creation-of-the-cosmos myth. A powerful stranger—Christ—
arrives one day and, after twice emerging from the tomb into which his
autochthonous opponents place him, rises into the sky as the sun,
destroying the "orderless," savage society that had sought to destroy
him, while at the same time creating the conditions for the emergence
of the "civilized" society of the myth's tellers, though without actually
accounting for them.

In outline this myth appears to be an ironic piece of social criticism,
taking the central story of Christianity, one of the conquerors' tools of
conquest, and subverting its "Christian" message by analogy to the
genocide of the conquest. Alternatively, the myth might be seen as
hiding, under the veil of Christianity, a purportedly indigenous conception of time as cycles of production and destruction. Yet both readings
are partial, representing the uses to which the myth can be put in

different contexts. As understandings of the myth they are inadequate, for they do not take into account the complexity of power and social identity at the heart of the myth itself, nor its relationship to social reality. The people of K'ulta vehemently reject their identification as descendants of the "primitives" of the story, thus precluding a simple *indigenista* interpretation. Rather, as a cosmogony the action of the myth is concerned with the definitions of space, time, and identity in the universe of social relations within which it is told. These definitions are themselves at the heart of a power struggle in the Andes. The question the myth raises for us, then, is how to read the relations of power present in the myth in terms that are both meaningful for the present-day people of K'ulta and congruent with the historical reality of domination.

Discourses on Power in Myth

Previous treatments of Andean myth have examined its relationship to history in the context of a purported Andean messianism/ millenarianism (cf. Ossio 1973a) and in light of the persistence and disruption of indigenous structures (cf. Ortiz Rescaniere 1973; Zuidema 1964; Wachtel 1977). More recent works, however, have rephrased the problem from that of identifying continuities in myth to that of examining the production of meaning and modes of interpretation.

Jose Maria Arguedas (1973), in remarks on a "syncretic" story from Quinua, has suggested that the Andean myth's reorganization of time is an artifact of its embeddedness in the dominant culture. The story identifies the indigenous with the past, the result of a temporal shift in which the historically derived biblical division between the Old Testament and the New Testament is transferred to the present, to account for the differentiation of social classes. The example is salient here in that it raises the possibility that Andean myth encodes what we might call a "strategy for domination," rooted in a temporal and cosmogonic distinction. Just what this equation of indigenous and past might mean is a question addressed in the Mesoamerican context by Warren (1985) and by a number of recent studies on Andean religion, such as Earls (1973), Harris (1982), MacCormack (1985a), Platt (1983), Salomon (1981), Taussig (1980a, 1984b), and Wachtel (1977). Without attempting a thorough discussion of the literature, we will discuss some of these works as they intersect with our own analysis, given that this frequently remarked problem of "temporal collapse" is a central one in the myth we present.

A 1973 essay by John Earls directly addresses the organization of power in Quechua myth, ritual, and belief. These forms, he argues, are best understood as serving to organize competing hierarchies of social relations, an interpretive strategy that enables him to explicate a ranking of cosmological forces at the local and global levels in terms of power relations between social groups. Earls argues that a disruption in the cosmological hierarchy represents the perception of a true political instability and hence becomes the conceptual basis for messianism. His argument advances our understanding of the role cosmological forms play in colonized or class-stratified societies and defeats the notion that, in the Andes, cosmological forms can be analyzed as virtual systems apart from their place in the historical context of power relations.

Michael Taussig has made the most thoroughgoing argument in favor of the role of myth and ritual as the "folk politics" of dominated groups. In *The Devil and Commodity Fetishism in South America,* he views belief in certain magical figures, such as the devil, as inherently defined by the colonial situation, in that these figures have arisen as part of a folk critique of modern capitalism (1980a:10). According to Taussig, the basis for this occurrence lies in an initial contrast between the (religious) fetishism found in precapitalist economics, which "arises from the sense of organic unity between people and their products," and the fetishism of commodities in capitalist societies, which "results from the split between persons and the things they produce and exchange" (1980a:37). He summarizes the results of hegemonic contact: " . . . in the colonial situation the zombies or spirits change to reflect the new situation rather than the precolonial spirit world. They are as dynamic and everchanging as the network of social relations that encompasses the believers, and their meaning mediates those changes" (1980a:231). Taussig uses the term "superimposition" to identify the way this change takes place. He finds that the cosmological forces and deities of pre-Hispanic times come to embody the contradiction that results from a new system of economic control being overlaid on an old system of reciprocity.

In his earlier work Taussig goes so far as to equate the introduction of a capitalist economy with the emergence of death and the devil as a focus of the proletarianized religious system. The limits of such an equation have been pointed out by Platt (1983), who marshals extensive evidence for a more complex understanding of the multifunctionality of both pre- and postconquest religious figures. In a more recent work, "History as Sorcery" (1984b), Taussig makes a stronger case for the internalization of colonial constructs of domination and their subsequent manifestation as channels of "wild power," either controllable or uncontrolled. He provides significant insight into the construction of cultural representations yet fails to describe how meaning is fabricated. For Taussig, the meaning of symbolic forms seems essentially to derive from, rather than help constitute, power relations,[1] so the development of meaning in individual myths and rituals is overlooked, or perhaps dismissed. In place of acknowledgment of any structured form of social constitution, we are left with the frail montage-like memory of the collective psyche confronted with the overwhelming pressure of institutional domination.

Tristan Platt's "Identidad andina y conciencia proletaria" (1983), which addresses the fabrication of meaning in colonized culture, provides a response to Taussig's thesis on Andean religion. Platt makes a historical argument for the reworking of colonial forms into Andean structures as a means of ensuring social reproduction. He contends that colonial and state labor extraction have been ritually reenacted as a form of sacrifice that serves to protect the autonomy of the group. This argument displays Platt's keen perception of the dramatic import of Andean ritual as it has developed historically.

Frank Salomon's "Killing the *Yumbo*" (1981) addresses similiar issues and provides an exceptionally detailed examination of the structure of an Ecuadorian fiesta-cargo ritual. In looking at the dramatic organization of the ritual, Salomon tries to account for the development and persistence of the disparity of meaning that seems to result from a dramatic juxtaposition of formal Catholic ritual and the expression of wild savagery in the *yumbo* dancing: "Perhaps the most distinctive trait of the *yumbo* complex in the Quito area is the development of an elaborate symbolic antiphony between the play of the 'savage' *yumbos*, which culminates in the ritual combat, slaughter, and resurrection called *yumbo huanuchay* or *matanza,* and the performance of folk-Catholic rites on the themes of religiously sanctioned hierarchy and community, which culminate in the display of the Host, token of Christian resurrection" (1981:163). He sees the function of this interplay as regulating structural ambiguities in the social identity of the participants—ambiguities that result from the historical development of Runa (highland Indian) society: " ... in terms of historical experience Christianity, no less than jungle shamanism, is the religious aspect of a foreign society with which one's own stands in a relation of intimate interdependency" (1981:194).

Salomon describes the context of urban and capitalist expansion in which this interdependency has developed (1981:164–65), but it is a context largely called upon to explain the inherent incompatibility of the juxtaposed cultural premises (1981:199) rather than the formation of the premises themselves. The historical process is not Salomon's central concern when he examines the forging of the new meaning system in ritual, since he equates this historical process with the derivation of the two contrapuntal ceremonial complexes from heterogeneous sources through bricolage (1981:196). Thus, he sees the ritual system as a necessary correlate, or derivative, of the cultural logic needed to mediate the contradictory reality by those who live in it.

Although he treats ritual and we focus here on myth, the narrative or dramaturgical structure Salomon (1981:199–200) defines in his exegesis is in many ways analogous to that of the myth we analyze. His treatment leads us to ask how the meanings of myth are related to extramythic cultural meanings. Does myth carry within it a deadweight of historical baggage, meanings presupposed by their tellers and with applicability to daily life only through active interpretation? Or are new cultural meanings established actively and creatively within myths, notwithstanding their relative conservation of form? Such questions seem to lead to a paradox in the works of Salomon and Taussig, one that apparently underlies much of the Andeanist discussion of where or when one finds the "truly Andean." In searching for the historical derivation of meaning, Taussig (1984b) overlooks the power of individual myths (or their telling) to create meaning, a capacity ascribed to the militantly "anti-structuring" qualities he attributes to shamanic practice. Salomon, in an exquisite analysis of dramaturgical form in ritual, seems forced to abandon the possibility that ritual elements bring to their part in ritual some presupposed historical structure.

In the pages that follow we seek a way out of this dilemma through attention to the narrative structure of the myth and also to the myth's— and the structure's—relationship to other forms of social practice. Our position is that Salomon's *yumbo* complex and Taussig's devil beliefs, like the myth of the destroying Christ, can best be understood as providing channels through which meaning systems may undergo revalorization. Given that the myths are, as we argue, about the creation of fully formed social agents and the constraints on such agency, ritual-dramatic and mythic narratives are called upon to make the universe of social action intelligible and to provide the text and context in which social actors can be "re-created." Neither solely creative nor fully presupposed, the meanings of the "elements" of myth (types of model actors or phases in their development) shift as these elements come into new forms of hierarchical relation, when in performance the narrative structure of myth or ritual is employed to comment on or change meanings and the meaning values assigned particular players, in the ever-changing lived forms of hierarchically constituted social action.

As a first step, then, in exploring this apparent dialectic between presupposition and creativity, history and virtual cultural logic versus effective and critical social practice, we must place the myth in the context of its telling. By so doing it will be possible to see this dialectic as a focus of the narrative development of the myth's plot, itself a calque of, and model for, the development of social actors in K'ulta.

Recontextualizing the Myth

In the Andes and among the Aymara of what is today Bolivia, "first contact" and the initial events of European colonization and cultural subordination took place far beyond the reach of individual memory, scores of generations in the past. When asking our Aymara collaborators in Ayllu K'ulta about such long past events as the Spanish conquest or the time of the Incas, the response was generally bewilderment: they assumed that we, like the priest, rural schoolteachers, and other city folks, had privileged access to such information. Their deferral to our supposed authority on such "questions of fact" undoubtedly resulted as much from centuries of usurpation of authoritative power by European officials as it did from the foreignness of the questions themselves. It did not mean, however, that K'ultas' myths are merely residual or underground history, left to the people after the co-optation of "legitimate" history by national society. Nor did we collect any revisionist "alternative" histories, though we believe something of that sort exists in the stories written and published by Aymara nationalists.

The Aymara related to us a myth about the founding events of the current cosmos, which occurred during the remote past (*layra timpu*), that is used to explain the junctures where past and present meet. Our friends told us versions of this myth, on several occasions, to help us understand the value of such significant social forms, of past and present, as Chullpas and wild foods associated with them, and of the sun and Jesus Christ. Myths such as this, held to be unquestionably true, define the terms in which history can be understood and in which the passing events of daily life, of ritual structure, and of recent history are embedded. They are the means by which their creators fashion and refashion a philosophy of history.[2] Through our analysis we hope to show how historical relations are incorporated into cosmological understanding, which is itself achieved in the practice of daily life.[3]

Jesucristu-Tatalantix Supaytinsi-Chullpantix

(Jesus Christ-Tatala and the Supay-Chullpas)

Tatala and the Supay-Chullpas were enemies. The Chullpas chased Tatala, a foreign, old man, and finally were able to kill him because they were many and he only one. They buried him in the earth and put thorns on top. They waited, then went away. Later they discovered that he had escaped. They caught him and buried him again, this time putting a large stone on top. They waited and waited, but when they left, again he escaped. They went after him. While following his trail, the Chullpas asked some other people if they had seen the fleeing old man. These people pointed out the ashes of his cooking fire, and from their appearance the Chullpas believed he was long gone. [Here the teller explains that this is a deceit in which the ashes (*sak'a sunchu*) only appear to be old.] Exactly at this point the Chullpas become frightened. They learn [or remember] that the old man would conquer them if he got away. They frantically build strong houses, with their doors facing east, to protect themselves from the heat and light of Tatala's fire. Tatala rises into the sky as the sun from the east, and the Chullpas die in their houses, burned and dried up by the heat. To this day, one can see their remains, and the sun, Tata Awatiri, continues to travel across the sky. Some of the Chullpas, however, managed to escape, by diving under the water of Lake Poopo. These became the present day Chullpa people.

Who Are the Chullpas?

The myth refers to one group of antagonists, the Chullpas, as an autochthonous people who lived before the sun existed, but the term *chullpa* has broader reference in use among K'ultas. The first time we heard this myth was in response to a question about the origin of the fishing people of Lake Poopo, who are themselves called Chullpas, otherwise known as Urus, Chipayas, or Moratos. Although distinct from one another, these groups are stereotyped as fishers and as hunters of water birds, as opposed to herders, and as gatherers, as opposed to agriculturalists. Although possessed of a kind of "wild" shamanic power, these groups are considered to be of particularly low status by K'ultas. In the K'ultas' view, gathering edible wild plants is a pastime for children or a pursuit of the destitute. So, too, they show disdain for the eggs sometimes collected from water birds and often sold to *vecinos* (townspeople) or used as gifts for visiting outsiders. That is, the birds and their eggs are "good" as food only for uncultured people. This association with water birds has special significance: birds are associated with original time and with the origin, continuing in the present, of domesticated animals such as llamas and alpacas.[4] In one version of a creation myth from Hualcan in Peru, similar to the one we analyze here, birds were the only life before the appearance of Jesus (Stein 1961:298).[5]

The view K'ultas have of present-day Chullpa people is stereotypical. In fact the Andean literature includes a number of articles debating the economic role of these groups at various stages in pre-Columbian and colonial history.[6] Although the Spanish misunderstood the taxonomy of production that defined Chullpas/Urus as inferior in Aymara terms, they assigned them a much lower taxation level than other indigenous groups because of their presumed inferior subsistence base. This suggests that at least the dominant native ideology concerning these groups was accepted by the colonial administration and incorporated into administrative policy, perhaps providing yet another structural route for its preservation.

Besides being a derogatory term for a present-day class of people, *chullpa* also refers to a particular kind of above-ground tomb found throughout the Southern Andes and to the ancient people who supposedly inhabited such tombs (interpreted as houses).[7] These people are thought to have lived on wild foods alone. Indeed, the Tatala myth discussed here was itself told as a story about the use of wild foods by these ancient Chullpas, who are considered to be unable to eat processed food. A currently told Chullpa story, akin to a ghost, or *condenado,* story, bears this out:

> A man, who is really a Chullpa asks hospitality of a couple and is fed generously of *quinua* soup. Upon leaving he hedges about where he lives, finally giving the direction, but warning the couple not to visit him. Sometime later, the male host, disregarding the warning, walks by the Chullpa's supposed house, but finds only ruins. Then, on the ground he sees bones, combined with the undigested *quinua* soup. Shortly thereafter, the man becomes sick.[8]

Besides highlighting the lack of reciprocity that often defines the relation between present and past in popular belief and stories about Chullpas, this story illustrates clearly the opposition between Chullpas and cultivated food and implies that subsistence differences are tantamount to living in a different state of nature.[9] The Aymara and Spanish conception of Chullpas/Urus as lacking knowledge of agriculture is in harmony with other characterizations of Urus and related "wild" people.

The relationship of Chullpas to hunting, and their consequent oppositional relation to domestication/cultivation, is a theme deserving more detailed treatment. Throughout the Andes wild animals are said to be the domesticated animals of the mountain gods of the *layra timpu* (underworld), and hunting them seems always to be associated with the appropriation of chthonic power. Conversely, the domestication of animals, although the mark of "civilized" people, distances them from the forces of the underworld as it differentiates them from Chullpas. We do know that hunting played a significant part in Aymara public ritual in the past, as, for example, in the description by Bertonio (1612:323) of vicuña hunting in naming rites. Of more interest here are the rituals portraying "wild" (outside the control of authorities) Choquela hunting people, called in to convey the wild forces still necessary in cultivated production, which are still enacted by Andeans in the Titicaca area (Cuentas Ormachea 1982). Both this rite and the chanku ritual hunt described for seventeenth-century Huarochiri (Urioste 1983:83) seem to be connected with efforts to ensure proper onset of the rains for agricultural purposes. In K'ulta certain kinds of wild animals are still hunted in order that fresh blood of certain nocturnal species might make men hard as stones in fighting. Similarly, and aside from a great many uses in curing, parts of other animals, such as foxes, viscachas, and the suri (the South American ostrich), are obtained as talismans, used to convey the animals' qualities to their carriers (cf. Platt 1978; Abercrombie 1986).

Ritual hunting, then, can be seen as a metaphoric catalyst for imparting to human authority structures the forcefulness of their "natural" analogues, in which the dominant members are chthonic deities. Domestication and the seasonally regulated forms of production thus made possible were consequent to, and themselves made possible by, the appearance of Tatala. As we shall see, the public rituals of K'ulta metaphorically apply the principles of the "domestication" and herding of animals—the "civilized" analogues of the Chullpas' hunting—to the hierarchical control over humans, an end made possible by following Tatala's example. Taken together, the qualities attributed to Chullpas/Urus amount to the opposite of "civilized," a negation against which ideas about what it is to be "civilized"—and "Christian"—achieve definition. This natural state, which signifies the past to K'ultas, is very much present in current Aymara understandings of geography.

In an insightful analysis based on the study of toponyms, Gabriel Martinez (1983) details an Aymara conception of the link between geography, natural forms, and the Chullpas. He discusses how the myriad toponyms that define Chuani geographic space may be organized into two interconnected conjuncts of relations, one centering on chullpas (also called wak'as or gentiles) and wild species of plants and animals associated with them, and the other related to wak'as (here also called demonios, not chullpas or gentiles) as well as metals, rainbows, and the wild animals of the gods. Martinez concludes that both conjuncts of terms describe marginal and dangerous zones that mark the border of the human world with the savage, either the past-below or the above-outside. We see, then, as surely as Western scientists read history in geologic formations, that Aymaras find social history alive in a system of botanical, zoological, and toponymic-geographic indexes. In these Aymara conceptions of space and time, the past, like the future, is nearby, immanent in the visible world and accessible via ritual practice, with the potential to break into daily life at any moment or place, in harmful or beneficial (and controlled or uncontrolled) ways.

It should be clear that the term *chullpa* can have various points of reference in daily life. How these points of reference are tied together and how historical processes are addressed in an articulated system of ritual and social space-time is subject to further discussion. Here we point out how the role of the Chullpas in myth grounds the definition of this social-sacred system by integrating what are present-day indexes of the past with a vision of cosmological history. The multivocality of the term *chullpa* —as it refers to remains of non-Christians, tombs, and "wild" people in the past and the present—is crucial.[10]

Remembered and more distant recognized ancestors of K'ultas, not surprisingly, also inhabit an ambiguous space, somewhere at the junction of *layra timpu* (the time of the Chullpas) and postsolar (and Christian) times. After death, K'ulta dead travel westward to an underworld kingdom inside Tata Muntu, a "world mountain" the location of which K'ultas do not know. The dead who have not completed or cannot complete their journey come as *condenados* to occupy the same near-space as Chullpas do, usually invisible but immanent in the physical world. That is, neither Chullpas nor dead ancestors have been completely banished by the ascension of Tatala and the separation of death. The association of Chullpas with the dead cannot completely account for the K'ulta tellers' ambivalence toward the Chullpas, however, as the absence of full identification of the teller with either side in the story (including identification with Tatala) must imply. The hyphenated title name Supay-Chullpa[11] makes this explicit: Chullpa refers to an ancestor, though a transformed inferior one; Supay designates an evil anti-god from the point of view of the external dominators.

The incompletion of this banishment is permanent, in spite of the best efforts of gods and humans, and along with the disruptive, generative, but uncontrolled interventions of Chullpa power it must be insistently and repeatedly performed in ritual, just as the failures in banishment must be related with horror in myth. Surely this eternal return of Chullpas and the dead expresses an ambivalence toward the process and the fact of their banishment in myth, insofar as this banishment comes to represent a decisive step in the historical transformation (and development in the life cycle) of its tellers. Although K'ultas refuse to identify the Chullpas with their own ancestors, since they regard themselves as children of Tatala (in some unspecified and ambivalent way), identification with the foreign conqueror is also incomplete. The ambivalence is radical and, given the fact that emulation of Tatala implies an acceptance of the conditions of a very much lived and ongoing form of social domination, impossible to resolve. A form of "domination-resisting" self-identification may be achieved through ritual enactments of the process described in the Tatala myth, but, like other unpleasant aspects of life (such as death and social hierarchy), it can never be accepted more than incompletely, ambivalently, and tentatively—and perhaps can be phrased and understood only when constrained in the context of myth and ritual or other "marked" genres and styles of speech and action.

Greg Urban (1985) has suggested that a linguistic feature representing a marked variety among the choices used in everyday speech can, in the context of a marked genre such as myth, be the standard unmarked style. Later in this essay we make a related point: that the marked role of the Chullpas in the myth helps to define the oppositions this term enters into in social, geographic, and ritual contexts of everyday life, even as it brings those contexts to bear in the larger narrative development of the myth. Within the narrative, these other usages become aligned to one another and to the system of meaning created through the plot itself. We also lay the groundwork for a synthetic interpretation of Aymara cosmology informed by an understanding of hierarchy reached through narrative.

In the myth related here the Chullpas are defined against the character Tatala; the sun is referred to variously as Tata Awatiri (Father Shepherd), Señor Jesucristu (Lord Jesus Christ), or simply Tatala (Respected Father). By contrast to the great number of tales about Chullpas, this is the only one we heard in K'ulta centering on the sun/Christian god. Generally, ritual (rather than myth) provides a public forum for demonstrations of the role of this supernatural being in the lives of K'ultas. As other studies (e.g., Earls 1973) have pointed out, the sun/Christian god is thought to be more remote and unable to affect indigenous life in a direct and spontaneous way, as do the underworld traces of *layra timpu*. We discuss the implication of this fact and how fiesta-cargo ritual gains access to the power of the sky deities in order to confirm the hierarchical ordering of power within present-day society. We also show that the ritual strategy for tapping solar power necessarily invokes a reprise of the narrative development of Tatala as civilizing, dominating agent, with special reference to the Christian notion of self-sacrifice and its transcendence.

Establishing Hierarchy: The Structure of the Narrative

The story recounted here is of an undifferentiated world that becomes divided. Initially the world is bountiful but unordered; there is no hierarchy within human society, just anarchy.[12] Nature, too, is unordered, with chaos portrayed as a lack of differentiation. The world is sunless and, in addition to its lack of diurnal alternation, lacks seasons. So, too, the Chullpas are not bound to the rhythms of agricultural and pastoral production: they live on wild plants and animals, forming a part of the natural order. This lack of differentiation in nature is at once parallel to and a cause of the lack of order in human society. It is only through the Chullpas' active role in a life-and-death struggle with Tatala that the human life cycle becomes bound to the cycles of nature, thus forming the basis for the human harnessing of this "natural," now cyclic energy for agricultural and pastoral production.

The plot unfolds such that the working through of the antagonism of the beginning between Tatala and the Chullpas leads to the disintegration of the initial situation without the full establishment of its opposite. At first, immortality is a complement to the other autochthonous features that characterize Chullpas, such as "natural" subsistence. Other Andean myths suggest that one characteristic of autochthonous beings is immortality.[13] Conversely, it is Tatala who at first appears as mortal. He is old and foreign, and it is his death that initiates cycles of life/death, creation/destruction, and foretells the eventual end of the Chullpas.

Tatala's triumph consists of his ascent to the sky and the resultant establishment of day/night alternation, thus creating the present world and the conditions for agricultural production. The ascent also brings about a differentiation between sky and underworld, so that the rise of Tatala to *alaxpacha* (the "above" or "upper" time-space) is paralleled by the relegation of the Chullpas to *manxapacha* (the "under" or "inner" world), where they remain potent supernatural forces. It is evident that the Chullpa "ghost" stories referred to earlier are based on the ever-present possibility of imbalance in this delicate system. Imbalance may also occur through catastrophic weather conditions associated with the sky god, prevention of which is one focus of much Andean ritual.

The structure of the myth as a whole is paralleled by individual episodes within it. The Chullpas' acts of burial prefigure their own mortality, while Tatala's deceit involving the cooking fire ashes foretells not only his future fiery destructive power but also the sun's role in agricultural production and the parallel role of fire in processing food. The structure of the myth is thus based on transformative actions that the antagonists originate but that ultimately transcend them.

As the cosmos is transformed, so the antagonists are transformed through their interaction with each other. These transformations appear as a series of reversals in stature of the antagonists. Tatala begins the story as human, old, solitary. When the Chullpas kill and bury him, they establish a temporary hierarchy based upon the division of space into within-under and without-above. This same spatial division, echoing as it does the division of Aymara geographic space by toponymic conjuncts, will ultimately describe the path of the sun at the end of the tale and in the present world; it will distinguish as well the destination of souls in their postdeath, partial banishment from the proper domain of humans. Yet Tatala overcomes death by defying barriers of thorns (ch''api) and stone (gala). Spines are used today as barriers to keep the dead and living apart: they are put across the road from hamlet to cemetery when a sick person's soul is in danger of taking flight or when a grieving, newly dead soul might come back to take a loved one. Martinez's (1976:65) treatment of toponyms connects "thorn" place-names to thorns with Chullpas. Other stories common in the Andes illustrate the power of these obstacles and their connection with sacred geography beyond ordinary human control.

Tatala's resurrections are described in this myth from the Chullpas' point of view. They stand guard at the tomb, leave, and return to find Tatala gone. They are progressively more horrified as the death-life cycle repeats itself, now not entirely in their control. It is during the Chullpas' final and unsuccessful pursuit of Tatala that their fate becomes known to them. The deceit of the cooking fire ashes foretells their end, serving as a metaphor for the control of temporality that Tatala, as the sun, will achieve.[14] At this juncture the active role of the Chullpas ends and their actions reverse. They abruptly turn around and return home, forecasting their destruction by heat from the sky. As a defense, they build small, fortified houses for protection.

The final action of the plot parallels the earlier actions but in reverse and on a higher and more encompassing plane. The destruction of the Chullpas is symbolized again in dominance from above, now from the sky. Similarly, the Chullpas have sealed their own fate of entombment; their last act, reversing all their previous actions, is toward the inside. At the conclusion of the myth both supernatural forces are remote from the earth: Tatala, as the sun, controls from outside the meteorological preconditions for successful human production; the Chullpas, banished to the underworld, define the limits of human domination of the earth itself.

Thus, the present-day cosmological order results from the actions of human-like agents. Cosmological bodies and events are invested with the creative agency and subjectivity of the people who tell the story. As deities, the forces the myth describes are the ultimate sources of social power and the ultimate constraints upon human agency. Indeed, it could be said that the object of most rituals in K'ulta is to align social relations and human subjectivity to the model provided in the K'ultas' humanized nature.

The Productivity of the Past in the Present

Even though the daily and seasonal alternations imposed by the process described in the myth imply reversibility in the relative hierarchy of the two cosmological zones, the myth nevertheless describes an ultimately irreversible process in which complementary forms of life-generating and life-destroying powers are divided and banished from the realm of humans. Living between the two zones of a now hierarchically ordered cosmos, today's Aymara must harness and balance, through alternation, what are opposed but complementary extrasocial forces, for the purpose of producing society.

The "conquest" of the story signals neither the complete elimination of the Chullpas nor the ascendancy of the sun as an all-powerful form; rather, the story describes the beginning of an alternation that is hierarchically regulated. The Chullpas exist to this day: as an index of the temporality of human life they exist as the ancestral tombs, which are powerful and dangerous forces; and as a reminder of the continuance of human generation they exist as the Chullpa descendants on Lake Poopo. Thought of as a more "natural" people, less encumbered with calendrical and productive responsibility and therefore inferior, these modern Chullpas are nonetheless ritually powerful because of their connection with (or embodiment of) *manxapacha* and *layra timpu*.[15]

The narrative development of the myth transposes an opposition between darkness and light, wet and cold, dry and hot, from the plane of this earth to that of opposed, otherworldly zones. Living between, but in neither of, the two zones of a now hierarchically ordered cosmos, today's Aymara must mediate the two by calling upon beings who have mediated the zones previously, whether through postdeath journey (ancestral souls), through proximity to both zones (mountain condors and saint-lightning), or by association with the negation of the contrast

(Chullpas, *condenados,* and the dead bodies of unbaptized infants, sometimes called *moros*).[16]

As we have pointed out for K'ulta, and as Olivia Harris (1982) has argued for the Aymara-speaking Laymis, Chullpas are closely associated with the ancestral dead, as the two come into play in seasonal processes. The K'ultas, like the Laymis, beckon the recent dead at the start of the growing season. Later, when continued rain means disaster for the crops, the last of the ghosts are dispatched to the *manxapacha* underworld in the post-*carnaval q'oyra* rite.[17] Shortly afterward, the rites of Easter reenact the burial and resurrection of Christ-Tatala. More generalized underworld forces are given special sacrifices and invoked, also for the purposes of agriculture, during the August and February seasons when the earth is said to be especially receptive. The *choquela* rite of the Chucuito area (Cuentas Ormachea 1982) also appears to be associated with these periods of opening.

The alternation of the rainy growing season (when *manxapacha* forces predominate) with the dry processing and exchange (when *alaxpacha* forces are at the fore) is also paralleled by diurnal alternations. One might argue that the postharvest return of the sun to predominance in the sky and the return of the dead to predominance below the earth create the conditions of extreme day/night temperature variation needed to "freeze-dry" the now-harvested crop. Freeze-drying is a critically important form of food processing in the Andes, which Murra (1984) has lauded as the "domestication of the cold," giving rise to the possibility of long-term storage; it is also the natural form of mummification the "dried up" *chullpas* (as entombed corpses) have gone through.[18] It seems likely, then, that the myth's description of the transformation of the Chullpas from wet- and dark-loving, "natural" humans into dessicated corpses with a role in the sustenance of modern Aymaras is also related to conceptions about alimentation, from cultivation to food processing to digestion.

In K'ulta, agricultural rites are superseded by herding-associated ritual, not surprising given the K'ultas' poor agricultural lands and their dependence on the trade of salt and animal products (in long-distance caravan or truck trade) for the acquisition of valley-produced foodstuffs. Pastoral life also provides a host of metaphors, peculiarly apt in the Christian context, which are taken up to form the K'ulta response to Tatala's productive journey.

The rites of August and February are oriented toward the herds, and the recipients of the sacrifices then performed are the hierarchically organized hill and mountain deities, including the local *uywiris* (herd caretakers) of household and hamlet and the *ayllu* and regional *mallkus* (condor-peaks) that rule them. As another kind of transformation of the "spontaneously generative" powers monopolized by the Chullpas of the Tatala myth, it is through these deities that the productivity of the herd is ensured, as human herders emulate the mountains' mythic ability to herd and control wild animals. Thus the libation sequences of sacrifices performed during all saints' feasts and life-crisis rites enact a litany amounting to the "genealogy" of hill and mountain deities ascribed to the animals, as the reassembled bones of sacrificed animals are returned to their source and placed in hilltop tombs.

Control of a herd—the mark of a fully adult and fully civilized K'ulta couple—is not achieved "naturally." Rather, in a succession of life-career rites beginning with marriage and merging into the fiesta-careers of *ayllu* authorities, independent households and herders are created through the intercession of solar power. The Lamb of God is, in K'ulta, the model par excellence of the ability to control a herd and thereby achieve adulthood, as well as the ability to complete the separation of the person from Chullpa-like childhood to achieve full humanity.[19] For a K'ulta man, adulthood is reached by independently exerting control over others, such as wife, children, and eventual wife-takers who perform what he considers the menial tasks of life, including, ironically, the actual activity of herding in the sense of taking animals to pasture. But the model provided by Tatala, as Tata Awatiri Awksa (Our Father Herder, as he is called in ritual), is of a herder of men. Thus the hierarchical control over other households implicit in political authority is conceived of as possible only by imitating Tatala's struggle of conquest.

This mimesis, like the process described in the narrative itself, can never be more than partial and incomplete. Not only are K'ultas ambivalent toward the historical finality of the domination of wild Chullpa powers by the colonizing powers of Tatala, but the incompletion or need for repetition is also a fact of social life. Each generation must repeat the process for itself; and each individual achieves the capacity for meaningful and effective action that characterizes the fully developed social agency represented by Tatala at the close of the myth. It is a process, however, that requires the permanent maintenance of a Chullpa within, a metaphoric Chullpa whose disorderly generative power conceals entropic tendencies that can never be fully mastered.

Perhaps this fearful cultural portrayal of preconquest Andeans as Chullpas precludes the possibility of a "return to preconquest" millenarianism. But both Tatala and the K'ultas need Chullpas for their development as agents and for the purpose of imposing domination and hierarchy. The Chullpas' resultant ineradicability, therefore, also precludes the completion of the hegemonic cultural transformation begun by Spanish colonists and their gods. In what follows we discuss the implications of this and show how the dominating power of Tatala and of the state can itself be turned to the purposes of cultural resistance.

Colonial/State Hegemony and the Meaning of Hierarchical Control

Conquest, domination, and the imposition of social hierarchy are central themes of Andean myth. Parallel to the hierarchically arranged sky and underworld of the myth related here are the like-named and hierarchically ordered moieties of K'ulta—*alaxsaya* (upper/outside) and *manxasaya* (lower/inside).[20] Interestingly, Platt (1978) reports what is clearly a variant of the present myth from Macha, an ethnic group neighboring K'ulta, in which the emergence of the sun (and subsequent differentiation of cosmic zones) is held to account for the origin of Macha's moieties.

The ranked but complementary moieties of the region can be interpreted as an introjection into society of the opposition between cosmic zones and their attendant deities. Like the cosmic zones, the moieties are locked into a permanent form of asymmetry in which the "upper" moiety remains "upper," though the permanence of the relative authority of moiety heads has disappeared with the colonial period. In today's moiety-level authority system (as in the cosmos), the valences of the terms to the opposition alternate, so that the higher ranked of the *jilaqata* and *alcalde* offices rotate yearly between the moieties.[21] The valences change in other forms as well. In the ritual battles (*tinkus*) that take place during saints' fiestas, there is an unpredictable give-and-take in which victory is not predetermined by the name of the moiety (though victory also remains subject to debate). Alongside this chance alternation are numerous other forms of more predetermined alternations, such as the annual exchange between moieties of ritual sponsorship roles in each of the town's major fiestas.[22]

It is through the system of collective fiesta performances that moieties, and the polity as a whole, are periodically re-created in the image of the cosmos as constituted in myth. However, it would be an erroneous simplification to assume that the myth serves as a static model of (or for) the symbolic attributes of a dual-organized society, perhaps as a rationale, logical or historical, for its origin and persistence. Rather, social processes, themselves understood in such forms as moiety organization, are couched in terms of hierarchization, played out in myth in the battle over death and regeneration. We suggest that it would be useful to reexamine fiestas, which have traditionally been considered conservative social forces, in this light. In doing so, the process of hierarchization encoded in ritual form is revealed as that process through which the very definition/formation of polities is enacted. In historical terms, it is this crucible in which power relations, and hence the very structure of domination, are forged.

As a state-defined entity, Ayllu K'ulta is a canton with a population spread among more than a hundred hamlets, themselves scattered across a large territory. Polity-defining (and authority-legitimating) activities are circumscribed, however, within a Spanish-founded, now usually empty, ritual center town, which is the locus of state and sky-deity intervention in local affairs. Such circumscription is apt, considering that the authorities constituted through the ritual system are the figures who mediate between the polity and the state. Thus, while moieties themselves express a parallelism with the hierarchy of the cosmos as a whole, the town-based public ritual (focusing upon sky deities) in which moieties actually meet seems to link the production/reproduction of the polity as a whole to the state/polity interface and to oppose this total order to the partial, submoiety social groups (such as household, hamlet, patriline, and *ayllu*) that are scattered across the territory. This is clearest in an apparent division between the rites performed in town (oriented toward the sky deities) and in the residential hamlets (oriented toward *manxapacha* deities). Seen in this light, the sequential structure of moiety-level rituals model and define the confrontation between the indigenous order and the colonizing state. To fully understand this confrontation, which parallels the dialectic of presupposition and creation in myth, one would have to work through a 400-year history of the articulation of Spanish-colonial and indigenous-Andean ideas about the relationship between "civilized" and "savage." Here we must be satisfied with a few brief comments.

Early Spanish sources, such as the Aymara dictionary by Bertonio (1612) and the origin myths collected soon after the Spanish invasion, indicate that the Aymara vocabulary defined fully "social" humans through their opposition to people of the presolar, predomestication age. These early sources show an identification, in Aymara terminology, of this autochthonous people with their supposed latter-day remnants in the hunting/fishing Urus and Choquelas, as we indicated earlier, as well as in wild animals and birds, all of which lived outside the frontiers of the hierarchical "community" of lords and subjects bound by reciprocal obligations.[23] Although the authors of these sources were Spanish, and we should suppose that they grasped and transcribed themes and definitions they found (and made) understandable in their own terms, we cannot see the Aymara self-definition in hierarchical terms as being a completely colonial imposition. The details of the taxonomy of natural productivity through which this hierarchical understanding is reached belies a colonial origin.

However, the project of conversion to Christianity and civilization, which justified the subordination of Indians in colonial rule, did presuppose and require the maintenance of Indians in the role of "pagans and savages" in a European opposition that in many ways resembles the Andean.[24] The project also required the resettlement of scattered populations that were previously unified through subordination to the hereditary indigenous elite into towns. The process derived from the European idea of *civitas*: civilization through orderly subordination to church and state representatives in a (social, not natural) human- and God-made world. Those who remained in the town and fulfilled their obligations to God and king (the feast sponsors and town authorities) would necessarily have been considered at least partly civilized; but in this scheme, those who fled—the majority of the populace, who returned quickly to their former, scattered settlements—presumably joined their *gentile* ancestors (or remained with them) in the category of lawless (rebellious) and Godless (idolatrous) savages.[25]

Today, the superimposition of these two parallel contrasts remains in the association of the town with the Christian sky gods of *alaxpacha* and the outlying hamlets with the relatively autochthonous deities of *manxapacha*. But this is not to say that the Andeans fully adopted the Europeans' terms. K'ultas consider themselves good Christians even as they recognize that they must keep some of their beliefs and practices out of the sight of the priest and other city people. It is their preconquest ancestors (the Chullpas) who, as non-Christians, have been assimilated to the category "natural man," with especially close ties to the chthonic powers that remain the raw materials from which "social man" is made.

Let us examine these ideas as they are played out in ritual. The temporal sequence of a fiesta performance moves from the residential hamlet to the ritual center town (the locus of church and state intervention in K'ulta affairs) and then back to the hamlet. This movement from periphery to center and back is accompanied by shifts in the focus of libations offered by fiesta sponsors. In the hamlet, libations are offered primarily in alcohol, to underworld forces (the mountains, plains, and ancestors that are close by and in which the hamlet is "rooted"). In the town, such libations are greatly attenuated in favor of libations in corn beer (*chicha*) to sky deities (sun, moon, and saints). The opposition between private and public performances may owe its existence, at least in part, to the idolatry-extirpating activities that accompanied the religious conquest of the Andes. However, this contrast in ritual performances does not emphasize the separation of the two social/cosmological zones but, like seasonal fertility rites, emphasizes their mediation. The power of authority comes from control over the meeting of the moieties and cosmic zones. Indigenous authorities, in turn, mediate by representing indigenous society to the state and the state (through tax collection, etc.) to the indigenous society. Authorities and ritual sponsors become "herders of men" only through a prolonged series of metaphoric, sacrificial equations among llamas, humans, and the gods. Hierarchical control of humans is gained by internalizing a quality both possessed by the solar Christ (Tata Awatiri) and present in the animal world (the *llantirus,* or "herd-leading llamas")—that of the one subsuming the many.

Very briefly summarized, fiesta sponsorship rites begin with a sacrifice of *llantiru* llamas (Spanish, *delantero*), dedicated primarily to chthonic *manxapacha* deities of fertility and "natural" production (the *uywiris* and *mallkus*). Through these sacrifices, and by presiding over the meeting of moieties and cosmic zones in banquet and *tinku,* the sponsor becomes a *llantiru* of the human herd (the herder of which is Tata Awatiri). Subsequently offering himself in symbolic sacrifice to the gods of *alaxpacha,* the sponsor is equated with the saint and with the solar Christ of which the saint is a fragment. The final sacrifice is of the saint image, whose "clothing" (layers of ponchos and carrying cloths) is removed and worn home to the hamlet by the sponsor and his followers.[26]

One might argue that the symbolic focus of these collective rites is the projection of the herder-herd hierarchy from the level of ordinary production (human to llamas) to that of production of the society as a whole, in which authorities are called *awatiri* (herder) and address their followers as *t"ama* (herd). But in fact it is the very power of controlling domesticated animals—the basis of "civilized" rather than a *layra timpu*-type society—that has been invested in the relationship between *alaxpacha* (and the state) and *manxapacha* (and indigenous society), that is, of having come from the domination of autochthonous beings by the solar Christ. If the rites of authorities represent a kind of submission to state hegemony, they are not conceived as such by their practitioners. Local control over their form represents control over the form in which hegemony is expressed, as serving local ends. So the ritual sponsors' and authorities' role, in mediating between cosmic zones and between the polity and the state, is that of appropriating from each (through the intercession of its opposite) what is necessary for social control. From the underworld to which humans have access through mortality, to the distant ancestors, and from "wild" intermediaries, humans may gain access to powers of growth and sustenance. From the sky gods, reached through rites partly imposed from the outside, comes (via a sacrificial pact) the power to harness such powers by subordinating them within a hierarchical order. In both cases society's appropriation of chthonic "generative" and *alaxpacha* "hierarchical" powers remains incomplete and its maintenance contingent on the repetition of sacrificial mediation.

The sacrifice involved refers us back to the Tatala-Chullpa myth. The death of the Chullpas can be viewed as a form of sacrifice, of autochthonous ancestors, upon which the present order and the present form of accommodated resistance to hegemony are founded. Platt (1983) cites a ritual practiced in Pocoata (a group neighboring both Macha and K'ulta) that phrases the "sacrificial" role of the constituted authority in terms of obligations to the colonial state. In acts referring to the dispatch of Indians to the *mita* of Potosi, it is the authority, as a *mitayo delantero,* who is sent packing to redeem the polity as a kind of offering to the mines and to the state. But all the while the ancestors, who did go to the *mita* (abolished in the early nineteenth century), are recalled as having laid the basis for the current order.

A similar rite of which we have only descriptions, since it ceased to be performed in 1978, took place in K'ulta during Todos Santos—confirming that the present order is based on an earlier, sacrificial pact between the dead and the state. In the K'ulta rite the *ayllu* heads feigned a dispatch of youths to the mines of Potosi while dancing in front of the cemetery with mummified black water birds hanging from their necks. The birds, like the authorities wearing them, were called *soq"a machura.*[27] Significantly, in other areas (see Allen 1982) this is just the term employed for what are called Chullpas in K'ulta. One sees here a strong connection between the authorities and the chthonic powers (the *uma haque* diving birds of Bertonio and the non-Christian dead), while the youths "sent to the *mita"* after having been "married" follow in the footsteps of the Christian dead in sacrificing themselves to the chthonic powers (via completion of obligations to the state) in order to produce fertility in field, mine, and household.

In contrast to the complexity and ambiguity within *manxapacha,*[28] the situation in *alaxpacha* appears to be more straightforward. The complete synthesis of pre-Columbian heroic sky deities with Christian counterparts makes colonial (and republican) hegemony, for the K'ultas, an integral aspect of the constituted social whole. The alternating ambivalence toward indigenous deities and Christian sky deities precludes either full identification with or complete rejection of one or the other. The antipathy between what are not only opposed parts of the cosmos but opposite sides of a long-running dialogue between "ethnic group" and hegemonic powers forms a complexly ordered dialectic through which society defines itself.

The fact remains that the Tatala-Chullpa myth falls short of being an Aymara Genesis. Indeed, the myth accounts for the creation of central contradictions in the culture and cosmos but leaves the earth, between the sky and underworld, vacant (unlike the creation stories collected by the chroniclers). We have just begun to understand the predicament— being at the same time of both eras and cosmic zones—that makes it impossible for the people of K'ulta to insert themselves into the story as products of either conquered or conqueror. A full treatment of this predicament would require the analysis of a social history that has not yet been written, tracing the vicissitudes of the conversion process, the succession of modi vivendi between indigenous polities and colonial and republican states, and a host of other issues.[29] It would also require a careful comparative analysis of pre-Columbian and modern world-inside-out creation myths,[30] as well as of Andeanized versions of the death and resurrection of Christ (and the substance of the texts and rites the priests actually taught). In the former story type, the destruction of an autochthonous people (clearly not the ancestors of the tellers) is followed by the creation of another race of human beings. In the Christian story, of course, the death of Christ follows the creation of humans and leads not to the destruction of his tormentors but to their redemption.

Concluding Remarks

We do not see this myth as just a mirror of the past in analogic form. Nor is it an ideological imposition, pure and simple, that has been filtered down through the exigencies of history and restructured along ideological lines for purposes either of resistance or "creolification." Both of these kinds of dialogue with history exist, of course, and myths can and are used to these ends when they are inserted, in the first case, in literary works and, in the latter case, in revisionist histories and political manifestos. These latter forms, themselves part of social life, are often later mythologized.

Although the myth related here may at first have seemed an apt metaphor of the Spanish conquest, it was clear to us that the tellers did not think of it in those terms. Nor could it be seen as an Indianized Bible story, put together from the bricolage of two religious systems to meet the religious needs of new Christians. It was precisely the uneasy fit of the myth with both the Christian resurrection myth and with what has been called the Aymara creation myth that brought home to us the centrality of the structural development of the plot itself, in interrelating, redefining, and creating new meanings for important but ambiguous aspects of the world as it is lived and acted upon. Myths, then, are much more than just historical precipitates; they are themselves continually becoming a part of history. Through their mythopoetic structures,[31] myths embody the emergent re-creation and distillation of cultural premises (they "talk about" history). They also are told in a historico-temporal context that provides a referential ground for the myth as a whole.[32]

Myths like the Tatala story are rooted in the plurality of culturally presupposed meanings of its terms. What strikes us as the "profundity" of such a myth derives from its multivocal subject matter (i.e., Chullpas, Tatala). The narrative structure of the myth revalorizes these distinct voices, as presupposed meanings are shifted and changed through the changing relationship of the protagonists in the myth.[33] This hierarchical structure of meaning makes the interpretation "permeable" to the larger purposes and debates of society. The mythic "process" described in narrative development also serves to comment on and revalorize a plurality of interrelated social processes, from food production to human development and maturation, to the "political" process by which K'ultas define themselves vis-à-vis state domination.[34] Specifically, the Christian resurrection myth here has become both a metaphor of and a vehicle for the narrative understanding of hierarchical control in Andean terms. The story of the Christ-Chullpa conflict represents a struggle between two superhuman forces that defines them as agents in its creation of the present world. This struggle, through the identity-defining transformation of the antagonists, regulates the cosmos and identifies the context within which their acts, and human acts modeled on them, can establish meanings. The story encapsulates an Aymara experience of the nature of social life and hierarchy.

The central metaphors and tensions of this story are based upon the same historical and religious understanding that gives meaning to the daily activities of the K'ulta tellers. We have seen that these involve the autochthonous Chullpas (though not as survivals of a romantic past) and the Christ figure (though not as a thin Hispanic overlay), which mutually define the past and therefore the present terms of social relations. In fact, the myth systematically reworks the hegemonic relationship of what were once two separate traditions. Moreover, an analysis that would insist on decomposing this system into its supposedly indigenous and Hispanic parts would thus completely distort the meaning built up in the myth in favor of a mythic history of its own making.

We have shown that such highly structured symbolic forms as myth and ritual cannot be viewed as conservative forces, preserving some original "precontact" cultural logic. Rather, they provide the active locus for the simultaneous distillation and recreation of the values (now presupposing the conquest and colonial domination) that motivate social action. This conclusion is, of course, congruent with the more generalized rejection of models that assume the existence of closed, autonomous cultural orders in a world where domination and colonization are all but inescapable. Latin Americanists—indeed, ethnologists in general—have been increasingly forced to face the problem, in efforts such as the symposium that gave rise to this volume. The wonder of it is that this theoretical sea-change should have been so long in coming to the Andes, where a full 450 years separates the ethnographic present from the Spanish invasion.

NOTES

The fieldwork on which this essay is based was carried out among the Aymara-speaking herders of K'ulta, an *ayllu*, "ethnic group," and canton in Abaroa Province, Department of Oruro, Bolivia, in 1979–80, and for briefer periods in 1981 and 1982. We gratefully acknowledge the aid of Thomas Abercrombie's Fulbright-Hays Dissertation Research Fellowship in 1979–80 and Fulbright IIE in 1981. We also acknowledge funding sources for his return visit in 1982: a Mellon award from the Center for Latin American Studies, University of Chicago; a Dissertation Research Abroad Fellowship from the Division of Social Sciences, University of Chicago; the Elizabeth and Melville Jacobs Fund of the Whatcom Museum; and Sigma Xi. We must also thank the people of Ayllu K'ulta for their collaboration in our research. This essay has benefited from the comments of a considerable number of individuals, beginning with the participants and discussants in the AAA symposium and including the editor of this volume, as well as from comments (on a penultimate draft) by Terence Turner, Rafael Sanchez, and Tristan Platt, and from the comments of an anonymous reader for the University of Illinois Press.

1. This insight, as well as a careful discussion of Taussig's use of the concept of ideology, can be found in Jaskol 1983.

2. Of course, this is not the only way in which K'ultas formulate past events. About remote times K'ultas also quote what others (such as schoolteachers) have told them, but this is considered a very untrustworthy sort of knowledge. About more recent events (such as those observed by the speaker or by someone who reported to the speaker), quite unmythlike "empirical" accounts (very familiar to us) are produced. Recounting of recent events is central,

for example, in the formal resolution of disputes in the court of K'ulta's rotative authorities.

3. This free translation was made by us from a version tape-recorded during an interview with a K'ulta research collaborator in September 1982. It conforms well to versions heard in other contexts (also in K'ulta, in 1979 and 1980) and is well known in the area. The two most typical contexts for telling myths are after dark within the family and during rest breaks in collective labor.

4. Flores Ochoa (1978) shows, as our field research confirmed, that along with the belief that the camelids themselves originated in springs, many color patterns are named after like-marked water birds.

5. Chullpas/Urus, like birds in general but especially water birds (after which the majority of llama and alpaca color/pattern terms are named), are closely associated with both the underworld (manxapacha) and the epoch in which it was predominant (layra timpu). It may be that, in the seventeenth century at least, the autochthonous people and their latter-day descendants were not just thought to eat such birds but to be these birds. Among Bertonio's dictionary entries are two for the same term: "Uma haque [literally, water person]: Los Paxaros de la Laguna, o mar"; "Uma haque: Qualquiera que trata en la mar, o laguna como los marineros, y uros &c." (1612, 2:374).

6. See, for example, Wachtel (1978).

7. For a description of chullpa tombs in the Titicaca area, see Hyslop (1976). See also the account of chullpa construction quoted in note 29.

8. This summary is of a myth recorded in K'ulta in September 1982.

9. This is consistent with the belief that "Hispanic" vecinos and gringos, who subsist through economic interchange instead of agricultural or pastoral work, are also products of a different cosmological order (Taussig 1980a; see also Harris 1982:71, note 24).

10. In a related version of the story, collected by Tschopik (1951), Tatala is referred to as an achachi (old man) and the Chullpas are called gentil jaqi (heathen people). Thus, "conquering sun" is referred to as an indigenous category of person, while the dominated people are designated by a borrowed Spanish term that specifies non-Christian. In the case under analysis, it is the dominator that has been semi-Hispanicized, while the defeated group is clearly named for indigenous cultural phenomena. A connection between indigenous tombs and conquered people that had been defined only by the end of the earlier myth is, in the present case, partly presupposed at the outset.

11. Supay was the Andean term chosen by Spanish missionaries to translate "devil." A graduated shift in usage from chullpa to supay is not evident in tellings in either Spanish or Aymara, nor between languages, although a historical connection was made by one teller who said that supays were the souls (almas) of chullpas. Other entities such as the uywiris and mallkus (types of mountain deities) were also said to take the evil supay form. For comparison see Hardman (n.d.) and Harris (1982). For a treatment of the semantic transformation of supay from ancestral soul to devil (and supay wasi from tomb to hell and mine), see Taylor (1980b).

12. Thus the portrayal of Chullpa society conforms to Bertonio's (1612, 2:89)

definition of the Choquela hunters as "Gente cimarrona que viue en la puna sustentandose con la caça." *Cimarrona* refers to those who are not under the control of authorities of any sort.

13. In a myth from Huarochiri, mortality results from a misstep in rites that had returned the dead to life in five days. Similarly, it is a misstatement that caused an original state in which game animals ate humans to be reversed (Urioste 1983:211, 37).

14. A similar deceit, also carried out through the control of temporality, is found in a myth reported by Rasnake (this volume).

15. According to Allen (1982), in the region of Sonqo, at least, the pre-Columbian tombs are unambiguously identified with *gentile* ancestors, not with an inferior, autochthonous people. But such ancestors are called *suq"a machulas,* which are a kind of black water bird in K'ulta. As noted in the text, mummified *suq"a machuras* are associated in K'ulta with the dead and with *layra timpu.*

16. In certain contexts this includes children, women, and wife-takers (see Abercrombie 1986).

17. In the *q'oyra* rite, an effigy of the deceased, feasted during previous rites, is forcefully dispatched to *manxapacha* by being thrown out of the hamlet on the western (sunset) path, along with the trappings of mourning. For men, the rite takes place during Carnaval, while the souls of women are sent on their way during Easter.

18. In the manufacture of freeze-dried potatoes (*ch'uñu*) and meat (*ch'arki*), the central process takes advantage of the alternation between the extreme cold of night and the temperate daytime temperatures and low humidity resulting from the strong solar radiation in the dry season. Water released from tissues through nighttime freezing is pressed out and evaporated during the day.

19. Thus, in all sacrifices the generative forces of the llamas, the blood and seed (chest fat), are poured and burned toward the east for Tatala, who himself has need of the generative power originating in *manxapacha.*

20. We note here the implications of the myth for understanding the institution of moieties which, following T. Turner (1983), might be analyzed as the projection to an intrasocial plane of a model of the domination of indigenous society by external powers. On the interpretation of moiety systems, see also T. Turner (1984).

21. In the case of cosmic zones, of course, "valences" (the relative predominance of *alaxpacha* and *manxapacha* in the affairs of humans, and also the strengths of zone-associated phenomena) alternate seasonally.

22. The interface of calendrical rituals and social organization and the structures of subsistence production is described and analyzed in detail in Abercrombie (1986).

23. This is particularly clear in a whole array of terms from Bertonio's (1612, 2:89) dictionary that identify people who, like the Choquelas, are "Gente cimarrona que viue en la puna sustentandose con la caça" (fugitives who live in the highlands, subsisting through hunting):

Puruma haque; Hombre por sugetar, que no tiene Ley, ni Rey.

Puruma vraq; Tierra por labrar, O la que ha mucho que no se labra. . . .

Puruma Caura; Carnero que aun no ha sido cargado.

Puruma, vel Cchamacapacha; Tiempo antiquissimo, quando no auia sol, segun imaginauan los indios, ni muchas cosas de las que ay agora.

Puruma camauisa haque; El que no acude a las obligaciones del pueblo. (ibid.:278)

Suni: Tierra despoblada.

Suni haque: Saluaje que nunca viue en poblado. (ibid.:327–28)

Pampa: El campo, o todo lo que esta fuera del pueblo, ahora sea cuesta, ahora llano. . . .

Pampa haque: Vno que viue a poco mas, o menos, sin consejo, ni prudencia.

Pampa haque, vel Puruma haque vel atimaa haque: Vno que no esta sugeto a nadie, que viue a su atuedrio. . . . (ibid.:246–47)

24. Indeed, their mutual assimilation is already visible in the 1612 dictionary entries given in note 23.

25. These insights owe a great deal to Pagden's *The Fall of Natural Man* (1983) and to understandings reached in many discussions with Rafael Sanchez.

26. Abercrombie (1986) provides a detailed description of these rites.

27. Our impression is that wearing the loon-like birds—with their affinity for water and ability to move between *alaxpacha* and *manxapacha* —was also done to bring on the rains. This is consistent with Harris's (1982) interpretation of the role of the dead in agricultural production. A contrasting rite is recorded in Bertonio (1612), in which a bird called Tunqui ("Un paxaro Grande como lechuca, que tiene las plumas amarillas"; 2:364) was used in a rite to prevent rain: "Tunqui aatutha. Leuantar este paxaro muerto en vn palo, como esperado para que no llueua, es supersticion de indios."

28. This subject is treated in depth by Platt (1983), and was underscored for us in discussions with Rafael Sanchez.

29. An analysis of the historical process by which the synthesis and displacement noted in the myth came about would have to address the question of ambivalence toward the Chullpas in the context of pre-Columbian forms as well. The occupants of many of the *chullpa* tombs were actually indigenous noblemen who were also, in their own way, dominating outsiders. Regarding *chullpa* construction, a witness to a *probanza* of the caciques of Cara Cara states that Tata Paria was:

> . . . senor de toda la nación de los caracaras de la dicha parcialidad (de anansaya) y de la de los quillacas soras carangas y chuyes y todas ellas le obedecieron y las hacía juntar en Macha y este testigo conoció muy bién al dicho tata paria siendo éste testigo muchacho y vió que le traían en onbros y yndios como gran señor. . . . y que éste testigo saue que todas las dichas naciones se juntaron para hacer le sepulturas/labradas de piedra y le hizieron dos la vna en macha y la ottra en caroata y que en aquél tiempo no se hacían sino a grandes señores como lo fue el dicho tata paria. . . . (AGNA 13, 18.7.2, Padrones Potosí 1612–19:f309r–v, testimony of Don Felipe Ochani, principal of Ayllo Paro of the Anansaya parcialidad and . . . "más de cién años de edad," dated March 21, 1612)

30. See, for example, Tschopik (1951) and Urbano (1981b). There is a remarkably similar version of the story recounted from the Department of Ancash, Peru, in Stein (1961).

31. The most well developed studies of this structure and its implications for myth as a genre are by T. Turner, most recently in 1985.

32. Myths are also historical in that they are always presented as tokens of a prototype (and thus governed by performance rules and permeable to contextual modification) and also that an individual myth may become an index of a social movement.

33. An example of a related process is the phenomenon of foregrounding developed in Havranek (1964) and Mukarovsky (1964).

34. It should by now be clear that we reject the structuralist tendency to dismiss or undervalue the importance of syntagmatic relations—the sequence of episodes—in narrative, a point more fully developed in T. Turner (1985). Indeed, we have argued that the sequence or plot in the myth discussed is itself of central importance in understanding multiple arenas of social relations. That is, the medium can be part of the message.

4

Time, Narrative, and Ritual: Historical Interpretations from an Amazonian Society

Jonathan D. Hill and Robin M. Wright

In the late nineteenth century, millenarian movements swept through indigenous societies of the Northwest Amazon. The movements centered on the Northern Arawakan societies of the Isana-Guainia drainage area and, at their zenith in the 1850s, also emerged in Eastern Tukanoan societies of the Vaupés basin. Several ethnographers have mentioned indigenous millenarianism and beliefs in messiahs (e.g., Koch-Gruenberg 1909; Galvão 1959; Goldman 1979), but they have not systematically inquired into the specific historical contexts of the movements or their basis in indigenous religion. In an earlier essay (Wright and Hill 1986), we provide a detailed interpretation of the nineteenth-century millenarian movements in terms of historical relationships between colonized peoples and nonindigenous colonizers of the upper Río Negro valley and some key symbols and beliefs in native Arawakan culture. In this study, our primary purpose is to explore narratives about the most renowned messianic leader of the nineteenth century, Venancio Camico, as part of a more general analysis of how native Arawakan peoples of the upper Río Negro conceive of and experience the relations between themselves and the past.

One of the most striking features of Wakuénai[1] narratives is the interpenetration of mythic and historical time frames. Wakuénai narratives about the mythic past are organized into several cycles that describe different stages in the creation of human, natural, and supernatural worlds. As the following analysis demonstrates, the mythic past is not a timeless, unchanging state but a dynamic, heterogeneous set of earlier and later past times. Wakuénai narratives include a historical dimension by integrating images of whites and their material culture into the framework of mythic past times. So, too, there is a strongly mythic quality to Wakuénai narratives about specific persons and events of past historical periods. History and myth intermingle in Wakuénai narratives; historical events are integrated into mythic time frames, and mythic events are woven into the historical past.

If myth and history are not separable phenomena in Wakuénai narratives, then it makes little sense to try to make a sharp distinction between them on an analytic level. Lévi-Strauss's (1966b:234–235) famous distinction between "cold" and "hot" societies has misled some anthropologists into believing that the central importance of myth in Amazonian societies indicates a total rejection of, or even an antagonism toward, any cultural expressions of time depth (Kaplan 1981:157). Carried to an extreme, the Lévi-Straussian dichotomy between the mythic and the historical leads to the conclusion that native Amazonians attempt to freeze historical events into an ahistorical, atemporal, mythic order. Kaplan argues: "This kind of thinking is typical of the ideology of a Lévi-Straussian 'cold society'. . . a mythic timeless order is in each generation re-established" (1981:159). Whether intentional or not, this conclusion has the unfortunate effect of denying the historical contemporaneity of native Amazonians and the researchers who have done fieldwork among them (Fabian 1983). By placing themselves historically "upstream" from their subjects, structural anthropologists impose an abstract conception of timeless mythic order upon societies in which such reifications are either absent or actively resisted. Sahlins's (1981: 70–72) attempt to extricate structuralism from the reification of myth into an abstract, ahistorical entity is ultimately unconvincing, for he insists on a reified conception of signs as "culture-as-constituted," or an atemporal structure.

However useful such abstractions may be to structuralist social science, they have no significance whatsoever in our attempt to understand how the Wakuénai interpret the past to themselves in their narratives. The Lévi-Straussian notion of a cold, timeless, mythic order, or Sahlins's concept of "culture-as-constituted" as atemporal structure, makes sense only in societies whose members have learned to use the power of written language to obliterate temporal otherness and heterogeneity, reducing time to an abstract entity that can be conceptually manipulated, abolished, and dominated. This subordination of time to an abstraction has its roots in the primacy of subjective, instrumental rationality over substantive rationality in Western culture since the Enlightenment.[2] As Jay notes: "The apparently objectivist bias of positivist thought in fact covertly expressed the growing triumph of subjective rationality, whose image of the natural (and human) world as a realm of dead exteriorities open to instrumental manipulation masked the fact that this view of the world was a human construct" (1984:73).

The past, whether mythic or historical, is nowhere experienced or expressed as an abstract, dead exteriority in Wakuénai narratives. The concept of timelessness is as foreign to Wakuénai culture as is that of abstract structure. Wakuénai narratives describe a past that is differentiated, complex, and heterogeneous, but these temporal frameworks are not, and can never become, cold abstractions because they do not exist in isolation from the sensuous verbal activity of oral narration. Also, ritual and ceremonial activities that socially mediate the relations between different mythic and historical past times and people living in the present effectively guarantee that the temporal relations established in narratives will not become reified into merely objective relations among things.

A consideration of Wakuénai ritual activities, and especially the highly elaborated musical language (malikái) of sacred rituals, is essential for any understanding of the temporal relations described in Wakuénai narratives. In Wakuénai ritual language, the mythic and historical pasts are given active expression in the present in order to integrate events into the memory of collective and personal traditions. The interpenetration of mythic and historical pasts that figures so prominently in Wakuénai narratives has its genesis in ritual language and practice. By giving active expression to the past in the present, ritual language does not aim at effacing the qualitative differences between past and present, as doctrinaire structuralists might argue.[3] Ritual language does not "re-member" something dismembered or recover the unity of an original wholeness (Jay 1984:68) in the same way that a Western historian reconstructs isolated events into a chronological narrative. Instead, Wakuénai ritual language restores a balanced relation of nonidentity and difference between the lived experience of people in the present time and the mythic and historical past times people describe in their narratives.

The following analysis focuses on temporal relations expressed in Wakuénai narratives, yet it is important that the mutual interrelations of ritual and narrative be kept in mind at all times.[4] The inseparability of ritual and narrative is particularly evident in the cycle of narratives about the primordial human being Kuwái and his mother, Amáru. The entire cycle of narratives provides a cultural typification of the human life cycle as experienced in sacred rites of passage. Similarly, Wakuénai narratives about the nineteenth-century millenarian movement led by Venancio Camico take ritual activities as either the explicit focus of the narrative plot or an implicit framework within which the plot becomes intelligible. Sometimes the entire sequence of activities in narrative runs directly parallel to the organization of ritual process. At other times the segments of a longer ritual occasion are inserted into a narrative sequence that, at least on the surface, is concerned with nonritual events. The predominant role of explicit and implicit verbal descriptions of ritual activities in Wakuénai narratives is a mirror image of the importance of ritual activities in the present as a socially mediated restoration of the balance between nonidentical past and present times. Verbal accounts of ritual activities in Wakuénai narratives socially mediate the relations between the present and the past in mythic and historical past times.

The Wakuénai

The Wakuénai are a Northern Arawak–speaking society of several thousand[5] fishers-horticulturalists living in the region of the headwaters of the Río Negro in Venezuela, Brazil, and Colombia (see Figure 1). Their society is organized into a number of exogamous, patrilineal phratries, each consisting of five or so patrisibs ranked in a serial order (Hill 1984a; Oliveira and Galvão 1973; Wright 1981), a pattern that has much in common with the ranked Tukanoan societies of the neighboring Vaupés basin (Chernela 1983; Goldman 1979; Jackson 1983). In the past, Wakuénai phratries were localized in discrete riverine territories within which basic aquatic and terrestrial resources were shared among affiliated sibs. The phratry as a whole acted as a defensive unit to protect its ancestral territory against permanent usage by outsiders from other phratries or ethnolinguistic groups. Historically, trade and intermarriage between phratries were used to reconstitute social groupings that had lost most of their members to forced labor campaigns or disease (Wright 1981). Interphratric exchanges of rights over basic economic resources allowed for adjustments to localized ecological scarcity. In the early nineteenth century, for example, the Hohódene traded rights to use garden lands in their homelands along the upper Aiary in exchange for rights to hunt and fish within Waríperídakéna territory along the lower Aiary and Isana (Wright 1981:18). In a similar manner, sibs or fragments of sibs fleeing political oppression by white missionaries, military forces, or merchants have been absorbed and reabsorbed into other phratries over the past 200 or so years (Wright and Hill 1986; Wright 1981).[6]

The history of Indian-white relations spans at least 250 years, perhaps even longer, in the Isana-Guainía drainage area. Jesuit missionaries

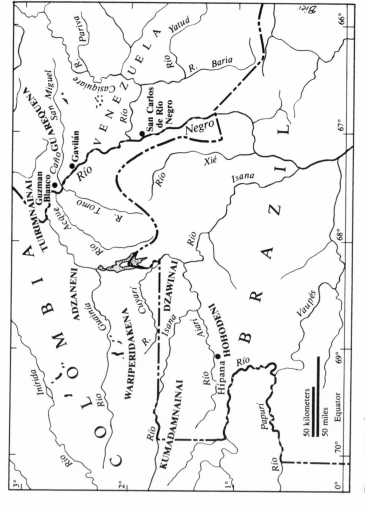

Figure 1. Northwest Amazon region centered on Wakuénai lands in the Isana-Guainía drainage area of Venezuela, Brazil, and Colombia.

arrived in the region during the early eighteenth century and introduced
the Tupían trade language, called *lingua geral* (Spanish, *yeral*), thus
initiating a process of *"yeralization"* among Northern Arawakan groups
which continues today.[7] Portuguese slave trading and warfare culmi-
nated in the 1740s and 1750s, resulting in the extermination of many
indigenous groups of the lower and middle Río Negro basin. The
Wakuénai, however, appear to have remained numerous throughout
this time and perhaps absorbed refugees from other societies (Wright
1981:134–35).

In the 1780s the Wakuénai began to suffer depopulation due to
epidemics of measles, flu, smallpox, and other exotic diseases brought
by the Europeans. Although Indian slavery had been officially halted,
the Portuguese government in Brazil instituted a system of relocations,
called *descimentos* (descents), using military force to capture the
Wakuénai of the Isana River and transport them to Manaus. Oral
histories of the Hohódene, a Wakuénai phratry of the Aiary River, recall
a time that appears to be very similar to the late eighteenth century.
Both documents and oral histories say that there were virtually no more
Wakuénai left on the Isana at that time. Only the collapse of the
colonial government at the end of the eighteenth century spared the
Wakuénai from total annihilation by giving them a few decades to
recoup their losses in relative peace (Wright and Hill 1986). Spanish
colonialism along the Negro-Guainía River in the late eighteenth century was somewhat less devastating for the Wakuénai but resulted in
the concentration of Baré, Mandahuaca, and other Arawakan societies
in mission settlements, called *reducciones* (reductions).

During the early nineteenth century the Wakuénai recovered from
severe population losses and regained a sense of sociopolitical order and
autonomy. However, the temporary slowing in the growth of non-native
political and economic institutions was soon followed by a more sustained and systematic development of the region in the newly independent states of Brazil and Venezuela. By the 1840s and 1850s the Wakuénai
were victims of an increasingly abusive "public service" program in
Brazil and an oppressive Indian labor system in Venezuela. The millenarian movement led by Venancio Camico, a Baniwa man from the
lower Guainía, emerged against this background of growing colonial
domination on the dawn of the Amazon rubber boom. Although his
movement was swiftly dispersed by Brazilian missionaries and military
force, Venancio and his followers escaped to a remote village on the
Caño Acque, a tributary of the Guainía that connects by portage with
the Cuyarí and Isana rivers. What was at stake in this movement was
the kind of transformation that the Wakuénai were to follow: whether

to become totally subservient to the whiteman's system of debt peonage or to seize the historical moment and carve out a ritual time-space in which a degree of spiritual and political freedom was possible. What Venancio's movement accomplished was a reorientation of social and economic relations in which the refusal to cooperate with the external, dominating order of the whiteman became elevated to the status of a sacred cosmological postulate (Wright and Hill 1986).

The division of Wakuénai ancestral lands in Portuguese and Spanish, and later Brazilian and Venezuelan, administrative sectors provided a strategic advantage for the Indians from the beginning of contact with the whites until well into the twentieth century. In the 1850s, for example, Venancio Camico fled from debt bondage in San Carlos de Río Negro and Maroa in Venezuela to start his movement among the Wakuénai of the Isana in Brazil. When Brazilian authorities broke up the movement, Venancio's followers fled to safety up the Cuyarí and Acqui rivers. After a brief imprisonment in San Carlos, Venancio escaped and went to live on the Acqui among his followers until his death in 1903. In the early twentieth century the Wakuénai and Baniwa of Venezuela escaped devastation by the military forces of Tomas Funes, a rubber baron turned dictator, by fleeing to the Isana River in Brazil. Many children and grandchildren of these refugees have returned to Venezuela over the past fifty years to found new villages along the lower Guainía.

Since the 1940s the transformation of Brazilian and Venezuelan boundaries from remote, colonial frontiers into modern, international borders has increasingly restricted the freedom of movement between the Isana and Guainía basins. This change was foreshadowed by a boundary resettlement between Venezuela and Colombia in 1936, when the border was moved eastward from the headwaters of the Guainía to Victorino, only a few miles upstream from Maroa. The Baniwa abandoned their villages along the Acqui and moved to Maroa and the Venezuelan side of the Guainía, apparently because the Colombian authorities interfered with village life and refused to allow the Baniwa to trade in Maroa (Hill, field notes). Wakuénai villages along the lower Guainía traded manioc products, fish, and game with the Baniwa, who became increasingly urbanized.

The movement of Wakuénai back to the lower Guainía in Venezuela was only partially a result of trading opportunities with the Baniwa. Beginning in the 1940s, Fundamentalist Protestant missionaries affiliated with the New Tribes Mission began to work among the Wakuénai of Colombia and Brazil. The missionaries caused a great deal of social strife among the Wakuénai by prohibiting brideservice and cross-cousin marriage, suppressing indigenous religion, and ostracizing sibs or fragments of sibs whose members resisted conversion (Hill 1983; Wright 1981, 1983; Wright and Swenson 1982). The lower Guainía of Venezuela was, and still is, one of the only parts of Wakuénai ancestral territory where the Protestant missionaries have no direct influence over indigenous affairs. Mission activities and international boundaries are two of the most important factors currently shaping the history of Indian-white relations in the upper Río Negro region. A variety of other factors of secondary importance further complicate Wakuénai relations with the representatives of modern nation-states, but these transformations are too complex for us to describe at any length here (see Galvão 1959; Hill 1984c; Journet 1981; Oliveira and Galvão 1973; Wright 1981).

Time and Space in Wakuénai Narratives and Ritual Language

Wakuénai narratives about the mythic past outline a complex process of cosmogenesis that began at Hípana, a village on the Aiary River.[8] The world of the mythic beginning was miniature in size and chaotic, for cannibalistic animals walked about killing and eating one another. Then, Iñápirríkuli, the Wakuénai culture hero and trickster, came into the world and began to rid it of the dangerous animals by taking vengeance against them. Despite the animals' unceasing attempts to kill Iñápirríkuli, he repeatedly subdues them and, through his extraordinary divinatory powers, creates order in the world. Underlying Iñápirríkuli's struggles is a fundamental social conflict between kin (Iñápirríkuli and his brothers) and affines, or "others" (the animals; Iñápirríkuli is married to a woman of the animal tribe), the resolution of which is the basis of human society (Hill 1983:39). The time-space of the mythic beginning is temporally but not spatially distant from the world of living people, for all actions take place at the sacred center of the world at Hípana, or the "navel of the world" (hliépule-kwá dzákare). It was a time before spatial distances came into being and when there were not yet any clear distinctions between male and female, human and nonhuman, living and dead beings.

A second set of narratives explains how the miniature world of the mythic beginning was transformed into the life-sized world of rivers and forests inhabited by people, plants, and animals. The central characters of this cycle are Iñápirríkuli, Amáru (the first woman), and Kuwái (the son of Amáru and Iñápirríkuli). Kuwái is an extraordinary being whose body consists of all worldly elements and whose humming and singing, referred to as "the powerful sound that opened the world" (kémakáni hliméetaka hekwápi), causes the world to expand and brings into being all living species and natural elements. He teaches humanity the first sacred rituals of initiation, yet at the end of these rituals Iñápirríkuli "kills" Kuwái by pushing him into a bonfire, and the world then returns to its miniature size. Out of Kuwái's ashes grow the plant materials for making the sacred flutes and trumpets played in initiation rituals and sacred ceremonies today. Amáru and the women steal these instruments from Iñápirríkuli, setting off a long chase in which the world opens up for a second time as the women play Kuwái's instruments. Eventually the men regain the flutes and Kuwái, Amáru, and Iñápirríkuli leave this world to go live in the various celestial regions from whence they are invoked in ritual.

A third set of narratives about the human past presupposes the existence of the mythic beginning and its transformation in the primordial human past of Kuwái and Amáru. In this set of narratives, human beings in this world (hekwápiríko) come into contact with powerful spirits from other regions of the cosmos. The narratives are closely related to Wakuénai concepts of illness, death, and their cure or prevention through shamanic ritual. Basically the narratives explain that human beings in this world can cross over into the worlds of the deceased as a result of excessive antisocial behavior. The demise of such individuals comes about when they return to the world of the living and tell people about their experiences in the other worlds (Hill 1983:226–32). By contrast, shamans and other ritual specialists routinely cross the boundaries between living and dead without bringing any harm to themselves or others, because they carry out these journeys through the sacred, musical language of Kuwái (malikái). Unlike the protagonists in narratives about the human past, ritual specialists do not return to the world of the living to tell about their experiences in the other worlds but enact these experiences in a language that differs from the language of everyday social life and can therefore be used to evoke other time-spaces without harming people. The protagonists in narratives invariably die when they tell others about the worlds of the dead, because in doing so they efface the differences between the time-space of human beings with those of other worlds by speaking about the latter in everyday language.

Before discussing the mediation of temporal relations in malikái, we must emphasize two major features of the temporal framework implicit in Wakuénai narratives. First, spatial movement, or expansion, is basic to the nature of Wakuénai ways of thinking about the past. The spatial movements of Kuwái and Amáru in the primordial human past are not described as mere journeys between places that already exist but as a dynamic process of creating spatial distances between places. The narratives do not arrange the space inhabited by the Wakuénai phratries of the Isana and Guainía rivers into a "mythic timeless order"; rather, they describe that space as a dynamic, temporal process in which an earlier spaceless time preceded the growth of the world in primordial human times. The transformational time-space of Kuwái and Amáru separates the mythic beginning at Hípana from the human past, resulting in a tripartite temporal framework, which is in turn matched by a tripartite division of the cosmos into the world of living human beings (hekwápiríko), the netherworld (íyarudáti) of recently deceased persons (lidánam, or "shadow"), and the celestial paradise (likáremi) of Iñápirríkuli. Thus, when the Wakuénai speak about earlier and later past times, they are also speaking about places and spatial movements. Conversely, the way in which the Wakuénai speak about and enact past times is most often accomplished through metaphors of place and spatial movement.

A second important point about the tripartite temporal framework in Wakuénai narratives is its paradigmatic nature (Whitten 1978:839–40). By this we mean that the evocation, whether in narratives or ritual language, of any one of the three time-spaces implicitly refers to both of the other time-spaces and to the relations among all three. When the Wakuénai speak about the birth and growth of Kuwái as kémakáni hliméetaka hekwápi (the powerful sound that opened the world) or enact this process in ritual language, they implicitly differentiate between the transformational time-space of primordial human beings, the earlier time-space of the closed world at Hípana, and the later time-space of the human past. Wakuénai narratives and ritual language restore balanced, nonhierarchical relations of difference between the present and a heterogeneous past. Although Iñápirríkuli's creation of the world in the mythic beginning was in many respects incomplete, it is never described as inferior in Wakuénai narratives, merely as different.[9] The more recent times-spaces of primordial and human beings only make sense by contrast to the indigenous understanding of an inchoate, or partially formed, social world that came first.

Wakuénai ritual language (malikái) differs from the dialects of everyday speech in several important ways. Although all native speakers can recognize the literal meanings of many words in malikái, only the specialists, called malikái limínali (malikái "owners," or chant owners), know all the nuances and allusions to narrative episodes condensed into the spirit names of Kuwái. The activity of performing malikái is called ínyapakáati and refers minimally to a voiced, aspirated exhalation of the breath made visible by tobacco smoke (see Hill 1985). Spirit naming in *malikái* is thus more than a simple verbal act and entails the audible, visible releasing of spirit names as musical tones. In talking about *malikái*, chant owners have little more to say about these musical sounds than that they are *kémakáni hliméetaka hekwápi*. By contrast, they are extremely articulate in speaking about the language of *malikái* (i.e., the spirit names themselves). Basically, all spirit names in *malikái* have two parts, or identities, one generic and the other specific. The double identity of beings named in *malikái* has its origins in the primordial human being Kuwái, who describes himself in narratives as "all things in this world" (*phiúmi hekwápiríko*).

In linguistic terms, *malikái* contains a system of generic classifiers in which each specific object, species, or person is categorized in one or more generic noun classes, which makes it possible to express profoundly contradictory images of the mythic figure of Kuwái. On the one hand, the chant owner can metonymically enact Kuwái's creation of the world by placing emphasis on generic categories that include many distinct individuals, species, and objects into a single compound entity. This process, called "heaping up the names in one single place" (*wakétaka nakúna papíniritsa*), is a relatively simple technique of naming a generic class of spirits and then filling it up (*wakámtaka nakúna*) with specific names. On the other hand, the chant owner can juxtapose a variety of different generic names, each with a complementary, specific name, to metaphorically enact Kuwái's creation of the world. The result of this process, called "chasing after the names" (*wapinétaka wátsani nakúna*), or "going in search of the names" (*wapinétaka wadzúhiakaw nakúna*), is a dynamic montage of unique metaphors highlighting the uniqueness of specific spirit names that exclude all but a single individual, species, or object on the basis of distinctive qualities. In male and female initiation rituals, chant owners perform a day-long series of songs and chants to "search for" the sib ancestor name of the initiate. The chants include the naming of places, beginning and ending at the "Center of the World" at Hípana on the Aiary River and covering an immense riverine area from Manaus to the middle Orinoco basin to the headwaters of the Guaviare, Inirida, Guainía, and Isana rivers. The mythic figure of Kuwái simultaneously encompasses both processual images, "heaping up" and "chasing after" the names.

The two processes of spirit naming in *malikái*, "heaping up" and "searching for the names," are semantic expressions of a relative hierarchy of structural levels that pervades Wakuénai sacred myths and rituals. "Heaping up the names," or categorizing specific objects, species, and individuals into generic classes, is a taxonomic principle that defines a lower-level pattern of relations. It is a classificatory operation in which the natural, social, and mythic worlds are organized into relatively discrete, bounded semantic classes, each of which is analogously constituted to all the other classes through the generic-to-specific relationship. The more dynamic process of "searching for the names" operates against the relatively static taxonomic principle of "heaping up the names" into discrete categories.[10] "Searching for the names" is essentially a process of transferring spirit names that are exceptionally powerful or harmful from the generic class to which they would belong according to the lower-level taxonomic principle into a different class of names on the basis of mythic connections. For example, in the process of "heaping up" the spirit names of edible bird species for the food of a newborn infant's parents, the chant owner names the yellow curassow in the class of umáwari, or fish and aquatic animal species. The reason for this shifting of a bird species to the class of aquatic species is that in myth the yellow curassow transforms itself into an anaconda. The higher-level process of "searching for the names" is thus a mythic principle of semantic transferal that overrides the lower-level taxonomic principle of "heaping up the names."[11]

In any given performance of malikái, chant owners make use of both taxonomic and mythic principles, but one or the other of the two is dominant. The relation between higher and lower levels is not an absolute opposition between dynamic and static but a relative contrast of more to less dynamic. "Searching for the names" is a semantic expression of transcendence through which processes of change, reordering, and transformation are given symbolic form. "Heaping up the names" is an expression of the basic order from which meaningful change and transformation arise.

Historical Interpretation in Wakuénai Narratives and Ritual Language

The hierarchy of mythic and taxonomic principles enacted in malikái and the transformational time-space described in narratives about the primordial human past of Kuwái and Amáru have become a basis for interpreting the history of Indian-white relations. As a mode of historical consciousness, Wakuénai ritual language and narratives do not form an atemporal structure of "conventional meanings" that absorbs or freezes the events of Indian-white history into a "mythic timeless order." The Wakuénai do not see themselves as the passive reactors to events initiated by whites or as recipients of the whiteman's culture. Instead, whites and their culture are classified through the taxonomic principle of ritual language so that they can be understood in relation to the more dynamic mythic principle of "searching for the names." In what amounts to nearly a reversal of the "cold" versus "hot" society distinction in structuralist anthropology, the Wakuénai interpret whites as a "heaped up pile of souls" who are less dynamic (though not totally static) than the Wakuénai and neighboring indigenous societies of the Northwest Amazon region, who possess powerful sib names, or souls, which must be "searched for" anew in each generation. Through the complex of narratives and ritual language outlined above, the Wakuénai view themselves as the principal makers and keepers of a sacred regional history, which subsumes the origins of whites and their culture in the upper Río Negro region.

The following version of the myth of sib ancestor emergence comes from a Dzáwinai chant owner of the lower Guainía River in Venezuela (Hill, field notes). The bulk of this narrative consists of a simple listing of Wakuénai sib names and their corresponding male and female tobacco spirits. Excluding the list of names, the narrative is reducible to the following underlying sequence of actions:

1. The white men were the first people to emerge from the hole beneath the rapids at Hípana, and Iñápirríkuli gave them all a single name (yárinárinái) and tobacco spirit (hérri hálepiwánai iénipé). "Later we will go to search for the names (nanáikika) of these people," explained the trickster-creator.

2. Iñápirríkuli searched for the names of all the Wakuénai sibs and gave them each a pair of tobacco spirits.

3. After giving names and spirits to all the Wakuénai sibs of the Isana and Guainía rivers, Iñápirríkuli continued to search for the names of Arawakan and Tukanoan groups of the Vaupés (Tariano, Uanano, and Cubeo). Although these groups formed part of the same search for sib names by Iñápirríkuli, they are distinguished from Wakuénai sibs by the phrase "after the white men" (hnetédali yárinárinái).

4. Iñápirríkuli ran out of names, for "there were too many people" (néni ñétim yúhakáwa). "Let's heap up these people and give them the spirit-name liwakétanhim dzáwi-ñápirríkuli" (the heap or pile of Iñápirríkuli). Iñápirríkuli gave the white men the name yárinárinái, and he named the places where they were to live Colombia, Venezuela, and Brazil.

In this narrative the relative hierarchy of semantic principles in malikái becomes a means for giving cultural form to an indigenous interpretation of the history of Indian-white relations in the upper Río Negro region. The arrival of the whiteman is not expressed as a passive experience that "happened to" the Wakuénai but as part of the same active process through which Iñápirríkuli, the trickster-creator, brought into being the ancestral spirits of the Wakuénai. The trickster-creator raised the whiteman's ancestors from the ground at Hípana before raising the sib ancestors of the Wakuénai and other indigenous groups, but he did not give the whiteman powerful sib names that must be actively "searched for." Iñápirríkuli announced his intention to search later for the whiteman's sib names, after searching for those of the Wakuénai and their neighbors. As is so often the case in narratives about Iñápirríkuli, the trickster-creator's words and deeds are in the final analysis shown to be clever deceptions that must be interpreted rather than taken at face value. In the final episode of the narrative, when Iñápirríkuli has run out of names because the whites are too numerous, the real intentions of the trickster-creator are revealed: to heap up whites as *liwakétanhim* rather than to search for their sib names (*nanáikika*). This denouement makes explicit the contrast between higher- and lower-level naming principles and the analogous contrast between indigenous peoples (*hwá nawíki*) and the whites (*yárinárinái*). The contrast is not a simple binary opposition of the Lévi-Straussian sort (i.e., Indian : white :: dynamic : static) but a continuum of more to less dynamic.

In the concluding episode of the narrative, Iñápirríkuli runs out of names because there are "too many people," and he names the places where the whiteman is to live. The indigenous view of history presupposes smallness of social scale but not rigidity. Sib names for several indigenous societies of the upper Río Negro region are added[12] to Iñápirríkuli's search after the white men, but the whites themselves are simply too numerous to include in this mythic process. The trickster-creator does, however, name the places where the whites are to live. Given the central importance of spatial movements and the naming of places in Wakuénai ways of thinking about the past, Iñápirríkuli's naming of these places is better understood as a metaphor for the active creation of a historical time-space the Wakuénai have shared with the whiteman for the past 250 years rather than a static, atemporal arrangement of space into a mythic order. The division of Wakuénai ancestral lands among Brazil, Colombia, and Venezuela was a historical process of great significance to the Wakuénai, for the spatial movements back and forth between river systems have been a key strategy for coping with the whiteman's diseases, economic oppression, military force, and missionary activity. Whereas the Wakuénai understand their history as a balanced relation between the rivers and forests they inhabit today, as well as the dynamic transformations of the closed world of the mythic beginning at Hípana during the primordial human past of Kuwái and Amáru, whites have struggled since the time of their arrival in the eighteenth century to divide the upper Río Negro region into separate administrative spheres of control. For the Wakuénai, it is the whites and not indigenous peoples who have treated their territory and its inhabitants as cold, ahistorical, and lifeless abstractions open to instrumental manipulations.

When not occupied in the search for new ways to reproduce objectivizing theories of "primitive" societies as history-less peoples (Goody 1977; Kaplan 1981; Ong 1982), Western historians and social scientists have wondered why it is that small-scale, nonliterate societies have been so reluctant to change their traditional beliefs and practices in the face of contradictory historical events (Lévi-Strauss 1966b; Sahlins 1981). From the perspective of the Wakuénai, the question of why they have perpetuated their unique complex of narratives and ritual language as a mode of historical interpretation is not important. Instead, the key question in Wakuénai historical interpretation is why have whites failed after so many years to become fully cultural, historical beings.

We have already hinted at an answer to this question in discussing the difference between Wakuénai and non-native interpretations of space. The Wakuénai contrast themselves as human beings defined in relation to natural species of the upper Río Negro region to whites as semihuman beings whose souls take the form of books and papers. Whites lack animal-shaped, collective souls (líwarúna) and powerful sib names (nanáikika), and thus they are unable to participate in Wakuénai history in an active sense. Nevertheless, whites are susceptible to indigenous witchcraft, since their souls are said to take the form of papers, or books, when they sleep at night. Thus, missionaries' souls appear as a Bible, traders' souls as a financial log, anthropologists' souls as field notes, and so on. Indigenous witches can avenge kin who have been harmed by a whiteman by entering the latter's home at night and tearing in half the book or papers that represent the whiteman's identity during sleep (Hill 1983:217).

From the Wakuénai perspective, whites have failed to become fully historical, cultural human beings because their books and writing have unnaturally divided them up according to occupational specialties. Whites are thus seen as beings whose alienation from nature and society leaves them vulnerable to the horrifying effects of indigenous witchcraft yet totally unable to become active participants in the creative, transformative powers of ritual language and narrative. From a comparative perspective it is important to note that people in nonliterate societies have often interpreted writing systems as a source of supernatural powers when coming into contact with literate peoples (Lévi-Strauss 1973a:298–300; Price 1983a; Rappaport 1985; Wachtel 1977). What distinguishes the Wakuénai interpretation of writing from these other cases is the overwhelmingly negative character of the power attributed to writing.[13] The Wakuénai interpretation of writing focuses on its effect of alienating people from nature and one another by dividing them into occupational specialties. In other words, writing is a symbol of social stratification and, because of the strongly egalitarian nature of Wakuénai social organization, is cast in a totally negative light. The Wakuénai view of writing is closer to the "atonal" philosophy of the critical theorist Theodor Adorno, who saw writing and abstract thought as sources of the subject's separation from and domination of the object (see Jay 1984:67). For both critical theorists and the Wakuénai, writing symbolizes the division of manual from mental labor and the resulting stratification of society.

The Wakuénai perceive a further linkage between writing and the whiteman's unnatural, unsocialized alienation. In counter-witchcraft songs, chant owners "heap up" into a single spirit name, *rupápera šru Amáru* (the paper of Amáru), the names of all exogenous diseases brought to the region by the whiteman. The category of Amáru spirits is used to name all the "hot things" (*tsímukáni*) introduced by the whiteman, including the powerful but useful steel tools the Wakuénai use in their gardening, fishing, hunting, house building, and other activities. *Rupápera šru Amáru* is the one member of the class of "hot things" that is not only powerful but unequivocally harmful and destructive. The linking metaphor of paper thus serves to connect the unnaturalness of the whiteman's souls, the division of labor in the whiteman's society, and the death and destruction of indigenous social groups due to the whiteman's introduction of exogenous diseases.

Historical Interpretation in Wakuénai Narratives about Venancio Camico

Wakuénai narratives about the most famous nineteenth-century millenarian leader, Venancio Camico, provide further insight into the nature of indigenous historical interpretations. As mentioned earlier, Venancio Camico's movement arose at a critical moment in the late 1850s when the Wakuénai were taking stock of the history of their relations with whites and deciding what to do about it. Essentially, Venancio's movement brought collective consciousness to bear on the historical dilemma of whether to stick together in opposition to the whiteman's plans for developing the upper Río Negro region or to become totally subservient to those alien plans. As the following discussion demonstrates, the cycle of narratives about the transformational time-space of Kuwái and Amáru has become a strategic resource for indigenous interpretations of Venancio Camico and his millenarian movement. Due to the paradigmatic nature of the temporal framework implicit in Wakuénai narratives and ritual language, the narratives about Venancio Camico do not set up a one-to-one correspondence between the millenarian leader and the primordial human being, Kuwái. Instead, the narratives portray Venancio Camico as a multivocal symbol of the indigenous past who simultaneously integrates within himself imagery of the trickster-creator (Iñápirríkuli), the primordial human being (Kuwái), and powerful shamans (dzáwináitairi, or "jaguar owners").

The following narrative about Venancio Christu was recorded by Hill among the Wakuénai of Venezuela in 1981 and is similar to one collected by Wright among the Hohódene of the Aiary River in 1977. The text explicitly focuses on the political struggles between Venancio and the territorial government. More generally, the narrative can be read as a struggle between the Wakuénai, whose source of political and religious power is symbolized in Venancio, and the whiteman, whose power is represented by the military and by an oppressive governor, Tomas Funes.

Venancio Christu and Tomas Funes

A man who knew about Venancio, who knew that he was a saint, who knew that Venancio could tell which people were sorcerers (dañeros) who had poison to kill others, told Funes about Venancio. Funes sent a commission of soldiers to fetch Venancio from his home on the Acque River. They took Venancio up to Funes's house in San Fernando where Funes asked Venancio if it were true what the others said about him, that he was really a saint. "No, this is false, what the others say. A saint is different because he doesn't eat manioc bread and meat. But I'm a normal human being and eat manioc bread and meat," Venancio replied. Then Funes asked him if it were true that he had many followers who brought gifts to him in payment for cures. Again Venancio denied what the others had told Funes. But Funes wanted to make sure that Venancio was telling the truth, so he ordered him to enter a coffin. Soldiers stood guard on all sides to make sure that Venancio did not run away. After Venancio had lain down inside the open coffin, Funes ordered it to be nailed shut, tied with a cord, and weighted with a rock. Then he sent his soldiers to throw the coffin into the Río Orinoco where it is very deep. After one hour, the soldiers raised up the coffin and took it back to Funes. When they opened the coffin, it was totally empty inside. The soldiers explained that Venancio must have escaped because the cord was not strong enough and the nails had not been placed very close together.

So they went to fetch Venancio and encountered him at his home on the Acque River. Again they ordered him to enter a coffin that was waiting inside Funes's home in San Fernando. This time they tied the coffin shut with a rope instead of a mere cord and spaced the nails only three fingers' width apart. They weighted down the coffin with a stone and threw it into the same deep part of the river. Again it was empty when they brought it back to Funes's house, and again the soldiers explained that there were not enough nails used to shut the coffin and that the rope was too thin.

The third time, they put nails very close together, only one finger's width apart, and tied the coffin shut with a very thick rope made of rawhide. After waiting the usual one hour, they raised up the coffin and untied the stone. This time they felt that the coffin weighed more than the other times and were certain that they had finished off Venancio. They told Funes so when they reached his house with the coffin, but they were all surprised when the coffin was opened and there was a huge anaconda (umáwari) inside. At that moment, Funes decided that Venancio was really a saint and that he could never kill him no matter how hard he tried.

Five months passed, and Funes sent his soldiers to fetch Venancio from his home on the Acque River again, just for a friendly talk. Funes told Venancio when he arrived that he now believed that Venancio was truly a saint since he'd survived three times underwater. Then Venancio pronounced a punishment on Funes, saying that he'd be killed one day in a revolt by his followers. Funes felt guilty about what he'd done and offered Venancio money, but Venancio wouldn't accept. Funes was very vexed about his refusal of his offer and continued to feel guilty until his death.

Tomas Funes was by all accounts a tyrant (Tavera Acosta 1927:199–200). During the 1920s, Wakuénai and Baniwa groups living along the lower Guainía fled from the terrorism of the Funes regime up the Guainía and its tributaries, such as the Tomo and the Acque. Other Arawakan societies, including the Baré, Mandahuaca, and Yavitero, suffered almost total annihilation during this period. "The rise and fall of the rubber baron turned dictator, Tomas Funes, was the culmination of rubber boom politics that decimated whole indigenous societies almost overnight" (Hill 1983:336). The conclusion of the narrative, when Venancio prophesied that Funes would be killed in a revolt, is accurate not only for Funes's regime but also for the late 1850s, when there were four attempted revolutions in the territorial government (Tavera Acosta 1927:183–84).

The narrative juxtaposes historical figures from two time periods by treating Venancio Camico, who lived in the mid- to late-nineteenth century, as a contemporary of Tomas Funes, who was governor of the Venezuelan Amazon territory in the early twentieth century. Although this telescoping, or flattening, of past historical times (see Roe, this volume) violates the canons of a literate, Western historiography, which aims at reconstructing "what really happened" in a chronological narrative, the juxtaposition of Venancio and Tomas Funes as contemporaries in Wakuénai narrative makes sense in terms of indigenous ways of thinking about history. In the narrative, Venancio Camico and Tomas Funes are separated by the spatial distance between Venancio's refuge on the Caño Acque and Funes's center of power in the whiteman's capital at San Fernando de Atabapo. Each episode in the narrative begins and ends with a spatial movement between the indigenous refuge and the non-native capital. Bearing in mind the importance of spatial movements and place naming in Wakuénai narratives and ritual language, it is clear that the successive journeys of Venancio Camico to the house of Governor Funes do not express a static, spatial arrangement but a dynamic, temporal process. Like the movements of Kuwái and Amáru in narratives and ritual language about the transformational time-space of primordial human beings, the movements of Venancio Camico in narrative are not mere journeys between places but the creation of a historical time-space that includes both the Wakuénai and the whiteman.

The "opening up" of this historical time-space is in each case constituted by a reciprocal pair of spatial movements in which Venancio is first forced to accompany Funes's soldiers to the whiteman's capital and then escapes to his refuge on the Caño Acque. Underlying the apparent flattening of time periods in the narrative is a deeper message about the history of Indian-white relations: whites repeatedly forced the Wakuénai to relocate outside their ancestral territories in the upper Río Negro region, and the Wakuénai repeatedly resisted assimilation by seeking refuge in remote headwater areas or by crossing the frontiers between colonial powers. Documents show that Venancio Camico was being taken to San Fernando de Atabapo by Venezuelan authorities in 1858 when he escaped to the Caño Acque (Wright 1981), and the flight of Wakuénai and Baniwa from the Guainía in Venezuela during the Funes regime to the Isana river in Brazil (via the Acque, Tomo, and Cuyarí rivers) is equally well documented (Hill 1983; Oliveira and Galvão 1973). The juxtaposition of Venancio Camico and Tomas Funes in narrative thus "opens up" a historical time-space in which the underlying theme of forced relocation versus return to safety, or slavery versus freedom (Price 1983a; Wright and Hill 1986), is of greater significance than a mere chronological recounting of "what really happened."

The struggle in which Funes and the military try to kill Venancio makes sense both in terms of Wakuénai historical relations with whites and also in the context of Wakuénai narratives about the mythic beginning and its transformations. More specifically, Venancio's struggle against Funes evokes the mythic deeds of the trickster-creator Iñápirríkuli, who always manages to outsmart his enemies and to turn their treacherous plans against them. One key symbol found in both the narratives about Venancio and those about the origins of Iñápirríkuli is the container (Wright 1981:536). In the latter, Iñápirríkuli's father-in-law tries to kill him by sending him into the middle of a new garden and setting fire to the garden periphery. Iñápirríkuli transforms himself and enters a small *ambauba* (Cecropia sp.) tree trunk. When the fire reaches him, the tree trunk/container bursts apart and Iñápirríkuli flies out, unharmed, declaring that he is immortal and cannot be killed.

In narratives, Venancio is a multivocal symbol of the Wakuénai past who simultaneously calls to mind the trickster-creator Iñápirríkuli and the primordial, monstrous, and world-opening human being Kuwái. Specifically, a strong parallel between Venancio and Kuwái is discernible in Venancio's ability to escape the combined forces of wood (coffin), metal (nails), vines (rope), water (river), and stone. This imagery implicitly evokes Kuwái, whose body consists of all worldly elements with the exception of fire. Like Kuwái, Venancio cannot be killed by any of these elements. Also, the container as a symbol of the primordial womb is a major theme throughout the set of narratives about Amáru and Kuwái. In the beginning of the cycle, Kuwái is stuck inside his mother's womb and has to be forcefully let out by Iñápirríkuli. Later, Kuwái transforms himself into a container when he eats the three boys who prematurely break their ritual fast. In both cases, whether it is the womb of Amáru or the belly of Kuwái, the narratives focus attention on the narrow escape from the container.

In the narrative about Venancio, the container as a mythic symbol of womb, death, and rebirth is extended to a new object, the coffin. Three times the coffin is closed, each time with a stronger rope (cord, rope, rawhide rope) and more nails (spaced widely, three fingers' width apart, one finger's width apart). The symbolism of Venancio's escape from the coffin resembles the sequence of narrative events leading up to the birth of Kuwái: Amáru is unable to give birth because she has no birth canal, so Iñápirríkuli blows tobacco smoke on her to make her unconscious and, with the help of three different species of fish, opens a passage to her womb so that the child, Kuwái, can escape. This sequence of narrative events is connected to the story of Venancio and Tomas Funes not only through the shared theme of narrow escape from death but also through stylistic features of the narratives. In the narratives about the birth of Kuwái, a series of three episodes tells how Iñápirríkuli called three different species of fish to open up a birth canal. A progressive action of opening up the womb is then recounted in three episodes. In the same way the story of Venancio and Funes is composed of a series of three episodes, with a progressive action of closing the coffin. Again, the symbolism of the coffin/container inverts the symbolism of Kuwái's birth even as it reproduces its narrative and semantic structure. Kuwái's escape from death in the womb comes at the beginning of the life cycle through a process of opening up, whereas Venancio's escape from the coffin comes at the end of the life cycle through a process of increasing constriction and closing.

The symbolism of Venancio's escape from the coffin is an indigenous image of the oppressive economic system the whiteman implemented during the rubber boom of the late nineteenth and early twentieth centuries. Their economic policies meant death, both physical and spiritual, for the Wakuénai and other native peoples of the Northwest Amazon region (see Chernela, this volume). The progressive tightening of the coffin with thicker ropes and more nails succinctly expresses these deathly transformations.

On the final try, the coffin is pulled out of the water and is found to contain an enormous anaconda. This animal continues to evoke the imagery of increasing constriction, since the anaconda kills its prey by squeezing it to death with its coiled body. By leaving an anaconda inside the coffin, Venancio symbolically reverses the processes of constriction and alienation by replacing an image of alien power, the coffin, with one of a more powerful, but equally dangerous, autochthonous power. For the Wakuénai, the anaconda is connected with the concept of adulterous, dangerous sexual relations and a reversal of the container/womb symbolism found in the set of narratives about Kuwái. Instead of expressing the theme of narrow escape from the womb through ritually controlled processes, the anaconda represents the child who refuses to come out of its mother's womb for fear of permanent separation, or death (see Chernela, this volume). The appearance of an enormous anaconda inside Venancio's coffin expresses a similar theme: the anaconda is stuck inside the container, whereas Venancio, like Kuwái and Iñápirríkuli, has escaped unharmed. At the same time the anaconda as an indigenous symbol of dangerous sexual power is used to create an image of the autodestruction of the whiteman's power structure through military rebellion.

A second narrative about Venancio Camico and his millenarian movement focuses attention upon the issue of how Venancio exercised spiritual authority over his followers and managed to keep his movement together despite the persistent weakness of his following. In the second narrative, we see how Venancio articulated the indigenous belief in shamanic journeys to the worlds of the dead with the Christian millenarian theme of Christ's death and resurrection during Holy Week. Venancio is at once a shamanic healer and a folk saint to whom promises are made, prayers offered, and respect given. He has acquired new power to punish disobedience and failure to carry out vows and ritual proscriptions.

Venancio's Annual Death and Resurrection

In Holy Week, on Friday afternoon, Venancio Christu told his followers that he was leaving this world for his house in the sky but that he would return soon. Privately, he told his wife to take care of his body and to pray for him while his spirit went to the sky. "We have to wait for Venancio two days, until late Sunday afternoon," his wife told the people after Venancio had "died." She told the people that they would all pray for Venancio and take care of his body during his spirit's two day absence.

Some soldiers and other white people arrived and asked what the people were doing, for many indigenous people had gathered to follow their leader's instructions. Venancio's wife explained to the outsiders that everyone was praying for Venancio and that they would continue to do so until Venancio came back in two days. There would be no dancing or drinking *aguardiente* until Venancio had safely returned.

But the woman broke her promise to Venancio and started a dance on Saturday while she was supposed to be leading the people in prayer. She told everyone that they could pray on Sunday and that would be enough. When Venancio came back, he would see that everyone was praying as they were supposed to be doing. She danced with the soldiers and other white men until she had danced in all the households of the village and with each of the men.

On Sunday, she led the people in prayer until Venancio returned in the late afternoon. Venancio's body arose, and he asked his wife what she had done while he was away. "We prayed the whole time," she claimed. But Venancio had seen that she danced with men while his spirit had been away. He punished his wife by waiting until she fell ill and, instead of curing her disease, handed her a piece of paper with instructions on it. The paper told her that she was permanently refused access to God through prayer. Then a devil with no legs or lower body came and made love to the woman. When they finished, the woman was also minus her legs and lower body. She went on dancing with the devil forever, using her forearms as feet.

Each year, Venancio died for two days during Holy Week. He told his followers never to cut any wood during his spiritual journey, since to break even a little twig would break their souls in half. Three brothers were sitting around talking the day after Venancio had left for the sky and one decided to test Venancio's claim by going outside to break a piece of wood. He went to sleep thinking that Venancio had lied, since he had broken wood and found it to be harmless. But the next day Venancio returned and called his followers up to be examined, family by family. When he got to the three brothers who had broken wood, he told them exactly what they had said and done the day before. The three were silent and afraid to answer Venancio. Venancio told them that a group of men would come to kill them as punishment for their deeds, and later that same day they were killed.

In addition to a number of specific, thematic connections between the narratives about Venancio Camico's millenarianism and those about the primordial human past of Kuwái and Amáru (see Wright and Hill 1986), both narratives illustrate a more general feature of indigenous ways of thinking about the past. In both sets of narratives, verbal accounts of ritual activities are a cornerstone of indigenous ways of expressing and understanding relations between the present and a heterogeneous past. In narratives about the primordial human past, Kuwái teaches the Wakuénai the ritual activities and language (malikái) which guarantee that the differences between the time-space of living human beings and those of the mythic pasts will never be "forgotten" or reified into merely objective relations among things. Likewise, in the narrative about Venancio Camico's movement, Venancio teaches indigenous people the ritual means for ensuring that the historical past of the nineteenth century cannot be "forgotten" or reduced to a dead exteriority no different from the present.

Although many of the symbols employed in constructing a verbal account of Venancio Camico's ritual death and return to life are drawn from Christianity, we do not see this borrowing of an alien cultural idiom as an example of syncretism but as a process of radically selecting only those ritual symbols and contexts from Christianity that make sense in terms of Wakuénai interpretations of history. The way in which Venancio Camico's death and "resurrection" are described in the narrative, for example, are better understood in terms of Wakuénai enactments of the death and rebirth of Kuwái in initiation rituals and the shamanic journeying to and from the Wakuénai worlds of the afterlife than as Christian celebrations of Good Friday and Easter.

Venancio's use of a written document to communicate the message of eternal castigation to his wife is entirely consistent with Wakuénai narrative techniques and the indigenous understanding of paper and writing as a negative power responsible for the unnatural, unsocialized alienation of the whiteman. A prominent device found in many Wakuénai narratives is the use of intermediary characters to deliver messages between principal characters. Wakuénai narrators often use messenger-figures as a frame for imparting highly significant information about major characters such as Iñápirríkuli, Amáru, Kuwái, and their enemies. One of the key episodes in the set of narratives about Kuwái, for example, comes during a dialogue between Kuwái and Kálimátu, a wasp-person sent as a messenger by Iñápirríkuli to lure Kuwái back to this world to perform the first ritual initiation. In the narrative about Venancio's annual death and resurrection, the use of a messenger-figure is replaced by Venancio's use of a written note. Given the connections the Wakuénai make in their ritual language and narratives between paper, the whiteman's soul, and the exogenous diseases brought to the region by the whiteman, Venancio's use of a written note to express his wife's transformation becomes perfectly intelligible. By dancing with the white soldiers during a period of ritual activity, the wife had permanently lost her collective, sib ancestor soul (líwarúna) and became like the whiteman, whose soul is made of paper.

In the legend, the paper message Venancio gives to his wife is doubly associated with disease and death, since Venancio waits until his wife has fallen ill and gives her the paper in lieu of a sacred cure. In some ways, this message bears resemblance to the Wakuénai practice of confessing evil omens (hínimái) to ritual healers. If an individual suffers from serious, life-threatening illness, a shaman may demand that the patient's kin confess unusual experiences, bad dreams, or open hostilities within the family, any one of which may be interpreted as an evil omen blocking the shaman's ability to bring back the patient's lost soul from the netherworld (íyarudáti). Evil omens are often cited as the cause of death when shamans and chant owners are unable to effect cures. The symbolism of Venancio's written message to his wife is rooted in the Wakuénai practice of establishing open channels of communication between healer and patient. However, the process of revelation versus concealment in the narrative turns the ritual curing process upside down. In curing rituals, important personal information is revealed by the victim or the victim's kin to ritual specialists in an effort to avert impending death. In the narrative, the ritual healer (Venancio) reveals hitherto concealed information from the sick individual (his wife) in full knowledge that the revelation will bring about her death.

Conclusions

For the Wakuénai, historical understanding is based upon the set of narratives about the expansion of the closed world at Hípana during the life cycle of Kuwái, the primordial human being. Metaphors of spatial movement and distance, such as the processes of "searching for" power-ful sib names and the naming of places in narratives, allow for the integration of events into the memory of collective and personal traditions. Time "opens up" and "closes down" at different moments in the life cycle of individuals and in the history of a collection of lives (Rosaldo 1980:23–24). Historical interpretation emerges in the interplay between the ends of a continuum ranging from more to less dynamic processes: from searching for spirit names to heaping them up in a single place, from escaping to the outside to getting stuck on the inside, from moving to safety to remaining in danger.

Wakuénai narratives and ritual language outline a complex, heteroge-neous past in which mythic actions and historical events intermingle. The past, whether historical or mythic, is different from the present, and both narratives and ritual language ensure that this difference does not become reified into a merely objective relation between dead, mean-ingless things. Nothing could be more alien to Wakuénai ways of understanding the past than the absurd notion that myth and ritual freeze events into a timeless order that effaces the difference between past and present times. The imposition of labels such as "cold societies" (Lévi-Strauss 1966b) and "mythic timeless order" (Kaplan 1981) upon Amazonian societies simply does not help in understanding how and why some of the most richly diverse traditions of oral narrative and ritual language in the world have been developed, and continue to flourish, in the Amazon rain forests.

NOTES

Hill's fieldwork among the Wakuénai of Venezuela was made possible by doctoral dissertation grants from the Social Science Research Council (SSRC/ACLS) and Fulbright-Hays in 1980–81 and by a faculty research grant from Fulbright-Hays in 1984. Wright's fieldwork with the Wakuénai of Brazil was made possible by a doctoral dissertation grant from the National Science Foundation. The authors wish to thank the Wakuénai of Brazil and Venezuela for their hospitality and cooperation, without which none of the analyses in this study would have been possible.

1. The term "Wakuénai" can be glossed as "people of our language" and includes the Dzáwinai, Waríperídakéna, Ádzanéni, Kúmadámnainai, and

Hohódene peoples of the Isana and Guainía river basins. These groups speak mutually intelligible dialects of the language Wáku, all trace their cultural origins to mythic emergence from the ground at a place near Hípana on the Aiary River (The Center of the World), and all intermarry. Wakuénai is used here in lieu of Baniwa, a *lingua geral* word designating all Arawakan speakers along the Isana and its tributaries in Brazil, and Curripaco, a name used in Colombia and Venezuela to refer to all Wakuénai groups. Baniwa and Curripaco are both inaccurate terms. Baniwa is the name of a distinct Northern Arawakan group living in Venezuela who seldom intermarry with the Wakuénai and whose language is not mutually intelligible with Wáku. Curripaco denotes a dialect of Wáku that is associated with the Ádzanéni phratry of the Guainía River and is therefore not an ethnologically precise term for the Wakuénai as a whole. The use of different terms reflects the geographical position of Wakuénai lands, some of which are in Brazil and the rest in Venezuela and Colombia.

2. The distinction between substantive rationality (*Vernunft*) and subjective rationality (*Verstand*) was of great importance to critical theorists of the Frankfurt School and paralleled Max Weber's more well known distinction between value and purposive rationality. Substantive, or value, rationality actively strives to reconcile the contradictions between thought-about and lived-in worlds, whereas subjective, or purposive/instrumental, rationality accepts such contradictions as "natural" features of an unchangeable world (Jay 1984:72–73). The hegemony of subjective rationality in the modern Western world is an ideological corollary of the technological domination of nature and the psychological repression of internal human desires. See Fabian (1983) for a critique of anthropological theory as a means of naturalizing, spatializing, and otherwise subordinating time.

3. Fabian's critique of anthropological theory and discourse makes a case for the pervasiveness of allochronism, or the use of rhetorical devices that result in a denial of the contemporaneity of anthropologists and their subjects (1983:32), in all varieties of nineteenth- and twentieth-century anthropology: evolutionism (the naturalization of time), cultural relativism (the spatialization of time into "culture gardens"), structuralism (the pre-empting of time), and symbolic anthropology (the aestheticization of time). Clearly, structuralism is not the only theoretical approach in anthropology and related disciplines that has perpetuated the allochronic discourse of nineteenth-century evolutionism.

4. See Hill (1983, 1985) and Wright (1981) for more detailed analyses of the interrelations between ritual language and narratives in Wakuénai culture.

5. Because of the division of Wakuénai lands among three modern nation-states, an exact population figure is difficult to obtain. The Venezuela indigenous census of 1981 estimates that 1,600 Curripaco (Wakuénai) live in the Venezuelan Federal Amazon Territory, including residents of urban centers as well as villages along the Guainía, Casiquiare, and Atabapo rivers. At least twice as many Wakuénai live in each of the other two countries, Brazil and Colombia, so that a minimal figure for the entire population is 8,000.

6. These processes of historical dislocation and reintegration were very much

in evidence both as memories of the past and as ongoing processes among the Wakuénai local groups with whom we worked. In 1980–81, Hill worked with members of the Dzáwinai, Waríperídakéna, and Ádzanéni phratries along the lower Guainía River in Venezuela. These local groups had all fled from their homelands along the Isana and upper Guainía rivers during the past thirty years, in part to escape the social pressures of New Tribes missionaries and their indigenous converts (Hill 1984b). Hill returned to the lower Guainía in 1984–85 to further document and analyze the social and ecological processes whereby the Wakuénai are currently adjusting to their historical dislocation. In 1977–78, Wright worked for several months with the Hohódene and Waríperídakéna of the Aiary River in Brazil. Through comparison of oral histories with written documents in Brazilian archives, Wright has demonstrated the continuity between Wakuénai groups living along the Aiary in the 1970s and the historical processes of phratric reintegration and exchange that took place in the late eighteenth and early nineteenth centuries.

7. The sib names published in Oliveira and Galvão (1973) are *lingua geral* equivalents of Wakuénai sib names. In Brazil, the Wakuénai are called Baniwa in *lingua geral*, a practice that helps to explain the terminological confusion about terms of reference for the Wakuénai as a whole.

8. The other remaining Arawak-speaking groups of the upper Río Negro region (Baniwa, Guarequena, and Piapoco) also consider Hípana to be their place of origin. In contrast, Eastern Tukanoan societies of the Vaupés basin do not all share a common orientation to a single place of origin (Goldman 1979; Jackson 1983).

9. In fact, the mythic beginning of Iñápirríkuli is actively constructed in Wakuénai food-exchange ceremonies (*pudáli*). In these dance-festivals the boundaries between host (kin) and guest (affine), men and women, and humans and animals are first established and then transcended in what amounts to a collective return to the precultural, presexual past of the mythic beginning (Hill 1984d).

10. T. Turner's (1977:58) reformulation of Van Gennep's model of rites of passage explores the theoretical ramifications of the idea that ritual structure consists of a relative hierarchy of structural levels, with higher levels standing in a relationship of "becoming to being, dynamic to static, and transcendent to immanent" to lower levels. For a more detailed application of Turner's concept of relative hierarchy of levels to Wakuénai chant-language and musical sound, see Hill (1985).

11. Dixon (1983:179–84) has axiomized a "semantics first" approach to understanding noun classes in Dyirbal, an aboriginal language of Northern Australia. In particular, he gives formal definitions for two semantic principles that are approximately the same as the "taxonomic" principles of Wakuénai chant-language (see Hill 1985).

12. At least two of the groups added to the "search" for Wakuénai sib ancestor spirit names have had historically deep relations of trade and intermarriage with the Wakuénai. The Wakuénai and Uanano have intermarried for several

generations. Historical relations with the Cubeo are also deep. At some point in the past, a number of Wakuénai sibs joined the Cubeo of the Cuduyarí River to form an entire phratry (Goldman 1979:26).

13. For an interesting comparison with Wakuénai ritual attitudes toward written language, see Guss (1986) on the Ye'kuana of Venezuela.

5

The Josho Nahuanbo Are All Wet and Undercooked: Shipibo Views of the Whiteman and the Incas in Myth, Legend, and History

Peter G. Roe

My interest in the interrelationships of history and myth among the Shipibo Indians of the Peruvian *montaña* accidentally began while I was researching the Late Prehistory of the upper Ucayali River. In excavations of the hitherto poorly understood eighth and ninth centuries A.D. Cumancaya ceramic complex (Lathrap 1970:136–45) at the type site of Cumancayacocha on the upper Ucayali, I recovered a staggering amount of whole and smashed vessels, the analysis of which yielded incontrovertible proof of the riverine Panoan cultural affiliations of their makers (Roe 1973, 1976; Raymond, DeBoer, and Roe 1975). These discoveries are relevant to the study of narrative traditions among the contemporary riverine Shipibo-Conibo peoples of the Ucayali basin, since one of their myths identifies Cumancayacocha as the origin site of their ancestors.

To paraphrase two variants of the myth, a large village of "Incas" (in a literal sense the Quechua-speaking members of the Andean empire conquered by the Spanish in the sixteenth century) lived there until one day either a woman shaman or the "Inca" poured flight medicine (*noiarao*) on the ground surrounding the village and it slowly rose. As the village levitated to the sound of drums and flutes, some pots fell to the ground and smashed (the explanation for the ancestral power-impregnated *quënquësh*, or pot sherds, which abounded at the site). The village flew over the Ucayali to descend either upon the mysterious Cerros de Canshahuaya on the lower Ucayali, downriver from Pucallpa, or at Masisea (see Gebhart-Sayer 1986a:16 on the Conibo; Roe 1982a:94, 139–40 on the Shipibo).

During the course of excavating sites in the Ucayali basin, my Shipibo workers discovered a ceramic artifact which they promptly (and in some hilarity) identified as a *shebënanti*. Archaeologists usually label any enigmatic artifact for which a technical function is not immediately apparent a "ceremonial object," and in this case they would be right. It was a small, slightly concave, baked ceramic rectangle with incised designs on one surface; the modern counterpart is painted with prefire designs in the Shipibo style. It serves as a "vaginal bandage or cover" and is an integral part of the Shipibo-Conibo female puberty rite, the *ani shëati* (big drinking). Applied after a radical clitoridectomy (Roe 1982a:93–112), it is discarded onto the midden after the girl heals, precisely where we recovered it. A veritable "Naven" in the Batesonian sense (Lathrap, Gebhart-Sayer, and Mester 1985:78), this ceremony was a "condensed metaphor" giving insight into the whole of Shipibo-Conibo cosmology. Since this ceremony and the artifact that is central to it are unique to the Shipibo-Conibo, the modern cultural affiliations of the archaeological complex seem clear.

We also recovered a cache of one pure native copper axe and one copper spokeshave at the site. Both of these artifacts were far too soft to have been actually used for technical purposes and must also have had ritual or ceremonial functions. Metallurgical analysis indicated they could only have come from the Andes to the west. In addition to documenting long-distance trade between the Andes and the jungle (Lathrap 1973:181), these metal artifacts indirectly supported the "Inca" (in the sense of a generalized "highlander") affiliation of the ancestral inhabitants of Cumancaya Lake.

Taken together with other similarities in the general artifact assemblage, there seemed little doubt that we had proof of the full fiesta and initiation complex in Cumancaya times and also of 1,000 years of riverine Panoan cultural continuity on the upper Ucayali. We also had the first secure archaeological context for Andean contact on the Ucayali, which validated "a historical kernel of truth in at least one Shipibo mythological account" (Roe 1982a:94).

These archaeological conclusions lead us to question the extent to which Shipibo-Conibo mythology, or at least one or more genres within it, is not "mythology" at all but rather carefully encoded oral history. Recently, Lathrap, Gebhart-Sayer, and Mester (1985) did just that by assembling a complex and powerful argument based on archaeology, ethnography, and historical linguistics, respectively, to isolate one genre of Shipibo-Conibo verbal art, the "Inca tales," as "literal" renderings of the historical past. My position here is slightly at variance but is reconcilable, inasmuch as I stress both the mythic and historical elements in these tales. Thus, I treat them as the overlap category of "legend."

Faced in a similar way with the apparently "historical" basis of a part of Shipibo-Conibo mythology, I set about collecting versions of the Cumancaya myth, other myths related to it, and information concerning the *ani šhëati* ceremony itself from older women who had undergone it (the ceremony passed out of currency in the 1950s due to missionary and mestizo pressures). The purpose of this fieldwork was to fill in some of the missing pieces in the ethnographic analogy employed in my earlier archaeological studies.

This essay encompasses a rather deep chronological column beyond the customary ethnographic present. It also alludes to time frames beyond the rubber boom of the last century and beyond even the era of the Inca Empire to the Late Prehistoric period of the Peruvian *montaña* during the ninth century. My experience suggests that not only is it appropriate to mention "legend" in the ethnographic context of myth and history, but it benefits the discussion to encompass prehistory as well.

Theoretical Considerations

Before discussing what "myth" and "history" are, one must ask why they exist and what they are intended to do. In his commentary on the papers in this volume, Terence Turner offers a compelling reason for the existence of history apart from the chronicling of facts: it serves to provide the members of society with a sense of "social agency." Through a record of things people did (history), individuals can recognize their unique ability to "make their own world" through personal and collective social action. A society thus lodged in history contains members who are not mere recipients of cultural gifts from the gods or spirits as recorded in myth. In documenting when and how others actively altered the conditions of life in the past, people are free to change other conditions in the present and thereby affect circumstances in the future.

Turner's analysis makes intelligible the common response of Shipibo informants to foolish questions about origins, such as "Where did the *quënë* [their unique geometric designs] come from?" The answer they often give—"The Inca taught us how to make them"; or "The World Boa [*Ronin*] instructed us to make even better designs" (Farabee 1922:96; Gebhart-Sayer 1985b:149, 153; 1984:10; Roe 1982a:88)—thus yields more insight into the general mythic viewpoint than it does into the phenomena at issue.

The durability of myth is shown by its seeming ability to "validate" its accounts via reference to the empirical, sensate world. It does so through a process of "reading in" (to use Boas's term for the variable assignment of "meaning" to geometric motifs) the etiological function of myth and folktale to nature. For example, the Shipibo note that the *jori*, or the green jay (*Cyanocorax yncas*), has purplish streaks below its beak. Their "Stingy Inca" myth says that these streaks derive from the bile (*tahui*) that leaked out when the bird ate the Inca's liver, and they remain the distinguishing mark of all the *jori*'s kin to this day. A Shipibo informant will point to the bird's beak as proof that the story is true. The whole landscape, from each whirlpool in the river to every strange tree along a well-known path, is filled with such palpable desiderata of the mythology. Only the most profound anomalies disturb this network of explanation. Yet the creators of myth are quick to attack chinks in their intellectual armor, and so the process continues.

Purely logical concerns do not give the whole reason for the existence of myths (Malinowski 1955a:108). Myths provide explanations of perceived features of nature via analogy and also furnish useful social charters for the cultural status quo. Yet, Beidleman (1980) has shown that myths and folktales do not merely reflect or support social reality but often invert it. By providing a simplified social stage of only a few actors (in contrast to the plethora of actors in a small face-to-face society), who are themselves simplified "cartoons" of single, and often extreme, human emotions (greed, jealousy) or actions (cannibalism, incest) rather than the emotional complexity and ambiguity of actual individuals, they "mind-game," or simulate, the usually disastrous consequences of behavior against the norms. Myths present incorrect behavior precisely to subtly reinforce the social charter underlying correct behavior. This "mythic schematization and inversion" is evident in the role of the "Stingy Inca" in Shipibo mythology.

Drawing upon these anthropological concepts, we may affirm that myths exist to resolve the contradictions of the imperfect matching of conception and action, by simplifying the social world and simulating behavior acceptable to the social charters of the status quo and showing, through the inversion of inappropriate (extreme) behavior, the disastrous consequences of contravening these social charters. The "contradiction" these Shipibo myths attempt to resolve is a novel but compelling one. The Shipibo, like other South Amerindians, are no longer alone. They cannot continue the luxury of dealing, both conceptually and in action, only with other similarly constituted "alien tribals." Such beings comfortably constituted their ultimate "other," the infra- or subhumans of non–Shipibo-Conibo cultural affiliation like the backwoods Panoan Cashibo, Amahuaca, the backwoods Arawakan Campa, or the riverine

Tupían Cocama (Roe 1982a:76–90). Against these peoples the Shipibo-Conibo stand out, in their own eyes, as paragons of civilization. All of these other groups appear as either "less than human" or "more than human"; that is, they are nonhuman and exist as minor ogres in the Shipibo "ethnoanthropological" (Magaña 1982) classifications of human beings, fit only to be killed and their young women "harvested" as captured wives. However, a technologically and socially more powerful set of beings has recently burst onto the scene in South America, forcing all of the Indians, at one time or another, to the brink, or beyond, of social and cultural extinction. These beings are the White Men, the Black Men, and the Mestizos (all capitalized as mythic beings) of Western state societies. Unlike their native enemies, whom the Shipibo managed to either raid or trade with in aboriginal times, the Westerners have engulfed them and still seek to exploit or capture their labor, goods, land, women, cultural allegiances, and souls.

One expects, and finds, the Shipibo-Conibo choosing the simple response of merely redefining the traditional subhuman, or anticultural (cannibalistic ogre = incestuous animal) mythic categories so that they can stuff these Westerners, their artifacts, and even their domesticates into them. Thus, the White Men, the Black Men, and so on, become just another kind of Aquatic Seducer or Forest Ogre in accordance with the aboriginal culinary code. Yet the real-world disparity of wealth and power between these intrusive aliens and the Shipibo does not allow the White Men to remain as just minor animalistic ogres. The Shipibo are caught between their admiration of the Westerner's machines and a desire for their wealth and social potency, on the one hand, and their contempt for the Westerner's subhuman, hairy appearance, libidinous (cannibalistic) tendencies, and stingy (anticultural) ways. They are torn by ambiguous and conflicting feelings about the Westerners, which they project in equally ambiguous and conflicting tales. As a reflection of this ambiguity, the Westerners in Shipibo tales often mutate into dual opposed figures. In short, the basic logical contradiction that Shipibo myths about White Men–Black Men–Mestizos attempt to resolve is: How can these new beings, who behave like the Failed Proto-Humans of the remote mythic past or the evil anticultural spirits of the current sacred periphery possess such wealth and power? Attributes like that ought to be the exclusive trappings of truly cultured beings like the Shipibo's own "Inca" culture heroes and mythic ancestors.

The dual answers to this conundrum are mirror images of each other. Some say the Shipibo's own ancestors failed by misunderstanding the intent of the Incas and, through greed or lust, brought poverty and powerlessness upon their descendants. Others say the Westerners are to blame since they stole power, wealth, and machines from the Incas, either by kidnapping them or stealing their treasure—or at least trying to. Hence the "original inequality" among White Men, Black Men, Mestizos, and Indians. While such answers are not unique, the "indirect" Shipibo "Inca transformation" of the Westerners is.

The Hypothesis

Perhaps due to their pivotal *montaña* position, wedged between the societies of the Andes and the Amazon, and their complex history of contact, first with the Inca Empire or even earlier Quechua-speaking "elites," and then with White Men and other Western aliens, the Shipibo have developed an intergrading set of narrative genres that addresses this conundrum. These genres range from mythologized "personal reminiscences," to thinly disguised oral history mixed with mythic elements, to myths proper, each of which roughly corresponds to a type of "past time" into which the Shipibo-Conibo readily sort the temporal loci of their tales (Gebhart-Sayer 1986a:1):

> 1. *Moatian icani*, or the *tiempo de Noe* (time of Noah) in Spanish, a remote and mythic "beginning time";
> 2. *Moatian ica*, or *Moatian ini*, the intermediate past of the "time of the Incas," after the time of creation but before the world of the "Grandfathers"; and
> 3. *Moatian*, the relatively recent past of the "Grandfathers" that encompasses the last fifteen generations or so, which chronicles the rubber boom and the smallpox epidemics of the nineteenth century.

The "middle time," or the "past time of the Incas," is really an overlapping, or "medial" (T. Turner n.d.), category between the remote mythic past and the recent "historical" past, since it incorporates some of the specificity and reliability of the recent past but also retains some of the fantastic or supernatural events and characters of the mythic past. It is the "legendary" past because it fits admirably within Malinowski's (1955a) hoary typology of "myth and folktale, legend and history."

I argue that all of these stories are "mythologized" to some extent insofar as they build upon a pre-existent and basal set of dualistic Magical Twins: the Sun and the Moon and their key animal avatars, the Yellow Jaguar and the Black Jaguar and the (Black Cayman-Anaconda) Dragon respectively. The Sun and/or his avatar was the benevolent "culture donor" who gave the secrets of cultural existence, like fire and cultigens, to humankind, thereby making life easier. The malevolent

Moon and/or his avatar was a "stingy," "culture-withholding custodian" who sought to keep humans in a state of nature and who, although defeated by guile with the help of bird intermediaries, remains the origin of all difficulties in this life and, ultimately, of mortality itself.

Through direct or indirect contact with the Inca Empire, the "Incas" were dichotomized into a Good Inca mapped onto the Sun and a Stingy Inca or Evil Inca mapped onto the Moon, but with the same mythic functions. (Still other secular tales record in very naturalistic detail the "cultural" consequences of this contact with an alien elite.) Then the Westerners arrived. At first they were generous, showering the Indians with wealth. But through the trauma of the rubber boom and the *patrón* system, they revealed themselves to be like the Stingy Inca, Yoáshico.

The Good Inca fled and the withholding aliens, who are assimilated with the Evil Inca, kidnapped him or took his buried wealth and now rule. Their god, either God the Father or Jesus, becomes the "Good Inca" and the Sun. But the Shipibo are not fooled and await the millennium, the return of the "real" Good Inca, who will bring with him the White Men's wealth and power while expunging their obnoxious physical presence. A new "Golden Age" (literally, for the color and "preciousness" codes coincide in attributing both kinds of "gold" to the Good Inca = Sun) will dawn, recapitulating the "beginning time" of mythic origins when the Good Inca first gave the people fire. The doomed Whitemen and their ilk will be "melted" in World Floods and/or "cooked = civilized" to death in World Fires. Since these future catastrophes repeat the disasters of the dawn of creation, they reveal that the Westerners were just another kind of Failed Proto-Human from the distant past, supernaturally eruptive into the regrettable present. Westerners masquerade as real people, but their goods and powers are nothing but the stolen patrimony of the Indians. The existence in the 1950s of an abortive but well-documented millenarian movement, centered on a new kind of "fire," shows that this "sacred topology," which warps the mythic past into the mythic future, has had, and may have again, concrete social correlates.

Whether this progression actually happened does not matter. What matters is that the Shipibo do not interact with or conceptualize about White Men and other aliens directly, as do other lowland groups. They have been through this before with the "Incas," whom they use, via the quasi-historical genre of their "Inca tales," as a "conceptual bridge" to understand, via a similar dualistic transformation, these new aliens. The Westerners become Incas also, and they are "two-minded" ones at that. The existence of a second genre of narratives, Shipibo "personal reminiscence" tales, which also inject myth into history and sometimes involve both "Incas" and White Men, shows that this transformation is not unique to the Inca tales. It is, in fact, the transformation of "legend."

Just as Malinowski (1955a:106) showed that legend is the medial point of conceptual overlap between myth and history, so too do the Inca tales of the Shipibo build a bridge from their memories of the White Men to personal reminiscences about them, and from thence to their folktales of the White Men and their companions. While the Westerners appear as "supernatural" Forest Ogres and Aquatic Seducers in the Shipibo myths, the Inca tales portray a singularly "nonsupernatural" aspect of even archaeologically verifiable historical accuracy. In these three genres we see the birth of myth out of history, just as they reveal the kernel of history in myth.

While the Inca tales readily fall into these categories, which other investigators also have recognized, the only term I have been able to elicit for these types is *moatian joi* (beginning time, word or story). Thus, there is a general term for "jokes," *shiro,* but no term for "trickster tale," even though the latter can be recognized as such and are common (Levy, personal communication, April 14, 1986). In addition to other forms, like origin myths, cosmological myths, and tales of ogres, Gebhart-Sayer (1986a) has recognized Inca tales, which I shall treat here as legends. Levy (n.d.:3) has defined stories of odysseys and trickster tales, and I have isolated animal seduction tales and "personal reminiscences."

What unifies these various kinds of myths, folktales, legends, and reminiscences, in addition to their respective subject matters, are a number of linguistic features that inform the anthropologist that he or she is not hearing ordinary conversation or speechifying. One such feature is the -ni suffix, which marks the tense of an action as the distant, unspecified past, that is, mythic or beginning time (Levy n.d.:22; see also *Moatian icani,* above). Another linguistic feature is the -*ronqui* attributive suffix. Like many South Amerindian languages, Shipibo is not only ergative and iterative in structure, but it also pays close attention to rules of epistemological evidence, that is, whether something is hearsay or was attested to by one's own eyes or ears. The suffix -*ronqui* is thus best translated as "they say" and connotes action of great antiquity and indirect attribution, with an implication of "ancestral truth."

It is on the level of subject matter, the identity and nature of the characters, and their activities in time and space that this loosely integrated set of genres reveals its coherence. I will discuss these aspects in terms of the dynamic or dual triadic[1] dualism evident in the Shipibo creation myth.

Of Proto-Culture and Supernature: The Domain of Myth

The Shipibo often begin their creation myth with the phrase (using the -*ni* and -*ronqui* suffixes): "They say that long ago, when animals could speak like people and people could turn into animals, that the heavens lay so close upon the earth that our ancestors could cook their food in the rays of the Sun, for they had no fire." The analysis of two long myths, *Páno Huëtsa Nëtë* ("The Giant Armadillo and the Other World = Light"; see Roe 1984) and *Ŝhopan Baquëbo* ("The Calabash Twins"; see Roe 1982a:63), shows how Shipibo myths are sacred stories, believed to be true, that deal either with Proto-Culture or with Supernature. These terms represent dual medial categories that derive from a binary set of Culture/Nature dyads—not the old "structuralist shell game" of creating a triadic classification out of opposed dual entities and their overlap, but an example of a more sophisticated "dynamic," or "interpenetrating," dualism than the static oppositional dyadic relations Lévi-Strauss (1969, 1973a, 1978, 1981) employed in his otherwise admirable summaries of Amerindian mythology. Figure 1 suggests that there are two categories of overlap between Culture and Nature (necessitating two Venn diagrams). What distinguishes one from the other is a shift in the point of view of the individual using them. *A*'s overlap with *B* from the point of view of *A* is something different (C1) than *A*'s overlap with *B* from the point of view of *B* (C2). This conceptual tendency to create new entities by shifting one's point of view is uniquely stressed in Shipibo culture, appearing in a number of different domains.

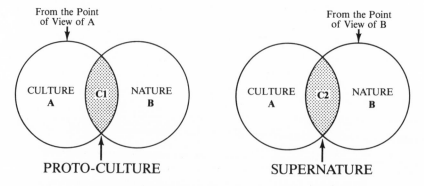

Figure 1. A schematic representation of dual triadic dualism.

Just as the Shipibo can play with "figure/ground" perception in painting, beadwork, and embroidery (by manipulating contrast in their *quënë* so that the background becomes the figure in one layout and, with a change of contrast, the same figure becomes the background in another; see Roe 1980, 1982b), so too do they weave warp-patterned textiles in "double-cloth" so that the figure on the front of the fabric changes contrast values with and becomes the background on the reverse side of the cloth (A. Rowe 1977). The same principle is present in Shipibo constellations, wherein both "positive" (star-to-star) asterisms and "negative" (black cloud) constellations in the Milky Way are emphasized (Roe 1983a). This frequent recourse to mentally "shifting gears" between the concepts Culture and Nature also produces dual medial zones that form the subject matter of their myths and folktales.

Proto-Culture

Proto-Culture is the first overlap category between Culture and Nature from the point of view of Culture. It is represented by the medial[2] fire, the false natural fire of the proximate Sun. That this fire was unsatisfactory because it merely "warmed" food rather than cooked it is evidenced by the subsequent attempts of the first animal-people to acquire "real" fire from the Dragon. This liminal time is populated by theriomorphic or anthropomorphic Culture Custodians, who possess the elements of culture, like fire, but use it "naturally," that is, by vomiting it forth when they want to cook with it and devouring it when they are done. They keep the fire hidden in their mouths or stomachs, away from human culture heroes (Roe 1982a:211). Since they know how to use fire but cannot make it, these Culture Custodians lack the key cultural trait of being able to generate transforming fire at will. Therefore they add a medial "rare" category to the opposed categories of "Raw" and "Cooked" in Lévi-Strauss's (1969) original system.

Once humankind has stolen fire from them, the Culture Custodians revert to being just spirits, *yoshi.* As such they can be kept at bay or killed by fire and other hot things like peppers and the colors red and orange. A curing shaman at Caimito noted, "As the *yoshinbo* ["spirits, group of"] all prefer the cold, you can easily deter them with burns" (Illius 1982:3), as well as burning substances like resinous incense and, above all, tobacco smoke (Roe 1982a:106, 208). Their cold and wet nature, the exhalations (*nihuë*) of their presence, like the humid, earthy, pungent vapors that rise from the rotting vegetation in the jungle after a heavy rain or cling to the land in the fog at night, are the stigmata they wear as "left-over beings" from the dark dawn of creation.

The other key element of Culture in Shipibo thought is cultigens. Not only do people refuse to eat their meat raw, they also eat "cultivated" food rather than strictly wild food. This is why "wild" foods like fruits and honey will always have "natural" connotations in their mythology. Just as the Shipibo have to steal fire from Yoáshico (The Stingy One), so too must they outwit him of his cultigens. He has in his garden plot all the plants the Shipibo will come to use, but he does not want to share them. He posts vipers and wasps on them to sting the luckless, animalistic humans and anthropomorphized animals who seek this gift of Culture.

As a symbol of animality, Yoáshico turns the unlucky animal-humans into real animals when they fail in their quest (Kensinger 1975:43 on the Cashinahua). If his stinginess, itself uncultured behavior, does not turn them into animals, then it forces them to behave like animals. It compels these first beings to become thieves who must steal the cultigens so they can plant them, just like the present-day animal thieves, the agouti and squirrel, who steal from humans' garden plots. Even worse, if Yoáshico accedes to their pitiful requests, then he gives them only toasted maize kernels with cynical instructions to plant them (of course, they do not grow); or he gives them tubers but chops them up so they too will not germinate. In either case, he is preventing them from "generating" culture. This is really why Yoáshico and other Failed Proto-Humans are doomed. While they may possess cultural items, they do not behave culturally. Their secretiveness is tantamount to stinginess with knowledge, just as their envy is equivalent to their meanness with things. This contrasts to the essence of true Culture and the truly "cultured" being, which is to share and reciprocate, in knowledge as well as with things.

Ultimately, in the absence of the Magical Twins as culture hero intermediaries, a helpful masculine-affiliated bird intermediary (a high, fast-flying, brilliantly colored bird, not a low, slow, dull-colored, female-affiliated bird) steals the fire and deposits it in the trees for future firewood. Other, but equally helpful, animal intermediaries steal the tubers and seeds. At that point, Yoáshico is challenged to an arrow duel and, being an ogre and therefore totally self-absorbed and stupid, he falls into a pit and dies, full of arrows. Birds come to bathe in his blood and so acquire their plumage colors in the local Shipibo form of the pan-Amazonian "bathing in the blood of the Anaconda" mytheme. The similarity of this Shipibo variant to the more common one, in which the protagonist is the Anaconda, proves that the anthropomorphic Yoáshico, or the Evil Inca, is really a transformation of the Dragon (Roe 1982a:90). Ever since his demise, people can generate fire or grow crops at will, just as they are free to share them with others because they now possess true Culture.

We thus have three states, not the simple two of Culture/Nature: (1) a state of Nature with no cultural items (fire, cultigens) and no cultural behavior (sharing/reciprocating); (2) a state of Custodial Culture with cultural items but not the ability to generate them and no cultural behavior; and (3) a state of Culture wherein items can be generated at will and shared on demand. Myths are rather like the "rites of passage of the mind"; they translate us from Nature to Culture in a Van Gennepian indirect tripartite process. In other words, myths are about the medial elements and behavior, how we got them and how we transcended them. But that is not all they are about.

Supernature

Myths are also about "unity." Following Dumont (1976), I call this facet "Supernature." Myths are tales about the "Golden Age," when all aspects of reality (time, space, and human/animal nature) were part of a single seamless unity. It is the function of myth to explain what that union was like, how it was lost, and how it can be regained.

In their creation myths, the Shipibo incorporate an integrated worldview that ties the differentiation of human/animal nature with the spatial segregation of the planes of the universe and the beginnings of temporal periodicity. Just as it represented union in lacking the differentiation of Culture from Nature, and hence was represented by Proto-Cultural fire (the heat of the Sun), so too was Nature primordially undifferentiated. If the current world of everyday experience is marked by an alternation of day and night, the Shipibo "beginning world" was uniform, either a continuous day, the *Nëtë Ehua* (day or world, great), or a night without end, the *Yamëcan Ehua* (night, great), the Eternal Night. Just as we use the diurnal/nocturnal alternation as the basis for our divisions of time, whether in minutes or seconds, the Shipibo speak of the position of the sun in the sky to mark the time of day, or of how many moons ago something occurred. Therefore, without this daily succession there was no time. Instead, it was always day, a world illuminated by a burning Sun that hovered motionless, too close to the earth, lethal in its unabated heat, the cause of a World Fire; or it was always night, a cold world dominated by a stationary Moon and filled with the waters of the *Jënën Ehua* (water, big), the World Flood, in whose dark waters carnivorous caimans and anacondas thrashed.

Just as time was homogeneous, so too was space. The separated worlds of the Underworld, the Earth, and the three superimposed Heavens of the current Shipibo cosmos (Roe 1982a:113) did not yet exist. Rather, they all nestled together, undifferentiated, as a single world platter. That is why the Sun lay close upon the Earth (Eakin, Lauriault, and Boonstra 1980:57; Tessman 1928:199).

The Shipibo case thus illustrates the general principle. In contrast to the "uniformitarian" X-Y grid of equivalent time and equidistant two-dimensional space, which locates persons and events in history (e.g., Ssu-ma Ch'ien lived and wrote his *Shih Chi* in Han Dynasty China in 200 A.D.), as Eliade (1959) noted in his distinction between sacred and profane space/time, the grid of myth is a deformable, three-dimensional, topological torus. While a nanosecond now may be equal to one in the Devonian, or a micron across the ice in the Arctic equal to one in the Antarctic for a scientist or a historian, one square centimeter in the Sinai desert is not equivalent to a square centimeter in the Old Temple, or the Dome of the Rock, in Jerusalem, nor is one day now the same as one of the six days of creation to a believer in the Judeo-Christian-Muslim tradition. This is the world of myth, the world of Supernature.

Sexed Space: Of Territories Sacred and Profane

The Shipibo model of social space is a concentric one. It is a kind of "sexed space" where the sexual division of labor is mapped onto horizontal zones. During the day, the center of the village compound is sacred to the extent that the central hearth is the women's domestic axis (Lathrap, Gebhart-Sayer, and Mester 1985:99–100) in this uxorilocal society. A Shipibo village is a loosely articulated affair built around residential compounds (Roe 1980), strung together in a linear fashion, like beads, along natural levees or old alluvial bluffs near the rivers or lakes. The carefully swept plaza, the *jëma*, which surrounds the residential huts and the cook sheds of each compound, is coterminous with the village itself (Siegel and Roe 1986). The *jëma* represents cleared cultural space bordered by the green wall of the jungle and the house gardens (Roe and Siegel 1982c).

Gebhart-Sayer (1985a:7–8) uses the indigenous concept of *quiquin*, "the beautiful," to describe the village and compound *jëma* as the "obvious confirmation of the contrast between culture and nature in an ocean of vegetation which threatens to engulf everything. All things ordered, predictable and trustworthy are found within the village, while the forest wilderness is unordered, arbitrary and full of dangers," especially for this riverine-oriented culture. Since another term used to describe the all-too-perfect "Platonic form" of *Nishi* (*Banisteriopsis* sp.)-inspired visions is *quiquin,* perhaps the Shipibo are striving, in the obsessive cleaning of their own "this-worldly" plazas, for the perfection of the "other world," the brilliant celestial *jëma*s of the Sky Spirits.

On the next ring out is the surrounding "profane intermediate region" of Nature, which encompasses the house gardens, secondary forest, and village garden plots, as well as the snaking paths that connect the compounds to each other, together with the canoe landing where the paths (*bai*) end. On the furthest concentric ring out, the world of Nature and Supernature begins, comprised of meandering rivers with their dangerous whirlpools (*toro*), vast swamps (*nëŝhba*), the feared deep forest (*ni mëran,* "forest," "deep in-side"), and, within the latter, the sinister isolated mountain (*ani mana,* "big," "hill"), outliers of the Andes. The riverine Shipibo particularly avoid the forest for there live the *yoshi* in their nature-fact huts, or hollow trees hidden beneath the gloom of the leafy canopy.

During the night this sacred periphery collapses into the sacred center and the Shipibo hasten to their huts (*ŝhobo*), their friendly fires, and the security of their cotton mosquito nets (*bachi,* "egg"). Even the bravest hunter hurries back along the paths lest he encounter in the dusk a wandering spirit hungry for human flesh (Roe 1982a:91) or, just as deadly, one that is lonely for human company. There are thus two domains: one leafy and the other watery, where these Forest Ogres or Aquatic Seducers can be found. As leftovers from primordial time, they engage in distinctly anticultural activities (cannibalism, incest) and lack cultural institutions like fire and cultigens. They can be "civilized to death" by "cooking" their raw essences in fire. Myths concern these supernatural beings and the Alien Tribals, like the backwoods Panoan Cashibo (Vampire Bat People), who are assimilated with them. White Men, Black Men, and Mestizos are the new occupants of this anticultural niche.

Since these domains are supernatural space, and sacred space is time, we also find that as one travels out into these remote concentric regions—the swamps, the forest, the mountains—or into the night, one goes back in time, to their time. Thus, there are three times in which stories about Proto-Culture and Supernature may occur: the remote antiquity of beginning time; the quasi-historical time of the "Incas," in which archaic things and strange events may still occur; and the present, but the present of the sacred periphery. To begin with the present, we start with "new myths," or personal reminiscences, proceed back to legends, and end with established myths set in the remote past.

In this class of narrative, a personal reminiscence becomes a legend and the legend behaves like a myth. In fact, these personal legends may eventually become assimilated into myths once they have been generalized. Below is one such instance of "walking into the ideology." My main informant, Manuel Rengifo, and I were discussing the "Incas," and he narrated this tale to me with a nonchalance that marked it as a bit of "real" personal history (field notes, text no. 67).

The Inca Who Was at Tsoaya Ihan[3]

It is said that in Tsoaya Ihan, the [water] was very transparent, crystal clear, during the time when the Shetebo[4] were new inhabitants there. The lake was clear all the way to the bottom. They say that one could see all kinds of things in there like *cabúri* [the *taricaya* water turtle, *Peltocephalus taricaxa*], *huamë* [the *paiche* fish, *Arapaima gigas*], and *amaquiri* [the *gamitana* fish, *Serrasalmus* sp.]. One could see them swimming about very clearly. When it was like that they say that the *chaiconi* [invisible, transforming humanoids] turned the mirror over and therefore now one can no longer see to the very bottom. One can see something, but not down to the very bottom. This happened in Nëtë Caya Ihan after the Shetebo had recently been killed off [in the Jënën Ehua]. The newly deceased Shetebo who had disappeared were there. The name of the lake was Nëtë Caya.

The Inca lived there after the Great Flood had exterminated the Shetebo. [They died] because they had buried his son. When they say that [the lake] was very clear one [man] headed toward the *caño* [intake/outlet rivulet] which debouches into Nëtë Caya lake. [The man] went there to go fishing. On the shore of the lake there was a house with an aluminum roof. Looking from the mouth of the *caño* toward the house [the man noticed that] there were men talking inside. But just as he got closer, looking [again, he saw] that the men had disappeared. Attracted [to this strange thing] the man approached closer and saw that the men were [really] no longer there. Only the eggs of their chickens and ducks and a lot of *bimpish* [the *guayaba* tree, *Psidium guajava*] remained.

The chickens and ducks had laid their eggs beneath the *bimpish* [trees]. The house was well closed in and they say that in front of its door there was very clean sand. Both the *shahuë* [the *charapa* mud turtle, *Podecnemis expansa*] and the *cabúri* were laying their eggs there. Thus the *caño* was then, they say. Now it is all closed in [overgrown]. Now nobody goes there. That is why there is now a lot of game that abounds there.

Then, during that time in the past, we ourselves had gone there. Arriving and looking around, [we saw] that it was like that. [I] went [there] at night and while I was there I saw airplanes flying around. [Even though] it was very late, in the middle of the night, the planes flew without lights. Only the roar of their engines, ROON, was heard. It was very mysterious. They were different from the planes which fly about over here [in Yarinacocha].

Note the narrator's shift from indirect ascription to direct personal reminiscence, thus confirming the tales. The tin-roofed, closed-in mestizo-style house and the mysterious airplanes mark these "Incas" as Westerners while at the same time preserving the "flight motif" of the ancient, indigenous Incas from the flight medicine of the Cumancaya myth (see Gebhart-Sayer 1986a:16 on the Conibo). Other mythic variants directly equate the airplanes with the Indian Incas to achieve symbolic closure: "When the Spaniards came, also many Incas fled into the Ucayali forest. From these people, too, the Conibo and Shipibo learned many things. These Incas still live today. They own airplanes and everything. They are in the sky and hide in the forest. They had intended to teach us how to fly in airplanes" (Gebhart-Sayer 1986a:25). The "airplanes" and "flight medicine" of the Incas are mythic transformations of the avian avatars of the Sun. Solar birds like the Hummingbird and the Scarlet Macaw are the "planes" that traditional shamans used to reach the Sun. Since the Good Inca is assimilated with the Sun, and the Westerners are merged with the Good Inca (at least until they refuse to share their things with the Indians), both Incas and Westerners will fly about in magical planes.

From the perfect meshing of myth with personal reminiscence legends to the tales of the legendary Incas, all the genres intergrade in Shipibo-Conibo oral literature. Thus the Inca tales, of which this is partially an example, are a truly intermediate type between myth and history. While some have stressed their historic content, I emphasize their mythic attributes. Neither view is wrong, save when they maintain exclusivity. The overlap between the two polar types is, in fact, legend. Rephrased, the Shipibo mediate history and myth with legend.

Inca Tales as Legend

Lathrap, Gebhart-Sayer, and Mester (1985) have presented a bold argument, based on archaeology, ethnography, and historical linguistics, respectively, that one genre of Shipibo-Conibo oral literature, the Inca tales, is not really "mythology" at all but rather precise oral history. They point out that these tales are surprisingly homogeneous, numerous, and conspicuously lacking in the sort of supernatural events that characterize myth. The three extract paleo-ethnography from these tales to reconstruct details of the past migration of a ruling elite and its grafting onto an old Panoan substratum, treating the Inca tales as the record of the social relations between that elite and the ruled from the perspective of the descendants of the ruled, the Shipibo-Conibo. Based in part on an argument I made earlier (Roe 1973), that prior to 800 A.D. the fine-ware component of the Panoan-affiliated Cumancaya complex revealed massive influence from the ceramic traditions of the Ecuadorian *montaña* far to the north, Lathrap, Gebhart-Sayer, and Mester (1985:66) identify that influence as deriving from the migration of a pre-Incaic, Quechua-speaking elite southward from the Ecuadorian Oriente along the flanks of the Andes into the Ucayali. In their opinion these are the "Incas" to which the tales refer, not the members of the historic Inca Empire.

Earlier authors, like Farabee (1922:96), who had the riverine Panoans beating off an actual Inca expeditionary force, or Waisbard (1958–59:24), who had all manner of exotic Andean populations migrating into and residing on the Ucayali, have offered equally literal reconstructions of population movements from the Andes, in spite of the lack of archaeological evidence supporting such "invasions." While Lathrap, Gebhart-Sayer, and Mester's thesis is more plausible, precisely because it incorporates archaeological evidence, Gebhart-Sayer (1986a:10) has also articulated a less radical thesis of indirect contact with the Inca Empire, via its *mitma* system of intentional colonization or via fugitives. These may have been the mechanisms that produced the specific Shipibo-Conibo "remembrances" of the "Incas" at a later pre- or postcontact time.

My command of Quechua linguistics is not adequate to evaluate the pre-Incaic argument, but my own Inca tales could lend credence to either of the more cautious positions: indirect contact during Incaic times, perhaps via trade, or postcontact Incaic colonization by highland Quechua fleeing to the *montaña* from the Spanish (as some highlanders are doing to this day). While I thus support Lathrap, Gebhart-Sayer, and Mester's historical reading of myth, I suggest that they have failed to notice the mythic elements in history. What they call "history" is really "legend." They are correct, however, that these tales form a specific genre in Shipibo-Conibo-Pisquibo oral literature. The tales also appear to be more common as one goes further upriver to Caimito, where Gebhart-Sayer worked, than downriver at Yarinacocha, Tsoaya, or Santa Rosa, Aquaitía, where I have done fieldwork. This is precisely as it should be, since in going upriver one approaches the Inca's Andean home.

The three are also correct that Quechua in general and Incaic knowledge in particular are pervasive and integrated influences in modern riverine Panoan culture (see Roe 1982a:86–90). Indeed, these riverine Panoans, and to some extent even the backwoods ones, have a veritable "Inca fixation" (Lathrap, Gebhart-Sayer, and Mester 1985:41; Waisbard

1958–59:24). The Incas act as benign culture heroes and are given credit for everything, from the invention of a portion of the design system to how one paddles a canoe! Yet there are also things the Panoans are credited with having before the Inca's arrival, in particular the female puberty ceremony, of which the "Incas" disapproved. This gives such attributions a "factual" aura since, if the Incas were just mythic culture heroes, they would be given credit for everything.

Lathrap, Gebhart-Sayer, and Mester's "literal" reading of Inca tales can be summarized as follows. As an Andean society with access to ore sources nonexistent in the alluvial lowlands, "they owned or introduced unknown techniques like flight medicine, how to catch large fish, how to use *Ayahuasca* [*Nishi*] and make fire, how to count days and soften stones, how to fly planes and make [metal] knives" (Gebhart-Sayer 1986a:7). Yet the Incas are also credited with the introduction of indigenous lowland crafts like pottery, textiles, and woodwork (Bardales 1979:34–35, 52–53). They brought in new cultigens too (Gebhart-Sayer 1986a:7). However, it was with their equipment that the Incas first instructed the Panoans in "high technology" and the use of stone axes and clubs, bows and arrows, "shining" or stone (probably metal) boats, and metal implements (Gebhart-Sayer 1986a:7). Being a stratified society, the Incas also brought class- or caste-based ethnic interactions. It is here that the texts take on an uncanny "historical" aspect (more so than with many of the above "gifts," like fire and cultigens, which traditional culture heroes also customarily bring in myth):

> For purposes of our argument the themes of the Inca cycle can be summarized: (1) The geographical locations, "Where the Inca lived" or "Where we lived with our Inca," are always precisely geographically described or even named. Among them Cumancaya figures prominently. (2) The Incas arrived on the Ucayali in groups, families, or as individuals, bringing along women, secretaries, workers, servants, and soldiers, traveling the Perené, Pachitea, and Urubamba rivers and using a footpath called [*bai nashua*] (broad path). Bridges are described and located. (3) They established themselves in already existing settlements and treated the Panoans as tributary subjects, servants, or communal workers. Intermarriage was problematic. . . . [4] The punishments for rebellious Panoans were hitting over the head and the application of poisonous animals. [5] They propagated communal work (nowadays called the *minga* among the Shipibo-Conibo) and collective ownership of the gardens. . . . [6] They gave the Panoans advice, settled disputes, and cared for them as far as food and clothing were concerned. [7] The Incas caused both quiet resistance and open rebellion. In one reported case they had to flee to the mountains from the Panoans. (Lathrap, Gebhart-Sayer, and Mester 1985:64–65)

Dualism and the Incas

My differences with this view tend to undermine the apparent historicity of the Inca tales. I contend that while Lathrap, Gebhart-Sayer, and Mester are correct that this genre is more historical than other genres in Shipibo-Conibo verbal art, it nevertheless also incorporates mythic elements. The first of these mythic aspects is the fact that magical or supernatural events do occur in these narratives, albeit less than in other stories. This is especially true in the case of the Cumancaya and *Incan* Baquë/Jënën Ehua cycles, where one sees the Incas miraculously surviving internment, causing World Floods, and engaging in magical voyaging and village levitation. These magical episodes argue for the mythologizing of historical tales.

Lathrap, Gebhart-Sayer, and Mester also ignore the repeated and obvious parallels between the Incas and the pre-existent Magical Twins: Sun/Moon = Dragon of riverine Panoan mythology. It is true, however, that many, not just two, Incas are mentioned in the Inca tales. This supports both the historicity of the tales and the analysis of the Incas as an elite population and not just a twin set. Indeed, the mention of specifically identified Incas (Curi Inca, Chëŝhë Inca, Inca Nima, Para Inca, Ŝhanö Inca, etc.) supports the social agency aspects of these figures as unique historical personages.[5] Yet, the behavior of these multitudinous characters polarizes into the two stingy/generous twins.

Furthermore, both the Stingy Inca and the Good Inca appear in the same myths as contending figures (whether as asymmetrical pairs like the evil father-in-law and the smart son-in-law or as symmetrical twins), and with the appropriate animal avatars (Snake-Anteater = Evil Inca/Jaguar-Eagle = Good Inca). Gebhart-Sayer (1986b:1) recognizes these equations and offers the following myth in support of the Magical Twins being equated with the Inca:

> Long after the Great Deluge and the ascension of the Good Inca = Christ to Heaven, the Bad Inca, who had stayed behind, inflicts the Long Night on mankind. During this time of perpetual darkness, giant cannibalistic Vampire Bats feed on people, and disease, earthquakes, inundations and fires produce continuous suffering. The Good Inca returns from the sky and "He first asked the Incas [these first people]: 'Who causes these catastrophes?' But no one knew."
>
> He then travels downriver with two companions: the Black Iron Jaguar and the Steel Harpy Eagle and comes to the tremendous foaming sea. There the Good Inca transforms himself into a small red [*jë*] ant and floats out to an island on the sea foam. There, in a White Man's style house he overhears the Bad Inca plotting further destruction for "[his] children," in spite of his wife's remonstrances. The Bad Inca tells her not to worry since

he is invulnerable. He has hidden his heart inside a *Coma* (a tinamou) and has placed the Tinamou inside a *Chaŝho* (red deer), which, in turn, he has placed inside his Iron Giant Anteater (*Ahua shaëu* [*shao* = "bone"], "tapir anteater").

The Good Inca overhears this, and sends his Iron Black Jaguar into the water to kill the Iron Giant Anteater of the Bad Inca. After a terrible battle the Jaguar kills the Anteater, but the Deer leaps out of its opened chest when it is dragged to dry land by the Jaguar. The Jaguar pursues and kills it, but out of the opened chest of the Deer flies the Tinamou. The Tinamou is pursued by the Good Inca's Steel Eagle which overtakes and kills it at the zenith. The Good Inca now rips the pulsating heart from the Bad Inca's chest. However, he goes back to the Bad Inca's house and hears his voice, his threats and the sound of the Evil Inca's wife cautioning him again. The Good Inca throws the Evil Inca's heart onto the table and the latter finally expires.

But the Bad Inca's soul travels far away to the country of the *Gringos,* probably the United States. *Mestizo* fishermen, *Mozos,* claim they saw him "there on the beach, all dressed in gold." After being presented to the President there he builds himself a golden house inside the earth beneath the President's palace. There he taught the *Gringos* how to manufacture machines, factories and airplanes. The narrator reports a U.S. missionary who showed him a picture of the Bad Inca (possibly Jesus) "youthful and beautifully dressed" inside his golden house. Being ignorant of who the Bad Inca really was, the missionary claimed that he was their God who had given them everything they owned!

Then the Good Inca returned upriver from the ocean to the Ucayali and "promised his people that until his next return no further catastrophes were to be expected, because the originator of the suffering was defeated." And indeed, "since that time, eclipses, storms, inundations, fire and earthquakes" have caused little suffering. (material in quotation marks is Gebhart-Sayer's; paraphrase, orthography, and identifications are mine)

As Gebhart-Sayer (personal communication, 1986) points out, "I think it will help you in your twin issue, as it is another instance where the two Incas appear together, even in an antagonistic constellation (almost like God and [the] Devil)." It is a syncretistic myth since it incorporates an aboriginal astronomical myth (the Black Jaguar is the Coal Sack, while the Tinamou is probably another Dark Cloud constellation in the Milky Way; the Deer is the origin of the Deer's Eye, a bright star in the Milky Way = *Chaŝhon Bai,* "Deer's Path"; see Roe 1983a), with modern imagery that accounts for the wealth and machines of the White Men and the Good Inca's "buried treasure" and his imminent return.

The positional and theriomorphic code relationships are maintained in this confrontation. The Good Inca is associated with the Sky and the Sun, the Evil Inca with the Water and the Lunar Subterranean realms. Each is assisted by an appropriate animal avatar "canoe": the Evil Inca with the Giant Iron Anteater and the Good Inca with his Giant Iron Black Jaguar. While no snake is mentioned for the Bad Inca, an ophidian combinatorial variant, the Giant Anteater, appears. The Iron Anteater is a transformation of the Iron Ácoro (Black Anaconda) Ship Serpent of Shipibo mythology (Harner 1980:91–92) on two grounds. In ethology the Giant Anteater (*Myrmecofaga jubata*) is one of the few animals capable of holding its own against that "super predator," the Jaguar, and appears in animal trickster tales as its enemy (Roe 1982a:190). On the morphological/analogic level, the long snaky tongue encased in the hollow bony tube of this edentate's mouth is linked to the similarly sinuous body of the snake (Roe 1982a:188–90). In turn, the bony tube is related to the blowgun, which is itself a transform of the Anaconda (Roe 1982a:52).

All of the other "encapsulated" animals of the Bad Inca have evil connotations, while both creatures linked to the Good Inca have positive linkages. The Shipibo link the Deer inside the Anteater to souls and corpses, the prey of the Moon, while the Tinamou is one of those laboriously flying "feminine birds" (Roe 1982a:63) that are opposed to the high-flying birds of the Sun = Good Inca like the Harpy Eagle. The battles between the avatars of the major figures repeat, in a minor mode, the clash of the major Magical Twins: the Good Inca and the Evil Inca. The rebirth of the Evil Inca in the land of the White Men is another variant of the *Inca Cani* (Withdrawing Inca) mytheme and sheds light on the "buried Inca" mytheme to follow.

This battle between the two Incas continues on another plane, that between in-laws in adjacent generations rather than between siblings in the same generation. Due to brideservice and uxorilocal residence, the son-in-law/father-in-law dyad is a point of some friction in Shipibo society. A father-in-law looks forward to a long period of service from an industrious and skilled son-in-law, while the son-in-law desires as short a period as possible and a rupture of the uxorilocal pattern to return to his natal compound. This fosters an avoidance relationship between these two males to minimize contact and friction.

In mythology, the correct relationship of a generous father-in-law and a dutiful son-in-law is inverted to show the dangers of incorrect behavior. Within the sibling set, the elder brother is assimilated with the role of wise and benevolent father and the younger brother with the foolish and malevolent son (the Good Inca and the Bad Inca, respectively). When in-law relationships are used, the age differences become morally reversed. Now it is the evil father-in-law who becomes the cannibal and attempts to kill and eat his smart son-in-law. Numerous Shipibo tales thus use dragonic figures, like the *Bi Yoshin* (Mosquito Spirit; see Roe

1983b), to represent the father-in-law, who makes excessive demands on his son-in-law (not just of his labor but also ultimately of his body). Since the Evil Inca has already been linked to the Dragon, we also have tales about the Evil Inca as a cannibalistic father-in-law who presents his hapless son-in-law with impossible trials as a pretext to eat him when he fails.

In this role, the Evil Inca becomes specifically identified as Yoáshico, the Stingy One: "After everybody had seen how bad this Inca was, another Inca came and defeated him. He married the daughter of the bad Inca. One day the new Inca went fishing on the lake. His evil father-in-law followed him to transform him into a heron, but the young Inca could avoid the assault" and the next day he ambushed and transformed his father-in-law into the sinister Manŝhanteo, the Toyuyo, or Jabiru Stork (Jabiru mycteria; see Gebhart-Sayer 1986a:18). This is a huge bird that, when seen from a distance on the playas, the Shipibo say looks like a soldier (sontáro; from the Spanish soldado) in white coat and black leggings. In another variant, the Josho Inca (White Inca; possibly, White Man Inca) acts in the Yoáshico role and is also transformed into a Jabiru with his followers as Herons (Manŝhan)—all aquatic birds.[6] Here the son-in-law is specifically identified as Rey Dios Baquë (King God, from the Spanish; child or son, from the Shipibo), or King God's Son, a form of the Baquë Mëraya (Child Shaman), son of the Sun (Gebhart-Sayer 1986a:20).

Thus, while these tales may refer to an alien elite in a historical sense, they are also a part of the Magical Twins mythic cycle. As the Incas have become mythologized by relating them to the dualistic culture hero Sun/Moon anticultural figures, history has become legend. Moreover, this prior experience with the "Incas" led the Shipibo-Conibo to do the same thing to the Westerners when they arrived. They too were mythologized, first into benevolent sun figures and then malevolent moon figures. The same fate awaited the Westerner's deities. This, in turn, leads to chiliastic expectations of the return of the benevolent Inca, who is still alive, perhaps buried, somewhere (Maxwell 1975:382).

The Inca and Chiliastic Expectations

The Shipibo-Conibo have elaborated the genre of Inca tales into a rich diversity of narratives and associated beliefs. These legends give cultural form to a variety of alien social practices and products which, from an indigenous perspective, are viewed in highly ambivalent terms: the Christian ideology of Good versus Evil, the inequality of trade relations between white/mestizo merchants and indigenous laborers, and the technological tokens (e.g., firearms and metal currency) of the Spanish conquest and colonial domination over indigenous Andean peoples. A detailed account of these narratives would require monographic treatment, so in the following discussion I select only those legends that deal with chiliastic expectations and the social relations between the Shipibo-Conibo and the white/mestizo/black outsiders. It is precisely the mythic aspects of their millenarian expectations (Harner 1974) that lead the Shipibo-Conibo themselves to affirm the historicity of the Inca tales and "the asserted former presence of the Incas on the Ucayali river" (Gebhart-Sayer 1986a:3).

Since the mythic past will loop back into the mythic future of the coming of the millennium, these historical tales become legendary in their prophecy of the future. The Shipibo seek to throw the switch of time, to return White Men and Black Men to the past from whence they came. Led by shamans, they will expel the Westerners by rebelling in the future. Then, the intrusive White Men will be revealed for what they always were, another class of Failed Proto-Humans awaiting oblivion through their "tragic flaws," greed and stinginess. True humans, Indians, will triumph, but with the White Men's riches.

My informants, when talking about the revitalistic cult of Wasëmea,[7] the rare female *mëraya* (the highest grade of transforming ventriloquistic shamaness) of the 1950s (Lathrap 1976:203), showed that this past was a proto-cultural one by affirming that she and her followers awaited the White Men's end in their thatched temples while cooking on a special "blue fire." This was their symbol, being a "new" fire different from the fire of the White Men. It marked the dawn of the new age, just like a new Sun, and showed that, like all Failed Proto-Humans, the White Men did not even know how to cook properly! The movement failed when the expected millennium never materialized. Yet the cult left behind a characteristic curvilinear design style that Wasemëa pioneered, as well as a feeling that she was an evil woman, a witch, who misled the people. Moreover, the resentment against White Men and Mestizos that was an element of that movement still exists, and a return of millenarian consciousness is always possible as acculturative and land pressures continue to mount against the Indians.

This vision bespeaks a more positive view of the "original inequality" between the Westerners and the Indians than the Shipibo "first theory" that defensively lays the blame on their own ancestors. The "second theory," in being more aggressive and showing greater pride, bodes well for the Shipibo's future relationships with Westerners. Only if the Shipibo have pride in themselves and their culture can they make the decisions to accept some and reject other elements of Western civilization. The opposite stance of total acceptance, which backwoods Panoans like the Iscobakebu have shown, deriving from a low self-image, is tantamount to cultural death.

The heart of the Shipibo's argument lies in their use of the pre-existent "culinary code" (Lévi-Strauss 1969) to portray White Men and Black Men as imperfectly made and, therefore, Failed Proto-Humans vis-à-vis the perfectly fabricated Indians, the legitimate inheritors of creation. The following myth completes the formula by asserting that White Men are underdone and doomed to melt away in the coming cataclysm (field notes, text no. 61).

The Creation of [the Races] of Mankind by the Inca

In ancient times, the Inca made men from the dust [of the earth]. After modeling the form [of one of the men] the Inca put him in a kiln. In a little while he took him out and the [man] left the kiln slightly undercooked. From this man descended the *Josho Nahuanbo*. Then [the Inca] made another man. After forming him [the Inca] put him in [the kiln] again.

Then [the Inca] took him out. When he looked at him [the Inca] saw that he was too well cooked; [he was] black. We ourselves call him [the ancestor of] the *Rashico*.

Then the Inca said once more, "The two whom I have made are not as they should be. Now I will mold another." Speaking thus, he made another one and put him in the kiln to bake him. Then the *Panshinshaman* [yellowish; in some contexts, reddish] person left the kiln. He was what we call the color of the Indians. When he had looked at him the Inca said, "He is good."

This tale, which completes the survey of genres, from personal reminiscence to historical legend and finally myth, shows how the Shipibo retain a sense of superiority over Caucasians, even while acknowledging the intruders' technical supremacy. The White Men/Black Men do not just erupt like their diseases, they also come from the distant past—unfinished and "rare." This myth bridges the domain of Proto-Culture to the creation of "proper humans," the Indians, by placing the fabrication of the protohuman White Men and Black Men before the origin of the Shipibo but after the Good Inca creator god. The Good Inca is assimilated with the beneficent Sun, who baked the wet mud of the newly emergent land after the waters of the World Flood receded with the heat of his day. Not only do White Men act like boorish intruders from the proto-cultural past, they are the Failed Proto-Humans of beginning time. Nevertheless, they have managed to live on into the present, via a mythic torus that has topologically deformed sacred time-space.

These modern intruders, original denizens of the dark and aquatic past, come from the sacred wet periphery and are doomed to "melt away" again into it when the Inca returns in a new golden day.

Just as the Shipibo-Conibo have elaborated their Inca tales into a rich genre of oral narratives, so too have they developed an extensive corpus of narratives and beliefs mythologizing the White Men and Mestizos and their cultures. These narratives can be understood as transformations of Shipibo-Conibo narrative genres in which the mythic-historical genre of Inca tales, or legends, serves as a conceptual bridge between Shipibo-Conibo consciousness of their own society and that of their relations with white/mestizo/black outsiders.

The Mythic Transformation of History (Legend)

I have argued here that the Shipibo have gone from history, through legend, to myth in their understanding of the intrusive Westerners. Moreover, this is a direct reflection of the actual history of Riverine Panoan experience with the "ultimate aliens." Perhaps there was a happy coincidence of their history, which breaks into two contrasting episodes, and the dualistic basis of Shipibo ideology. During their first halcyon era of contact with the Spanish, which started in 1557–1691 with Franciscan and Jesuit missionaries competing for the souls of the natives by being lavish in their gifts of iron and cloth, the whites were likened to an earlier experience of "culture donation" and generosity on the part of the Good Inca. When later demands for labor and cultural change turned these benevolent beings into the Bad Inca, the Conibo erupted in a massive rebellion (1693–98), which closed their homeland to the Spanish (DeBoer 1981:31–37).

Another period of rapprochement ensued, which turned into the nightmare of the rubber boom and *patrón* exploitation (Tessman 1928:11–12). The present is marked by systematic encroachment on the part of the surrounding mestizos, mostly the acculturated descendants of the riverine Panoan's hereditary enemies, the Tupían Cocama, and an increasing politicization of the Indians themselves, as an indirect result of the bilingual educational program instituted by the North American Evangelical (S.I.L.) missionaries operating out of their huge aerodrome bases on Lake Yarina. It is no wonder that the present imagery of the Whites, Blacks, and Mestizos should tilt toward the "dragonic" end of the symbolic continuum. Ironically, the present spottily applied educational system is bringing in historical information on the Inca Empire, a central and proud element in modern Peruvian national identity, which appears to corroborate the historical basis of the Shipibo-Conibo's own legendary Inca tales. Thus the stage is set for the continuing interaction of myth and history in the form of nascent millenarian movements.

Conclusion

We have come a long way from Thunder, Black (Evil) Jaguars, Anacondas and Caimans, swamp-dwelling and cave-inhabiting anthropomorphic spirits, to Inca gods, Aquatic Seducers, Forest Ogres, and millenarian saviors. To appreciate how the Shipibo have intellectually "digested" White Men/Black Men as recent historical intrusives, we must also understand how they dealt with earlier pre- and protohistoric "Inca" arrivals. Fundamental to this uneasy process of social adjustment is the profound ambivalence that the quasi humans elicit and the Shipibo myths reflect. On the one hand, the Caucasians are the historical "winners," triumphant in their superior technology and social organization. Thus they and their mestizo progeny are the inheritors of the indigene's wealth from a golden age. But they do not want to share. Their inhuman (greedy, cannibalistic) character aligns them with ogres and the "untamed" forested, mountainous, or watery sacred periphery. They are anticultural figures, doomed to be obliterated by a mythic topological looping, a deformation of mythic time-space. The present periphery becomes the remote precultural past; the White Men are assimilated with Monkeys, Dwarfs, and Giants, the Failed Proto-Humans of the first worlds.

Curiously enough, the present domination by Westerners offers hope for a perfectable future. Through an Indian messiah (male or female), who will emerge from the earth while mayhem rains from the heavens, the currently rampant aliens will be smitten. Thunder will seal the White Men's doom, just as Thunder assimilated their initial harquebus/machine-gun victories. Indians, who once disdained the flashing weapon, will now embrace it and drive the *Viracochas,* whom they once welcomed, into the waters from whence they came.

While it might appear that the Forest Ogre, the Evil Inca, and the White Men all obey Roland Barthes's (1984) "obsessional play of symbolic substitutions," one taking the place of the other in an endless gyre, as they "continue to function as algorithms to be used by mythic thought for the carrying out of the same operations" (Lévi-Strauss 1981:537), all is not just ahistorical structure. The dynamic dualism of the Shipibo system is also responsive to the exigencies of history. Perhaps, however, in their case, we find a happy congruence between history and the paradigmatics of oral tradition. The long and curiously "binary" pattern of historical contact between the worldly and widely traveled "canoe-Indian" Shipibo and the Westerners led them to differentiate these aliens into dualistic beings like their native supernaturals, at first benign and now malignant. This may have replicated an earlier period of contact with the expanding Inca Empire and perhaps an even earlier, but equally expansive, lowland Quechua-speaking "elite."

It is not just a matter of ahistorical structure, or of unstructured history, but of a "structural history" that orders dyadic historical episodes into dualistic figures and then mythically projects these figures upon the "mirror world" of the future to hasten the millenarian return of the remote past. The Shipibo, like their backwoods Panoan kin, endured periods of contact with whites and their associates that bifurcated into initial halcyon encounters and subsequent exploitative confrontations. No wonder they transmuted the aliens into polar figures just as they earlier transformed the "Incas" into binary beings.

The Shipibo, Conibo, Pisquibo, Cashinahua, Sharanahua, Cashibo, and Amahuaca have all responded to the new arrivals' greed by interpreting it via an underlying reversible dualism, as the actions of the Culture Custodial-Witholding Dragon and his Failed Proto-Humans, like the Shetebo. This dualism was manipulated by an equally basal "culinary metaphor" such that Gold succeeded Meat even as the "raw" Forest Ogres and Aquatic Seducers and the "rare" Failed Proto-Humans became first the Evil Inca and then the Stingy White Men and thieving Mestizo. Just as we are beginning to see the history that lies behind myth (Lathrap, Gebhart-Sayer, and Mester 1985) and transmutes it into legend in the lowlands, and the myth that underlies "history" in the highlands (Zuidema 1982), so we can now begin to interpret the mythic structures that fold time and encode it into space in both of these vast culture/geographic areas.

NOTES

The research on which this essay is based took place initially in the central Ucayali basin under the support of a National Endowment of Humanities Fellowship for eight months during 1981, principally at the well-known village of San Francisco de Yarinacocha, near Pucallpa. I gratefully acknowledge this support, as well as that of the National Science Foundation through its LOCI grant program and the University of Delaware via its Grant-in-Aid program. The latter supported an additional month of observation during 1982 at the village of Santa Rosa on the upper Aquaitía River. Additional thanks are due the University of Delaware Research Grants program for making possible another two months of fieldwork in the lower Ucayali basin during 1984 in the village of Tsoaya, near Contamana. Write-up time was provided by the Centro de Investigaciones Indígenas de Puerto Rico, of which I am curator. Thanks also to fellow specialists in South Amerindian studies with whom I have had productive discussions about some of the ideas presented herein: Catherine Allen, William Crocker, Angelika Gebhart-Sayer, Bruno Illius, Dominique Irvine, Daniel Levy, and George Mentore. Special thanks are due Robert Carneiro for generously sharing with me all his field notes on the Amahuaca relating to mythology, which he collected with Gertrude Dole during their 1960–61 fieldwork among the backwoods Panoans. Of course, none of these scholars are responsible for any of this study's shortcomings.

1. While I did not formulate my conception of "dynamic dualism" (Roe 1982a) with reference to either W. Crocker's (1983) definition of "triadic dualism," as he deduced it from the symbolic oppositions of Ramkokamekra Canela thought, or Isbell's (1978) cognate "reversible dualism" of highland Quechua conceptions, it is compatible with both and argues for profound cognitive similarities between South Amerindian groups of even differing ecological and sociological settings. A summary of this concept is provided in Hugh-Jones's review (1985).

2. I am here using T. Turner's (n.d.) concept of medial fire, which he independently devised for his discussion of the gift of fire of the Jaguar in Northern Kayapó mythology. I have already discussed why, being a Jaguar, it freely gave fire to humankind, while similarly structured tales in other groups like the Shipibo, but involving a stingy reptilian Dragon (usually a giant Black Caiman), make the humans steal fire from him (Roe 1982a:201).

3. Here the -ronqui suffix was used to mark this story as a myth. Yet later it intergraded seamlessly into a "corroborative" personal reminiscence. At that point in the text the -ronqui suffix was deleted. Sehuaya or Tsoaya Ihan is an oxbow lake near the mouth of the Pisqui River. It is located across from Contamana, downriver from Pucallpa. Plagued by hordes of mosquitos, this area is little frequented save for a small Shipibo settlement there. Because of its isolation, this lake is rich in fish, supernatural events, and beings like the Chaiconi. Unlike the muddy Ucayali, this still lake has relatively clear water, at least until it is obscured by microscopic plant growth (hence the "mirror" symbolism).

4. The Shetebo are an extinct (or assimilated) subgroup of riverine Panoans who, historically, were located on the lower Ucayali river. They followed the fate of the Cocama (Myers 1974:147) and were wiped out early by their contact with European diseases while the Shipibo were just emerging from their sheltered position on the lower tributaries (DeBoer 1981:33–34). The Shipibo then moved out into the main river and pre-empted Shetebo territory. The Shetebo therefore function like Failed Proto-Humans in Shipibo mythology. Their misfortune has

been transmuted into greed and envy and their death through disease into death by drowning in the World Flood. This fate was punishment for their burial of the *baquë mëraya* (child, highest class of shaman) son of the Inca god. Today a few Shetebo remain near Tsoaya but are acculturated into the dominant Shipibo ethnic group.

5. Bardales (1979:9, 36) records a Conibo text that affirms the existence of three, not two, Incas. My Shipibo informants insisted that there were only two principal ones, Yoáshico (Stingy Inca), who was also called Shanö Inca, and the Good Inca. There are several explanations for Bardales's version. First, it could simply reflect subcultural variation. Second, his texts were produced for the S.I.L. (a.k.a. the Wycliffe Bible Translators) and therefore might have trinitarian biases, since he is an acculturated and indoctrinated informant (we know that the S.I.L. texts are aberrant in other details—principally their total paucity of sex, which makes them highly suspect among the otherwise "earthy" Shipibo-Conibo narratives). The third reason may be a simple literate bias on Bardales's part to create symmetrical Incas for all three riverine Panoan subtribes: the Shipibo, Shetebo, and Conibo.

6. The reverse can also happen, as when Yoáshico changes his *rayos* (son-in-law) into a *Manshanteo* when he sees him standing in the water, poisoning fish as he had requested him to do amid a group of the Stingy Inca's "soldiers." Yoáshico fulfills his animalistic function by turning the son-in-law into the Jabiru and the soldiers into Abo, the *Manchaco* Heron (see Bardales 1979:19, 41 on the Conibo). Many of these aquatic birds have sinister connotations in Shipibo cosmology: they are associated with the water, a low-lying, anticultural realm; they often eat dead or stranded fish and thus act like a carrion-feeding Vulture; and like a Vulture, some of the forms, especially the *Manshanteo* and the *Abo*, have naked heads or necks (*tëcho*), "without plumes, naked, corrugated." Thus they are tabooed as food and can *copia*, or bewitch, causing analogous skin afflictions in the children of men who contravene the taboo. This is why one of the *Manshanbo* (the Heron group), the *Josho Manshan* or White Heron (*Casm. alba*) has a putrid-smelling (*pisi*), bloodlike (*bia*) "wind" or "essence," *nihuë* (see Illius 1982:6 on the Conibo). The negative associations of this "liminal" bird group (which overlap between watery and airy realms), their disgusting feeding habits, and their disease-inflicting nature, go a long way toward explaining why the *Manshan*, or *garza* (Spanish), group can become, in songs, "the [frozen] metaphor for *mestizo[s]*" (Levy, personal communication, April 14, 1986).

7. Her cult center was in Painaco, on the lower Ucayali. Wasemëa never married, being joined like a nun to the spirits. Apparently she did not use *nishi* either but relied exclusively upon strong native tobacco, *romë*, as a hallucinogen. While postmenopausal women are "honorary males" since they are no longer involved in the naturalistic feminine "wet" cycle of menstruation, lactation, and parturition and can "study" *nishi* and thus become shamanesses, I got the strong impression from talking with several male informants that the real objection to Wasemëa was her sex. She was a pretender to the wrong role, that of

the mighty masculine *mëraya,* and thus is remembered as a kind of witch. This male view is not shared by women, judging by the pride that Casamira and other women artists I interviewed took in being the stylistic successors of Wasemëa's revolutionary curvilinear (*mayaquënëya,* "curved [line] design, with") design style.

6

Images of Resistance to Colonial Domination

Roger Rasnake

Much recent thinking in anthropology has led to the conclusion that social life is imbued with paradox; contradiction seems to be an unavoidable prerequisite for ongoing social action. The inevitability of contradiction becomes especially clear when one attempts to trace out the connections between the social order and shared systems of meaning. This understanding of the importance of contradiction is not rooted in a single theoretical approach; rather, the existence of apparently irreconcilable oppositions in thought and action is a theme that has been developed from a number of perspectives in anthropology. In fact, one might argue that the failure to recognize paradox and contradiction is indeed a failure to do modern (i.e., late twentieth-century) anthropology.[1]

Where we see the paradox in the link between social action and shared systems of meaning to be centered is, of course, fundamental to our theoretical analysis, and the point where we locate the nexus of the problem leads to various (though not necessarily mutually exclusive) methods. Discussions about the relationship between the symbolic realm and the social order can center, of course, on both symbolic action (ritual) and symbolic formulations in language (myth); however, in line with the overall focus of this collection of essays, I would like to give primary attention here to myth. It is through these forms of oral expression, presented as narratives in the Andean case to be discussed, often with dramatic inflection and participation by the audience, that the concepts and values of fundamental importance to the group are articulated. These narratives are rooted in the perception that the contemporary social order is a product of past conflict between two distinctive cultural complexes, which are presented within the myths as drastically irreconcilable. And as this contradiction between cultural worlds imbues the tales with their own force and dynamic, it also reflects and comments upon the present reality of inequality and domination experienced in social life.

While myth takes first place in this discussion, ritual is closely related to such expressions in the sense that the content of symbolic action refers to the same principles of spiritual power and to the same realities of cultural domination as those depicted in myth. In the case at hand, therefore, ritual must also enter into the analysis to show a broader range of contextual *significata* than that expressed in the myth presented, sets of meanings that are relevant to the overall context of interethnic and interclass relations. Toward the conclusion of this essay, then, I turn briefly to ritual to show how such symbolic action complements and expands on the concerns expressed in the myths to be discussed.

Ritual and myth are traditionally seen as closely linked, but determining which is to have analytic primacy was once the source of considerable conflict in anthropology. This debate is less relevant for the situation presented here. Rather, I argue that Yuras strive to maintain a certain (though not absolute) coherence in the shared meaning-world they create, a coherence that is worked out in both myth and ritual. Coherence need not imply the now rather threadbare conceptualization of culture as an "integrated, seamless whole." A more fruitful approach is to see culture as more loosely integrated, a complex of historically created symbolic forms that are, indeed, reproduced but can be reformed and reinterpreted (or even consciously extirpated) when circumstances change. In this approach, culture is related much more closely to social practice.[2] However, as Max Weber argued decades ago, there exists in human society a pressure toward creating coherence in shared symbolic frameworks. The coherence between symbolic action and verbal expression is therefore real yet relative.

Nor, as was stated earlier, does this pressure toward coherence suggest a failure to recognize contradiction or paradox. Indeed, precisely the opposite is the case. In both ritual and myth, elements of contradiction are presented by the actors for analysis. In ritual, contradiction is expressed in the ambiguity of key symbols and the actions carried out in relation to them.[3] In myth, the values expressed symbolically within the narrative itself often present the observer with inconsistencies or contradictions between those values and social action. The way that contradiction is to be understood has been developed in a number of different ways within anthropology. Without attempting an exhaustive catalog, several of the current approaches can be characterized as follows.

First, people (i.e., the people studied) present the anthropologist with a mythic vision of the world that seems very inconsistent with their life in society. In a sense, they tell us that they do one thing, then they go out and do another. Alternatively, several competing mythic visions, mutually inconsistent, refer to the same social reality, which is to say that sometimes the people tell us (and do) different things than they tell us (and do) at other times. These are, of course, separate problems. The first is that of the distinction between the observer's model and the actor's model, between etic and emic, or, to use Fortes's (1978:10) original phrasing of the issue, between the anthropologist's view and that of the native. This is now so obvious to us that we take it for granted.[4] The second problem is that which arises from the situational use of shared cultural beliefs expressed in myth and ritual. Focusing on this leads to an approach that recognizes that social-structural principles can indeed be in conflict, a situation that may call for varying legitimations at different times by different groups. In ritual studies this insight has been the keynote for the advances made by those who identify themselves as processual analysts or as followers of an action approach (Cohen 1979).[5] For the study of myth, Leach (1954) has provided an important precedent for this perspective in his analysis of the legitimating myths of Kachin lineages.

A second approach has been that of the French structuralists, in which the contradictions are conceived to lie primarily at the level of thought and to be resolved in thought. The contradictions are real, in the sense that the symbolic process, in the form of myth, takes into its consideration oppositions rooted in such aspects of existence as subsistence patterns, or principles of social order, or the relations between neighboring groups. But the resolution of the oppositions takes place, in structuralist thinking, in the conceptual act of reducing the contradictions to the symbolic form itself: the myth. The contradictions become a means to demonstrate, out of time, the nature of human thought.

This is not the place either to elucidate the many advances of structuralism or to criticize overly its shortcomings, but it is clear that the focus on thought removes us from action; and that the programmatic goal of understanding the commonalities, cross-culturally, of *pensée* makes the understanding of praxis a lesser priority. Nor is structuralism, in its effort to get to the nature of thought, terribly interested in seeing the relation of particular symbolic forms to particular processes in time. These are, after all, only the "mechanical models," the surface data that are only the beginning of the process of analysis. The "meaning" of the myth is not its utility as a legitimator of conflicting social principles, as Leach originally suggested, or even its usefulness as a tool of the powerful to manipulate a dominated class. Rather, the meaning lies, as

Lévi-Strauss once wrote, in the idea that "myths signify the mind that evolves them by making use of the world of which it is itself a part" (quoted in Murphy 1971:176).

Yet another major approach to the relationship between the social and shared systems of meaning has focused on class-structured societies. This approach positions the nexus of the contradictions in the contrast between a people's symbolic expression in myth of their identity and of their perceived situation and what seems to be, from the outside, the real objective circumstances of at least some of those who share that symbolic framework. We are referred to the question of false consciousness and the related issues of mystification and, to use Marx's (1977:387) term, "celestialization." While more recent formulations of the relationship between "superstructure" and the determining, underlying socioeconomic relationships see the two as subtly and flexibly linked (e.g., as found in the work of Godelier [1978] or Bloch [1983]), the model, as used by more doctrinaire scholars, has actually phrased the problem in a way not unlike the first formulation in recognizing a contrast between the "native" model and that of the "observer." Here, however, the observer views society with an eye to the typical social relations created in economic activities, with a focus on relationships of power, control, social class, and the ability of one group to impose a superstructural meaning-world on another. Here, too, we see contradiction and paradox, although the paradox is explicable in terms of conflicting class or group interests (Lefebvre 1977).

A fourth approach, the one I adopt here, is a development of the third. It too focuses on conflict in class-structured societies, but it calls for an emphasis on practice that the French structuralist model would consider epiphenomenal and that the more traditional Marxist model would eschew in favor of a stricter determination of superstructural characteristics as a reflection of the relations of production. This "practice-centered" approach, which has been described by Ortner (1984) and is perhaps best exemplified by the work of Bourdieu (1977) and Comaroff (1985), leads us to see the relation of myth to the social order in complex, stratified societies in more dynamic terms of social action and cultural process.

From this approach, and consistent with the view of culture outlined above, I would argue that it is more fruitful to see the "internal" or "experience near" models—the myth—as a struggle to come to terms with perceived contradictions within the social order. I make the assumption that within contradiction there is a push toward a dialectical resolution.[6] That is, the subjects' model addresses the present situation with a consciousness of transformation as well as an awareness of the past. Symbolic forms, and especially myths, thus picture the past as an arena in which the present situation of paradox was created. Myth becomes history—the mythic vision becomes imbued with a consciousness of time and transformation—and, at the same time, history becomes myth—"real" events in the past, events the observer confirms from other sources as actually having occurred, are modified and shaped not only to conform to principles of order in a particular cultural tradition but also to express the contemporary perception of the meaning of past events; and this is done in such a way that the remembered transformation creates a contradiction, or a paradox, that is yet to be resolved. Mythic formulations reveal a shared cultural reflection on the past as it is lived in the present. In terms of a comparison with a more structuralist approach, this shift could be expressed in epigrammatic terms as a move "from opposition to dialectics."

The Yura of Southern Bolivia

The Yura, an Andean highland group, are Quechua-speaking corn farmers, peasant cultivators who have managed to retain their small plots stretched along narrow rivers in steep, arid valleys. They number about 5,000 and occupy a well-defined territory of some 2,000 km^2 (or 750 square miles). Like many other groups in Bolivia, they retain a conscious local ethnic and organizational unity throughout the entire area, even though they are dispersed in over 100 named settlements and villages.

Today, the Yura, like most other Indian peoples in the Americas, find themselves at the bottom of the class structure of contemporary Bolivia.[7] They are well aware that urban folk consider them by nature to be inferior; they know as well that they can only avoid exploitative relationships with urbanites and government representatives by constantly struggling to retain what rights they have gained in the last decades and by making strategic alliances, individually and collectively, with members of other social groupings. The Yura also recognize their material poverty, which the present economic crisis of Bolivia has, if anything, made even more extreme.

In the specific context of the Yura today, the great majority of *comunarios* (or ethnic Yuras, the members of the various *ayllus*) find themselves confronting the relative power of a group of mestizo-ized *vecinos* ("neighbors" of the town), who reside in the canton capital and who control local political and economic power. The *vecinos*, who are Spanish speakers, identify with urban culture and maintain strong links to the urban social order. Their economic base is largely founded on sales of consumer items (especially alcohol) to the comunarios; and this, plus their virtual monopoly on state-recognized local-level positions of authority, grants them considerable political control. The mestizos also engage in agriculture, though at a remove in terms of their own direct labor. While they do not control major extensions of land, they have been able to acquire choice parcels through purchase or expropriation at the death of comunarios (often justifying the latter by claiming unpaid alcohol debts). They mobilize labor to work their lands through asymmetrical ties of obligation with the comunarios, based on common residence as well as on fictive kin ties and implied coercion (expressed most often when comunarios come to the central village to carry out official business, such as requesting birth certificates or registering to vote; see Harman 1987).

Vecinos therefore represent, both symbolically and actually, the penetration of the state into the countryside, into the heart of the Yura ayllu. Vecinos consider the Yuras to be uncivilized, ignorant, or, in moments of pique, indios brutos (brutish Indians), a grave insult in Bolivia. The Yura look at the vecinos as rich and powerful but also as greedy and cruel, with no sense of the proper human values of hospitality, reciprocity, and mutual support. While willing in some contexts to refer to them by the respectful term wiraqucha, Yuras also see the vecinos as q'aras, or people "stripped" of ethnic identity and of the human qualities they deem essential. These hierarchical and exploitative social relations, while mitigated by certain social conventions such as compadrazgo ties which "personalize" the vertical links, are nevertheless an everyday social reality for most comunarios, a dimension of social life that must be dealt with.

Historical research has shown that the Yura were a segment of a larger ethnic unit, itself part of a polity that had been incorporated into Tawantinsuyu, the Inca Empire, for only a few decades before the Spaniards invaded the area in 1538. The Yura briefly formed part of a large encomienda given in turn to two Spanish adventurers, then were made direct tributaries of the Spanish Crown. For centuries the Yura, like all other Andean groups in the region of the vast silver complex of Potosí, suffered the depredations of forced labor in the mines and the extreme pressures of the taxation policies of both the colonial and republican governments (Rasnake 1982:131–237).

Four hundred fifty years have passed since the Spaniards first invaded these southern Andean highlands. Yet that key historical event remains a basis for understanding the present. The sequence of stories that recount the changes brought about by the Spanish invasion endows that event, by association, with a world-creating power, a power that is not used, at least at present, as a legitimation for struggles within the group but is called upon as a means to comprehend, and to confront, the realities of what we might call "national powerlessness," of class subordination in the wider social context. At the same time this pivotal event provides an affirmation of another kind of power, the Yuras' perception of what I call their "chthonic power." That is, the world of today is characterized by the real paradox of oppression by an alien elite, yet by a partial independence from that oppressive world; by conflict and compromise with those "outside" forces, yet by a limited, carefully cultivated autonomy.

Yura Vision of the Past: The Tales of Tyusninchis

The Yura do not normally articulate their situation of powerlessness and their struggle for autonomy through abstract verbal concepts in an explicit formal discussion. Rather, this expression has largely taken two forms, that of oral tradition and of ritual action. In the stories the Yura tell each other, and in their participation in public and private ritual, these themes are communicated through the formulation of an apparently paradoxical view of their past and their role in history. A thorough analysis of the ritual expression of that ambiguous appropriation of the past, while essential for a complete understanding of the Yuras' ongoing symbolic reproduction, is outside the scope of this essay, and I shall only briefly turn to it in the concluding analysis.[8] But this ambiguous expression in stories, in myth, also yields important insights into the Yura view of themselves and their relation to the wider society, and these verbal forms are the focus of my discussion here.

My use of the term "myth" is a conventional one, for to distinguish myth from other kinds of tales is a Western categorization that the Yura do not make on their own. That is, the Yura themselves do not make an explicit division between stories that are especially "sacred" (itself a problematic concept) and those that are told primarily for entertainment. The three stories that follow, like all such tales, are labeled *kwintus* (Spanish *cuentos*, "stories"). *Kwintu* is a general term applied to many kinds of stories, all of which are said to be "of another time," in a time separate from the present. Within this broad grouping of *kwintus* the Yura make no verbal subcategories.

Categories can be delineated, however, in such contextual aspects as when the tales are told and in the nonverbal cues communicated during the telling. The three stories summarized below, for example, were recounted in a context of high interest, in a serious, though conversational, way. Although these stories are not without humor (especially the first one), they were not told primarily for their entertainment value. They were described as a representation of *unay tiempu,* a term loosely translated as "olden times."[9]

These stories contrast dramatically with other *kwintus,* among which are the widely known trickster tales of Atuq Antonio ("Anthony the Fox") and others involving anthropomorphic condors and bears. These latter *kwintus* also refer to the origins of human practices and features of the world; but the way in which they are told is quite different from that of the stories recorded below. This second grouping of tales is told dramatically and mimetically; the teller may play the different roles by moving about, exaggerating or masking his (or, less often, her) voice, and by adding sound effects. The goal of these latter tales, in which performance plays a central role, is to entertain and especially to provoke laughter.[10]

It is from the first kind of tales that I offer three examples of the Yura conceptualization of the past and its relation to the present. As we shall see, of the three "myths" from Yura oral tradition, certain aspects are, from the observer's point of view, more "historical" than "mythic," while others would be deemed more fantastic. Nevertheless, an analysis of these "myths" suggests ways that the Yura understand the nature of social conflict in the world and how it came to be.[11]

Tyusninchis and the Chullpas

The first world was a world of darkness. The people, called Chullpas,[12] planted their fields and harvested their crops in darkness. Their crops were rocks, not the food crops of today. And their "master," their god [Amunku], was the moon. They lived in a world illuminated only by moonlight. It was to the moon that they made their offerings. The Chullpas had towns, the way we have Potosí; they had towns [and nations?].

(It's said that over in Wistira they had their church. There are just rocks there now, walls here and there. I wonder what it was like; but that must be where one of their towns was. Their town may have been just like the village of Yura. In that nook there, there is a huge rock, and that is where their bones have been found.)

But in the fullness of time, Tyusninchis [our god] appeared,[13] Tyusninchis who is the sun. His arrival brought with it a rain of fire (*nina para*). The Chullpas, fleeing from the light and in order to escape the fire, ran into their houses and into caves, into mines and to desolate mountain peaks, but not before they were all dessicated and destroyed. In this turning over of time (*timpu tijrapi*), the Chullpas' time "finished up." None of the Chullpas were left over, none survived. They all died out. These people were also called "Tyus Yayas" [God the Fathers].

After that, then, the Olden People appeared, the "Olden Parents" [Jach'a Tatas].[14] The Olden People came to these places and made the fields that we plant today. They named the mountain peaks, these Early-Time Parents. These people were of Tyusninchis; Tyusninchis must have made them.[15] We are the grandchildren of the grandchildren, a long time later, of the Jach'a Tatas. "Jach'a" means "grandparent." Like animals, they multiply, they multiply, and from these grandparents we came along. The Jach'a Tata, and ourselves, we're called "Tyus Churis" [God the Sons].

The Jach'a Tatas knew everything, just as the Old People know everything now. We younger people don't know as much. We seem to be forgetting these things, not talking about them as much.

Now, until what year will we be here? They say that we too will all die off, and the birds, those that fly about now, will become the people of the next age. They will be called "Tyus Espiritus" [God the Holy Spirits].[16] It seems that the birds will become the people. What will they call us? Maybe there will be another rain of fire, or an earthquake. What will the world be like then? Will there be mountains? Maybe not? Will it all be one flat plain? Will the peaks be even bigger? Will it be dark? If Tyusninchis dies, who will there be?

This story recounts the creation of the present world and suggests the significance of the role of Tyusninchis. In the next tale Tyusninchis takes on human qualities. Although the Yura tell a number of stories in which Tyusninchis is depicted as a person, the one recorded here is perhaps the most popular tale of this genre: Tyusninchis's escape from the "devils."

Tyusninchis and the *Yawlis*

Tyusninchis lives in the world as a child, yet as a very powerful one; and his presence in the world angers a group of "men" who set out to pursue and destroy him. [In most versions Tyusninchis is on foot; the men, usually referred to as *yawlis* or *yawlus* (from the Spanish *diablos*) are on horseback, and in some versions they are wearing fine silver armor. Tyusninchis is sometimes depicted as being alone. At other times he is accompanied by his mother, while in yet another version he is traveling with Santiago. In this case, the two ride on Santiago's "little white horse."]

One day on his travels to escape the *yawlis*, Tyusninchis passes by a field where a man is planting.

"What are you doing there?" he asks. The man, an ill-tempered sort (*machu machu runa*), shouts back, "What's it look like I'm doing? I'm planting rocks."

"Ah, so be it," says Tyusninchis, and journeys on. He soon passes by another man in his field, who is also planting.

"What are you doing there?" Tyusninchis again calls out.

This second man was a much more respectful person. "Oh, my lord, I'm planting all the things we eat, maize, potatoes, uqa, broad beans," the man answers.

"Good," answers Tyusninchis. "Now if some men come by on horses asking about me, you tell them that you saw me when you were planting this field."

"Very good, sir, I'll do that," the man replies.

Tyusninchis goes on. Night falls, then morning comes. When the first man goes to his field the next day, he sees that there is nothing left but rocks everywhere, no food, just rocks. The second man also goes to his field the next morning and finds that everything he had planted has, miraculously, grown during the night. The corn is tall and ready to be harvested; the potatos are ready to be dug.

The *yawlis* ride by the fields of the first man and ask him about their prey. This time the man decides to be more forthcoming and answers that Tyusninchis passed by when he was planting.

"When you were planting? When did you plant? Fool, there's nothing there but rocks!"

The *yawlis* go on to the second man, down the valley. "Did you see a young boy go by here?" they demanded.

The second man remembered what Tyusninchis said. "Yes, sir, I did. He came by when I was planting this field."

"Oh, no, that must have been months ago. Look, the field is ready to be harvested. Let's turn back; he has escaped us."

Before an analysis of Yura concepts relating to Tyusninchis is developed further, let me recount one last tale to link these images more clearly to a comprehension of historical realities through myth. From an outside observer's point of view the following tale, while it discusses the powers and characteristics of Tyusninchis, also introduces elements we would identify as "historical." It is not appropriate to make such a distinction in Yura categories of thought, however, for we find similar actors and modes of action in their explanation of the distribution of wealth and power that we found in the flight of Tyusninchis from his pursuers. This tale, like the two previous ones, is thought to describe the origins of the present social world and explains the nature of its contradictions. The existence of the Incas in the tale is intriguing, for as opposed to other areas closer to the center of the Inca Empire, Yura oral tradition has very little to say about the Incas and about any changes they may have wrought in the past. Indeed, much of what the Yura have to say may have been learned in the few grades of elementary school that many men and some women have completed. The following tale is about the "Inca King," although he is identified with the figure of Tyusninchis.

King Inca, the Spaniards, and the Mines

You are familiar with the *kinsa rey*[17] [the staff of authority that the indigenous leaders of Yura carry while in office]. That staff, they say, was the *bastón* [Spanish, "cane"] of the King Inca. That's what he used to walk around with.

It seems that the Spaniards, when they showed up, wanted to kill the King Inca. Because of that, he became angry and ordered all the precious metals, like silver, to disappear inside the mountains. Before that, they say that the metals were outside, lying around on the ground like rocks for anybody to pick up. They weren't hidden like now. But because those Spaniards, turning fierce, killed him, he put all the metals away inside the mountains, just by the power of his words, just by saying so. The only way you can get them out now is by working with your strength, your blood, your effort. That's why we have to work so hard to bring the metals out from the center of the mountain. The miners will sometimes pour libations to the King Inca, then. That's a story they used to tell me.

It seems to me that maybe King Inca was Tyusninchis. But he won't come back; all that he left us was his staff.

If those Spaniards hadn't come, I wonder what would things be like now? If the Spaniards had not come and made the King Inca hide the minerals, we would probably all be rich; there would be plenty for everyone.

It may be that the Incas used to have the mines worked. But that too was taken over by the Spaniards. When the Spaniards came, they made all the people work in their mines; wherever they could, they opened mines; they descended on us like ants to do this. People went to work at Potosí, at Jalantani, at Porco. They used to work very, very hard. The Postillones[18] used go to the mines for half a year, sent off there to work, and they died there, died off. They would go, carrying their bundles on their backs, Yuras from every river valley. They went year after year to work for the Spaniards, leaving at Christmas and at the festival of San Juan in June. They would leave weeping, because some didn't come back. Some got sick, others were lost in the mines. The Spaniards made people work too hard; they were terribly abusive.

The Stories Examined

These three tales, while they may be told in different contexts, nevertheless are linked to an overall view of the events of the past and of current class relationships. Let me briefly suggest how these aspects of oral tradition can be linked, focusing on the Yura concept of Tyusninchis, the Sun.

Starting with the first tale of the ages of the world, it is clear that the story of the creation of the present, as told in the destruction of the Chullpas, creates a mythic vision of the past. Before this world there was a previous cosmos, one that existed as a kind of total reversal of the present age. People lived, traveled, and worked in darkness; they raised "natural" (and inedible!) crops as opposed to the present-day "cultural" ones. They had as their principal divinity the feminine and "weaker" moon. It was they who left the ruins of the past that are still evident in these dry highland valleys.

Along came Tyusninchis, the Sun, who destroyed, through his brilliance, that ancient, dark world and created a new earth to be peopled by the Yuras' ancestors. These ancestors "humanized" the world and made it the cultural place it is today, the significance of which is perhaps best expressed by the fact that the Jach'a Tatas named the mountain peaks, which are, along with Tyusninchis himself and Pacha Mama (Earth Mother), the principal aspects of divinity to which the Yura still make their offerings.

Despite the fundamental changes that take place, the tale reveals little dialectical sense for the transformations that occurred; in terms of human action, the changes seem somehow unmotivated. As for a perception of the conflicts that underlie present hierarchical social relationships, little is revealed; without further contextualization, the events seem to have occurred in a vacuum.

In the second tale Tyusninchis plays a more human role. In contrast to the anonymous world destroyer-creator in the tale of the extermination of the Chullpas, he acquires something of a personality. To be sure, this tale repeats a theme of the earlier one, in that the people of the first age, Tyusninchis's enemies, will not be sustained in the present time. Here, the *machu machu runa* (*machu* can mean "angry" but also "ancient") who answered Tyusninchis disrespectfully ends up planting rocks, as did the Chullpas in the darkness. This genre serves a function of "etiological tale" as well; in other versions of the *yawli* story, further episodes recount the creation of certain important features of Andean life, like coca leaf.

But the important thing here is the centrality in the myth of Tyusninchis. In this case Tyusninchis represents the Yura; he is their spokesman and culture hero. His ability to escape armored horsemen through quickness of wit and a special relationship to the natural world is one model available for the Yura to understand lived hierarchical relationships; it also reinforces the conception of their own chthonic ties to the valleys and peaks that comprise their territory. The *yawlis*, while they may be called "devils,"[19] were nevertheless in their equestrian imagery quite clearly European; the social order depicted in the tale becomes, through their introduction, more complex than was the case in the first story and more reflective of the nature of real social conflict. The *yawlis* were outwitted and were unable to impose their will on Tyusninchis or to destroy him; his chthonic power defeated their seemingly superior ability to force him to submit.

The third story reveals a different historical consciousness than the earlier two. While the primary actor in the first two is Tyusninchis, or the Sun (whom the Yura conceive to be the power who, with Earth Mother, grants them life and sustenance), the third places King Inca in the central role. King Inca is an ambiguous figure in that he, too, is perceived as a figure from "outside," from beyond the valleys of Yura. Yet in this story he is also identified with (or somehow similar to) Tyusninchis; as a stand-in for the Yura culture hero, he is assaulted and killed by the Spaniards, who, as the second segment reveals, came for the great mineral wealth of the land.

In retribution for his own murder, King Inca mystically wrests the wealth away from the Spaniards by plunging it deep into the mountains. But here is the paradox that results from King Inca's actions: if he had not hidden the minerals in the mountains, today the people, the Yura *comunarios*, would be wealthy, not poor. The effects of King Inca's revenge become even clearer when the role of the Spaniards in forcing the people to work in the mines is recounted. That is, although the mythic revenge was intended to punish the Spaniards for their greed and their violence, those who in the end suffered the consequences were precisely the Andean people, the workers sent into the mines to "retrieve" for the Spaniards what King Inca had hidden from them.

That Tyusninchis is a major refraction of divinity in Yura thought is confirmed in symbolic action. Conceived at the highest level of generality, he is in ritual contexts not only a recipient of offerings alongside Pacha Mama but is in fact joined with the feminine fertility principle that Pacha Mama represents. This pairing is most evident during the Yura festival cycle in the winter season of Chirao, between harvest and planting. The feminine principle of divinity is propitiated at the "big fiesta," a festival right after harvest dedicated to the female "patron saint" (actually, an image of the Virgin Mary) for the entire territory. The masculine power of Tyusninchis is celebrated some six weeks later at Corpus Christi.[20] The latter ritual, which takes place in late June, occurs when the sun is at its lowest point in the sky. The Yura believe that without the offerings made and the libations poured at Corpus Christi, the power of Tyusninchis would falter. Likewise, since Corpus takes place in midwinter, the fertility of the fields is, in a sense, suspended. They can only be renewed through the sun's reinvigoration, accomplished by means of the different acts of the festival.

In Catholicism, Corpus Christi celebrates what its name implies, the body of Christ, that is, the Host. But as the bemused Spanish priest who has for years led the annual procession in the plaza of the village of Yura realizes, this solemn act, for the Yura participants, is "about" Amunchis, "Our Master," the Sun. He also recognizes that the associated European symbolism encourages this perception: the gold monstrance into which the wafer is placed is a perfect replica of a medieval image of the sun.[21]

This apparent lack of orthodoxy addresses in ritual action what are central concerns for the Yura participants. In the procession around the central square at Corpus Christi, as happens at all such processions during the annual festival cycle, the Yura reaffirm and reconstitute their conception of the social order. Each corner is assigned to one of the four major *ayllus* that incorporate all Yura; one half of the square "belongs" to the Upper Moiety, the other half to the Lower Moiety. The procession around the square thus takes Tyusninchis, in his "churchly" form of wafer and monstrance, through the microcosm of the four *ayllus;* and at each corner, where the priest says a prayer and offers a blessing, Amunchis "shines" on his people.

The ambiguity of this ritual action is evident when we consider that it is the priest, a representative of the church and always an outsider to the Yura, who has the authority to preside over this important event. Thus, at the same time that the Yura recognize their dependence on their seemingly Andean creator and lord, Tyusninchis, they also recognize that the definition of their lord does not come strictly from within the confines of Yura territory but relies on outside forces to "complete" the conceptualization. More than that, the Yura, in their awareness of the power of the state either to ensure their ownership of lands or to alienate their source of subsistence, know they must show obeisance to that power.

Beyond the festival of Corpus Christi, Amunchis receives further ritual attention and offerings, most notably at the *q'uway* of sheep, goats, and llamas. This family-level celebration requires the main participants to climb to a nearby mountain peak before dawn to make a series of ritual offerings to the sun as it first reveals itself over the eastern summits.

Perhaps most significant in terms of ritual action is the identification of a masculine power, here conceived in intermediary terms as the mountain peaks, with the *kinsa rey,* the Yura staff of authority. In all Yura public rituals the *kinsa rey* is the major representation of the powers of the group and of its incarnation, identified with the indigenous authorities who carry it. As I have shown elsewhere (Rasnake 1982:chap. 6), the staff derives its power from the mountain summits, which, as we have seen here, are themselves linked with the Jach'a Tatas—another manifestation of the chthonic theme. Yet these summits are also joined in Yura thought with Tyusninchis: he strikes them first and last in the day, and the *mallku,* the male condor (another incarnation of the mountain peaks), is the creature that comes closest to his face. The power that inheres in the *kinsa rey,* then, gives the Yura their land and its productivity (for the land would be barren without the sun's warmth), their sense of unity as a clustering of groups (for the Yura native authorities carry the staff at all ritual moments when they act for the group), and their human authority (the elders only take on their roles by receiving the *kinsa rey*).

Tyusninchis is therefore the incarnation of the active life principle, the provider of light and warmth, the "essential other half" (to use Isbell's [1978] phrase) of an encompassing unity with Earth Mother which makes life possible. He is the maker of the present world, the creator of the founding ancestors, and the bestower of the world upon the Jach'a Tatas for them to name and inhabit. He destroyed the first age's dark beings to make ready an illuminated world for his people. In the associated form of King Inca, he gave the Yura one of the most important symbols of group unity and ritual authority, the *kinsa rey,* in which inheres the sacred power of the mountain peaks. And around this ritual symbol, this mythic nexus, revolves a powerful series of concepts basic to the Yura understanding of the world and their place in it. These concepts reflect important aspects of the contemporary Yura reality: the relative economic and social autonomy of the people; the Yuras' success in retaining control of their lands and resources (due substantially to the strength of their *ayllu* organization); and what has been their determined "traditionalism" in the construction of a social identity in the face of strong pressures for change. In this we see the chthonic power expressed in "real" life experience.

Yet the ambiguities of Tyusninchis must also be seen as part of the complexity of the concept. Tyusninchis in ritual action is the object of attention at the festival of Corpus Christi. But the priest's frustration with the identification of Christ and Sun is not wholly warranted, for the Yura are not attempting to deceive him. This is not a case of wily peasants pretending to go along with a European superior while laughing at him behind his back.[22] Rather, as we might expect in the case of a multivocal dominant symbol such as this, Tyusninchis is both the Sun and an acknowledged image of the power of the dominant society.

Tyusninchis as the Sun in the story of the Chullpas destroys a malevolent world for his people; but he is also the crucified Christ hanging in
the church of the central village of Yura, an image of suffering brought
to the Andes by the Spaniards. When asked about stories of Tyusninchis,
the Yura tell the sorts of tales the *yawli* story exemplifies. But I was also
told of Tyusninchis being nailed to a cross. For example, one version of
the *yawli* tale, told by an elderly *vecina* (a woman of the small
Hispanicized local elite), had Tyusninchis accompanied by his mother,
the Virgin Mary, and the pursuers were called *judios;* that is, the escape
through Andean valleys was depicted as the flight into Egypt.[23] Here, a
melding has taken place between the autonomous Andean Tyusninchis
and the Christian ideology that the dominant society has imposed.

This "confusion" is, it seems to me, a recognition on the part of the
Yura of the inherent opposition and contradiction of social life, especially the felt powerlessness in relation to the dominant classes. In terms
of the myths, Tyusninchis is from the Yura perspective their own
spiritual entity, but he also belongs in essential ways to the dominant
society. He gives the Yura the power and legitimacy to farm their lands,
to live in their valleys, and to call the land their own; he provides for
their welfare. But Tyusninchis came to this world at the same time as
the invading Spaniards.[24] The Jach'a Tatas, the Tyus Churis, were
created simultaneously with the arrival of the Spaniards, and their
existence was always a struggle against the outside oppressors. Tyusninchis
thus stands in an ambiguous relationship to the Yura: he gives them
life and is the source of their chthonic power; but he also placed over
them (or at least somehow acquiesced in the existence of) a race of
outsiders who control and exploit them. At the same time Tyusninchis
is in an ambiguous relationship with the Europeans: he flees from
them, and he magically hides the wealth of the mountains from them;
the power of the mountain peaks, which he controls, is denied them. In
some stories the Europeans are his pursuers, identified with "devils."
Yet he seems to support them in their power, and his image in the
church is in their control.

Around this figure of Tyusninchis the contradictions of class relationships are reflected upon in mythic discourse. The past is understood to
have "begun" with the inequality inherent in the society created by the
Spanish invasion, and the dynamic of that encounter is continually
rehearsed in mythic language. In the course of that discussion we can
see various means of picturing that struggle as well as a shift toward a
"historic" consciousness, from a world of darkness to a consideration of
the mining *mita.*

But the contradictions, while historical, do not exclude a further synthesis in mythic terms. Adopting a mode of thought that is wide-spread in the Andes,[25] the Yura assert that this world, which began with the Jach'a Tatas and the Spaniards, will also end. A new age will begin and birds will become human. In a new "turning over" of time, the contradictions inherent in the struggle between Andean chthonic power and elite political power will finally be resolved. However, resolutions of one historical moment become the beginnings of another; and, as has been said, all social life is characterized by paradox and contradiction. Thus, the third age, the age of the Dyus Espiritus, will not, in Yura thinking, be an age of universal equality. The birds may become the people of the new age, but they, too, will have to struggle against a new set of "masters." Who, the Yura rhetorically ask, will the oppressors of this new age be? The myth thus provides comprehensible images for understanding social complexity. It is also a way to image a transformed world that is an alternative to the present but one still shaped by the real contradictions of experience.

Conclusion

Myths are indeed "good to think" (as Lévi-Strauss [1963b:89] wrote in another context about symbolic forms) because they serve to structure thought; from this perspective they confront certain existential dilemmas of life and order them, using the concrete elements of existence as signs in a system of meaning. This form of analysis of myth may well reveal certain universal patterns basic to the human psyche. It is the point of this essay, however, that in the Andean case, and perhaps in many class-structured, "traditional" societies, myth is, at another level, also a kind of symbolic strategy in which myth-makers attempt to encompass within their formulations real social (and not just logical) contradictions, social contradictions that came about in time, in lived history. This dialectic between experience and symbolic form is a kind of mytho-praxis (Sahlins 1983:526ff.) in which present realities can only be under-stood by reference to the mythic re-creations and transformations of the past. The tales present and preserve history; they "actualize" it and thus provide an ambiguous legitimation of complex social formations—in this case, of the class and power relationships that resulted from the Spanish invasion.

In the myths recounted here, the Yura reflect on the ambiguities inherent in their position of relative powerlessness in the wider context of social hierarchy and oppression. That is, the myths permit reflection on the paradoxes created in a situation in which political power is held by an alien group who work in terms of a worldview drastically different from the Yura and who are in a position of control in the regional and national political system. The myths do not resolve the paradoxes created by this social reality, for such contradictions could only be resolved through a real transformation of the social order, one that would be, in mythic terms, yet another world reversal, an event that would be as monumental in its significance as the destruction of Andean autonomy and the creation of the colonial state. And even then, as the Yura picture it, social hierarchy and exploitation would not end.

The myths serve not only to structure thought but also to structure action. They create an arena for the construction of a social identity that is very much at odds with the vision of the dominant urbanized elite, by defining a world in which Yura identity is integral to the very nature of things, in opposition to a wider context of power relations that negates that identity. In this sense the myths are a strategic license for social action. Despite the ambiguities of the role of the divinity Tyusninchis, these historico-mythic formulations serve to profoundly confirm the Yura in their own localized power (a symbolic conception I call "chthonic power"), which is one form of shared symbolization of their identity. The myths act as a vehicle for the expression of the Yuras' conception, in a particular time and at a particular place, of their unity as a social group. They validate that unity, with its organizational complexity, not as a simple charter, but as a symbolic challenge.

NOTES

The original work in Yura upon which this essay is based was carried out from October 1977 to November 1979, supported by an Inter-American Doctoral Foundation Fellowship on Social Change. Additional research on oral tradition was undertaken in July 1984, partially supported by a grant from Goucher College.

1. As opposed to the structural-functional approach of the earlier part of this century, for example, which assumed that the symbolic, that is, myth and ritual, "functioned" in almost a mirror-image way to maintain and undergird the social system (Radcliffe-Brown 1965:153–77); or the functionalist, which saw myth as a simple "charter" for the present social order (the classic statement of this being, of course, Malinowski's [1955b]). Both of these models lacked dynamism and tended to be very ahistorical.

2. See Comaroff's (1985) study of the reformulation of the religious framework of the Tshidi Tswana in a historical context of increasing incorporation into the oppressive state of South Africa.

3. I have discussed just such symbolic ambiguity, expressed in the festival of Carnaval, for the Yuras of the Department of Potosí (Rasnake 1986).

4. Geertz (1983:55–70) has challenged the absoluteness of this distinction between the two models.

5. Cohen (1979) offers a useful discussion of recent work based on this approach. Again, most of these studies focus on ritual action, such as V. Turner's (1957) classic study of Ndembu village fission. Such studies as Gluckman (1942) and Swartz, Turner, and Tuden (1966) provide the "classic" statements of the perspective.

6. The dialectical approach received an explicit (if very psychologistic) formulation in Murphy, *The Dialectics of Social Life* (1971). Since that time the term has come to be used not for an explicit theoretical framework but for a perspective that argues for a multicausal approach which sees symbolic as well as social and material factors as dynamic elements in an interactional model.

7. Social mobility is perhaps more possible in Bolivia than in other countries with smaller indigenous populations.

8. I have dealt elsewhere, in considerably more detail, with the analysis of ritual aspects of Yura public life (Rasnake 1982:chap. 6; 1986).

9. Since I usually requested the telling of *kwintus,* I cannot be certain of the range of contexts in which these are told. It is significant, however, that these particular tales, as opposed to the second grouping of *kwintus,* were always told indoors. Indeed, when the three recorded here were related, it was late at night; we were inside a dwelling and the stories were told jointly, by several present, who would add elements and comment on aspects already mentioned. Earlier in the day, as had happened many times before, questions had been asked that should have elicited these stories. When the conversation was outside in the courtyard, however, the *unay timpu* stories recorded here were not told. Yet I found no explicit labeling of these stories as being in a separate category of *cheqaq,* or somehow "true," an opposition that Allen (1983) reported.

10. These latter *kwintus* are told outside and children are ideally present and participating. Many informants told me that these were the stories they heard from their grandparents and other older people when they themselves were children. Thus, while not finding in Yura the same categorization as Allen (1983:41) did between *kwintus* such as these and the *cheqaq* tales referring to supposedly lived events, I do find a performance difference that leads me to argue that the tales relating to the deity Tyusninchis carry a different symbolic weight from those of Atuq Antonio and related stories. Future research needs to focus on this issue more closely.

11. These stories are composites told to Inge Harman and me at different times during our stays in Yura. The first one combines tales told by members of two related households, first in June 1981 and then in a more complete form on July 20, 1984. The version of the latter date is considerably more complex. The translation in English reproduces the tales accurately but is not a word-for-word transcription since several tellers combined forces to tell the tales. While this method diminishes possible contextual differences in the telling of the tales,

I reiterate that these tales were told at our request and in very similar contexts. I feel confident that the tales represent a core concern of Yura oral tradition. Since these tales were not told in my presence in other contexts, I unfortunately do not have the data for a more complete contextual analysis.

12. As in other parts of the Andes, *chullpa* refers both to the dried human remains of pre-Hispanic burial sites and to the sites themselves. These burials are what is left of the people of the past age. The Yura argue, quite rightly, that if they were from a later time, they would have been buried in the cemeteries associated with the churches.

13. There is a sense here in which there was no intelligible human reason for why Tyusninchis appeared at this moment and not at another. Rather, it was akin to a kairotic event, one that comes about in the fullness of time, determined by deity and not by humans.

14. *Jach'a* is, like many "ritual" words in Yura Quechua, from Aymara; in that language it means "big" or "tall" (Cotari 1978:109), but as the text reveals, to a Yura, Jach'a Tata can mean "Grandparent."

15. Again, human motives are not at work here. Tyusninchis destroyed the *chullpas* so that he could begin the second age, so that, as one Yura put it, "We, who are here as *cristianos*, might come into being." For a Yura, that is explanation enough.

16. This recounting obviously incorporates a Joachimian view of history, in which the world is divided into three ages of the Trinity. The particular origin of this phrasing of an Andean stage theory no doubt lies in early missionary work. But its appropriateness for an Andean worldview is amply documented in the work that has been done on Andean concepts of the various ages of the world, especially the considerable attention that has been paid to Guaman Poma, but also in the case of other Andean writers (Duviols 1980; Ossio 1973a, 1973b, 1978; Salomon 1982; Wachtel 1973; see also Urbano 1980).

17. I have elsewhere analyzed in some detail the significance of the wooden staff carried by the *kuraqkuna*, or elders, that is, the traditional authorities of the Yura *ayllus* (Rasnake 1982:313–43). The *kinsa rey* has a wide range of meanings, including a special relationship to the *jach'aranas*, or mountain peaks, which I now understand also to be identified conceptually with the Jach'a Tatas.

18. Although in recent times the Yura applied the term *postillón* to *ayllu* members who took turns carrying the mail between the city of Potosí to the northeast and Tomave to the west (and later only between Porco and Tomave), they also use the term to refer to those who in former days went to Potosí to work in the mining *mita*.

19. A number of people did not see a connection between the Quechua word and its Spanish root.

20. The ideological union of the two is clear in the way people refer to them when not using the formal names. The two festivals in succession are said to be the "mother's" (*mamalaqta*) and the "father's" (*tatalaqta*).

21. The Yura do not need the monstrance to remind them of the identifica-

tion of Tyusninchis with the sun, for this is revealed and reinforced in daily, face-to-face interaction. Each time the Yura have occasion to refer to Tyusninchis or Amunchis, they glance up toward the place in the sky where the sun is located.

22. Here, the concept of syncretism seems particularly unenlightening if it means some sort of mechanical mixing of indigenous religious symbolism with that of the European world.

23. This version may indicate one of the roots of the story, although among the Yura the tale has been thoroughly molded to an Andean form and content.

24. This is clearly enunciated by the Yura, who state that the Jach'a Tatas never lived independently of the Spaniards.

25. Both the ages of the world, as discussed in note 16, and the idea of cataclysmic moments of cosmic chaos and world renewal, or *pachakuti,* seem to be quite ancient ideas in the Andean world, even if the former has taken on a European phrasing. The concept of the *pachakuti* was fundamental to Guaman Poma's conception of the past and his periodization of history; its importance for an understanding of the Andean ideology expressed by this key author has been analyzed by a number of ethnohistorians (e.g., Duviols 1980; MacCormack 1985b; Ossio 1973b; Pease 1973; Wachtel 1973). The modern representations of the concept of *pachakuti* are to be found in such cultural forms as that of the widespread expectation, in southern Peru, of the return of Inkarri (Arguedas 1956; Gow 1976; Muller and Muller 1984; Pease 1978; Valderrama and Escalante 1978; Ossio 1973a; Urbano 1981a). The concept of the three ages, described in the third tale, reveals a similar conception (Urbano 1980).

7

Cerebral Savage: The Whiteman as Symbol of Cleverness and Savagery in Waurá Myth

Emilienne Ireland

"A myth is a dream that many have begun to tell."
—observation by a Mehinaku man[1]

The initial focus of my research among the Waurá was not myth and symbolic systems but political and social organization. It soon became clear to me, however, that I would have to understand their myths in order to learn very much about the Waurá at all, for they use myth not merely to structure their notions about the cosmos in some abstract and unconscious sense but as an acknowledged frame of reference for nearly every activity in daily life. Allusions to mythological characters and events crop up constantly: in casual jokes and banter, in public rebuke and private criticism, as the irrefutable rationale for political institutions such as chiefly privilege, and even in the highly secret content of sacred chants, the knowledge of which is in itself a major source of political power. In fact, myth is an essential part of the context needed to understand Waurá statements on almost any subject. And so it is that myth is a key to understanding Waurá perceptions not only of the whiteman[2] but of their historical experience with him as well.

Until recently, the best-known studies of myth in lowland South American societies have examined myths primarily as arrangements of intellectual artifacts (Lévi-Strauss 1973). It has frequently been suggested that such an approach be balanced by analyses that also take account of the nonintellective aspects of these myths (Maybury-Lewis 1969; Geertz 1973a); recent work has done this in illuminating ways (E. Basso 1985, 1987). Like the Kalapalo myths discussed by Basso, Waurá myths about the whiteman are concerned not merely with patterns of characters and events but also with "how enacted emotions give meaning to particular contexts" (E. Basso 1987:351). The prominent role of emotion in Waurá myth is particularly obvious when contrasted with the marked emotional restraint, even detachment, generally displayed in other Waurá oral genres. Accordingly, I will begin by examining general notions the Waurá hold about the whiteman and then illustrate the contrasting ways these notions are expressed in myth as opposed to historical narratives and song poems. I also will discuss the extraordinary affective intensity of these particular myths, a social dimension unexplored in any other form of Waurá oral expression. Waurá myth serves as both an explanatory system that makes sense of what seems incomprehensible and a means of dealing with the disturbing emotional impact of traumatic historical experiences. Contact with the whiteman has been profoundly traumatic for the Waurá, and among Waurá oral genres, only myth fully explores the feelings of fear and helplessness resulting from contact, specifically from catastrophic disease epidemics and the sudden perception of technological inferiority following exposure to manufactured goods.

Background on the Waurá

The Waurá comprise a village of about 127 virtually monolingual Arawak-speakers who subsist mainly by fishing and horticulture in the lowland tropical forest region of Central Brazil. The village is located on a tributary of the Batovi River in the southern part of the Xingu National Park, a large government-administered indigenous reserve on the Xingu River. The research on which this discussion is based was conducted during eighteen months in the village between January 1981 and September 1983.

Unlike most of the other peoples discussed in this volume, Waurá experience of outside contact has been largely indirect, through disease epidemics and manufactured goods, as opposed to direct, day-to-day economic and political subjugation (cf. Reeve, Hill and Wright, Chernela, and Rasnake). There are no roads leading from Brazilian towns to the Waurá village; nor is there an airstrip. Access to the village is not only physically inconvenient but restricted by government authorities as well. Consequently, visitors arrive only infrequently, perhaps two or three times a year, and consist mainly of medical personnel, researchers, photographers, journalists, and government functionaries, most of whom stay in the village for less than a day and then leave, communicating with the Waurá through gestures and the rudimentary Portuguese that a few Waurá have picked up. Virtually all other communication with the outside world is through Posto Leonardo, a small cluster of buildings beside an unpaved airstrip, operated by a government administrative agency. Since the Waurá must walk nearly seven hours through the forest to reach the post, they generally go there only to obtain Western medical treatment or when post functionaries are distributing a government shipment of fishhooks, ammunition, or other manufactured goods to the local tribes. Occasionally, Waurá obtain permission to take government planes to São Paulo or Brasilia for medical treatment or to trade artifacts for manufactured goods. As a result, many Waurá men, and a few Waurá women, have been to a city or town. Such excursions are infrequent, however, and the Waurá do not have direct or unrestricted access to the outside world.

Also in contrast to some of the other societies described in this volume, the Waurá remain essentially autonomous in the management of their internal political affairs. Unlike most contemporary Amerindian communities, in which the local political leader is a middle-aged man, fluent in the national language, who acts as a power broker in relation to the dominant society, the Waurá chief is the oldest and most conservative man in the village, a man who stubbornly disdains to speak Portuguese and who discourages contact between his village and non-Indians. Indeed, other Xingu chiefs have told me he is the last of the traditional chiefs in the region. The Waurá's conservatism is recognized by neighboring tribes, who alternately admire their faithfulness to the old ways and look down on them for their ignorance of modern Brazilian society.

Despite this seemingly moderated and benign contact experience, the Waurá have been profoundly affected, even traumatized, by the entrance of the whiteman into their world. Their perceptions of this experience are expressed in casual conversation, in popular aphorisms, in formal complaint songs, in historical narratives, and in myth. But the treatment of this historical experience in the various genres is anything but uniform. As I will show, these perceptions surface in strikingly different ways depending on genre, context, and other factors.

The Waurá View of the Whiteman and the Experience of Contact

The Waurá's ordinary conversational observations on the whiteman are generally negative. The whiteman is seen as intellectually clever but morally repugnant. In the Waurá view, self-control over violent aggressive impulses, compassion for children, and acceptance of the responsibility to share material wealth are all basic attributes of human beings. Those who lack such attributes are considered either malevolent witches or monstrous, not-quite-human creatures.

The Waurá are puzzled by the whiteman, whose extraordinary ability to make tools and objects is in bizarre contradiction to his manifest inability to get along with others without constant resort to physical violence or the threat of it. Neither can the Waurá understand why this strange creature, blessed with fabulous quantities of material wealth, does not know how to share and indeed seems to lack ordinary human compassion. The whiteman is not ashamed to ignore suffering of others who are hungry and impoverished, even when they are children.

Thus, despite the generosity, friendship, and camaraderie the Waurá may display toward individual whitemen, there is a general and vague perception that non-Indians as a group are not quite human. This view is reflected in the two uses of the frequently heard Waurá expression, "the whiteman is not human" (aitsa īyáu kajaipa). The first, often accompanied by an appreciative chuckle, is a compliment, usually voiced in reaction to some new article of Western manufacture: "Wow! That whiteman, he's not human! He really knows how to make things." The second, however, reveals an underlying sense of fear and distaste toward whitemen: "The whiteman is not human; he's bad. He is angry, violent, and dangerous."

This is certainly not to say that the Waurá view themselves as perfect or their own behavior as above reproach, for they are the first to point out that their behavior frequently falls short of their own standards. However, they are quick to add that selfish or violent behavior, and especially cruelty to children, is considered shameful and that people who openly behave in these antisocial ways lose the respect of the community. A Waurá who indulges in such behavior typically will hide or try to deny it.

What amazes them about the whiteman, the Waurá say, is that he does these things with no indication that they are shameful and wrong. A Waurá man who loses his temper typically will keep a low profile for days, hoping people will forget his disgraceful behavior, or at least pretend to forget it. But when the Waurá make a trip to Posto Leonardo and listen to whitemen trade stories over dinner, they are horrified to hear them actually boast about fights they have gotten into and people they have punched or physically intimidated.[3]

Similarly, while the Waurá frequently grumble about having to share food with the children of parents who are sometimes too lazy to provide for them, they nevertheless do share the food. It may annoy them to have to do so, but it would be unthinkable for someone who has food to openly refuse a hungry child. The Waurá are particularly disturbed that the whiteman is not ashamed to ignore such suffering.

> The whiteman is not like us. He is so clever at making objects that he does not seem human. How does he know to make these things? He surpasses us completely. We are not skilled that way.

But even though he is so clever, he is also very ignorant. For whitemen do not live as human beings. I have been to your cities and seen hungry children sitting on the streets begging for food. People pass them right by and don't take pity on them. Maybe they think they are dogs. That is what the whiteman is like. He has no shame. He even beats and kicks his own children; this too I have seen. This is not the way human beings behave.

That is why the whiteman is so angry and brutal. He mistreats and abuses his children when they are small, and so they grow up filled with the anger their parents have put into them, and do not know how to be men.

Look at the whiteman. He shouts and yells and bullies everyone around. His father has not taught him anything. When he hears evil words, he does not know how to listen quietly. Instead he returns them in kind; foolishly he spills his angry words like water slopped on the ground. He becomes violent and has no control over himself.

In addition to these overall moral concerns, the Waurá have more immediate reasons for their strong negative feelings about the whiteman. At the end of the last century and again around 1954, the Waurá, along with countless other American Indians, suffered devastating measles epidemics which they recognize to be a result of white contact. The initial epidemic, the Waurá say, was brought to the area by the very first whitemen to visit their village, led by one whom they call "Tsariwa."[4] The pestilence he brought reduced them overnight from three large villages to a single small one. The remaining village site, formerly called "Deer Place" (*Yutapwihi*), was renamed "Tsariwa Place" (*Tsariwapwihi*), in memory of the catastrophe that occurred there.

Although the Waurá have since moved to their present village site, about two days downstream, they still speak proudly of Tsariwa Place as their last true village. There once had been a great circle of fine houses, they say, not like the mere handful, most of them small and in poor repair, in the present village. The Waurá were numerous then, and unlike today, the chief's oratory at dawn was complemented by the ritual replies of formally recognized auxiliary chiefs (*inamula ipalukaka*). Many of the old ceremonies performed at Tsariwa Place have since fallen into disuse, and even the vast *piqui* groves, tended lovingly by generations of Waurá ancestors, now lie abandoned, like the graves of the ancestors themselves. And so Tsariwa Place, the last of the traditional, archetypal Waurá villages, bears the name of the whiteman who annihilated it, a bitter irony not lost on the Waurá.

The second measles epidemic, which took place more than thirty years ago, was also a turning point in Waurá history. Despite the lack of reliable census data for that period, it is safe to say that the Waurá lost about half their remaining population. This disaster remains so important in their history that the Waurá commonly reckon time in living memory as "before the measles" and "after the measles."

In compiling genealogies, I found that of the thirty-one Waurá who are still alive and who lived through the last epidemic, nearly 70 percent lost a first-degree relative, that is, a parent, child, spouse, or sibling; and over a third of all survivors lost two or more such relatives, that is, a mother and a husband, or a wife and two children, and so on. As a result, many children were orphaned by this disaster. I refer here not to adults, such as the Waurá chief, who lost a beloved parent, or to children who lost only one parent, but to children who were too young to marry and suddenly found themselves with no parents. Of all the Waurá alive today who lived through that time, nearly 20 percent were such orphans.

The Waurá describe this terribly traumatic experience in their historical narratives:

> Suddenly in every household, people were sick and dying. Our mothers and fathers, our children and our wives were all dying in their hammocks, and there was nothing we could do. We tried to bury them with dignity, but we were too weak ourselves, and could only dig shallow pits and push them in. They were not even cleansed or painted or prepared for their journey. Because the graves were so shallow, the dogs just scratched away the dirt, and ate the arms and legs of our dead.
>
> People became frantic with fear. Some of them untied their hammocks and took their families into the forest to escape the disease. We tried to stop them, but they wouldn't listen. Afterwards we found only their bones, picked clean by the vultures.
>
> As the days passed, we were too weak ourselves to do anything but wait for death. There was no one to bury the dead. People died in their hammocks and their corpses began to rot in the same house where others lay dying. Infants lay against the bodies of their dead mothers, crying with hunger, but no one listened to them. People went outside to defecate and collapsed behind their houses. There they died, and there the vultures came to eat them.

Not surprisingly, memories of this episode are so painful that some Waurá still cannot talk about it, even more than thirty years later. Several of my female informants had to change the subject when they became choked up and began to weep. Even the chief, a man of formidable emotional self-control, abruptly ended one of our interviews after mentioning that his mother had died in the epidemic. He stood up and told me that the whiteman had killed off all his people; and then, apparently not wishing to comment further, retired to the solitude of his hammock.

The Whiteman in Waurá Oral Literature

In view of some of these strong negative associations with the whiteman, one might expect to find him linked to images of anger, fear, and hostility in Waurá oral literature. To my surprise, however, I found this was generally not the case. Although the chief expressed resentment toward the whiteman for bringing the measles epidemic that killed his mother, such sentiments generally do not surface in the standardized historical narratives told in the men's house and by the hammock fires at night. As in the narrative above, the facts are allowed to speak plainly for themselves, without any embellishing metaphors or explicit appeals to emotional response. Such narratives typically are recounted with impressive dramatic skill, but unlike myth, they maintain a markedly unemotional tone.

I should emphasize that I refer here not to myth but to what the Waurá distinguish as "mere truth" or "mere factual accounts" (kamalajita). Since this distinction is important both to the Waurá and to my argument, it merits clarification.[5]

The Waurá term for any formal prose-style narrative is aunaki (story), a broad category that includes two distinct genres: myth (aunaki yaji; literally, "true," "real," or "great" stories) and historical accounts (aunaki in the unmarked form). When pressed for a qualification of aunaki, Waurá typically added some deprecatory suffix, such as -ta (mere), -tsái (little), -juti (inferior), -malū (worthless), or -ipwitala (a mere imitation of). Or they said simply, "Aitsa aunaki yaji, kamalajita": "It's not a great myth; it's just a fact, something that happened."

Because I still did not understand the distinction between "myths" and "mere facts," I asked the Waurá what appeared to be the next logical question: "Aren't the great myths factual? Didn't those things really happen?" Their reply, seemingly evasive, was actually quite precise. I was missing the point, my informants said, because the great myths refer to events that happened long, long ago. Of course they were "true" (kamalaji), the Waurá insisted, adding, "Well, that's not really for us to know. People didn't witness these things, after all. They've only heard about them for a very long time."

And so I found I could predict whether a given narrative would be classified as a myth or a historical narrative by asking whether anyone had witnessed the event (iyau inubawi). If the item were a myth, the answer would be, "Oh no, this happened long ago"; if a historical narrative, my informant would pause to recall specific individuals. Unlike myths, historical narratives consist of detailed factual descriptions of actual events firmly fixed at a specific point in time—for example, "When it happened long ago, my grandmother's first child was still in the womb." An interesting exception to this rule is discussed later.

It should be noted that such narratives are not merely personal reminiscences. All *aunaki* are community property, ritually recounted with impressive dramatic skill before a respectful audience. The standards for performance are high, and only the old people, and among them only those with a reputation for eloquence, take on the challenge of performance. As one accomplished storyteller explained, searching for an analogy I could understand, "It's like talking on the radio. Your words come out smoothly, but your heart is tight within your chest, because you're always thinking you're going to mess up." Historical narratives are not conversational anecdotes but a formal narrative genre, as their classification with myth under the general term *aunaki* rightly implies.

Another genre that describes the Waurá experience with the whiteman is *kapwijai,* a special type of public complaint song central to numerous ceremonies. These songs are like myth in that they are full of metaphor and allusion, but they are like historical narratives in their treatment of the whiteman. *Kapwijai* maintain a cool distance from any reference to the undeniable pain and terror in the Waurá's historical experience of the whiteman. In these songs the whiteman is either ignored or treated in a lighthearted and sarcastic manner, as in the following verse in which a young man sings humorously about his desire to learn Portuguese:

> Well, mama, you're gonna miss me,
> 'Cause I'm gonna go off and work for Old Baldy
> I'm gonna learn how to talk gibberish:
> mbla-mbla-mbla-mbla-mbla! is all I'll say
> when I come back.

This ritualized use of sarcastic humor about the whiteman has been described for other Amerindian societies (K. Basso 1979) and should not be taken as a sign that the subject is not a serious one. As one shrewd observer points out, "Indians have found a humorous side to nearly every problem and . . . the more desperate the problem, the more humor is directed to describe it" (Vine Deloria, quoted in K. Basso 1979:3). However, it is worth noting that such songs, when treating other topics, are by no means always lighthearted. In fact, they can be very serious and somber, since they frequently serve as vehicles for the public accusation and denial of witchcraft and even as direct challenges to chiefly authority. Yet among the scores of examples I taped during Waurá ceremonies, I have found none that reflect the powerful negative associations with the whiteman one might expect in light of Waurá historical experience of contact.

The Whiteman in Waurá Myth

There are two areas of Waurá life in which reactions to even the most disturbing aspects of contact with whitemen are acknowledged and expressed: dreams and myth. Gregor's (1981a, 1981b, 1983, 1984) description of the sinister role of the whiteman in Mehinaku dream life is entirely consistent with my own Waurá data. This is not really surprising, since the two communities are so closely related that the Waurá call the Mehinaku "our other selves" (apawanau). For the Waurá as well as the Mehinaku, a dream of the whiteman is a harbinger of disease and possibly death. In Gregor's (1984) sample, 48 percent of all Mehinaku dreams showed some level of anxiety, while 91 percent of dreams about the whiteman were fearful. Historical narratives and public complaint songs seemingly avoid disturbing and emotionally charged symbols, while dreams of the whiteman are typically dominated by threatening, even terrifying images: disfiguring diseases; fires raging out of control; bombs falling from planes; whitemen who imprison, shoot, dismember, rape, and murder the dreamers and their families. A common element of these dreams is that the whiteman is the aggressor and the dreamer is his helpless victim.

Waurá myths are strikingly similar to Waurá dreams in their symbolic treatment of the whiteman. As in dreams, the whiteman appears in myth as a monstrous, frightening, deadly creature. In one important respect, however, myths and dreams about the whiteman are different. In their dreams about the whiteman, the Waurá are typically helpless and terrified, while in their myths they confront the whiteman in the same gruesome incarnations but are not defeated by him. While the dreams are generally disturbing, the myths are ultimately reassuring.

The anxiety about the whiteman seen in Waurá dreams is eloquently expressed in their creation myth, an epic they refer to as their "true" or most important myth. The whiteman is not mentioned until the very end, when the Sun is distributing various defining attributes to all the tribes of humanity. I have condensed that passage here:

The Sun offers a rifle to the ancestor of the Waurá, but the Waurá merely turns it over in his hands, not knowing how to use it. The Sun takes the rifle from the Waurá and offers it to the ancestor of the dreaded warlike "wild" Indians who live to the north of the Waurá. This Indian is also baffled by the rifle, and so the Sun takes it away again and this time hands it to the ancestor of the whiteman.

The whiteman immediately lifts the rifle to his shoulder and fires it successfully, thus laying claim to the superior technology that would be his. The Sun then gave hardwood bows to the Indians, with which they were well satisfied.

Next the Sun passed around a gourd dipper from which each man was asked to drink. The ancestor of the Waurá approached, but found to his horror that the dipper was filled to the brim with blood. He refused to touch it, but when the "wild Indian" was offered the dipper, he readily drank from it. When the Sun finally offered the dipper of blood to the whiteman, he drank it down greedily in great gulps.

That is why the whiteman and the "wild Indians" are so violent today; even in ancient times, they were thirsty for the taste of blood. To the Waurá, however, the Sun gave a dipper of manioc porridge. And that is why the Waurá drink manioc porridge today, and why they are not an angry and violent people.

This myth reveals the whiteman as clever, and perhaps even superior in a technological sense, but it also reflects the profound moral repugnance the Waurá express toward all warlike and physically aggressive people. Furthermore, unlike other forms of Waurá oral literature, this myth deals openly, though in a safely removed, symbolic way, with the deeply disturbing emotions the whiteman evokes in the Waurá, revealed here by the jarring image of drinking blood.

Perhaps the most interesting Waurá myth about the whiteman is one that does not purport to be about the whiteman at all. The Waurá explain that this myth is about the Kustenau, an extinct Arawakan tribe that, like the Mehinaku, was closely related to the Waurá. The Kustenau were completely wiped out by the first measles epidemic that swept through the Upper Xingu region at the beginning of this century. The myth describes how two spirit-beings called Atujuá fell from the sky as omens of the demise of this people. The Waurá term *Atujuá* refers to whirlwinds and waterspouts, and the Atujuá spirit is traditionally represented in Waurá ceremonies by huge disklike masks that are spun around their axes, knocking down and scattering people and objects and generally creating chaos. The masks are striking objects, about eight feet tall when worn, in which a man's head and upper body are completely hidden inside an upright disk (see Figure 1). There is so much room inside the masks that the Waurá traditionally used them for

Figure 1. Two masked *Atujuá* ceremonial dancers chase a village woman. Note that the traditional *Atujuá* mask completely covers the head and upper body of the dancer. Drawing by Muri.

sexual horseplay, where a male dancer would invite a woman to join him inside the privacy of the mask by parting a curtain of straw and having her climb on his back. The reader will notice that the descriptions of the Atujuá spirits in this myth in no way resemble the traditional spirits of Waurá ceremony and are instead an intriguing aberration:

> Long ago, a pair of Atujuá spirit-beings fell from high in the sky. This happened during the last years of the Kustenau. My mother wasn't yet born at that time, but my grandfather may have witnessed it. The Atujuá spirits were harbingers of death; that is why the Kustenau all died out.
>
> One morning, just before dawn, two strange creatures were seen falling from the sky. They were approaching the village like huge storks, making a deep whooshing sound as they fell through the air.
>
> They fell into the forest, burning the trees in the area where they landed. The Kustenau all went to see the strange dead beings. They saw that their body paint and ornaments were the same as ours. Their ankles and feet were smeared red with *urucum*, their cheeks were painted with the proper black designs, and their hair was well trimmed. Macaw-feather armbands were tied around their arms, their wrists and knees were bound with cotton, and their ankles wrapped in bark. Around their necks were fine shell necklaces.
>
> But they were scrawny, hairy, and white-skinned; they were monsters. Their skin was covered with small brown moles and spots. Hair grew out of their faces. Their belts were not shell belts such as we wear, but snakes that had been tied around their bodies. Even their bellies were very hairy. And their legs were covered with straw fiber. From the waist up, they looked like men, but from the waist down, you couldn't see any skin, only straw. They filled the air with their danger and power; just to touch them burned like fire. They were an omen that the Kustenau tribe would soon die out and vanish.
>
> The Kustenau all took pieces of their hair and ornaments and used them to make witchcraft fetishes. That's just like those Kustenau, they really were terrible witches, all of them. Not just the men, but the women, and even the little children, all knew how to work witchcraft, and did, too. That evening at dusk, they were all busy, shooting witchcraft darts into one another.
>
> That's all they did. At night their victims would sicken and die, and they would keep right on shooting darts into others. Those Kustenau were very bad people. We're not like that. They killed each other with the fetishes they made from the bodies of the dead spirits. That's why they all died out, they killed themselves off with their own witchcraft. If you visit their old village, there is no one there. Not even a single person. They have all vanished.

"Didn't the whiteman's diseases wipe them out?" I asked. "No, it was just their own witchcraft," my informant answered.

Analysis

A feature that makes this myth unique among the nearly 100 Waurá myths I collected is that in the opening lines the narrator refers to a specific point in time, one that is within memory of recent generations ("My mother wasn't yet born at that time, but my grandfather may have witnessed it"). Such reference is precisely the feature that otherwise identifies a text as being a historical narrative and not a myth, but when I asked the Waurá about this, they insisted the Atujuá story was a true myth, or *aunaki yaji.* In most respects this seems reasonable, since the metaphoric style of the Atujuá text conforms to that found in all Waurá myths and absent from their historical narratives.

Presumably, the unexpected historical reference is a function of this being a relatively new myth. The Kustenau were still thriving until the end of the last century, and so this myth about their extinction could have come into being only since then. In any case, this example illustrates that while the criterion of historic specificity may, for the anthropologist, conveniently happen to categorize collected texts into two groups conforming to Waurá notions of myths (*aunaki yaji*) and historical narratives (*kamalajita*), the Waurá themselves may be using quite different criteria when they draw this distinction. In the Waurá view, this story is a myth despite its taking place in recent memory. Clearly, the Waurá believe that what makes a myth a myth is not merely a matter of history or the lack of it.

What, then, does make a myth different from a text of a different genre? This question leads to perhaps the most interesting aspect of the Atujuá myth: the Waurá do not overtly associate the monstrous beings with the whiteman. This is intriguing because the monsters are described as hairy, bearded, white-skinned men with freckles and moles and even a trouserlike garment from the waist down. More to the point, the monsters are associated with the extinction of the Kustenau tribe, which was wiped out by whiteman's diseases shortly after first contact. Yet when I asked directly whether these creatures did not represent the whiteman, the Waurá flatly replied they were not whitemen but monsters. As far as they were concerned, the myth was about the extinction of the Kustenau and not about the whiteman.

I would be inclined to argue that the striking resemblance of the Atujuá monsters to the whiteman is not merely coincidence and that the monsters in fact represent a Waurá view of the whiteman. However, I am also willing to grant my Waurá informants their separate point that the myth is not really concerned with this issue, in any event. After all, we should not be too quick to put ourselves at center stage of any story in which we happen to play a part. That is, it probably does not matter whether the Waurá actually think of the Atujuá spirits as symbols for the whiteman. What is important to the Waurá about this myth, as they readily point out, is that it makes sense of an event that is otherwise incomprehensible in Waurá terms.[6] It offers an explanation for the sudden extinction of an entire people. We should remember that the Waurá do not subscribe to our own germ theory of disease; instead, they believe that all deaths of young and middle-aged people are caused by witchcraft. Traditional Waurá theories of disease simply cannot account for an epidemic of communicable disease, unless it is viewed as the result of an epidemic of witchcraft. What must be explained, in the Waurá view, is not the physical disease itself but the moral breakdown that created it.

That is precisely what this myth does. The Kustenau, as they handled the bodies of these deadly creatures, were infected not with physical disease but instead with an epidemic of social and moral sickness. Because the Waurá see physical illness as being caused by the social ill of witchcraft, it is only natural for them to view an epidemic of physical disease as the product of a breakdown of traditional social and moral codes. As the myth describes, immediately after contact with the deadly creatures, the Kustenau returned to their village and all began shooting witchcraft darts into one another, the very embodiment of the logical extreme of social chaos.

Thus, it seems appropriate indeed that the spirit beings bear the Waurá name Atujuá, belonging to the spirit of whirlwinds and waterspouts. Of more than forty-five ceremonial spirits in the Waurá pantheon, Atujuá is apparently the only one that represents a destructive natural physical force. The vast majority of these ceremonial spirits are associated directly with animals, fish, and birds; a handful, such as the spirits of the sacred flutes and bullroarers, are associated with ritual objects that in turn represent fish or fishlike creatures. There are a few others, such as the ghost-spirit, associated with the dead, and Yamurikuma, the spirit that presides over ceremonial expressions of female dominance. But there appear to be no ceremonial spirits of thunder, lightning, fire, windstorms, rain, and so on, even though the Waurá quite readily personify most of these forces in their myths. So the Atujuá spirit is unusual, if not unique, in that it represents a destructive natural force associated with chaos and disorder.

Just as it is appropriate that the spirit-beings bear the Waurá name of Atujuá, so also is it fitting that they be in the physical image of the whiteman. Recall that the spirit-beings of the myth are unlike the traditional Atujuá figures of Waurá ceremony, which are huge, upright disks of straw, revealing almost no human feature, no glimpse of face or arms or torso, only the dancer's feet protruding from the bottom. The upper part of a traditional Waurá Atujuá is a nonhuman shape made of straw, with human legs below, but the mythic Atujuá is precisely the inverse: apparently human above the waist, with straw leggings below. The Atujuá of the myth is neither a true human being nor a proper ceremonial spirit but instead a bizarre aberration, an anti-being that, like the whiteman he resembles, fits into no traditional category in the Waurá world. The mythic Atujuá creatures combine symbolic associations with both the traditional Waurá Atujuá spirit, a natural physical force of chaos, and the whiteman, whose unnatural way of life is viewed by the Waurá as one of moral chaos and disorder.

But if it is the whiteman who is morally polluting, then why do the Waurá lay the moral blame for this disaster on the Kustenau? Why not blame the whiteman, or at least the Atujuá beings who seem to represent him? In fact, this question points to an essential dimension of this myth: despite its disturbing aspects, it is profoundly reassuring. Only wicked people are destroyed. Disease epidemics cannot without warning erase an entire tribe of innocent people from the face of the earth. Therefore, although the Kustenau became extinct, the Waurá need not fear it could happen to them. In the words of my narrator, "Those Kustenau were very bad people. We're not like that."[7] Similarly, the creation myth in which the whiteman acquires superior technology and reveals his bloodthirsty nature is reassuring in the end. Although the whiteman may be technologically superior, the Waurá are shown to be morally superior; the whiteman's way of life, however apparently seductive, is unworthy of emulation.[8]

So it seems that, in the Waurá case at least, myths about the whiteman operate on several levels at once. First, and in the most literal sense, they provide explanation of otherwise incomprehensible events. They make cultural sense of what the Waurá so revealingly call "mere truth" or "mere facts." Second, in describing the destructive impact of white contact, and especially of disease epidemics resulting from contact, myth openly deals with a subject that is typically too painful to confront in other, more literal contexts.[9] Yet myth goes beyond this, for it not only deals with the subject in a general sense but actually explores some of its most disturbing emotional associations. In the creation myth, the whiteman is seen as completely surpassing the Indian with his skill and cleverness, but he is also seen as a gruesome drinker of blood. Likewise, in the Atujuá myth, the frightening, physically ugly and morally repugnant images of the whiteman are all graphically described. This kind of exploration is something that generally does not occur in other forms of Waurá oral expression. Not in historical narratives, nor in complaint songs, nor in curing chants, but only in myth do the Waurá distance themselves from "mere facts" (such as the literal identity of the bringer of measles), while at the same time going to the heart of another kind of truth—powerful emotional associations that simply do not surface in other genres of oral expression.

In addition, myth is more than just a mirror of physical, social, or psychological reality. Indeed, as the Waurá point out, myths are not "mere facts." Myth can transform the very perception of reality, not only in the sense of rewriting the history of specific events in the past, but in the sense of making statements about the present and the future as well. As Turner states in his commentary, "mythic and historical texts . . . are not to be understood primarily as . . . representations of the events of contact . . . [but] as programs for the orientation of action within the situation of contact." And so it is that in their Atujuá myth, the Waurá have taken a historic tragedy of monstrous proportions and transformed it into an affirmation of their own moral values, and of their destiny to survive as a people.

NOTES

Research for this essay was supported by the Organization of American States, the Yale University Concilium on International and Area Studies, the Smithsonian Institution, and the Library of Congress Folklife Center. For advice and assistance throughout my research, I owe special thanks to Tony Seeger, then at the Museu Nacional in Rio de Janeiro, and to Pedro Agostinho, Charlotte Emmerlich, Bruna Franchetto, Jennifer Stuart, and Eduardo Viveiros de Castro. I am also grateful to Ellen Basso, Janet Chernela, Tom Gregor, Ken Kensinger, Joanne Rappaport, and Judith Shapiro for comments on earlier drafts of this essay; to Jon Hill, for being a sensitive and forbearing editor; and to my husband, Nat Heiner, for patiently reading through more drafts than all the others put together. Above all, I am indebted to the Waurá. Their perspective on the whiteman and his way of life inform not only my thinking in essays such as this but also my personal notions of how a life should be lived and how to raise my own child in the whiteman's world.

1. Thomas Gregor (personal communication, 1985).

2. I have chosen "whiteman" as a gloss for the Waurá term *kajaipa,* referring to non-Indians in general, including Brazilians, Europeans, and Americans, whether white or black, as well as Orientals. While the awkward term "non-Indian" might be more precisely descriptive, the Waurá themselves use the Portuguese equivalent of whiteman, *branco,* as a gloss for *kajaipa.*

3. Compare Keith Basso's (1979:55) description of the Western Apache view of

the whiteman as overbearing, arrogant, and tactless: "Whitemen are angry even when they're friendly."

4. Conceivably, this individual was Karl von den Steinen (1886, 1894), judging from the date of the epidemic and the Waurá's claim that the whiteman came a second time, within a few years of his first visit.

5. The Waurá distinction between *aunaki yaji* and *kamalajita* seems parallel to that in Quechua between narratives about mythic time-space (*unai*) and those about historical time-space (*cauchu uras*), described by Reeve in this volume.

6. Compare Lifton's (1967:462ff.) discussion of Japanese postwar monster films and their relation to the bizarre and monstrous devastation of atomic bomb exposure. Godzilla, the most famous of these monsters, is brought to life by the Bikini test explosions and thus is, like Atujuá, causally associated with an overwhelming catastrophe of inhuman proportions.

7. Compare the similarly reassuring message of the Godzilla films, in which Japanese scientists save their people through courage and technical mastery. Although in historical experience the atomic bomb victims were tragically helpless and overwhelmed, in the monster films the would-be victims are competent, resourceful, and firmly in control of their own destinies (Lifton 1967:462).

8. Keith Basso (1979) describes a similar message in Western Apache jokes about the whiteman.

9. Compare the marked emotional numbing and detachment displayed by atomic bomb survivors when describing the horrible details of their experiences (Lifton 1967:31–35).

8

Political Memories and Colonizing Symbols: Santiago and the Mountain Gods of Colonial Peru

Irene Silverblatt

In 1535 the Spanish delivered a fatal blow to the Inca resistance when they successfully broke the siege of Cuzco and devastated native ranks at the fortress of Sacsahuaman. Over seventy years later the Andean chronicler Felipe Guaman Poma de Ayala wrote down remembrances of this momentous event in the history of Peru:

> Santiago . . . the apostle of Jesus, at that moment when the Christians were completely under siege, made another miracle in the city of Cuzco. Those who witnessed the event say they saw Santiago come down from the sky . . . preceded by an enormous clap of thunder, followed by lightning that fell on the Inca fortress of Sacsahuaman. . . . The Indians became frightened when they saw the bolt of lightning, and terrified, they said that Illapa, [the god of] Thunder and Lightning had fallen from the sky to chastise the Indians and lend support to the Christians. Santiago came down to earth in this way to defend the Spanish. [And the Spanish] recognized him [right away] and said they saw him mounted on a white horse with many bells, well-armed, brandishing his unsheathed sword with which he wounded and killed many Indians. [And the saint] dismantled the siege which the Indians, under the orders of Manco Inca had tried to impose. . . . Since then, the Indians call lightning Santiago, because this saint came to earth like lightning, Illapa, when the Christians, in desperation, invoked him, crying out "Santiago." At the same time, these pagan Indians, when they heard him and saw the way in which he came to Earth, were terrified, frightened, and thus, they witnessed this miraculous occurrence. (Guaman Poma 1956, II:33–34)

This essay traces the colonizing career of Santiago—a killer of Moors and since the Spanish conquest a killer of Indians—who with colonial irony became the protector of the Indios he was commissioned to conquer.[1] Soldiers fighting under the banner of Castile brought Santiago to the New World, confident that he could dominate the heathens of the Inca Empire just as he dominated the recalcitrant Moors of the Iberian peninsula. Castilian victories bore witness to Santiago's prowess, thus bolstering the Spaniards' faith and adding a new dimension to the indigenous one: Santiago's victims also claimed him as their patron, but in peculiarly Andean ways.

Once colonial rule was firmly implanted—after Manco Inca's rebellion was quelled and the nativistic Taki Onqoy movement, when Quechua gods were ready to battle Christian saints, was crushed in the 1560s— Peruvian peasants created a novel religious doctrine. Colonial Andean faith thus fused the saint of conquest with Illapa/lightning and the mountain gods—native deities representing power and domination. The problem to be explored here centers on the significance of this merger.[2] The Andeanized Santiago's history as a patron of the vanquished allows us to understand how Indians experienced, grappled with, coped with, challenged, and endured the lived realities of colonization. His transfigurations, imaging the very different relations of power and economy instituted by colonialism, also suggest appraisals of life's possibilities—strategies for social action—and provide clues to the activities and kind of future Andean peoples envisioned.

In this essay I critique contemporary studies of Andean beliefs that have overlooked dimensions of power and history in the construction of meanings. Long popular in studies of Andean symbols, structuralist models, in their hunt for sets of ordered invariants, have tended to neglect the dynamic trajectories of Andean traditions.[3] Projecting structures of contemporary myths onto the pre-Columbian and colonial past, such approaches suggest a timeless continuity in the peasantry's means of interpreting their world and minimize the ways in which power and class infuse and twist cultural constructions of reality. Along similar lines, others have simplistically turned Christian symbols into cloaks for native gods, thus denying the complexity and depth of meanings incorporated in the culturally fused divinities of Peruvian peasantries. This excursion into Andeanized Santiagos and Hispanified mountain gods contributes to an emerging field of scholarship that focuses on the history of imageries and anchors them in the power-charged social relations that constitute their human creators.[4]

If this exploration contests the image of timelessness with which anthropology has bestowed Andean peoples, it also challenges their image as victims, responding ciphers, to the West's dominating structures of power.[5] Indians have shaped their colonial worlds (Stern 1982),[6] assisted by the mind's knowledge and by the less articulate but power-fully felt understandings of the soul. Indianized Santiagos' amalgamating, ambiguous, transforming semblances contributed to these forms of knowledge and understanding by concentrating and condensing the historical experiences of colonization. Intertwining history and remem-brances, re-presenting the past, Hispanified mountain gods charged powerful political images in the memories of the "present." They augured portentous ethical contrasts, hinting of resistance to the perceived immo-rality of colonial social relations; but they also, even simultaneously, resonated the aura of the new masters and could be frightful colonizing symbols in league with the powers that be.[7]

Spanish and Andean Divinities of Power

Let us look briefly at the Spanish Santiago (Figure 1). Jesus had nicknamed this apostle Son of Thunder because of his monstrous temper, and the likeness of thunder to the flash given off by fired harquebuses made Santiago eminently suitable as a soldier's mascot (Arriaga 1968:215). Santiago's abilities to defeat the heathens had been proven in the Old World, where he divinely led the campaign to wrest the Iberian penin-sula from the Moors—hence his nickname, Santiago Mata-moros (Moor killer). The conquistadores hoped to transport this saint and his powers over pagan objects of conquest to the New World. Before firing their weapons, Spain's army would always shout his name. The association of thunder with gunshot—deemed responsible for Spanish victory—helped produce Santiago's mystique (cf. Gow 1980:279–81). Cuzco's notables (all of Iberian descent) named Santiago the patron of the vanquished capital of the Incas since "he, through his miracles, played a large part in [its] conquest and pacification, fighting on the side of the Spanish against the Indians" (Esquivel y Navia 1901:114).

It appears that by 1560 the Spanish likened their saint's iconography to his new role as killer of Indios, Santiago Mata-indios. The chronicler Garcilaso described a painting of Santiago on the wall of the Cuzco cathedral that faces the plaza, in which Santiago "is seated on top of a white horse grasping his leather shield in one hand and his sword in the other and many Indians, wounded and dead, were thrown down head long at his feet." Indians seeing the painting, Garcilaso continued, would declare, "A viracocha [white man] like this one was the one who decimated us in this plaza" (Gisbert 1980:197–98). Writing around the time of Garcilaso, Guaman Poma also recollected how Santiago struck

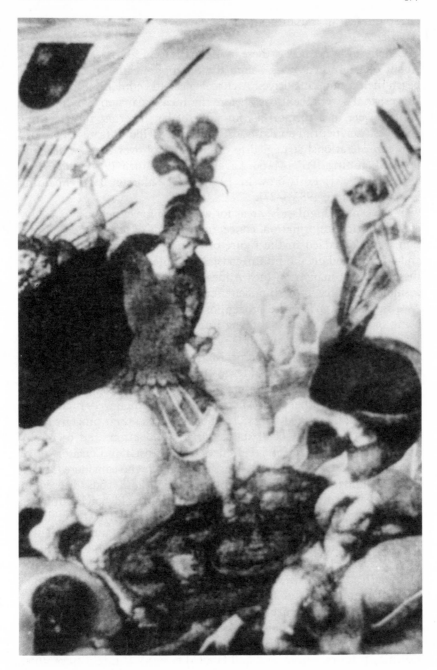

Figure 1. The Spanish Santiago: Santiago Mata-moros.

terror and fear in Indian hearts as he paved the way for Spanish victory (Figures 2, 3).

Conquest was not new to those living in the Central Andean Highlands. About one hundred years before the Spaniards came, the Inca lords began their conquering drives. Archaeological and ethnohistorical sources suggest that several centuries before the Inca expansion, the highland polities were in a turmoil as, for want of better terms, these "ethnic enclaves," seigneurial domains, or stratified chiefdoms (some organized into confederations) struggled to extend control over land, water, and people (Lanning 1967:141–56; Lavallée 1973; Murra 1964, 1967, 1968, 1978:62–82, 131; Rostworowski 1977, 1978; Salomon 1986; Spalding 1984:42–71; Stern 1982:3–27).

In the central highlands, areas for which we have the most extensive ethnohistorical information, conceptualizations of power and domination were embedded in the figure of Illapa (Thunder and Lightning) and his descendant mountain gods. A complex divinity, Illapa ruled the heavens of many non-Inca Andean peoples. He was an impressive cosmological force, providing beneficial rain as well as brewing storms. As a mountain god or the progenitor of others, he guarded the well-being of livestock, herds, and the human beings dependent on them (Polo 1916:6; Cobo 1964, II:161; Duviols 1974:277–78; Arriaga 1968:22).

Thunder was also a conqueror. Many Andean peoples conceived of Illapa as the father of or actual legendary founder of some of the descent groups that constituted an "ethnic enclave." These heroes were portrayed as the subduers of other local Andean kindreds, which were then joined as one internally ranked polity. Thunder gods and their progeny had a keen sense of politics, social status, chiefly obligation, and hierarchy that mirrored the political experiences of their highland creators. Like curacas, or local chiefs, humans of superior rank who considered themselves Thunder's direct descendants, the mountain gods dressed in exquisite, elegant cloth and ate from silver and gold bowls—fineries that suggested their privileges and powers. Mountain gods might be more capricious than local chiefs, but Andeans' understanding of power and its limits tempered divine impetuousness (Hernández Príncipe 1923; Zuidema 1973; Ávila 1966; Arriaga 1968:128; Archivo Arzobispal de Lima [hereafter AAL], Leg. VI, Exp. 11).

While membership in an ethnic enclave guaranteed all constituents access to basic subsistence resources, and while customary kin-based obligations of mutual assistance and aid ensured access to labor, a higher-ranking strata (probably emerging with the ranking of kindreds) did enjoy privileges over land and labor. The curacas might have stood out with their finer garments and goblets, but their decision-making

Figure 2. Santiago in Peru: Santiago Mata-indios.

Figure 3. Santiago Mata-indios, according to Guaman Poma (1936:f.404).

powers, and their means to commandeer the labor of others, were constrained by deeply entrenched Andean expectations demanding chiefly
largess, chiefly concern, and the inviolability of products garnered from
the fields and herds of others (Murra 1978:62–82; Hernández Príncipe
1923; Spalding 1984:72–105).

After the Inca conquest, when *curacas*, their polities, and their gods
paid homage to Cuzco, chiefly prestige items became insignias of roy-
ally legitimized middlemen in imperial politics and religion (Hernández
Príncipe 1923; Cobo 1964, II:161; Molina 1943:25). As ethnic enclaves
lost their autonomy, so did their mountain gods, who were constrained
to show obedience to Cuzco. Nevertheless, by creating positions for
Thunder and his lineage-founding sons in the imperial cosmological
hierarchy, the Incas legitimized the worship of local gods. Some peasants accepted the imperial version of divine order, others were more
skeptical, but all retained faith in their mountain gods' traditional
capabilities (Cobo 1964, II:161; Silverblatt 1987:40–47, 81–108; 1988).

The actions of Thunder and the mountain gods bespoke lessons in
coercion—in the arbitrariness of power and its economic consequences.
As guardians of herds, and hence of mortal well-being, these divinities
could take away what they provided, and mountain gods were not
beneath using this capability to force polities into their religious sphere.
A Jesuit priest, working in the north-central highlands of Peru, uncov-
ered a fascinating legend of the Yaramate, who were coerced by the hero
Tumayricapa into joining his group of devotees. The Yaramate had no
intention of owing allegiance to Tumayricapa and his brother. But gods,
being more powerful than mortals, got their allegiance—or better said,
stole it. Tumayricapa pilfered a Yaramate llama, knowing by divine
prescience that Yaramate shepherds would soon be searching for their
missing flock. When Tumayricapa saw the herders approach, he snorted
white hail (one of Illapa's meteorological specialties) from one nostril
and pinkish hail from the other. Humbled, the Yaramate asked, "Why
did you take our llama, father (*tayta*)?" Tumayricapa replied, "Is it true
you have called me 'father'?" After determining that the Yaramate
meant what "father" implies (i.e., obedience), Tumayricapa said he
would receive them as "children (*hijos*)" (i.e., provide for them) on the
condition that they owe him obeisance. "If they didn't," Tumayricapa
warned, "he would destroy them and their means of livelihood" (Duviols
1974–76:278).

This paternalistically phrased tie makes clear both the hierarchy
and the economic basis of political inequality among the Yaramate.
Tumayricapa did not initiate a customary relationship of mutual aid
and responsibility by giving; rather, he imposed a relationship of ine-

quality by taking. Andean peoples recognized hierarchy between them-selves and their gods (and between themselves and other mortals) as beginning with force and the ability of one group to deny or diminish the well-being of another. Nonetheless, a second Andean lesson was expressed: power brought with it certain obligations. Tumayricapa was a father and was expected to provide for his children.

Andean mountain heroes expressed understandings of power, which included an acquiescence to and reliance on hierarchy. Central high-landers saw themselves as dependent on powerful, dominating forces, associated with the prerogatives of mortal chiefs, for their livelihood and welfare. The latter perception was bound to the specifics of Central Andean power relations, which included morally sanctioned obliga-tions and responsibilities on the part of those in power to the not-so-privileged. Even the Incas paid lip service to chiefly obligations of generosity.

Of course, the Incas were not chiefs but imperial lords. Nevertheless, the nature of the institutions they did impose on the Andean peasantry was tempered by traditions rooted in chiefly ethics: they were obliged to generously host those working on state lands; they did not interfere with subsistence production on what they redefined as community land; ideologically committed to the material welfare of those they conquered, they acted as giant redistributors of Andean products (Murra 1978:135–97). Some mountain gods, as myths tell us, seemed co-opted by Inca largess; others were skeptical and encouraged rebellion (Silverblatt 1988). But in any case, the mountain gods, armed with their Inca experiences, embod-ied notions of political morality that colored peasant understandings, expectations, and critiques of the profound changes Santiago fore-shadowed.

Making Sense of Colonial Disorder

The Spanish invasion imposed alien economic, political, religious, and conceptual structures on Andean society. The economy of Spain, oriented toward the emerging market economy of Europe, saw in its new-world colonies the opportunity to accumulate great wealth. The political institutions imposed on the colonies worked to ensure that Spain's colonizing aims were met. The ideological underpinnings of these institutions embodied an evaluation of the universe—of the qual-ity of the relationship between society and nature and between social groups—that was foreign to the Andean peoples being colonized. Buttressed by a worldview in which nature and humanity were becoming increasingly defined in relation to their market value, and by a theology that divided the world into competing forces of good and evil, colonial secular and religious authorities attacked the social foundations of Andean culture that were incompatible with the colonial enterprise. Yet, ironically, to transform Andean society into a colony of Spain, Spanish authorities also required the labor and political stability of a self-subsisting peasantry. Thus certain community structures of production—including community jurisdiction over land and resources and the morally charged traditions of mutual assistance and obligation—were reinforced under the colonial regime (Silverblatt 1987:109–11; Spalding 1984; Stern 1982).

Like their Inca predecessors, the Spanish used local chiefs to mediate between ruling authorities and the peasantry. As colonial middlemen, *curacas* were primarily responsible for ensuring that Spanish tribute along with other economic and political demands were met. However, the colonial regime rewarded Andean chiefs with the material perquisites of an expanding mercantilist society; and as privileged members of the conquered caste, *curacas* had one foot in the alien Hispanified universe of their conquerors. *Curacas* could dress in European finery, eat from European dishes, go to special schools to learn the European language, engage in European commercial transactions, even buy and sell property. Able to acquire the skills and savvy needed to manipulate colonial institutions, some chiefs used these skills to benefit their constituents. Yet their privileged access to colonial sources of wealth afforded them a material independence—unknown under the Incas—from the peasantries who were dependent on them and whose welfare they were obliged to protect. No longer constrained by the traditional arrangements limiting their economic and political activities, some local chiefs affronted and violated customary Andean morality (Spalding 1970, 1973). *Curacas'* divine forebears—now amalgamating mountain god–saints—bore these contradictions in their souls.

Colonized Andeans tried to come to terms with their new experiences, and in the process Santiago, or someone similar,[8] was adopted by Indios living in Peru's central highlands. Divine Spanish and native images of power sputteringly fused as colonized Quechua created a new Andean religion inseparable from the political realities in which it was spawned. This new religion carried colonization's complexities, incongruities, and conflicts at its core, and it brooked difficult burdens. It was compelled to grapple with an alien form of colonization that increasingly defined peasants and their production in mercantilist terms and, for the most part, disregarded any statutory responsibility for their material welfare. It had to contend with an alien vision of humanity, one that

declared Andeans to be of a different race than their masters. And it was
a religion that had to confront a growing differentiation within the
peasant community itself, one that set Hispanified chiefs apart from
their common kin.[9] Broad contradictions motored the colonial process—
overlaying encounters of class and culture: lord and peasant, Spaniard
and Indian, *curaca* and commoner, exchange and subsistence. Penetrating native communities, these contradictions probed Andean experience and parented discordant—even ironic—religious representations
of colonial circumstances of living.

Andeanized Santiagos: An Indian Challenge

By the seventeenth century Santiago had become deeply entrenched
in native religion. Yet even though clerics struggled to implant Christian doctrine in the hearts of Andeans—part of the colonizing mission to ideologically dominate native peoples—they condemned the
Andeanized Santiagos they discovered as devil-inspired. The Indians
had taken Santiago too much to heart, and the prelates, finding Santiago
invariably linked with Illapa and fearing a "cover-up," felt obliged to
censure certain venerations of the warrior-saint. Aware that pagan
Indians named those with a religious calling after their divine sponsors,
and unearthing a plethora of Santiagos apprenticed to the ministry of
Andean divinities, the church banned indigenous children from being
called Illapa, Rayo (lightning, in Spanish), or Santiago (see Arriaga
1968:205, 214–15, 275). But the saint was not simply Illapa's cloak; he
was not simply a disguise for idolatry.

Andean mountain gods, magically able to change their appearance,
assumed a new persona that emulated the Spanish saint. This transformation appeared so commonsensical to native Peruvians, seemed so
unremarkable, that Andeans like the chronicler Guaman Poma—as
well versed as he was in Catholic doctrine—called the pre-Columbian
thunder god Santiago-Illapa (Guaman Poma 1956, III:121). Peasants
asked by idol-hunting priests to list their local deities included one
called Santiago Dawn (Duviols 1971:336). And when an indigenous
healer from another central highland village appealed to his mountain
god for help, it was Santiago who appeared: "Resplendent, shining,
dressed in gold and he would burn [anyone who could] look at him . . .
and he entered [the room], making a noise like the sound of spurs . . .
and they began to sing and chant to him: you who are dressed in gold,
dressed in yellow, now you come crossing mountains, plains and valleys"
(AAL, Leg.1, Exp. VIII, f.91). The mountain gods' inventors, experienc-

ing the changed conditions of living evoked by the Spanish invasion, transformed the deities who reigned over the Andes' heights: Illapa and Santiago had inextricably merged, forging a god kin to, but nonetheless differing from, either of his progenitors.

After the Spanish conquest, Andean mountain gods adopted the new trappings of power that marked colonial society. Now they might be called "saint"; now they might even ride mighty stallions and wear the gold and silver ornaments of the colonial elite. Andean peasants were well aware that the Spanish conquest marked a period of profound transformations in Andean power relations. The interpenetrating Santiago–mountain god imageries—born out of the submersion of indigenous peasantries and their leaders into the ascendant colonial world— expressed those changes as they exposed a developing calculus of native possibilities. These prodigal sons of Thunder, by whatever name they were called, comprehended the duplicities of colonialism, its conflicts and cracks, as indigenous peoples interlaced memories of their pre-Columbian lifeways with emerging understandings of their living experiences under colonialism.

As Hispanified mountain gods—with their protracted gestation over the decades-long period when Spain cemented its highland rule— chronicled that dominion, they simultaneously challenged it. Even if seventeenth-century Andean resistance did not directly confront state power, nativized Santiagos defied intended Iberian monopolies of ways of living and conceiving the world. In rejecting Spanish cultural dominance, Andeans kept alive an indigenous ethic that retained an explicit moral—and implicit political—challenge to colonial society. Thus, even as they were incorporating the preeminent Spanish saint of conquest into Andean religion, native peoples consciously condemned anything church-related as an abomination. In the highlands of Lima, after 100 years of colonization, local religious leaders would incite their indigenous brethren to denounce Spanish practices and gods. Indians should not eat Spanish foods, drink Spanish beverages; but, most important, they should avoid the church, its rites, its saints. Colonial Andean religion traced its constituents' deteriorating conditions of life to the unwarranted attention they were giving foreign gods at the expense of their own (AAL, Leg. II, Exp. 6).[10]

The vigilant eyes of the Spanish, in conjunction with peasant political weakness, made it impossible for natives to forsake the rites of Catholicism, which both religious and secular establishments demanded of their Indian subjects. So they would go to church, with mocking hearts, and make phony confessions to the priests. Yet they surreptitiously removed their dead from the Christian cemetery and reburied them, according to custom, in caves on their community's heights. Keeping alive the rites of their ancestors, these *comuneros* secretly worshiped their Illapa forebears and lineage founders during lavish feasts held twice a year (AAL, Leg. II, Exp. 11).[11]

Aware of the peril in flouting their obligation to participate in Christian rites, villagers from Cajatambo also celebrated lavish feasts to their town's patron saint, San Pedro. But before engaging in any festivities, they would beg permission of their native gods. Shamans tell us that their divinities always conceded, albeit reluctantly. So with the prior consent of mountain gods, Cajatambinos duly worshiped San Pedro, and afterward, San Pedro's burlesqued wooden image watched over the authentic festivities celebrated in honor of Illapa's son (AAL, Leg. II, Exp. 11). In their conscious separation of the Catholic world from the native one, Cajatambinos—although they deferred to Spanish dominion—paid homage to their past by comparing it to the present. Thus they contested the legitimacy of the present political order (and probably derived the strength to endure it), armed with the remembered morality of their native gods—even if native gods, by now, could be called Santiago.

Native gods had been burned, driven underground, by the extirpators of idolatry. Keen to the Spaniard's ever-deepening grip over the highlands, while well versed in the nuances of public rituals of power, Cajatambinos resignedly encouraged their constituents to sham displays of Catholic devotion. However, Hispanified Thunder and Mountain learned well from their Iberian masters. Discovering catechism lessons on the immortality of the soul, Cajatambinos bestowed their shrine-idols with eternal life. So even though Father Avendaño had physically destroyed Illapa's son and descent group founder, Guamancama, his soul lived on in colonial Andean religion. He was even remade in a wooden image: not unlike the wooden images of saints, which, with consummate irony, native people derided as so much foolishness (AAL, Leg. VI, Exp. 11). Christian ideology was turned to the service of indigenous resistance.

If elements of Catholicism gave added life to Cajatambo's divine heroes, then it should not be too surprising that Iberian Catholicism's foremost warrior saint, Santiago, could also be drafted to serve in the defense of native religion. Idolators from a hacienda in the province of Cuzco gathered to wish havoc on the Spaniards. Happening upon a heretical reunion in the hacienda's chapel, a horrified priest records:

> . . . they made offerings of *medio reales* [Spanish money], portions of coca, and small jugs of *chicha* [maize beer], and they called for the devil, naming him Santiago, and then a phantom appeared about one yard tall,

mounted on a white horse, who descended from the chapel's roof. They spread two little jugs of *chicha,* coca, a certain type of stone they call *mullu,* on shredded hay and chewing coca they invoked him and said, "Come, Santiago, Apuhuayna [young lord]." [Hearing] these words, the phantom would come down from the roof in great shining splendor, sometimes in the midst of lightning. The phantom would answer them, "I will help you, as long as you don't confess, don't hear mass, don't pray in Church but just dedicate yourselves to my cult," and having said this he would disappear. (Esquivel y Navia 1901:222)

Thus Santiago, the warrior-saint who was to redeem the New World for the Spanish, could do battle for those whom he was commissioned to vanquish. Santiago, or Santiago figures, represented a forceful understanding: that if the Spanish could not be banished from the Andes, they could at least be held at bay. This was an insight yielded by the peasant experience of over a century of compromise and struggle in the colonial Andes. And it was a perception expressed by and in the totality of Santiago–mountain god's often incongruous and caustic imageries.

Andeanized Santiagos and the Indian Compromise

Mountain gods—guarantors of peasant well-being—reflected on traditional Andean social forms and the character of life they represented: they stood for a time past as well as for the persistence of customary relations into the present, through, though often in spite of, colonial pressures. However, as Andeans perceived the growing hold of Spain on their communities, they judged their welfare to be also dependent on the ability of their sponsors to manipulate foreign economic and juridical institutions. Christianized mountain gods—colonial hybrids—captured these bitingly discordant, yet mutually spawned tendencies. While indigenous peoples longingly discerned their Hispanified gods as natives, and so relished the pre-Columbian ethos they embodied, they also discerned these gods as Europeans, bent on fighting battles—and exacting demands—increasingly defined along Spanish lines (Figure 4).[12]

Mercantilism was unknown to the central highlands before the arrival of the Spanish, and as Andean communities were becoming tied to the colonial market economy, their gods reflected the changed circumstances of their creator's lives. Mountain gods even started to make the same kinds of claims on their devotees as the colonial establishment. The *comuneros* of Hacas, following Andean tradition, maintained community herds to support their gods' celebrations (cf. Hernández Príncipe

Figure 4. Christianized mountain god: Santiago as protector of pastoral life.

1923). Not content with the pre-Columbian economics underlying this religious practice, Guamancama, the mountain god of Hacas, required that Indians, in addition, purchase a llama for the festivities held in his honor. Guamancama ate from plates of gold and silver, like his pre-Columbian forebears, but he was not content and also insisted that his devotees give him offerings of *moneda,* or silver coins (AAL, Leg. VI, Exp. 11).

Objectifying in Guamancama their understandings of these trans-forming conditions of life—the penetration of mercantilist economic relations and the ensuing powers that accrued to those who participated in them—*comuneros* tied their god's behavior and his prestige to a mastery of the exchange relations that were spreading throughout the Andean countryside. Guamancama demanded and captured the market's mystique, not unlike his Hispanified Indian counterparts with their privileges to own property and independently enter into commercial transactions. Now commoners tended to perceive their well-being as dependent on the only Indians who could attain the market's magical fruits of profit and power—gods and *curacas.* So even while Guamancama railed against European contamination and immorality, he too was participating in, while his subalterns produced for, colonialism's most polluting and underhanded institution.

At times Andeans would transform their gods completely into gringos, or *mistis* (whites). Thus *misti*-gods, divine Indian advocates in colonial courts, would mediate as "lawyers" on the side of their human subjects. Sometimes they would intercede to get unwanted priests out of villages; at other times they would fight against unscrupulous creoles who were trying to steal Indian land. But gringo-gods were also supplicated by their Hispanified mortal descendants, who apprehended their divinities' commercial savvy and prayed them into astute business partners (AAL, Leg. VI, Exp. 11, AAL, Leg. I, Exp. 12).[13] Andean gods, like school-trained *curacas,* could now intervene in the entanglements of inequi-ties of colonial Peru. Yet by doing so they harbored a potential danger: Hispanified mountain gods, like colonial society's Hispanified Indians of privilege, could overlook their native roots, constituencies, and responsibilities. Moreover, with their legendary successes in the market, courts of law, and bureaucratic maneuvers, mountain gods—perhaps unwittingly, perhaps not—were encouraging acquiescence to the colo-nial way.

Andeanized Santiagos captured peasant understandings, sentiments, and fears of their cracked world and of the larger political reality encapsulating it. *Comuneros* sensed that as colonialism became more firmly entrenched it was only as well-heeled elite in colonial relations that their gods could attain the power of saints (i.e., embody the hope of being able to manipulate, with some success, the political-economic relations that produced saints). Ironic indeed that it was not the orthodox Santiago who constrained native feelings for their possibilities in the colonial world. This was not the Santiago of the church's campaigns to indoctrinate compliance to the colonial order but a more insidious, profoundly persuasive Santiago, all the more so for his less conspicuously conventional demeanor.

A Dialectic of Challenge in Compromise/Subversion in Rule[14]

The Andean peasantry lived as a dominated class under the Incas, and even parochial mountain gods like Tumayricapa glimpsed procedures of exploitation and acquiescence. Nevertheless, neither this experience nor its imageries could fully comprehend how Andean lives and mountain gods would be transformed in the colonizing process. The Spanish conquest of the Andes transformed the character of the power relations that bound the peasantry to the larger society which dominated it. Unavoidably fused with their Iberian doubles, Peruvian mountain gods provided Andeans with certain understandings of their history under colonialism as well as of their experience of its new configurations of authority. They imaged hunches about native possibilities and strategies, representing an indigenous calculus of how to challenge and endure a colonial future. Yet even as Spanish provocations were animating this vigorous counterculture, which was defying, or at times taming, colonial demands, Andean opposition was being tethered by colonialism's terms for existence.

As the return of the pre-Columbian order seemed increasingly remote, mountain gods—while tenaciously clinging to their traditional figures— took a Hispanified turn. Believing in an Indianized Santiago or a "*mysti*-fied" mountain god might have diffused the despair felt by the powerless in colonial society, offering solace, even hope. Peasants, too, if only in the dreams of religion, could partake of the goods and power needed to survive in a world dominated by saints and a growing market economy. But herein also lay the limits of those dreams— limits that were inherited from the pre-Columbian past. Andean peoples, for decades indebted to a hierarchy of lords and chiefs, still perceived their welfare as dependent on these mortals' mirror images: the gods, who lived in the Andean mountains and skies.[15] Now these divinities, transformed through the colonial experience, were *misti*-fied, and native representations intimated an unavoidable dependence on these culturally (even "racially") alien forces to recreate meaningful and decent lives.

In religion and ritual, Andean peoples validated the political hierarchy and economic relations in which their mountain god–Santiagos participated. In accepting this hierarchy, in consenting to its force, they expressed a conviction that their survival was tied to the system of power over which their mountain gods exerted influence. This consent was the flip side of a hegemony that, constraining visions of life's possibilities, successfully delimited the forms of resistance that it could take.[16] As their bonds to a money-loving, legalistic, bureaucratic mountain god tightened, Andeans' sense of their own redemption and of the new social order they might struggle to achieve increasingly engaged the colonial society their gods aped—even while defying it.

Seventeenth-century Christianized mountain gods challenged colonialism's moral ascendancy and cultural dominance; and they decried any characterization of Indian peasants as passive victims of European rule. Andeanized Santiagos encouraged resistance, but it was a resistance contained within the boundaries of colonial power relations. Nativized Santiagos presented an oppositional view, one that fought to minimize the polluting effects of the Hispanic world. However, even if Christianized mountain gods preached to keep the Spanish universe at arm's length, they only whispered an alternate vision of radically restructured power relations.[17]

Nevertheless, these messages of accommodation in defensive struggle, resistance-in-acquiescence, became essential, humanizing strategies for survival in a world in which rebellion seemed doomed and was thus only vaguely perceived as a viable alternative. Santiago–mountain gods, preaching defensive resistance, were most likely offering realistic appraisals of the outcome of insurgency. Yet with their understanding and sensitivity to the peasantry's conditions of life, they also offered hope of change through their obstinate moral challenge to the present. These Hispanified mountain gods/nativized saints embodied the didactic memories of colonized history, memories that spoke of ethical distinctions and violations of morality. These understandings were not lost even if they appeared muffled by imageries, dazzled by *monedas* and spurs, that counseled accommodation.

As Santiago–mountain gods counsel vigilance, they also caution us of the intricate, nuanced, deceptive means through which power infuses cultural symbols and images; of how power saturates the process of living in a class-fractured world. They remind us of the ways in which dominant political orders are privileged in their attempts to shape interpretations of life's trajectories. Ironic fellows, they point to the tenacity of colonizing imageries which occasion the very memories that challenge them. Mountain god–Santiagos, nativized saints, condensers of history, also put us in our place, reminding us of the partiality of our own reconstructions of social pasts and presents.

NOTES

This paper has benefited from generous colleagues and generous research support. The participants in the symposium were all helpful; and in particular I want to thank Jonathan Hill and Terry Turner for their thoughtful criticisms and encouragement. I am also grateful to Richard Berger for his helpful suggestions and insightful comments. Others who read (or were forced to listen to) Santiago's various versions include Michael Taussig, Sabine MacCormack, Billie Jean Isbell, Kay Warren, Nan E. Woodruff, Julie Saville, Rayna Rapp, Lucy Salazar, Jeffrey Quilter, the Spring 1987 Andean ethnohistory seminar at Yale, and the University of Illinois Press's anonymous reviewers. Thank you all for your good advice. The American Philosophical Society, along with the College of Charleston's Faculty Research and Development Committee, graciously underwrote the initial research on this project. I was able to continue my research and work on revisions in relative calm, thanks to fellowship support from the Smithsonian Institution and the Social Science Research Council.

1. Any discussion of Santiago and his transformation from a killer of Moors to a killer of Indians owes a tremendous debt to the pioneering Peruvian scholar Emilio Choy (1979).

2. Others who have looked at the fusion of Santiago with Andean divinities— but with different understandings than those presented here—include Fuenzalida (1968) and Gow (1980).

3. See Isbell's (1985) new introduction to her structuralist-inspired book, *To Defend Ourselves: Ecology and Ritual in an Andean Village* (1978), which questions and evaluates structuralism's contributions to Andean studies.

4. Some of the analyses that most inspired this critique privileging the social history of symbolic construction and the ways in which power relations infuse imageries include Nash (1979), Lears (1985), Thompson (1974, 1978a), Williams (1977), and Warren (1978); and see especially the pioneering works of Taussig (1980a, 1980b, 1987) and Genovese (1974, 1981).

5. Among the growing literature emphasizing human agency in the construction and reproduction of society see Medick (1987), Karp (1986), Giddens (1979), Bourdieu (1977), and Thompson (1978b).

6. Stern's book is a masterful study of how indigenous peoples in the Ayacucho region vigorously limited and shaped colonial policy. Other Latin American studies that analyze how native peoples actively contoured colonial institutions and rule include Farriss (1984) and Wasserstrom (1983).

7. Much of this discussion of history and the ethical imperatives of historical memory is indebted to Taussig's (1987) provoking insights (see especially pp. 366–92). The growing emphasis on "resistance" in the social science literature on the peasantry can be assessed in the works of Scott (1985, 1986), Larson (1983), and Crummey (1986). See Taussig's (1980, 1987) studies analyzing cultural and imagistic forms of resistance to capitalist penetration in South America.

8. It should be noted that all mountain gods did not take on the name Santiago, even though in appearance they emulated that saint.

9. Spalding (1970, 1973) and Stern (1982, 1983) have greatly contributed to our understanding of the ambivalent role of the *curaca* in colonial Andean society.

10. Stern (1983) has perceptively suggested that Andean religion might have been used by the peasantry to tether *curacas*, who were overly attached to the Hispanic world, in an attempt to mitigate internal community divisions.

11. Under colonial rule the indigenous worship of ancestors was a challenge to the secular and religious establishment. However, since the Incas encouraged the maintenance of local cults and actually incorporated them into state religion, they did not consider local religious activities to be heretical or defiant (unless that practice openly denied the superiority of the Inca). Thus the significance of local, peasant worship must be analyzed from the perspective of the larger political/religious system of which it is a part. In any case, peasant traditions do not simply persist but are actively reproduced; and in the colonial Andean context they were "preserved" at risk.

12. The notion of contradictory consciousness described here is based on the work of Gramsci (1973).

13. Clearly, mountain gods embodied different meanings for the two strata that comprised the Indian colonial community.

14. The dual notions of "accommodation in resistance" and "resistance in accommodation" come from the work of Genovese (1974).

15. See T. Turner (1985) for a penetrating study of precapitalist notions of fetishism.

16. "The dominant culture," as Williams (1977:114) argues, "at once produces and limits its own forms of counter culture." The oppositional ideologies developed by the Andean peasantries in the seventeenth century can be illuminated by Williams's insights, based on the work of Gramsci. The indigenous struggle for withdrawal from the seventeenth-century colonial state did not represent an independent vision, comprehending radically restructured power relations. Thus Andean peasant resistance could be ensnared in and constrained by hegemonic structures even though the peasantry repudiated the Spanish regime and denied its governmental legitimacy. (See Williams [1977] for the complexities of hegemonic orders and the emergence of alternative and oppositional visions.) While this study looks at the limited and limiting nature of oppositional ideologies from the perspective of exploited groups, it presumes its dialectical counterpart (i.e., the advantages of those in power to realize and insinuate their visions of society). Of course, the church, whose evangelism was

an ideological arm of colonial rule, played an integral part in this process, even though it was not the orthodox Santiago (the one preached about in Catholic doctrine) who constrained native conceptions of their possibilities. The fact that Santiago represented hegemonic concepts in ways not even conceived of by priests intent on indoctrinating acceptance of colonial rule through church dogma, is a fascinating dimension of Santiago's profoundly persuasive and insidious powers as well as of the still unclearly understood processes underlying the creation of hegemony. For a provocative analysis of hegemony in the U.S. South—which stands as one of the earliest applications of Gramsci in English and still one of the most brilliant—see Genovese (1974).

17. Peasant involvement in the great Tupac Amaru rebellion might have been experienced in part as a response to the call of their colonial indigenous gods for justice. Indigenous resistance in the seventeenth century, no matter how enveloped within the confines of colonial society, prepared the ground for the more violent activities and disruption of the century that followed. This essay does not deny the potential for radical action in the past or in the future; nor does it deny the role of a morally outraged Santiago in stimulating political action (cf. Pease 1974). It is, after all, a study in social process understood in terms of potentials and possibilities: not only what was but—with an eye on tendencies and limits—what might have been.

9

History, Myth, and Social Consciousness among the Kayapó of Central Brazil

Terence Turner

This essay addresses the nature of historical consciousness among the Gê-speaking Kayapó of Central Brazil, and more specifically the relation between the mythic and historical levels of Kayapó consciousness of their relation to Brazilian society. The Kayapó have had contacts of one kind or another with the Brazilians since the beginning of the last century (but for most of them peaceful relations with the state began only in the 1950s). More generally, this essay is concerned with the differential expression of mythic and historical modes of consciousness of the contact situation in different cultural genres and its implications for ethnographic investigation of social consciousness among preliterate societies such as those of lowland South America.

The work of Lévi-Strauss and other structuralist writers on lowland South American cultures has perpetuated certain romantic notions about the nature of social consciousness in these societies, such as that they lack a notion of history, either of themselves or of their contact with Western society, having instead a totally "mythic" formulation of social reality. Implicit in this proposition is the more general assumption that myth and history are mutually contradictory, incompatible modes of social consciousness, the former tending to give way to, or decay into, the latter when the native social order, conceived as an internally static, unself-conscious system in its pristine, precontact state, is disrupted by the irreversible historical changes imposed from without by Western society.

Three seldom examined assumptions seem to underlie much of the discussion of indigenous South American societies' formulations of their experience of contact with Western society. The first of these is that contact with Europeans or contemporary national societies is so unique in their experience, and so disruptive of their cultural orders, that their cultural representations of contact tend to take fundamentally different forms from their representations of themselves and of other native societies. In specific terms, it is frequently suggested that the irreversible changes forced upon native societies by contact with Western society constitute the latter's first experience of "history" at the level of collective consciousness. The implicit or explicit corollary is that indigenous societies lack historical consciousness of themselves and therefore represent the development of their own institutions and social divisions only in "mythic" terms. Myth is to history, in other words, as native society is to Western society (or more precisely, the native society's contact with Western society).

Another pervasive assumption is that of the homogeneity of indigenous cultures' social consciousness, both of themselves and their contact with Europeans. It seems often to be taken for granted that each indigenous society possesses a single, internally consistent view of its own origin and structure, or at any rate of the origin and structure of Western society insofar as the latter relates to itself.

A third assumption, distinct from although related to the last, is that of the inconsequentiality of genre to investigations of social consciousness among preliterate peoples. If it can be assumed that an indigenous society has only one conception of itself and its relation to the Western world, then it seems an easy (if not logical) step to assume that the expression of that conception in any one genre can be taken as representative of its expression in all genres. The form of expression, in other words, makes no difference to the content that is expressed, at least at this fundamental level of cultural meaning. Some such chain of assumptions would seem to be responsible for the way in which the analysis of a single myth or historical narrative is often presented, without further qualifications, as representing the whole thought of a society on a given subject.

These assumptions are obviously at variance with the notion of genres as formal-thematic unities in which specific sorts of content tend to become associated with specific forms of expression, as developed within Western literary scholarship and instantiated at the intercultural level by anthropological investigations of folk genres. It follows that any investigation of a culture's collective forms of consciousness of a subject like history or contact with Westerners must be careful to canvass all of the genres in which the culture expresses aspects of the subject in question.

The present study of the mythic and historical dimensions of Kayapó representations of contact with Brazilian society develops a critique of these assumptions by way of an attempt to contextualize them in several different dimensions. One of these dimensions consists of placing Kayapó accounts of the origin of Brazilians, shotguns, and so on, in the context of their accounts of the origin of other native societies and of subgroups of their own society. Another is the influence of the dialogic context (who is speaking and to whom) on the terms of the discourse itself. Under "terms" I specifically include the "mythic" or "historical" character of the discourse and, within these broad categories, the specific type of mythic or historical formulation involved, "myth" or "anti-myth," or "major" or "minor" historical mode. Here I point out instances in which the social relation between the speaker's group and the group that is the referent of the discourse appears to have a bearing on the nature and level of that discourse.

As a third dimension of contextualization I stress the relevance of the cultural genre of the discourse to the mode of consciousness ("mythic" or "historical") expressed in it. The major genres considered are narratives with culturally prescribed story lines, which comprise the Kayapó genre of *mē tum iarên,* or "tellings about the old ones," which is the typical vehicle of myth and also of one type of historical account, and extemporized oratory, which is the characteristic medium of historical discourse directly bearing on matters of contemporary concern. The Kayapó data, when placed in this multiply contextualized perspective, appear to contradict the assumptions about Amerindian, and particularly lowland Amazonian, social and historical consciousness I have just reviewed.

It is clear, to begin with, that among the Kayapó the type and level of social discourse about contact with the Brazilians varies as a function of the genre in which it is expressed. The same is true of the context of performance and the performer's relation both to the parties being addressed and those being referred to. The same Kayapó who, as a bedtime story for his children, may tell a myth of how the Brazilians came from giant caterpillars, may later find himself delivering an oration to the adult members of the village in which he recounts, in relatively straightforward historical terms, the story of the group's contacts with the Brazilians. Still later, the same man may lecture visiting Brazilian officials about the same events, now deploying them in a different rhetorical mode, predicating conditional constructions of the present and future in terms of the past, in terms that combine historical and mythic argument. In this latter mode, historical and mythic statements are advanced to support claims, assert obligations, and threaten reprisal, all in a manner calculated to extract the support of one sector of the alien Western society against the depredations of another sector of the same society.

If one were to look only at standardized Kayapó tales or myths about ancestral times (*mē tum iarên*), one would get no idea of this diversity of thought and consciousness. In the simplest terms, one would be biasing one's sample in a way that would tend to exclude the historical aspects of Kayapó consciousness simply because those aspects are not usually expressed in Kayapó culture in the genre of traditional tales.

This is an appropriate place to clarify the nature of the Kayapó cultural genres in question. The Kayapó themselves do not make the distinction between "myths" and "historical" accounts. Both myth and accounts of past events preserved and retold for their own sake are lumped in a category variously denoted by the terms *kukràdjà,* "thing which takes a long time to tell," or *mē tum iarên,* "sayings about the old ones." The former term includes all lore of any kind, from ceremonial songs to the directions for starting an outboard motor. The latter category is more specific, denoting only narratives of the type described. Such tales are mainly told to children as bedtime stories.

Oratory, called "teaching" (*akrê odja;* literally, "teaching standing up") is also an important Kayapó genre of communicating cultural lore and wisdom. It is practiced by men of the older (father-in-law) stratum of the "fathers'" age set (*mē kra-re*), which includes chiefs and ritual specialists. It is the prescribed accompaniment of all weighty social occasions such as collective rituals, gatherings in the men's house, or debates over collective decisions of any kind, as well as a solitary pastime for the more self-pleased and insomniac members of the older male population. There is an elaborate oratorical style, involving a considerable number of phonetic, intonational, and vocabulary shifts from normal speech. In contrast to the tales comprising *mē tum iarên,* oratory is intended for an adult (and primarily male) audience.

Taken together, the Kayapó data on myth and oratory lead one to wonder how much the widespread assumption of the essentially ahistorical, "mythic" form of lowland societies' cultural consciousness of themselves and their contacts with Western society owes to sampling errors arising from the omission of those genres, like oratory, that more closely correspond to what in literate societies would be identified as prose, in contrast with relatively poetic forms like myth. The same reservation applies to the attribution of the inception of historical consciousness to the experience of Western contact. Both assumptions are contradicted by the Kayapó evidence in several different ways. The Kayapó possess a variety of cultural formulations of events in their own history, ranging from minor village schisms through the division of their tribe into major subgroups and their encounters with non-Kayapó indigenous peoples to their various forms and levels of contact with Brazilian society. Some of these are in forms we should call mythic and some in terms we should call historical. There can be different myths dealing with the same event, existing side by side with relatively "historical" versions of it.

This is certainly true of the first encounters between the Kayapó and Brazilians, which may be represented in the form of myths of the "origin" of Brazilians and their characteristic possessions—firearms and commodities—or of relatively objective accounts of early fighting, plundering, peacemaking, relations with the first Indian service agents, and the growth of dependency on Brazilian commodities. The forms of the "mythic" accounts, moreover, are essentially similar to those in which the Kayapó recount the origins of other indigenous peoples and subgroups of their own people. They also possess "historical" accounts of the latter. The Kayapó, in other words, possess both "historical" and "mythic" accounts of themselves, of other native peoples, and of their contacts with the Brazilians, and in either mode their accounts of the latter show no special forms or features that distinguish them from their accounts of the former.

Two Myths of the Origin of Brazilians

There are several different Kayapó myths of the origin of Brazilians and their characteristic cultural accoutrements—firearms and commodities. The texts of two of these stories follow. The first narrative is the only Kayapó myth of Brazilian origin with known cognates in other Gê groups. The story of Angme kapran is known from the Apinaye and under the name of Auke from the Eastern Timbira groups. The Eastern Timbira variants were analyzed by Da Matta (1970) in an important article I have discussed at length in my commentary on these essays. The Angme kapran story was not told among the three Kayapó groups (Gorotire, Kuben-kran-kên, and Porori-Kretire) with whom I worked. Two Kayapó variants of the story have been recorded, one from the Irã'ã-mrãyre and one from the present-day Tchikrin of the Cateté. The

Irã'ã-mrãyre version was collected by Nimuendajú (n.d.) in 1940; the Tchikrin variant, by Vidal (1977:265–66). Only Nimuendajú's (the shorter) variant is presented.

Angme Kapran (Irã'ã-mrãyre)

Angme kapran was a *wayanga* [shaman] possessed of great power. He had a son, who however paid no attention to him. Angme kapran always went about with a bundle of arrows on which was perched his tame yellow macaw. The men hated him and wanted to kill him. They knocked him down and tore him into pieces: they also killed his macaw and burnt up his arrows. But that very afternoon he returned safe and sound to the village with his arrows and the macaw. After they had thus tried several times in vain to kill him, they finally threw his body into a big fire and heaped firewood on top.

When the women were going to the plantation the next morning, they heard the reports of guns. Following the sound, they got to a big house with many doors. In it there lived a white man who owned cattle, horses, and poultry, as well as a plantation with a kind of maize very different from the Indians'. It was Angme kapran. He had made gunpowder from the ashes of his flesh, the gun out of the bones of his lower leg, the cattle out of his anklebones, and the maize from his teeth. As the women came past, he called them to him, fed them, and then locked some of them up in his house. The rest, who had recognized him, went to the plantation after this delay, and then returned to the village, where they told that they had found Angme kapran. So all the people went to get the women who were still locked up. His son also came along and presented himself, but the medicine-man answered that he did not want to have anything to do with him, seeing that he had paid no attention when his father was being maltreated. He let one of the captive women go after another, then scared away the Indians with gunshots. They were terrified and never more returned to him. (Wilbert 1984:106; source: Nimuendajú n.d.)

The Origin of the Shotgun (Kretire)

Iprēre emerged among us Indians, and was the one who went around making people. Later he went off to live alone with his children. It is said that he shot a tapir with an arrow and went off in search of it, following a track left by its blood. A snake was seated near where the tapir passed by, and without delay Iprēre followed on. It is said that the snake spoke like this: "Where did you come from?"

"I shot a tapir with an arrow. It ran off, and I went after the track left by its blood in order to kill it," answered Iprēre.

"No, it's already gone away. You didn't kill it. Why did you act like that?" said the snake.

"I shoot animals with arrows. I kill some of them, but others I just manage to pierce, as in this case. I follow behind in order to kill," answered Iprère.

"No, it's already run away. You shot it but it fled. Now tell me, where is your wife?" asked the snake.

"My wife is far away together with my children. I'm here to kill animals for them to eat. As I walked by I shot an animal and followed its track so as to kill it," stated Iprère.

"Well, it has already fled. Go back home; turn around and go on back. Tomorrow fetch your wife, and come and sit beside me so I can show you how to do something. I will show you at once how to make a shotgun so you can make one yourself to kill animals, from the very spot where you happen to be standing at the time. Then you can do the same as I do," said the snake.

They say that those were the snake's words, and that Iprère went back where his wife was, together with his children and mother-in-law.

"Tomorrow morning we're off to visit someone, so he can show me his work. Let's see if I manage to do the same as he does, and kill animals from the spot where I stand. I shot a tapir but it ran off and I went in pursuit. Someone told me that he'd show me how to do what he does," Iprère said to them.

At dawn they set off for their visit. It's said that the snake showed him how to do it. He explained everything. He showed him all the inside of the gun.

"Go on, you can do it yourself," said the snake.

Iprère sat down and made one himself.

"It's ready," exclaimed the snake, and made ammunition for it, adding: "That's the way you do it. With this you will be able to kill animals from the spot where you stand. Go on, try it out on your mother-in-law." It's said that he addressed his mother-in-law through his wife.

"Tell your mother to stand over there, so I can try out the shotgun on her."

The mother-in-law went off to stand in a weed-free spot.

"Go on then, try it!" said the snake.

Iprère took aim and fired. She cried out and fell to the ground.

"That's it!" the snake said. "That's the way to do it. That's what you must do with animals so you can kill them from where you stand, so as to stay put. When you shoot animals with arrows, and run after them, you end up exhausted. So now you've seen what I do."

The snake had shown him how to make a shotgun, and his mother-in-law was laid out cold. When her bones were clean [of flesh] Iprère remade her. He was the one who used to go about making people, so he brought his mother-in-law back to life. Then he showed the whites how to make the shotgun. He only showed the white men. The Indians had arrows to shoot animals with, whereby they managed only to kill some of them, as when Iprère was born. One must have the know-how to be able to kill well with arrows.

"You shall kill well with arrows," Iprēre said to them. And it's as he said it would be. Iprēre made shotguns. The snake showed him how to make shotguns for the white men, and Iprēre gave them the gun. He gave the Indians arrows. That's the way it was. (Wilbert 1984:257–59; source: Lea n.d.)

The story of Angme kapran, as I have noted, is the Kayapó version of the origin of the Brazilians common to all of the Eastern Timbira and Apinaye as well as the easternmost Kayapó groups. In its Kayapó variant, it conforms to Da Matta's (1970) model of the Timbira versions as "anti-myth" (see also my commentary in this volume); that is, it accounts for the origin of Brazilian society and possessions (above all, firearms, but also the sheer wealth of trade goods of all kinds) by an inversion of the structure of the principal origin myth of the indigenous culture and its characteristic possessions (above all, fire and the bow and arrow).

In the latter myth, the culture hero, as a boy, is abandoned in a nest of macaw fledglings, with which he becomes for a time metaphorically identified. He then grows up among Jaguars, who bestow upon him the cooking fire and the bow and arrow. His possession of the reproduced bit of fire is the basis of his return and reintegration into human society as an adult and, simultaneously, of the constitution of society itself as a self-reproducing system whose structure is based on the generalized form of its fundamental productive process (the production of social-ized adults, which is symbolized by the process of cooking and fire-making; see Turner 1985).

Angme kapran is distinguished as the possessor of a yellow (adult) macaw. This is an unnatural color for a macaw, obtained by plucking out its feathers and rubbing its skin with a substance that causes the new feathers that grow to be an artificial color. Angme kapran's macaw has shed its fledgling's plumage (associated in the culture origin myth with normal social childhood), but instead of growing normal adult plumage, it has developed a deviant, artificially induced plumage well suited to the emblem of a shamanic loner like Angme kapran.

The culminating attempt to destroy Angme kapran and cast him out of society takes the form of burning his body (a use that is itself the metaphoric inverse of the use of fire in the origin myth to transform an unsocialized youth from outside society into an integrated adult mem-ber of society). This act proves ineffective in the sense intended, since Angme kapran not only rises phoenix-like from his ashes but trans-forms them into the new products of Brazilian civilization. The fire, as an instrument of socialization and social reproduction, has thus been transformed into an instrument of desocialization and the reproduction of asocial products outside the control of the native society. This inverse transformation of the functions of the most fundamental possession of native culture epitomizes the inefficacy of all action framed in the terms of indigenous society vis-à-vis Angme kapran.

The twin themes of the inversion and alienation of the power of reproduction and the relative powerlessness of the native society over the Brazilian are the major constituents of the message of the anti-myth. Related to the first theme is the contradictoriness of Angme kapran with the ordinary process of social reproduction within the native society (he kills his wife and his brother's wife and kidnaps many of the women, either withholding them from the native society for a period or actively using them to reproduce his own society). Related to the second is the ambivalent behavior of Angme kapran at the end of the story, alternately giving out presents, killing, and kidnapping, but above all acting in total independence of the native society and quite beyond its power to influence or constrain.

Seen in the framework of these broad themes, the second of the two myths given here is also an anti-myth, fundamentally similar in its structure and message to the story of Angme kapran in spite of its surface dissimilarity. The successful reproduction of the alien (snake) weapon by the Indian demiurge, Iprēre, leads immediately to his asocial treatment of his mother-in-law as a game animal (he shoots her for target practice at the snake's suggestion). Iprēre's successful reproduction of the mother-in-law after the flesh has rotted off her bones leads directly to his distribution of the gun to the Brazilians and the bow to the Indians. In the first instance the extrasocial reproduction of Brazilian firearms is presented as directly incompatible with the reproduction of native society (the wife's mother-daughter's husband relation being the core of the uxorilocal extended family, which is the basic unit of social reproduction in all Gê societies). In the second instance, the rotting of the mother-in-law's flesh, leaving only her white bones, is analogous to her burning in a fire (Kayapó dead are entombed in domed graves resembling earth ovens, and the rotting of the flesh of the corpse is thought of as a process of gradual transformation of the dead person from his or her social form to that of a ghost, pure white like bones or ashes, who is ready as such for full integration into the society of the dead; the parallels with the metaphor of cooking as socialization are patent, but here the transformative process is obviously in the reverse direction, that of desocialization). The reproduction of the mother-in-law as a social being after her reversed "cooking" by Iprēre thus resembles, in inverted form, the reproduction of Angme kapran and the caterpillars as asocial beings after their burning. The point is that this act of social reproduction, restoring to Indian society its own form of reproduction, is the context for the permanent alienation of the reproduction of the shotgun to Brazilian society and the contrastive allocation of the bow and arrow to the Indians.

The alienation of the power of reproduction associated with Brazilian culture is thus once again achieved as a function of the neutralization of a process of desocialization by fire (i.e., a metaphoric form of "burning"). In this case, the undoing of the fiery transformation allows a social element to return to its place in society, thus permitting social reproduction to continue, rather than achieving the same result by the expulsion of an antisocial element whose presence in society was preventing that process from taking place. The fundamental logic of the two cases is the same, as is their message about power relationships: that is, the power of reproduction of Brazilian society, epitomized by firearms, is incompatible with the ordinary processes of transformation and reproduction of indigenous society; it represents an inverse transformation of those processes; it is more powerful than they; and it manifests its power in the structurally appropriate form of inverting the effects of indigenous social transformations.

I have emphasized the structural similarities of these stories, but I do not want to overemphasize their similarities at the expense of their differences. The point is worth making that when these two myths and the several other known Kayapó stories of the origin of whites are taken into account, there is clearly no single Kayapó myth of the origin of Brazilian society or its relation with Kayapó society. There are, rather, several such accounts that emphasize different substantive aspects of Brazilian society and Brazilian-Kayapó relations within a common structure of basic assumptions and relations. One characteristic Kayapó theme that comes through strongly is the importance of the sheer numerousness of the Brazilian population and its implications for some special capacity for reproduction; another is clearly firearms; another, the abundance of commodities; another, hostility. The terms in which the differentiation of Brazilian and Kayapó societies along these dimensions is accounted for in the myths do not, however, imply the end of Kayapó society or the contradiction of its mythological logic. On the contrary, as we are about to see, they are very much the same terms in which the Kayapó account for aspects of their own social history and their experience of other Indian peoples.

Two Stories of the Origin of the Juruna

The Origin of the Juruna (probable provenience: *Mẽ Kran No Ti*)

A long time ago there were no Juruna. Then the Kayapó made a long journey away from the village. The young boys were shooting at a termite. Then the latter took the boys by their arms and threw them into the water.

The boys stayed in the water where they grew and became the Juruna. Afterward the Kayapó killed many Juruna. They killed them because they were no longer Kayapó. (Wilbert 1984:55; source: Verswijver ms.)[1]

The Origin of the Juruna (provenience: Gorotire)

In a certain tree lived a large caterpillar. It was black and its head was decorated. It was shamanic [*wayanga*], and at night when the men went out hunting it took on human form and seduced the women.

A boy told his father what was happening, and the father decided to stay awake all one night to make sure the boy was right. That night the caterpillar did not turn into a man, but the Indian saw the caterpillar's children come down from the tree to look for their mothers. After they had had enough to eat, the little caterpillars returned to the tree.

The man, wanting revenge, set fire to the tree, and the heat made the caterpillars pop with cracks that sounded like gunshots. But the big caterpillar did not die with his children. He ran to the river and swam away, raising and lowering his body above the water in the same way that caterpillars move on land.

Later on, by way of the same river, the Juruna Indians appeared. They are called *ngo-iren* [water-paddlers] by the Gorotire because they make canoes and like to travel by water. The Juruna came armed with shotguns, weapons that the Gorotire were not familiar with. And so they thought that the Juruna made noises with those weapons to avenge the cracks caused by the Kayapó fire, which burned the bodies of the tribe's ancestors. (Wilbert 1978:153–54; source: Banner 1957:65–66)

Both of these stories account for the origin of the Juruna in the same terms by which the origin of Brazilians is explained in stories already presented. The second story, of the origin of the Juruna from caterpillars, is particularly striking in this regard, being obviously the same story as that of the origin of the Brazilians from caterpillars. The Juruna may have acquired guns before the Kayapó, and this story may reflect the experience of the Kayapó with gun-bearing Juruna from a time before they themselves possessed firearms. Be that as it may, the overriding point of these examples is that the same mythological terms are used by the Kayapó to account for the origin of the Brazilians and of another indigenous people. The advent of the Brazilians, it would therefore seem, is not seen by the Kayapó as presenting special problems from the standpoint of their mythic system as a whole.

Two Stories of the Origin of a Kayapó Group

The Children of the Snake (Origin of the Gorotire)
(Tchikrin of the Cateté)

A woman went every day to the garden and her husband remained in the village. She roasted potatoes in the garden and sent them back by her little boy to his father in the village. She stayed in the garden to weed.

One day the father became angry and said to the son, "Why doesn't your mother bring the potatoes herself, why is it always you who brings them? I am angry. I am going out to the garden to see for myself what your mother is up to."

Arriving at the garden, he said, "Where is your mother weeding? There are no weeds cut, they are all standing high."

The man went in search of his wife, and finally discovered her together with a snake. The snake had its tongue out very close to the woman's eyes, and the man could see that it was copulating with her. He said nothing, but returned to the village.

In the afternoon the woman returned from her garden and made an earth-oven for roasting potatoes. Then she sat down close beside her husband. "Don't sit beside me," he said to her, "for you stink of snake."

"Why?" she answered, "there is no Indian snake."

He replied, "I have already seen that you have a snake lover."

The husband left on a collective trek. He took his son. They went very far away.

The wife was pregnant. Her belly was very large. She gave birth alone, to many children, boys and girls. They were Indians, but grew very rapidly, like corn. In three or four months, they were already big.

One day the husband said, "I am going back to the village to see my wife."

In the morning, he left, alone. Arriving in the gardens next to the village, he heard the children of the snake crying.

He thought to himself, "Who came here and killed my wife?"

He looked and saw the snake children; there were many of them.

He returned to the forest to tell the other Indians. They asked him, "What happened?" The man said, "Other Indians came and killed my wife."

The Indians wanted to return together to the village to attack the intruders.

The husband said, "No, there are too many." So they went back on trek, and afterwards made new gardens elsewhere.

The snake's children are the Gorotire, they are very wild and aggressive. (Vidal 1977:243; my translation)

Origin of the Gorotire (Irã'ã-Mrãyre)

In the beginning the Kayapó inhabited a single large village, so large that it required a whole day to make the circuit of the house-ring. The youths, in preparing for a festival, were practicing a number of songs. Then they went hunting to obtain meat for the festival. In the meantime the family heads danced in accompaniment to the songs that belonged to the youths. When the latter returned and discovered that the men had appropriated their songs, thereby rendering the ceremony impossible, they grew very angry. They consulted an elder familiar with the tracts toward the west. In the evening this elder went to the plaza and called the youths: "Come here. All of you get together. Tomorrow I want to eat *kruot-ti* [*Hoplias macrophthalmus,* a fish that occurs in the Xingu but not in the Araguaya region]." The other villagers were surprised at this request, but the elder made all arrangements for the next day with the two leaders [*nga-djwoyn*] of the youths. The following morning they left the *aldeia,* taking their girls along. Almost all the youths were in the party. They marched westward and founded a village of their own. Then they made war arrows, returned, and fought the *mẽ kra-re* [mature men's age set] who had insulted them. They increased in numbers, forming the Gorotire. (Wilbert 1984:57; source: Nimuendajú ms.)

These two stories are remarkable as accounts of the same event in the development of Kayapó society (the origin of the Gorotire as a distinct group of Kayapó) but in opposite ("mythic" and "historical") modes. It is probable that the two stories are not possessed by the same Kayapó groups: that is, the Tchikrin (traditional enemies of the Gorotire) may lack the second, "historical" story, while the Gorotire and the other Western Kayapó groups derived from them appear to possess only the latter. I have heard this "historical" story told in each of the villages in which I worked (all of which, like the contemporary village of Gorotire, are offshoots of the ancestral Gorotire village). I have never heard the "snake children" story told in any of these groups, and believe I would have if it had existed in them. This point is probably significant. The Tchikrin, who are themselves descended from neither the Irã'ã-mrãyre nor the Gorotire but were for long bitter enemies of the latter, have produced a "mythic" version of their origins, whereas both the direct descendants of the historical fission, the latter-day Irã'ã-mrãyre and Gorotire, preserved the same "historical" account. Level and mode of social consciousness appears to be a function of contextual factors, in this case the distance and hostility of the relationship between the speaker's group and the group that is the object of discourse.

However this may be, the basic point remains that in the second story we have a quite plausible "historical" account—in what I have called in my commentary the "minor" mode of historical consciousness—of an actual event, the fission of the ancestral village of the Gorotire and the Irã'ã-mrãyre, which must have happened about 1850. Moreover, this account is preserved in the form of a narrative not dissimilar to mythic narratives, although it lacks their characteristic appeals to extrasocial agency. I suggest that the narrative has survived in this form because it succinctly formulates one of the main structural tensions in Kayapó society—that between the bachelors' and mature men's age sets—in a way that also gives dramatic warning of the results of letting this tension get out of hand. In other words, it is in the most relevant sense a representation (and cautionary tale) of the present as well as a story of something that happened in the past. In its capacity as a generic pattern of the present, couched in terms of a unique series of events in the past, this tale resembles myth; and it is this resemblance that doubtless accounts for its preservation in the mythic genre of *mẽ tum iarẽn*. "Historical" consciousness among the Kayapó is thus clearly not confined to contacts with Western society. Yet, as the first story shows, the Kayapó are capable of "mythologizing" events of the historical past of their own society in the mode of anti-myth usually reserved for accounts of the origin of Brazilians or non-Kayapó indigenous peoples.

Political Oratory in an Interethnic Context

The context of the following speech was a visit by Dr. Olímpio Serra, then head of the National Park of the Xingu, and a group of his assistants and medical personnel to Kretire village in August 1976. I was there making a series of ethnographic films with a team from the British Broadcasting Company, and we filmed and taped chief Rop ni's welcoming speech to the Brazilians. Rop ni spoke in an open hut surrounded by Kayapó, with the Brazilians seated on either side of him. His opening remarks were in Kayapó and were obviously directed more to his own followers than to the Brazilians, although he may have been speaking partly to the camera, since he knew I would make a translation of his remarks. Partway through the speech he switched to Portuguese.

Speech by Chief to Visiting Delegation of FUNAI Officials, Headed by Dr. Olímpio Serra, Then Director of the Xingu National Park (Kretire)

Here in Kretire village, named for my brother [the late chief Kretire] many people, I and many who followed me, were angry with the Brazilian ranchers encroaching on our land. Because of this other Brazilians came to persuade us not to fight: first Claudio and Orlando [Villas Boas] and then my kinsman, my brother here, Olímpio, have come to my home, amongst those who follow me and who want to destroy the ranches, and I have spoken to them.

The Brazilians, in the old days, never roamed these lands, but only my ancestors, in those times of no sickness and no fighting. Only the forefathers of us Indians were here then. Now we are few. Today, so soon after our ancestors' time, we are scattered into disunited groups, and you, with your ranches, call upon us to give up our land. Never! I will not agree to this!

Did not my own grandfather, my grandfather who was born before me, who lived before I became flesh and before you Brazilians, too, became flesh, despise the things of the Brazilians? Did he not warn me, long ago, of these things? He told me, "You—you are an Indian, a true Indian, therefore never drink the liquor of the Brazilians!" Yes, he said so! But now the young people, those only now growing up, are forgetting this advice. They are not listening to the older people, they are drinking the Brazilians' liquor and acting crazy, fighting and killing one another. It is very bad. Now I—I, Rop ni, I have enjoined all those Indians here with me in the park not to drink Brazilian liquor. I have counseled peace and an end to fighting, I have spoken to the people. Yes! And now our brother Olímpio has come and sat down beside me, so that I may speak to him too! So it is!

[Speaker now shifts to Portuguese]

As the ranchers are out to steal our land, I ask why they need more of this land here in the park? The president, the former president of Brazil wanted to give us more land. The boundary of the park was set at Upuaní. The road was planned to run on the other side of the great waterfall, leaving the park much larger, and so we were satisfied, no? But now, today, the [road-building] tractors have cut our land in half. It was [FUNAI] President Bandeira de Melo who cut off our land in this way. Therefore we were very unhappy with him. Then the ranchers tried to steal even more land from us. Why don't they look for land somewhere else? Well, I am not giving any more pieces of our land here to anyone. If any rancher comes into our land here, then I shall fight. I can and I will fight the ranchers. If I am forced to kill ranchers, then I shall return to the jungle, like my grandfather who fought the Brazilians before. This is what I will do.

Orlando and Claudio [Villas Boas] helped us very much. Orlando, Claudio wanted to bring more of us here, more Indians into the park. Here in the Xingu National Park. Then Orlando left, and Claudio too left, and now it is Professor Olímpio who is helping us here. Because Professor Olímpio now stands in the place of Orlando and Claudio as the friend of the Indians here in the park, the Xingu Park. So, if the ranchers come into our land here, I do not want to have to kill them. I don't want to start fighting and killing the ranchers who are trying to steal our land here. I am not crazy. We have children, we have wives. So when some of us want to go and fight and kill more [ranchers] like our grandfathers who fought so hard and killed so many—who knows how many they slaughtered—each man of them, with his war club and his strong arm—who knows how many perished at their hands—each of them must have killed ten Brazilians— each single war club took the lives of ten people—this is what I would do again.

But Orlando and Claudio Villas Boas did not want this, did not want us to go back to fighting again. They did not want us to kill more people. They didn't want that at all. All right! Professor Olímpio now is here and can hear what I am saying to you. Professor Olímpio, too, does not want more fighting and killing. Because it is very bad. For a long time my grandfathers fought constantly, killing people; but now, today, we don't want to kill more people. And I think that this is right and good for us, for we don't want to kill any more people. We will only do so if the ranchers come into our land to "break something" [quebrar uma coisa, a colloquialism that is the rough equivalent of the English "raise hell"]! If any rancher shoots at us, we are going to shoot back. This is what I will do. All right! It is this that I want to tell you. Any intelligent person today realizes that, whereas our grandfathers were simply Indians, today we also need things from you [Brazilians]. My grandfathers despised these things of yours, of you "Caraíba," or as we call you, in our own language, kuben. In the language of another tribe of Indians, my kinsmen, they call you "Caraíba." Well, it is the kuben who want to get rid of us here. So I am not going to allow any ranches on our land.

No follower of mine will go out of the Park to associate with other Brazilians in other places, because I know that that way your Brazilian diseases will be brought back to us, and they are very dangerous to us. In the old days, before the Brazilians made peace with us, we were increasing. Today we are decreasing because of your diseases. These diseases are very dangerous to us Indians. That is why I don't let any of my people here leave the park to visit any of the ranches. Only a foolish person, a stupid person would do this, because he would end up bringing diseases back to the rest of us. Therefore I don't allow it.

Long ago, my ancestor (his name was Iprẽre, in your language you call him God, Jesus Christ; in our language we call him Iprẽre). . . . (tape ran out at this point; source: Turner field notes)

This speech shows considerable sophistication in the rhetoric of historical interpretation and argument. In the first section, delivered in Kayapó and obviously intended primarily for his own people, Rop ni couples an account of his respected grandfather's advice to spurn the things of the Brazilians, especially their liquor, with a statement of his own, clearly identifying himself with the legitimizing ancestral figure and criticizing the contemporary generation of young men who are challenging his authority. He reviews the historic shift from the time before the arrival of the Brazilians to the present in terms of demographic decline and political fragmentation resulting from disease and fighting, in an indirect reminder to his more belligerent followers of their relative weakness in relation to the Brazilians and the consequent importance of his role as mediator. He emphasizes this role at both the opening and conclusion of the Kayapó portion of his speech, reminding his listeners that on the present occasion, as on others, the Brazilian officials come to him to attempt to mediate conflicts arising from Brazilian incursions on Indian land. Altogether, this presentation of the facts of contact with the Brazilians is well designed to reinforce the speaker's authority vis-à-vis his followers, on both internal and external grounds.

In the second part of the speech, addressed directly (in Portuguese) to the Brazilians, Rop ni presents the same facts in a quite different light. He speaks of the shift to dependence on Brazilian commodities as an accomplished fact, which "any intelligent person realizes," rather than as a mere vice of rebellious youth, and he lists this as one of the considerations, from the Kayapó point of view, that militates against reopening hostilities with the Brazilian squatters. With respect to the possibility of armed conflict, while protesting his devotion to peace and his diligence in restraining his followers, he also reminds his visitors in the most dramatic terms of the Kayapó record of warfare against the Brazilians and threatens to "return to the jungle" to fight again if necessary (thus asserting the Kayapó will to forego the fruits of peaceful relations with the Brazilians, including the commodities he recognizes they have come to "need"). Rop ni's concluding peroration on the feats of the culture hero Iprẽre, unfortunately missing from the tape, included a version of the story of the origin of shotguns given earlier (the informant happens to be the speaker's sister). In the context of the speech, the mention of the shotgun story was apposite in stressing the establishment of separate and complementary modes and, by implication, spheres of existence for Indians and Brazilians. This in turn implicitly legitimizes the speaker's claims for the inviolability of Kayapó land in the Xingu as the basis of the Indian "sphere." "Myth" and "history" are thus deployed side by side in a dialogically sophisticated performance in which different modes and levels of consciousness are synthesized into an effective rhetorical unity.

Rop ni's threats of armed resistance, incidentally, were not empty. A few years after this speech, members of his group combined with members of the other Kayapó village on the upper Xingu killed a dozen Brazilians on one intrusive ranch, and forced the evacuation of several others through exchanges of gunfire in which there were Brazilian casualties (no Kayapó were killed or wounded). These actions actually resulted in the restoration of a considerable tract of land (that to which Rop ni refers as having been severed by the road, BR-080) to the Kayapó by the Brazilian government. Rop ni's recitation of the warlike deeds of his ancestors and contemporaries, and his stated willingness to risk the benefits of peaceful commerce in defense of his people's land, was no mere exercise in hollow rhetoric but the expression of a fully historical consciousness, capable of formulating the possibilities and risks of present action in terms of an understanding of the conditions and effects of actions and events in the past. It thus exemplifies the dynamic role of historical consciousness as the repository of alternative courses of action in the present, which may (and in this case, did) become decisive ingredients in present action. History, in this dynamic and vital sense, reflexively makes itself.

In both parts of his speech Rop ni displays what I have called in my commentary both "minor" and "major" levels of historical awareness. The former involves consciousness of the contingent causal relations among a set of events that does not result in irreversible change in the native social order, nor is it determined by that order (examples are the actions ascribed to Gen. Bandeira de Melo in shifting the announced boundary of the Xingu Park in such a way as to cut Kayapó land in half, or the secular decrease in the Indian population as a result of contact diseases). The latter involves the realization that certain events or conditions have had irreversible consequences for the social-cultural order. An example of this is the speaker's consciousness of the implications of dependence on Brazilian commodities. In both parts of his speech Rop ni argues from specific actions or events as causes to their specific effects in shaping the contemporary situation of his own and other Kayapó groups (diminution of population, dispersion of groups to scattered territories and accompanying political disunity, loss of land to Brazilians, dependence on Brazilians for commodities, but also the historical fact and future possibility of armed resistance, and so on). Yet this same speaker, at the end of his speech to the Brazilians, is capable of launching into a mythological excursus on the feats of the culture hero Iprère and the way in which he defined the relationship between Indians and Brazilians by giving the shotgun, which he had learned to make from a snake, to the latter.

Rop ni did so, of course, because the myth incidentally legitimizes the point he had been arguing on historical grounds and thus supports his argument on a different (and, from his point of view, more absolute and incontrovertible) level. He thus exemplified what I suggest on general theoretical grounds (in my commentary in this volume) is a commonplace, if not universal, principle: that "mythic" and "historical" consciousness are not mutually exclusive but are complementary ways of framing the same events, which can, and usually do, coexist in the same culture, indeed in the same utterance by the same person. This situation certainly has its counterparts in our society: witness the speeches of our current political leaders; or our vaunted tradition of narrative history, which in the practice of many historians rests squarely upon the Hobbes–Locke–Adam Smith myth of society as the creation of a multitude of mutually independent, rationally self-interested individuals.

NOTE

I am greatly indebted to my colleague Bill Hanks for his careful critical reading and many valuable comments on an earlier draft of this essay.

1. The provenience of the myths published in Wilbert's collection is given by tribe but not usually by village or subgroup. It is probable that this story was recorded among the *mẽ kran no ti* Kayapó of the western Xingu drainage, since Verswijver has worked principally among that group.

10

Indian Voices:
Contact Experienced and Expressed

Alcida Ramos

In the 1950s the anthropologist Darcy Ribeiro prophesied that the Indians of Brazil would become so deculturated by contact with whites that they would eventually lose their ethnic identity and be transformed into "generic Indians" (Ribeiro 1970:222), stigmatized by whites and left with none of their specific cultures or traditions. Ribeiro's pessimism was understandable given the constant loss of territory, depopulation, exploitation of resources and labor, and armed persecution. For nearly five centuries, Indian group after Indian group had faced the same problems, which led many to extinction and others to precarious survival. But the image of the alienated generic Indian is a fiction. Ribeiro's prophecy has not come true.

What has happened since the fifties is the birth and growth of a political pan-Indian movement in Brazil. In the early seventies the first regional Indian assemblies took place, initially sponsored by a progressive branch of the Catholic church (CIMI, Conselho Indigenista Missionário). At these assemblies Indian leaders organized around the need to claim rights granted by the Constitution and by law but constantly threatened by both private and official actions. The União das Nações Indígenas, as the Brazilian Indian movement is called, was created in 1980.

As a result of this pan-Indian movement, meetings and speeches by Indians have clearly demonstrated Indian identity with a specific tradition. These people are not just Indians, they are Shavante, Terena, Kaingang, Makushi, Guarani of such and such a place, and so on. They often evoke the past, when their cultures were different from what they are now, before the effects of contact, but nowhere in their discourses is there a trace of the cultural void imagined by Ribeiro. The common cause of the political arena has unified the Indians and, at the same time, reinforced their ethnic distinctions.

The Indians have transformed "Indian" from a derogatory term used by whites to a key concept in their own politics of contact. The "generic Indian" is no longer the last stage of a defeatist, down-and-out, no-future-in-sight existence; rather, it has become a mark of otherness vis-à-vis the nationals. The appropriation of "Indian" by the Indians has exorcised the heaviest spells of discrimination associated with the term. Of course, this does not mean that there is no more discrimination; now it is expressed in other ways: for example, *bugre* in the south, *caboclo* in the north. But "Indian" is no longer a dirty word. In fact, it has gained legitimacy by the use to which it is put and the context in which it is used. The "Indian" is now a well-known political figure in the national scenario.

For the purpose of discussing some of the ways in which white society has affected indigenous traditions of symbolic expression, I shall present, in translation, three speeches delivered by Brazilian Indians to white audiences at meetings organized by whites in major cities of Brazil. These meetings took place during a period of military control of the government, when both Indians and whites felt the weight of repression and censorship. For better or worse the Indian question was one of the very few political issues that could be discussed in relative safety. Many whites took advantage of this to air their own frustrations, while the Indians used the unexpected opportunity to vent centuries-old grievances. Sympathetic whites crowded into formal auditoriums and improvised quarters to hear and applaud Indian speeches, often delivered in garbled Portuguese but always potent, vivid, and aimed at the common enemy— those in power.

These speeches, when looked at with a critical eye, begin to make more sense as texts. If we distill from them the rhetorical matter that makes up the individual styles, we can find a number of clues about expectations, viewpoints, life trajectories, and political options of the speakers in terms of interethnic relations. We can better understand these speeches if we see them in the context of the symbolism of contact. All of this leads me to reflect on what anthropology has offered by way of theoretical guidelines on this subject and to question some deep-rooted assumptions, particularly about history and "peoples without history."

The Indians Speak

The themes are recurrent, the moods are comparable, the images of the whiteman are similar. Among the hundreds of Indian speeches, these are as telling as any others. I will not explore these speeches to their full capacity, for a symbolic interpretation is beyond the scope and space constraints of this essay. No life histories were collected, but my own familiarity with the last two speakers has allowed me to go beyond the personal marks left by them in their speeches.

(The speech that follows was delivered by Augusto Paulino, a Krenak Indian from the state of Minas Gerais, to an audience of forty-four Indian leaders, six anthropologists, three lawyers, and one Catholic bishop, under the sponsorship of thirty-seven support groups, professional associations, and university branches. The meeting, organized by the Pro-Indian Committee of São Paulo, was held on April 26–29, 1981, in the city of São Paulo. See Comissão Pró-Indio 1982:26–27.)

Dear brothers, I'm here to present this weak figure who has been suffering for many years. He has been suffering for 22 years. I'm going to tell you the little story of the Krenak, what has been happening for 22 years. Over there in our territory, since the time of the SPI, the Post Chief began. . . . We had many head of cattle, we had 900 head of cattle, 600 sheep, 300 animals, it was well organized, we had everything, then they began to sell away till there was nothing left; they took us away from there to Maxacalis. We didn't like it, they went back, on foot, 92 days to go back. We arrived, camped on an island. There arrives Captain Pinheiro and said he was going to liberate our headquarters. Our liberation began again, he took us there and we began to work, making gardens and gathering cattle, we were starting again. He built a jail, opened up everything. We began to organize the land again. But then the *fazendeiros* got suspicious that we would occupy the whole territory. They began to wander around, took us away again, now to the Fazenda Guarani. Well, they took us to Fazenda Guarani way over at Crenaque. At that time they built a jail, everything, then they brought Indians from Amazonas, Indians from all over the place, were arrested, beaten up. That was in 1968, they took us away to Fazenda Guarani. The Indians didn't want to go, but they tied them up, put them in jail, left them there two, three days starving. They took us to Fazenda Guarani. We stayed there seven years. In seven years we began to discover the law, went back again. We were camping in our own territory again, we got there and also they had destroyed everything. We went on camping and they wanted to remove us again. But then we began to know the law, going this place and that. They left us alone. We are camped there in 13 *alqueires* [630,200 square meters]. We want to organize the territory, to get ahead. Then they came up, gathered together, came up and asked us how much land we wanted to organize as our territory, saying that our land up there is 1,950 *alqueires*. To get organized, to get the work done we are only 80 people, used to be 600. People died out . . . the older ones were missing the place, wanted to come back but couldn't. Talked about it, they arrested, beat us up, and people died. And there we are, 80 people in 13 *alqueires*.

Some people tried to get us 250 *alqueires,* which would be fine for us, but they didn't agree. Then, we went to the police chief in Valadares and he said, "But what do Indians want so much land for? Indians are lazy, don't work, this Krenak Indian who doesn't work, what does he want land for, he can eat fish and game." Well, in the old days the Indians had game to eat, had a lot of fish. Nowadays, how can the Indian live, 80 people within 13 *alqueires* of land? What is there to eat? Then, I ask all of you, brothers, here, to participate and we will be very grateful. And I ask you all not to weaken, face the battle, for the toad that stops is eaten by the snake. The toad always hops a little bit forward. We can never stop, for it's been 22 years since I've been suffering, but now, with God's will, I'm getting ahead, even if I hop one meter today, two meters tomorrow and, with God's will, I'll get there. Even if it is to leave to my children, my nieces and nephews, my cousins, to my community, I want to leave something. Thank you very much, all of you.

(The speech that follows was delivered by Alvaro Sampaio, a Tukanoan Indian from the Vaupés region, to an audience of Indians, lawyers, anthropologists, and other professionals who work on Indian issues. The panel was organized by the Brazilian Bar Association, Rio de Janeiro chapter, and took place in the city of Rio de Janeiro on November 18, 1981. See Ordem dos Advogados do Brasil 1981:81–84.)

I'll stand up because I can't talk while I sit here. Usually at the Indian assemblies I have attended the chief stands up when he speaks to give a better audience. I was born in mid-village in the State of Amazonas where there was no room, no doctor and I had never imagined that I would speak to intellectual people like these present here. And why is this? My presence here has a meaning, precisely to give a message. It is a message that will serve many people well, but for others it will be an alert. The discrimination the Brazilian Indian has been suffering from the times when this country was discovered to these days means that our country knows in fact—and conceals it—that which is called racism. In this sense the great mass of whites and the small number of Indians and the way of subordinating our fellowmen is not in accord with the dictates of law and justice. FUNAI, lately using the Indian Statute just like in the first times the white civilization used, in front of them, its word, has disarmed us so that we lose our lands. And FUNAI continues to do this. It places the Indian under the Indian Statute in order to do a better control. No one likes to be subordinated to others, listen to words, or be alienated, since man's principle is freedom. To be unable to participate, or to speak to one's superiors as, for example, the Indian to FUNAI, right in the middle of a country like Brazil, right in the times of democracy, this is not called democracy. To us it means imperialism and anti-democracy. The way of regarding the Indian, when the Indian begins to discover that his way and his destiny are not right, that's what makes us come to the big cities and give the public opinion a different knowledge from that it would never have. For, when we arrive here you're forced to listen and take this message to your families. Because the problem of the Brazilian Indian is not his alone, but of the Brazilian people. I'm speaking in this way because very often my word has been useful to many people. Emancipation and, lately, these criteria that FUNAI is throwing over the Indians, what does that all mean? Are we in full harmony? Myself and Marcos Terena, who is the president of the União das Nações Indígenas, are working, in the meantime, in front of the indigenous communities because many, as I have told you, are still asleep. And we are a proof of this. That the indigenous communities are exploited, omitted in any way and that they are innocent in front of people like us. For instance, I know what tricks FUNAI is playing over us; and nobody defends the other in this case. We are forced to speak like this, not because we want to, but because somebody forces us. It is the Indian Statute: the justice which is not done, and the law which these men ignore. And, unfortunately, gentlemen, lawyers, we have within FUNAI lawyers who study all day long to change the Indian Statute, and this Statute can't be changed because what it contains has never been put into practice. Even a few days ago, on the 12th of this month, me, Marcos Terena, my cousin Carlos Fernandes Machado, were having an interview with this new president. In accord with our non-governmental organization, we wanted to have been received as members of the board of directors of the União das Nações Indígenas. Unfortunately, our organization is a pejorative being to the nation. And we don't understand why. We don't understand why. To be an Indian inside this nation means to be shameful for other nations. It means a regression to the progress of Brazil. But to steal the Indian land, to commit injustice against him, that's what the people don't consider in fact. By people I mean men who are competent, who say they are competent, but in front of the indigenous eye they are not. Our conversation with the new president was like this. He found the word "Nações" can't be. In fact, we also know this. He said to us: "you must have the spirit of Brazilianness [brasilidade], Brazil is great and must be still greater." I answered: "That's why we came here to talk. Because very often we, Indians, the leaders, have most responsibility, more than any president of FUNAI or perhaps even of the Republic. If Brazil is great, it must be equal for all, not just for some people." I wanted to say this to him because so far the Indian had not spoken up and been heard in his international and national demands. That's why the Indian has his problems with land. That's why we go on insisting until he listens to what we want to do. He also said, the president, that we are picking a fight within the nation. No one is picking no fight, when he's making a claim. A son, when he goes to his father to claim his rights, the father gives. Many of them were misunderstood. On the other hand, the Indian becomes that who existed in the old days. But, in reality, the Indian continues to suffer in front of our eyes; it is the Indian himself who is looking for a way to self-determination. Self-determination doesn't mean separating from Brazil and be in the government. It means a desire of the Indian to participate in what the whiteman is participating, in the national communion, for we have the same ambitions as any whiteman and the same rights, but we can't say that, from one day to the next, we'll turn into whites. Because that's not up to us. This is outside our principle. I can't change, transform the president of the Republic into a Tukano, from one day to the next, because it's impossible. There is no law for it. Many of those military men who are in high positions, at the top of FUNAI, want to use the Indian as military and we feel ashamed. What will other military men say about these people? They have a pejorative idea of the indigenous communities. We can't stand being exploited any longer. No one likes to be exploited. For these words I've just said I take responsibility. Be this as it may, I think the Brazilian Bar Association will also join the Indian struggle to put Order and Justice in our Brazilian society.

(The speech that follows was delivered by Marcos Terena from the state of Mato Grosso do Sul, on the same occasion as the previous speech. See Ordem dos Advogados do Brasil 1981:76–80.)

I'm very pleased to be here amid scientists from law, anthropology and social fields. Having heard these remarks about the Indian issue in the country I feel a bit shy because we have just heard that, according to the criteria of Indianness, the Indian has to have the primitive mentality. Well, in front of a podium of wise people in the relevant subject matters, I have to declare myself an Indian and I proudly say this to you and say another thing; something that in my heart, in front of all this pile of papers which I know what it is, but many Indians don't even know exists. Well, what I have to say is that I feel highly honored with the opportunity you give me tonight; in this opportunity I can speak and I hope I will also be heard so that everything that has been debated here will be useful for our work, but that it can also be reverted as a concrete benefit for all Brazilian Indians who, who knows, would like to be here, but can't. The privilege given to me provides me with the chance to, in my name and in the name of my family, the Indian family, also thank all of you who are in this house, a house I consider to be of men dedicated to the law and to what is right.

For several centuries those men who were named Indians were able to live in peace, with their own customs, their own traditions, what is called culture. But one day into their homes, Indian homes, came men who at first showed themselves to be friendly, but later, deceitfully, betrayed the trust put in that relationship. Until very recently, only a few years ago, I think in the '70s, we heard—perhaps many of you have also heard that right now, in the middle of the 20th century, there were people proud of saying that they were Indian hunters, a fact I consider shameful for a nation which sees itself as potent as many others and which I consider the greatest in South America.

Although there has been, since 1910, a federal agency for the protection of these people who were the first inhabitants of this country called Brazil; although powerful instruments have been created which the whiteman respects (and if he does not respect, at least he fears) which are called laws; although this kind of support exists, the Indian continues to be abused in his rights, respect for which very often depends less on the law, I think, than on solidarity and human respect. Today, looking around me as an Indian, as a Brazilian, knowing two societies, two civilizations, I have worried a lot about law, about justice, because many times I've heard that people who have killed a fellow human being have not been imprisoned. On the other hand, I have also heard of people who were in jail for a long time without having committed any fault or murder. In analyzing things of this kind I only think, not as an expert like you gentlemen, but with the sensitivity of a human being who has always respected the most basic things, from a small twig falling off a tree, to the whole universe, I know that there is in the country a law called Constitution; I also know that there is a law called Human Rights; also another called Geneva Convention and, particularly to deal with Indian affairs, there is a law number 6001 called the Indian Statute, not to speak of the various international agreements and recommendations to which Brazil subscribed and took a position vis-à-vis other countries. In all this maze of laws, decrees, recommendations, of endless legal paperwork, is the person of the Indian, an Indian who, even though massacred, cheated and forgotten, reappears as a myth, as a thing that doesn't exist. Very often, in the minds of Brazilians, what I call the majority society, there is that Indian who comes armed with arrows and clubs, painted in various colors, good to be photographed, to be made stories over, who makes pretty crafts and who is a source of funds both to FUNAI and to those who exploit that sort of thing. For some he is naive, savage, stubborn; for others he is an obstacle obstructing progress. Everybody talks, everybody debates the Indian issue, but no one has ever shown concern or, if he has, has not been heard, with what was really in the heart of the Indian, besides distrust or perhaps fear. FUNAI is here a guardian of the Indian. The laws are here to protect the Indian, and I ask you: where is the Indian? Where is the Indian going? I ask a very specific question of you who are listening to me tonight: in what way have you cooperated with the Indian? Today you're here, listening to my speech. My hope is that, by talking to you, I am contributing to alert you about things Indian. The Indian is also a Brazilian, although he has his own language, his own customs, his own world, a totally different world. I act and speak like an Indian because the Indian wants to speak and be heard; to respect but being respected too; and to participate, gradually and harmoniously, somehow, as a Brazilian; and more, as a native Brazilian. His culture, his customs, his traditions must be respected as sacred and valuable for each and every people. Why does the whiteman use malice to cheat the Indian?

Why doesn't the whiteman respect the value the Indians put on land, according to their conception of it? Land is a fundamental element for the survival of Indian peoples. I believe the mere fact of your being gathered here, under the roof of the Brazilian Bar Association in Rio de Janeiro, is in itself an attempt to comply by exercising real Justice in the application of the laws in defense of these peoples called forest dwellers [*silvícolas*]. The demarcation of Indian land is essential for the definition of what Indian territory is, but I think it will have been useless to demarcate if there is no Indian to inhabit it. And a population will have a chance to grow and be strong if it has medical assistance and education. I also think that FUNAI's role is clear in the law. There is a specific law about it. It wasn't the Indian who invented it. It wasn't the Indian who asked for it. But it's there. I think the law exists and FUNAI exists. They're there. What is lacking then? I think that what is lacking is to find effective ways for FUNAI to defend its wards, to defend the Indians. When I see the Brazilian development programs I feel that Brazil is moving, at a fast pace, toward development, toward its interior, toward what is called progress. Will the law and goodwill alone be enough to give security and self-defense to peoples who only know how to make a living off the land? I hope that, within your possibilities, something concrete can be done, something that is really geared toward the Indian populations, which are few. As someone here said, demarcation should be easy, but it isn't. I would like you to think of those Indians who, right at this moment, who knows, are sleeping with empty bellies. Perhaps it doesn't depend completely on FUNAI, but on all those who feel themselves to be Brazilian and who can say so with pride. What I can say to you is that I am proud of being able to speak as an Indian and transmit this message because, in the same way as you're listening to me, there are many people who call themselves Brazilians and don't like to raise the subject. I hope that you of the Bar Association, anthropologists, sociologists, all of you who can hear me tonight will make of the Indian movement or of the Indian cause not just an excuse to say "I'm defending the Indian," but think of means for you to help the Indian, the Indian who is in his village. I consider myself privileged because I've learned your language while you haven't learned mine. I consider myself privileged for going to the University, while many of you struggle for years to do the same and don't succeed. Thus, my message is that you must regard the Indian from the point of view of the law, based on the organizational structure such as FUNAI, the government agency, to find a way for you to collaborate toward the growth of the Indian side by side with you, and not as an isolated society, as someone has said. A different society, by all means, but with the same feelings as any Brazilian, who knows how to love, to feel, and who wants to find in you also the thought that it is possible to join efforts to make our country less small, less mean about the Indian issue.

Speeches as Texts, Audiences as Readers

Frozen on the page, these speeches lose a gamut of communicative links with the audience—fleeting facial expressions, voice inflections, pitch, pause, speed, gestures, looks, innuendos of all sorts—only to gain the permanence of the recorded message, untrimmed, unqualified, unaltered. In the written version there is no mediating gesture, no sympathetic glance, no emphatic silence. We who read them have to content ourselves with this impoverished rendering of the speakers' dialogic effort. But, although the gesture is unseen, the silence unheard, and the glance no longer caught, the speech turned into text acquires a force of its own. We who were not there to see and hear the speakers, even though away from them in space and time, are able to appreciate their message, understand their plight, and interpret their posture. The ephemeral moment of the spoken word is transformed into fixed discourse to which we can turn again and again to discover new, even surprising meanings. The congealed text, a contribution from the world of the whitemen (Goody 1968), can then become an effective tool in the struggle of the Indians against the very same whitemen.[1] For most Indians in Brazil and elsewhere, orality is the privileged medium of communication. But they increasingly recognize that the written word is more powerful and appropriate in contexts such as legal claims, political manifestos, or whenever the only way to be heard is through literacy.

The three speeches translated here can be displayed and commented upon, reaching a different, if not wider, audience simply because they were originally written down. In contrast to the speed of events surrounding the politics of contact, these speeches, in their textuality, have gained a permanence in some ways equivalent to the memory of peoples without writing. The fixity of the written text fulfills the whites' need, to which the Indians comply if they are to hold the whiteman as their interlocutor. Writing is thus transformed into one more political tool.

For an English-speaking readership I have translated the speeches from Portuguese. This act raises another set of considerations. Particularly in the second speech, I had to face the problem of its incongruities, some grammatical, some lexical, but on the whole much subtler than those in the first speech. These incongruities give the second speech a very special flavor; but how do we transmit that in a foreign language? Given that translation is always an act of treason (captured in the saying "traduttore, traditore"), I began with two alternatives: to find equivalent incongruities in the English language, which I am ill equipped to do, not being an English speaker myself; or to ignore them in translation, present the text in English, and point out that the incongruities exist in the original. In the end I opted for a third alternative: literal translation from Portuguese. The oddities thus produced are probably greater than the original text deserves, but my intention is simply to call the reader's attention to the disjointed, yet catchy, character of some of the utterances. Sampaio's speeches, which in a grammatical sense are slightly out of sync, have always seized his audiences in a way that is more powerful than, for instance, Terena's flawless speeches in Portuguese.

Let us now examine each of the speeches and try to capture some of the components of individual style in this political genre. Each reveals something about the speaker, his political trajectory, his position vis-à-vis whites, the multifaceted contact situation, and the Indian movement.

The first speaker, a Krenak Indian from the state of Minas Gerais, reveals a mode of expression quite common among Indians who are making their first appearance in the field of contact politics. The well-being of his own people is his main concern. Nothing in Paulino's discourse indicates a commitment to the indigenous movement at large; rather, he appeals to his companions as an audience for his telling about his people's sufferings. His particularist speech has the same tone as many others uttered in similar contexts of Indian meetings: a long list of grievances against the whites, responsible as they are for the depletion of resources, the invasion of traditional territories, anxiety about the future, lack of communication, and disrespect for indigenous ways of life. This Krenak man is representative of those Indian leaders whose point of reference is the immediate community and who have not as yet grasped the sociopolitical meanders of the national society.

The passage from the traditional politics of persuasion to the imposed politics of coercion, exercised by the Brazilian state, is vehemently portrayed by Paulino in terms of stark, naked violence. Arrests, beatings, forceful removals, expropriations—these are some of its ugliest faces. The epitome of such violence was the establishment, referred to in the speech, of the Crenaque jail for Indians, which was in operation for several years. In just a few words the speaker summarizes the long history of this type of treatment, common to so many other Indian peoples and intensely lived by his people in a matter of two decades. The condensed language, the use of metaphor and parable (e.g., the toad and the snake) give his individual style a candor that is so often the strength of indigenous discourses in Portuguese. Paulino's understanding of the whiteman encompasses not a simplified, stereotyped opponent but a complex, multifaceted other: the captain who helped to relocate his people, the police chief who disdained the capacity of the Indians for work, those anonymous friends of the Indians who tried to get more land for them. In about twenty years this man continually has had to expand his horizon to accommodate all these figures and situations previously unknown to him. He reaches forward in search of a solution to his people's problems, hoping to achieve a satisfactory modus vivendi, good enough to be passed on to the coming generations, even though the "good old days" are gone forever. Punctuating this tragic story is the poignant theme of the longing that kills, the well-known tale of old people who want to return home and, unable to adjust to a new environment, simply give up and die.

The other two speakers exhibit a much greater fluency in political discourse and a much greater familiarity with the ways of the whiteman. The second speaker is a Tukanoan Indian from the Vaupés region in the Northwest Amazon. He was educated by Salesian missionaries and as a youth went to Manaus, was in the army for a while, then tried to enter the university there before becoming involved in the Indian movement. In 1980 he participated in the fourth Russell Tribunal in the Netherlands, where he denounced the activities of the Salesians as ethnocidal. This cost him much anxiety due to the campaign the missionaries launched against him among the Indian communities. His expressed desire notwithstanding, he has not gone back to live with his own people, spending his time in São Paulo, Manaus, and other South American countries where he interacts closely with the Peruvian and Ecuadorian Indian movements. He has had a very important role in the Brazilian Indian movement as a vehement spokesman for the defense of Indian rights against FUNAI, missionaries, and most whites. The aggressive tone of his discourse reveals much of his life history. His sometimes vociferous speeches unveil his personal drama as a young Indian: the conflict between the ideal of returning to his people and the urge to go on with the political struggle at the national level.

Sampaio's discourse also shows a strong effort to involve the audience by using expressions and references that come from the political context of the whites themselves. The imagery is directly political with its most "civilized" accent: the military, the concept of autodetermination, the notions of imperialism and democracy, the desideratum of equal opportunities—these are all symbols in political discourses by Brazilians who were opposed to the military government. The appeal to these symbols is particularly great for an audience made sympathetic by the common experience of being ruled by a regime of force. In spite of frequent semantic incongruities, Sampaio delivers a powerful message, and his anger is not lost on his audience/readers. His discourse suggests a difference between sense and meaning: while at times the sense is fuzzy, the meaning is quite clear.

Most important in this speech is the reference to "nations within a nation." Banning the designation "União das Nações Indígenas," the military authorities and, I must add, the civilian government that followed them, have argued that such a proposition conflicts with national security by representing a potential cleavage in the country's sovereignty.[2] It is argued that to propose the establishment of nations within the Brazilian nation is to be unpatriotic, particularly on the part of the Indians who carry different traditions, speak different languages, and are said to be highly manipulable by foreign interests. Furthermore, to create Indian nations would go against the official policy of integrating the Indians into the national society. The reference to *brasilidade* by the president of FUNAI is a condensed way of expressing this policy: from being the first occupants of the land the Indians have been turned into a threat to national security. The tone of confrontation in this speech is a reaction to such distortion. Sampaio's speech also reveals a most cherished notion that the Indians should be equal to whites yet maintain their cultural differences, which is entirely at odds with the official interpretation of what integration should be (i.e., a total melting of the Indian population into the undifferentiated mass of Brazilians).

As deeply involved in the Indian movement as Sampaio, the third speaker shows a completely different style. Also a youth who left his village to study in the city (first in Campo Grande, then in Brasília), Terena joined the movement just before the creation of the União das Nações Indígenas, which he served as one of its first presidents. As a pilot he tried for a long time to work for FUNAI, being turned down repeatedly by the colonels who ruled the Indian Foundation in the seventies and early eighties. His tendency to salvage FUNAI as a legitimate organism for the defense of Indian rights is quite visible in his speech, albeit expressed in a critical manner: FUNAI's establishment as the result of the whiteman's endless laws, which are made without consulting those affected by them. Amid the tangle of legal paperwork, the Indians remain helpless, unless the whites adopt a more engaged and committed stand.

Although very critical of the performance of the Brazilian government regarding Indian policy and treatment, Terena has held on to his conviction that working from within the system is as valid as confrontation from outside. For this he has paid the price of mistrust from companions and supportive whites, who have accused him of being co-opted. His discourse has elements both of criticism and hope in the possible effectiveness of FUNAI to care for the Indians' interests. It contains much of his political project of being part of the system in order to change it, without relinquishing interest in the movement.

Terena tries to use the whites' own weapons—education, for instance—to fight them.

As in Sampaio's speech, the different-but-equal theme is ever present in Terena's speech. Whites must recognize that the Indians are Brazilians too, as capable, or more so, of handling aspects of white society, such as the national language or the universities. The double sense of *brasilidade* appears quite clearly if we compare the meaning attributed to it by the president of FUNAI in the second speech and that given to it in the third. The two men obviously are not speaking of the same thing. While the former implies the dissolution of Indianness, the latter affirms the opposite: Brazilian Indian yes, but still, and above all, Indian. Terena's apparent apology for the great Brazilian nation is a skillfully constructed trope, designed to reach a critical coda: Brazil will not mature as a developed nation if its Indians continue to be treated as "a myth, as a thing that doesn't exist"!

Terena's appointment in 1984 to the position of chief of staff for one of the most progressive—some would say grossly populist—presidents of FUNAI, a civilian in the military era, was received with ambivalence. But even those who were suspicious of Terena's authenticity granted that his and other Indians' appointments were historically important. For the first time Indians were placed in the higher echelons of the FUNAI bureaucracy; for the first time the Indians themselves were in charge of part of the government body of which they are wards. However, this achievement can be viewed as a double-edged sword, for a new breed of "Indian" emerged, the *Indio funcionário* (the bureaucratic Indian), a category of apparently self-interested, job-hungry young men who would rather oppose the Indian movement than risk their newly acquired positions. Once again the authorities succeeded in the practice of "divide and conquer." As the political face of the country and of the FUNAI changed in the mid-1980s, this trend was in part replaced by another short-lived surge—a rash of Indian candidates to the House of Representatives on the eve of the drawing up of the new Constitution. Among these candidates were Sampaio and Terena; none of the Indian candidates were elected.

The Symbolism of Contact

To say that indigenous societies are not static is to say the obvious. Even if we view them as "peoples without history," it is widely recognized that the various mechanisms of their internal dynamics can and do result in considerable changes as generations come and go. Most observers now agree that when the West intruded, the Rest was already in motion. Nevertheless, it is impossible to minimize the impact of Europeans on indigenous peoples. The advent of the whiteman is an undeniable "founding event," to use Ricoeur's (1978:40) phrase.

Interethnic contact has produced the figure of the Indian for whites and the whiteman for Indians. The image and influence of the whiteman have precipitated a whole range of symbolic elaborations for indigenous societies, from myths to millenarianism to political movements. There is virtually no Indian society left on the South American continent that is unaware of the whiteman. His image, transformed into so many local versions, pervades the modes of thought and modes of being of most indigenous peoples. By penetrating the Indians' lives, interethnic contact has contributed to the renewal of Indian traditions. And since tradition is constantly being reshaped—for a static tradition, as Gadamer (1975) says, is a dead tradition—the phenomenon of contact comes to feed into this process of ongoing transformation. Even amid the most vicious forms of domination, ranging from slavery, labor exploitation, punitive expeditions, and land usurpation, to disease transmission, no Indian society has endured contact without exercising some sort of creative reaction. The influence of the whites is not limited to their incorporation into speech genres and modes of expression. In fact, this very incorporation creates states of mind and affect that predispose the Indians to interact with whites in certain ways; and this, in turn, contributes to the character of contact.

At the root of the transformations triggered by contact is the passage from a system characterized by the politics of persuasion to one defined by the politics of coercion. Indians accustomed to conducting their lives on the basis of group consensus are apt to be shocked, if not traumatized, by the imposition of the rule of force or threat of force brought to them by the whites, be they administrators, free-enterprise invaders, or missionaries. It is the enforcement of this politics of coercion that gives the contact situation its particular character of domination and inequality.

The political arena of which the three speeches presented earlier are part is one of several spheres in which the whiteman looms large. For now let us assume that the symbolic realm of contact can be divided into three orders: mythic, historical, and political. Each one would generate its own symbolic arrangements, its own discourse, its own praxis. Among these orders, the politics of contact is the most recent manifestation and should be understood as part of a larger symbolic universe that also contains the myths and historical narratives that make use of the figure of the whiteman. For each order there is a genre; and sometimes there is much blurring between genres.

What distinguishes these genres is not so much the symbols proper as the use that is made of them and the audiences to which they are addressed: for instance, time is suspended in myths, past-oriented in the case of "old times" narratives (or future-oriented in the case of millenarianism), and concerned with a progressive present in the political arena of interethnic contact. Whereas in the mythic genre events are neutralized by the use of metaphor and allegory, and in the historical genre events are controlled by hindsight, in the political genre they are confronted by actions that are specifically directed toward white society. Different from myths and historical narratives that are produced for internal consumption, to be told around the household fire or in the village plaza, political speeches delivered in lecture halls, church basements, or the National Congress require the actual presence of whites. A genre that until recently was foreign to Brazilian Indians, the speech of protest has become their main vehicle for visibility as legitimate social agents in a country that shuns official recognition of its undeniable multiethnic reality.

Most national Indian leaders operate both in white society and in indigenous communities. On the one hand, they are exposed to the traditional expressions of their own people; on the other, they pass on to their people their own experiences in the interethnic camp. To what extent the ingredients of contact politics feed into the mythic and historical genres of the communities is yet to be properly investigated, but it would be surprising if the former did not influence the latter. It is to be expected that events from the political field are incorporated into an ongoing stream of interpretations that contribute to the dynamic character of specific indigenous traditions.

From Compartmentalized to Holistic Thinking

Returning to the issue of different orders in the symbolism of contact: if the division of a "totality" into portions is of great heuristic value for the purpose of describing, analyzing, and communicating our acquired knowledge to an audience, then, our language being what it is, especially in written form, there is a risk that such division might take on an aura of "reality," replacing the originating context. In truth, reification happens all the time. The hardening of our disciplinary language creates a reality of its own, follows its own path, and imposes its own rules and interpretations. If we say, or write, often enough that the story of the anaconda giving birth to the people in the Vaupés is a myth and as such is a static exercise in bricolage, we end up fixing the story in a rigid category, which is then quickly exhausted by our analytic logic. Once a myth, always a myth; and who would dare call it politics or history? Actually, in the mythic order, as in other orders, there is already a universe of commentary about life, the world, time, space, stasis, and movement that transcends any attempt to slice up lived experience. The rationale for separating spheres, be they myth, history, politics, geography, or whatever, is not in the indigenous discourses themselves but in our need to organize ethnographic material into familiar categories in order to make sense of it in our own terms and in those of our readers. Ironically, in our attempt to capture totality, we compartmentalize and tend to forget that this categorization is only an "as if" proposition.

The indigenous way of thinking as revealed in what we, not they, call myths, narratives, and so on, challenges the habits of compartmentalization that anthropology has inherited along with the scientific premises of Western rationalism and empiricism. Our difficulty is to perceive and express a holistic, undifferentiated, semantically blended universe of cross-cutting messages. But, while we cannot reproduce the original context in which this blending occurs, it is not impossible to do an intelligent and intelligible rendering of it. I see the indigenous political movement as a passage from holistic thinking to compartmentalized thinking, a necessary device if the Indians are to make themselves effectively understood or heard by the whiteman. However, that does not mean that they must replace one mode of thinking with the other. Rather, if they have learned to use our mode of expression without abandoning their own, why can't we do the same? If we try to blend the genres, we may find that under a rhetorical mode we have called "mythic" there is a sense of history which, obviously, encompasses the political sphere of contact. How can we be so sure that all those myths of the whiteman, of the beginning of agriculture, the building of the universe, the creation of disease and death, are not manifestations of an indigenous historical consciousness that we do not recognize as such because they come in a package that does not fit into our compartments? Conversely, much of what comes to us as historical facts may, under closer scrutiny, turn out to be as fictitious as our conception of what myths are.[3]

It would certainly be wrong to take myth for history if we transferred to the Indians our premise that history requires objectivity and the assumption of a realistic unfolding of sequential events, as opposed to mythic bricolage. However, if we accept that language is bricolage, how can history or politics, or even science, not be bricolage, since it is human and everything human happens in language (Derrida 1970:256)?

If history, like myth, is a concretization of bricolage, or fiction, as Certeau (1986:199–221) argues, then the categorical opposition of these genres becomes somewhat dubious.

It may be objected that, since the category "history" is a Western concept and invention, it is not fair to use it for something other than what it is intended to be. Here again, there is the risk of letting words crystallize, eliminating the possibility of a candid wide-angle look at otherness at its most otherliness. It is legitimate for us to organize the universe into categories that we can understand, so long as we do not reify those categories. We should not confuse heuristic value with empirical value. Furthermore, we must be aware of the ever-present tendency in Western thinking for the former to have supremacy over the latter. If we need to separate some things as myths, others as history, and yet others as politics, it should be clear that we do so at our own risk and for our own benefit; we must recognize this separation for what it is, that is, an operational device rather than an ontological reality. To insist on dividing "primitive" from "historical" societies is to add to the intellectual apparatus of domination, to build a sort of indigenist Orientalism (Said 1979).

So far anthropologists have played the role of translators to white audiences. But more and more we will have to face the issue of communicating with the peoples from whom we learn. We are getting closer and closer to a time when our articles and books will have to be written with Indian readerships in mind. Will we know how to do it? Will we be believed? Will we know how to respond to their questioning or challenging interpretations which, necessarily, will be different from ours? And, perhaps most difficult of all, will we be able to reconstruct our language in such a way as to do justice to the amazing wealth of imagination and aesthetic resourcefulness we find in the field? (For example, we may question whether a Portuguese version of this essay would be readable and/or acceptable to the Indian leaders about whom I write. And even if it were understood by them as an intellectual exercise, what about the ethical problems it raises?) Is it, in other words, possible to avoid the tendency to objectify our subjects of study in our pursuit of anthropological understanding?

For centuries the whiteman has been the Indians' most imposing "significant other." Far from being "peoples without history" with "totemic" minds, the Indians are and have always been engaged in interpretations and reinterpretations of contact. Their historical consciousness does not follow the path of a Western-style historicity, and if we are to adequately capture the expressions of this consciousness, we must revise our attitude toward categorizing the world. We must benefit from influences outside the field of traditional anthropology, not the least significant of which are the examples of the Indians themselves.

Interethnic Indian: A Political Actor in Search of a Role

Brazilian Indians are increasingly using literacy as a weapon in their political actions. They recognize that orality has a limited efficacy in a world in which the hegemony of the West has been established via the extraordinary power of the written word. Indigenous peoples are now articulating their traditional ways of expression with the adoption of Western channels such as writing, tape-recording, radio, and television. But it seems that these new media are not displacing old modes of thought; rather, they are providing indigenous peoples with more effective means to conduct their struggle for recognition as legitimate others.

What do Brazilian Indians do with these new media? There are two trends: one seeks equality through similarity with whites; the other tries to achieve equality through equivalence. The first emphasizes the need to occupy spaces that have always been taken by the whiteman; the second tries to show that the Indian ways of being are as valid as those of the whiteman.

In contrast to the Shuar Indians, for example, who refuse to enter directly into the state machinery of Ecuador, some Indian leaders in Brazil have shown a strong tendency to go into party politics. The degree of success has been minimal and the results somewhat disastrous. Witness the career of the Shavante leader Mario Juruna: elected by an urban constituency of Rio de Janeiro (and not his native Mato Grosso), Juruna was used by his party leaders as a symbol of oppression under the military regime, as a representative of a dubious Brazilianness emanating from the dispossessed, long-suffering, helpless Brazilian people. At a time when no white voices had the freedom to protest, Juruna, illiterate and ignorant of the complexity of national politics but protected by his Indianness—that is, he is a ward of the state—was encouraged to bombard the government with caustic criticisms which nearly cost him his office in 1983. As the political climate of the country opened up, Juruna was no longer useful. Following his involvement in a senseless scandal over accusations of corruption, he was gradually discarded from the political scene and failed to be re-elected in 1986. Like a ghost, he now wanders the rooms and hallways of the National Congress in Brasilia.

More realistic and enlightened, the leaders of the União das Nações

Indígenas, both at the national and regional levels, have opted for grass-roots, unspectacular, long-term work at consciousness-raising in the communities, emphasizing Indianness as a value to be preserved. Several of these leaders have been pressured by the church to avoid confrontation with the government, and as a result they have been pushed into the background of the indigenous movement.

While the regional leaders have the possibility of combining militancy with community life, those who operate out of cities, such as São Paulo, Brasilia, or Manaus, are cut off from the everyday routine of the indigenous world. They travel regularly to the villages, but, at least in some cases, they are virtual outsiders, albeit "kinsmen" who are welcome for bringing news and hope. Radio programs and television and newspaper interviews with these leaders are not infrequent, and their eloquence can move listeners, viewers, and readers, who, expecting to hear and read broken Portuguese, are often surprised by their articulateness.

The cost of political activism to Indian leaders can be extremely high. Heavy drinking, marginalization at home and elsewhere, generalized distrust of the world, anguish, psychological confusion, and even assassinations are some of the burdens that make the life of most Indian leaders in Brazil a personal drama that is sometimes more than they can endure. Add to all this the ever-present possibility of manipulation and co-optation as an instrument to undermine their integrity, and we can sense the predicament facing a critical Indian fighting against the current.

In dealing with indigenous discourses about whites, the adage that "always the meaning of a text goes beyond its author" (Gadamer 1975:264) could not be more appropriate. The unveiling of layers of meaning contained in the three speeches presented here is an exercise in interpretation of the equivocality of symbols. The same symbol can be used for one purpose by a speaker and for the opposite purpose by another. The image of FUNAI and the notion of Brazilianness are examples of this equivocality. What emerges from the joint voices of the Indians is that their movement is a rebellion against political invisibility. In their collective cry to be seen and heard and taken into consideration, the Indians appeal to the efficacy of certain symbols they know will strike home among whites. In this they are no different from the powers-that-be when the latter invoke, for instance, the image of the flag, the sound of the national anthem, the idea of Union, of *brasilidade,* in an attempt to amass popular support and build legitimacy.

The multidimensional character of speeches such as those reproduced here emerges in both genre and style. The context is interethnic, the genre is political, the styles vary from individual to individual, revealing a bit of the life history of each speaker. In the performative act of delivering a speech, the Indians are turned into actors engaged in communication with a specific audience. Who are the possible audiences for an Indian speaker performing a political act in an interethnic situation? Most of the time they have been Indians in assembly or white sympathizers, be they anthropologists, lawyers, journalists, students, or members of other minorities. There are also occasions when the audience is composed of bureaucrats or politicians. For each of these various modalities of listeners a different rhetorical effort is made, putting to test the stylistic versatility of the speakers.

Speeches transformed into texts are a valuable tool for understanding the trajectories of Indian leaders along the road of interethnic contact. Because they are permanently available, texts can speak to us in several ways at different times, providing us with a variety of angles from which to study the messages they contain. A sensitive look at textualized speeches can give us some insights, preliminary as they may be, into what recondite corners of the speakers' personalities have been most affected by the violence of prejudice, discrimination, and social injustice. For example, the tone of the speeches—some delivered in a tortured language, some in open confrontational style, some in cautious compromise, most of them as desperate pleas for justice—tells us a great deal about the speakers. Like actors in search of a role, Brazilian indigenous leaders keep struggling to establish a place in national society on equal terms with whites, a place from which they can express themselves directly to the nation's authorities without the intermediacy and frequent misrepresentation of their custodian, the National Indian Foundation. Like actors on a gigantic stage, they strive to be acknowledged by the public in their roles as citizens of a double world—the Brazilian nation and their own societies.

Texts such as these can be the starting point for ethnographic encounters sufficiently dense to reveal the intricacies inherent in the process of forging an interethnic being. But besides opening a door to the understanding of a certain human type—the "interethnic Indian"—such texts also lend themselves to certain theoretical explorations in anthropology, with the potential to uncover dimensions that, until recently, had been left unexplored. The complexities of Indian/white relations in South America indicate that incursions into fields of thought traditionally outside the immediate range of anthropology may not only be opportune but perhaps necessary if we are to pursue our quest for a deeper understanding of what it is to be an Indian in this century on the South American continent.

NOTES

My thanks to Mariza Peirano for her critical reading of this essay.

1. An equivalent device, the tape recorder, was effectively used by the Shavante leader Mario Juruna in his meetings with governmental authorities as a political instrument that allowed him to catch many a lie and cause much embarrassment when those lies were picked up by the press. The tape recorder played an important role in the image making that led Juruna to be elected to the House of Representatives in Brasilia in 1982 (Hohlfeldt and Hoffmann 1982).

2. In the late 1980s, the military branch of Brazil's civilian government argues for the military occupation of the country's northern border. Part of their rhetoric in justifying this position is their fear that the Yanomami Indians who live both in Brazil and Venezuela may organize themselves as an independent nation. To give substance to such rhetoric the military are carrying out what is known as Projeto Calha Norte, a massive plan for the installation of outposts, complete with full-size runways, banking agencies, and other facilities, right in the middle of several Yanomami villages and among other Indian groups in that vast region.

3. See, for instance, Galeano (1981:204–14) for a version of the history of the "Paraguayan War" that is completely different from the version taught in Brazilian schools.

Commentary

Ethno-Ethnohistory: Myth and History in Native South American Representations of Contact with Western Society

Terence Turner

General Issues

History, Myth, "Cold" Society, "Hot" Society

The current theoretical discussion of the relation of culture and history can be seen in the broadest terms as a continuation of the perennial struggles of anthropological theory to reconcile the notions of structure and individual, society and culture. These issues are very much to the fore in this collection of papers, and we have the organizers of the 1984 AAA symposium entitled "From History to Myth in South America" to thank for having chosen a theme that so aptly focuses the relation between cultural form and historical social action. As a group, these essays well exemplify Cohn's (1980:215, 217) remark, made in a slightly different but parallel connection: "Studying [anthropology] in an historical mode would shift the anthropologist away from the objectification of social life to a study of its constitution and construction.... What started as a new kind of [anthropological] history will bring us back to questions about the construction of culture."

This said, perhaps the best thing about this collection of essays is the way they go beyond the assumptions implicit in the title of the symposium. South American cultures, as they richly demonstrate, do not simply absorb "hot" historical events into "cold" mythic structures. They have their own forms of historical consciousness, which coexist and interact with mythic formulations of various kinds. Furthermore, in many cases myth can be seen to provide the foundation for historical awareness and action, rather than serving as a device for suppressing or preventing them.

The relationship between myth and history, in brief, appears to be fundamental to the formation of social consciousness throughout the South American continent, and it is more various, more subtle, and more dynamic than that implied in the terms of the original call for papers. As the historical record itself makes clear, myth in South America has not been merely a passive device for classifying historical "events" but a program for orienting social, political, ritual, and other forms of historical action. This is attested in the most dramatic way by the many messianic rebellions and resistance struggles led by mythically chartered leaders in all parts of the South American continent, a number of which are discussed in the essays in this volume. Not only "from history to myth," then, but also, and equally, "from myth to history."

Another important point: the formulation "from history to myth" implicitly treats history as a category of concrete social events (such as the first contact between Western and indigenous societies), in contrast to myth as a form of collective consciousness or cultural structure. The historical experience of the native peoples of South America, and specifically their interaction and conflict with European conquerors and encroaching national societies, thus becomes magically transformed into the theoretical program of two converging orthodoxies, namely, American cultural anthropology and French structuralism. This program may be concisely stated: isolate and focus upon pure cultural form to the exclusion of social dynamics; dismiss disorderly event and unruly action as irrelevant to ordered structure; declare the irrelevance of material, "causal-functional" relations to "logico-meaningful" patterns; and thus pass from the apparent anarchy of parole to the essential, underlying truths of langue. As most of the essays in this collection amply demonstrate, however, this theoretical agenda, whatever its resonances with the ideological history of the late twentieth-century Western world, only mystifies the dialectical interplay of history and myth, society and culture, event and structure, in the tortured histories of native South American peoples and their struggles to preserve themselves and their cultures against the encroachments of Western civilization.

An important point this formulation overlooks is that history is not merely a record of concrete events but also, like myth, a form of social consciousness. It thus leads us to omit the whole critical question of the historical consciousness of indigenous societies from the agenda. From this omission it is a short and easy step to the Procrustean dichotomy between mythic natives and historical Westerners: that is, "cold" societies and "hot" societies.

As many of the essays in this volume bear witness, however, historical consciousness is well developed and widespread among native peoples
of the Amazon and the Andes. This is not merely a "cultural" point: it is
central to the continuing ability of the peoples of both regions to make
their own histories at the level of concrete events. Not only "from myth
to history," then, but "from history to history."

Moreover, since the same South American peoples who have developed
their own forms of historical awareness also in most cases possess lively
and well-developed mythologies, it seems clear that myth and history
cannot be conceived as mutually incompatible modes of consciousness
or as consecutive stages of cultural evolution. Rather, they must be
considered in some sense complementary and mutually informing (a
relation to be discussed later in more detail). Not "from myth to history,"
then, but "myth and history together," in parallel, as two sides of the
same coin.

Shifting the focus of the discussion to myth and history as complementary modes of social consciousness, or, if one prefers, cultural
structure, raises a whole series of questions that have received surprisingly little attention in the recent anthropological literature on history.
Foremost among these is that of the distinctive criteria of history and
myth as comparative cultural categories. This question, in turn, leads to
another. Once clearly distinguished from each other, are history and
myth to be understood as essentially uniform in their various cultural
manifestations, or do they vary significantly in ways related to the
societies in which they arise? Another question already raised in passing is that of whether the two modes are, after all, contradictory and
incompatible, perhaps associated with different types of society or levels
of cultural development, or rather complementary, or at least potentially compatible aspects of the same cultural formations. If the latter,
does this relationship hold only for very simple societies like some of
those in the Amazonian lowlands, or does it hold at all levels of social
complexity? Finally, what is the relation between myth and history as
modes of consciousness and the genres, contexts, and structures of the
texts (narratives or other cultural forms) through which they are
expressed? These questions clearly involve a number of fundamental
issues of anthropological theory.

Another major focus of recent anthropological theorizing to which
this volume contributes is what I have elsewhere called the "peripheral situation" (Turner 1986) of interaction between native societies
and the expanding frontiers of Western capitalism, and in particular
the relationship between this situation and the genesis of modern
anthropology. By concentrating on indigenous forms of consciousness

of interaction with Western societies, the contributors here seek to invert the terms of the perspective from which our discipline arose. Anthropology was born out of the discovery of Otherness: the social, physical, cultural, and religious alienness of the non-Western peoples encountered by Europeans and their descendants in the past six centuries of Western expansion and imperialism. By examining the images of Westerners and Western society formed by the Others during this process of Western expansion, the contributors to this volume enable us to see ourselves as the others' Others, or in effect as the objects of other anthropologies. This exercise, as many of these essays demonstrate, can not only be instructive in revealing the terms and categories in which others have represented their experience of contact with the West but can also become a potent context for reflecting on the fundamental theoretical categories of Western anthropological and historical perspectives.

It is important to be clear that, in focusing a discussion of the relation between history and myth on the interaction between indigenous and Western societies, we do not assume that contact with Europeans or local Western societies marks the first involvement of native cultures in the dynamic processes of conflict, contradiction, and change that we call history. In some recent writings (e.g., Sahlins 1981, 1985), the unique events of the first contact between the native society and the alien Europeans tend to be pressed into service as a historical metaphor for the theoretical myth of the alienness of historical events as such to the cultural "structure" of the "cold" native society in question. None of the contributors here appear to fall into this fallacy of misplaced Fahrenheit. To think in terms of "cold" societies, as several of these essays point out in so many words, is all too often to commit the double error of failing to recognize the role of social dynamics and historical contradiction in their formation and reproduction and of ignoring the events and changes the members of such societies themselves find significant (the latter point is well put by Rosaldo 1980:27–28).

It is, in sum, essential not to slip into facile theoretical dualisms in which the complex relation between native and Western societies is represented by simplistic polarities like culture : society :: structure : event :: myth (as the epitome of cultural structure) : history (as an unstructured series of "conjunctures" or social interactions). Rather, we must begin, as do most of the contributors to this volume, by recognizing in theory as well as in fact that the "structures" of native sociocultural systems are formed by social and historical processes involving conflict and change. Conversely, the situations of contact between native and Western societies do not consist simply of "events" but generate their own structures. Western myths about both native and Western societies play as much of a role in the generation of these structures as native myths.

The transformation of native cultures through contact with Western society cannot be conceived as a collision between eventless structure— a mythic langue—and unstructured event—the historical parole. The cultural order of a non-Western society, pre- as well as postcontact, cannot be understood simply as a structure of categories or symbols unimbricated in social processes of action, conflict, and change. It is, rather, at once a precipitate and a dynamic component of such processes, constituting at the same time their representation and their motivating values. Native societies' cultural representations of their encounters with Western society can therefore be understood only as attempts at the integration of one global sociocultural structure of actions, symbols, processes, events, and conceptual categories by the members of another.

Social and Cultural Dimensions of Historical Representation

Interethnic contact as event and as situation. The focus on the historical encounter and continuing interaction of indigenous and Western societies raises a number of challenging theoretical questions. Chief among these, as Comaroff (1985:3) puts it in a work that addresses in exemplary fashion many of the themes of this volume, are the interconnected problems of recognizing the appropriate global unit of analysis and of taking due account of the complexity and specificity of the sociocultural systems that form its constituent subunits.

The initial contact between a native society and a Western colonial or national society constitutes an "event" for both societies. Starting with that initial event, however, contact becomes a "situation of contact," a system of interaction with a structure of its own, which includes aspects of both societies, each of which in turn has structures of its own. As Cohn (1980:218) has remarked, " . . . one of the primary subject matters of an historical anthropology is, to use Balandier's term, the colonial situation. This is not to be viewed as 'impact,' not as 'culture contact', but as a situation in which the European colonialist and the indigene are united in one analytic field." The structures of the situation as a whole and of each of its constituent subsystems change in relation to one another, that is, they have histories. These histories are composed, at the lowest level of organization, of sequences of events; but the sequences themselves have structural properties, that is, they constitute processes, hierarchies, and contradictions.

Balandier (1955:33) characterized the "colonial situation" in Africa

in terms of the imposition of domination on an autochthonous majority
by an ethnically and culturally distinct, technologically superior minority,
ideologically supported by religious, political, and other claims to intrin-
sic superiority. This formulation, with its stress on the domination of
an autochthonous majority, fits the Andean countries better than the
Amazonian lowlands, but Cardoso de Oliveira (1964:27–29) and his
students have adapted it to the situation of "interethnic friction" between
Brazilian native peoples, who in the Brazilian context constitute small
ethnic minorities, and Brazilian national society. His general formulation of this adaptation of Balandier's notion of "situation" is that of a
" . . . syncretic totality [which takes the form of a] situation of contact
between two populations, 'united' by diametrically opposed, although
interdependent interests" (Cardoso de Oliveira 1964:28).

"Situation," "process," "structure," "event." A "situation of contact"
is a sociocultural structure conceived as a historically developing process.
It may be contrasted in this capacity to the notion of "event." Events may
constitute the units of processes, the form in which they manifest
themselves. As forms of appearance, however, they may obscure as
much as they reveal of the structural connectedness of the process or
processes out of which they arise (as Braudel [1980] insists). Myths and
indigenous historical narratives of interethnic contact typically represent it as a sequence of events (e.g., "how the whitemen appeared,"
"how the first shotgun was made"). Analysis, however, reveals that such
narratives typically order the events they recount according to schemata
representing the processes that constitute the structure of the ongoing
situation of contact.

The essence of this structure is its character as a process of conflicted
interaction, of "interethnic friction" rather than conformity to a shared
normative or cultural pattern. This implies that the native society will
represent this structure to itself in terms of the pattern of action that
comprises its own differential relation to the situation (e.g., resistance,
submission, avoidance). Such patterns or structures of action (i.e.,
processes) are typically represented as sequences of events in forms of
cultural consciousness such as myths or histories, through which the
actors attempt to articulate their nature and meaning to themselves.
Events, in other words, constitute the forms of appearance through
which cultural actors define the subjective meanings of the collective
structures and situational patterns that provide the general framework
and orientation of their acts.

This is what makes events of primary interest to the native mythogra-
pher or historian and the anthropological or historical interpreter alike.

It is why myths, rituals, and at least the less self-conscious sorts of histories present situations and structures through the medium of narratives or enactments of events. It is, conversely, why events, either as units of stories or as social happenings, cannot be accepted by the analyst in the form in which they overtly present themselves but must rather be interpreted in relation to the social and cultural structures that inform them. This interdependence between structure and event has emerged as the focus of one of the major aphasic syndromes of recent anthropological and historical thought, with structuralists and *Annales* historians stressing structures to the exclusion of events, and post-structuralists and vulgar Geertzians focusing on events or performances to the exclusion of structures.

The point for present purposes is that the mythic and historical texts with which these essays are concerned are not to be understood primarily as what most of the texts overtly purport to be, namely, representations of the events of contact. Rather, they must be understood as programs for the orientation of action within the situation of contact and as keys for the interpretation of interaction within that context. Representations of events are able to serve these purposes to the extent that the structure of the situation becomes the schema through which they are organized, interpreted, and re-enacted in consciousness. The specific manner in which the structures in question are encoded and enacted as events, on the other hand, conveys the specific subjective meanings of those structures and situations to the tellers of the tales, the celebrants of the rituals, the orators, historians, dancers, and shamans of the indigenous societies we seek to understand.

Reflexivity, reproduction, and Otherness. The concern of the authors of this collection of essays for situating the myths, rituals, and historical narratives they discuss in their social and historical contexts makes it possible to suggest a few tentative generalizations about the relation between the forms of South American native societies' representations of Western Others, their own sociocultural structures, and the situations of contact through which their interaction with the dominant society is organized. To begin with, focusing the discussion on other cultures' representations of Otherness is a strategically apt context for foregrounding the reflexive dimension of sociocultural structures so commonly overlooked by culturalist approaches not grounded in a context of social interaction. Surely, the most fundamental epistemological question posed by ethno-ethnohistory is precisely how the Other is defined as Other. The answer can only be: in contrast to the self. How then does a society define *itself* as such? The answer, in pragmatic terms, is: by reproducing itself as a totality. Reproduction (the reflexive production of production) is of course a social process, but it is also a cultural structure (or structure of cultural structures) consisting of the conceptual forms of (re-)productive activities and the values toward which they are oriented. A society's representation of itself, then, is constituted of the operations (i.e., culturally represented forms of actions) comprising its process(-es) of self-production. It follows that its representation of its relationship to another society should take the form of some transformation of the process(-es) of reproduction that form the basis of its representation of itself.

A comparative survey of the data and analyses presented in this volume amply bears out this hypothesis, not only with respect to the *content* of indigenous societies' representations of contact with Western society, but to their *form* as well. The textual structures of the myths, historical narratives, and rituals described in these essays can be seen to constitute cultural encodings of the basic processes of reproduction of the societies from which they are drawn, transformed in terms appropriate to the representation of the relation of the society in question and the Western Other in the situation of contact.

Mode, Genre, and Text as Dimensions of Cultural Structure

This volume's concern with the mode of consciousness (history and myth) manifested by indigenous cultural representations of interaction with the West entails a concern with forms of expression as well as with underlying sense. As has already been emphasized in the discussion of the relation between situational structures and their representation in terms of events, the two are interdependent in the generation of meaning. As a general proposition, then, the content of social consciousness cannot be understood apart from an appreciation of the cultural significance of its forms of expression. This proposition opens a critical perspective on a series of issues that lie close to the heart of the current anthropological discussion of the relation of anthropology and history.

One of these issues is clearly the cultural significance of the forms themselves: what is implied by a mythic as distinct from a historical representation of one's own society's relation with an alien society? And, incidentally, what precisely do we mean by myth and history as cross-cultural categories, presuming that it is possible to speak of them as such? To understand the terms in which other cultures have formulated their historical interaction with our own society is to understand their ethnohistories of us—to do ethno-ethnohistory, so to speak. The special merit of this enterprise is that it forces us reflexively to clarify our own notions of history and specifically our conception of the relation between social (historical) context and forms of social consciousness, whether the latter take the form of history or myth.

The general question of form embraces not only the generic mode (myth or history) of such representations but also their more specific genres (both culturally and analytically defined) and, at a still more concrete level, the details of textual structure and performance. The representations analyzed in this volume include examples of various narrative genres as well as such non-narrative genres as oratory, dance, and ritual. Several of the essays demonstrate the ways in which genre and textual structure are integral to the meaning of the representations they discuss, as well as their relation to their historical and social contexts. Most concern themselves with the propositional meanings coded by the forms of the texts as wholes and avoid the reductionist tendency of much recent cultural analysis (here I have structuralism and some strands of American symbolic anthropology primarily in mind) to treat texts in their culturally constituted forms merely as arrays of symbolic elements to be extracted and recombined, without regard for text or context, in simple associational patterns or models congenial to the methodology and ideology of the analyst.

History and Myth as Modes of Cultural Consciousness

Basic Definitions: History, Myth, Time, and Social Agency

Myth and history: Basic definitions. The first step in dealing with these questions is obviously to clarify what we take to be the essential features of myth and history as modes of social consciousness. "Myth" may be defined as the unself-conscious projection of structures of the existing social order as the framework of events that logically transcend the limits of that order, notably, those responsible for the origins of that order itself or the origins of alien societies. The unself-consciousness of the projection means that the forms of the existing social order, although in fact the historical products of human social action, assume fantastic form as the products of superhuman deeds or presocial, natural or supernatural beings. Myth, in other words, is a fetishization of the process of producing society, or of history in the most essential sense of the word.

The characteristic move of mythic thought is the projection of the existing order of experience as its own formative principle, but in a fantastic, asocial form inaccessible to the world of ordinary social life. This means in practice its projection as a peculiar form of time: a dual time, in which the original coming-to-be of the existing sociocosmic order, or some aspect of it, is represented as a qualitatively distinct mode of time, which not only precedes but continues on another level to frame the complementary mode of time, that of everyday social activity, in which the social world is directly lived, known, and recreated.

From the perspective of myth, then, the sequence of events constituting all of postcreation (everyday) time is seen as determined by the structure of society and cosmos fixed in pre- or supersocial mythic time. The power to create or change the forms and contents of social existence, or social agency in the full sense, is not seen as being available to inhabitants of the contemporary social world. Such power was exercised only by the ancestral mythic figures, although it still streams through and around the everyday world in the mythic time dimension, where it may be contacted and tapped by special ritual means. Contemporary social persons can only reproduce the forms created by the mythic ancestors and thereby participate, within the limits of the received forms and, as it were, at secondhand, in the role of social agents.

"History" as a mode of social consciousness is the opposite of myth in these respects. It takes as its point of departure the awareness that social relations are not (at least within the time span of the events in question) predetermined as the result of actions or events in an inaccessible past but are in significant respects shaped by individual or collective social action in the present (or in a time continuous with the present). The operative principle in "historical" as opposed to mythic consciousness, in other words, is an openness to contingency, an awareness that the existing social order emerges as the effect of particular actions and events even as it constrains them. History, then, is rooted in a consciousness of creative social agency as a property of contemporary social actors (or at least *potentially* contemporary actors in the sense of persons belonging to a social world and time continuous with those of the historians and their audiences). It is not primarily defined as a form of awareness of the past but as a mode of consciousness of the social present. This consciousness of the present as actively determined by the social beings who inhabit it is what gives the past its historical significance as a sequence of acts and events that have contributed to creating, and thus may to some degree explain, the present.

The time of history, in contrast to mythic time, is thus by implication a homogeneous time in which the self-reflexive capacity to create the forms of social order is not fixed within a distinct, qualitatively differentiated phase of time but is present, at least as a potential, in the actions and events of the contemporary everyday world. As Lederman (1986:22) has argued, historical consciousness in these respects may become an important component of the realization of the consciousness of the potential for social self-determination from which it springs:

> Not only is the dynamism of Mendi [Papua New Guinea] social life reflected in their constructions of the past; one might also argue that that dynamism is predicated on their "historical" constructions. Their knowledge of past events, and particular sorts of changes, is a condition of contemporary cultural innovation. . . . Accounts of migrants preserve the possibility of mobility. . . . Clan names preserve the possibility of alternative social alignments. The past is a reservoir of alternatives for contemporary people to draw on."

Myth and history in social context. History and myth, in short, are modes of awareness of the social processes through which the forms of social existence are created, reproduced, and transformed. In the words of the historian J. G. A. Pocock (1962:211–12),

> . . . historiography [which Pocock defines as "social awareness of the past and its importance to the present"] is a form of thought occasioned by awareness of society's structure and processes. . . . the activity of remembering and preserving the past must be studied as a social activity. Awareness of a past, then, is a social awareness and can exist only as part of a generalized awareness of the structure and behavior of a society. . . . Since all societies are organized to ensure their own continuity, we may suppose that the preservation of statements about the past . . . is in fact society's awareness of its continuity.

Pocock's formulation is excellent as far as it goes, but it does not differentiate between mythic and historical modes of social consciousness as we have defined them. What then are the conditions under which a specifically historical awareness can arise?

A case in point is the birth of our own historical tradition in ancient Greece. Classical scholars like F. Jacoby have attempted to account for the differentiation of Greek historical thought from its mythic substratum in terms of the combination of the skepticism of the Ionian philosophers and their conception of inquiry ("historia"). However, as M. I. Finley (1965) observed, this combination by itself produced only metaphysics, not history. For the latter, he argues, a third component was crucial, namely, the development of the polis, and perhaps in particular the Athenian polis, which " . . . introduced politics as a human activity and then elevated it to the most fundamental social activity" (1965:300). Following Finley, then, historical consciousness arose in

Greece in the context of the differentiation of a sphere of social interaction devoted to the determination of the forms and contents of social relations through self-conscious social activity.

Finley's explanation of the development of historical consciousness in Greece converges with the definition of history put forward here: the critical element in each case is the consciousness of social agency, that is, the power of members of society to shape their own social existence. I suggest that Finley's formulation applies more generally. We should expect to find historical awareness developing in any context of social relations in which members of a society experience themselves as shaping, through their interaction, significant aspects of their social existence. This experience must be of an intrinsically social or collective character, that is, it must transcend the memory span as well as the normal sphere of social relations and activities of individuals. Such contexts may be relatively restricted—for example, an exchange network in which particular kinds of valuables are traded and accumulated over generations. In such a case the stories of particular valuables and their successive owners and transactions may constitute a genuine store of historical consciousness, however concrete and limited in scope (I take this example from Lederman 1986). The contexts may, of course, be far more inclusive and generalized, as in the instance of the Athenian polis.

The point of Lederman's example of the Mendi exchange network is that social contexts favoring the development of forms of historical consciousness are not the exclusive property of complex societies like the Athenian polis or the Inca Empire. They may exist in relatively simple societies, such as many—but not all—of those in lowland South America. I am not suggesting that history is a cultural universal. There are simple societies that appear to lack culturally elaborated forms of historical consciousness (as distinct from individual reminiscences), just as they may lack institutionalized contexts for collectively managing their social affairs. My point is simply that there is no empirical or theoretical basis for the assumption that because a society is relatively simple (i.e., lacks classes, the state, or writing) it must lack collective forms of historical consciousness. There is, in concrete terms, no theoretical or empirical basis for assuming that indigenous South American cultures, either in the Andes or the Amazon, had or have no alternative to the representation of their experience of contact with Western society in purely mythic form. For some, at least, as several of the essays in this volume attest, genuinely historical formulations are not only a possibility but a reality.

Varieties of History

The heterogeneity of social pasts. Greek (and Roman) history was essentially concerned with politics: it is possible to speak of a single classical historical tradition with a relatively uniform view of what is significant in the present and therefore the past, defined in relation to the same aspect of contemporary society (its political institutions). Nothing in Finley's formulation, however, implies that there need have been only one social context for the exercise and experience of self-determination, or only one form of historical consciousness in Greek culture if there had been more than one such context. That was the way it worked out in Greece, at least as far as the written documents attest, and this is of course the only instance with which Finley was concerned. In a generalizing, comparative mode, however, it is necessary to recognize with Pocock (1962:213) that the awareness of the past within a particular society is rarely the simple awareness of the continuity or reproduction of a single structure: "...a society will have as many pasts as it has [structural] elements of continuity...[and] there is no *a priori* reason why these different awarenesses should grow into a single awareness."

Pocock's point has been borne out by anthropological studies, which have shown that different formulations of the past, defined with reference to different spheres of social activity, often coexist in the same society. Cases in point are Cohn's (1961) description of the different conceptions of the past of the twenty-three caste groups making up a single Indian village and Lederman's (1986) account of alternative Mendi codings of historical relations in terms of collective clan names or individual exchange networks. Multiple pasts, of course, imply multiple presents, a point familiar to citizens of contemporary Western societies, in which every important political persuasion, class, gender, ethnic, religious, or other important social category has its own historians, producing charters for its own perspective on social reality.

Modalities and paradoxes of historical time: Continuous and discontinuous conceptions of the past in relation to the present. The proposition that historical time is continuous with the present and therefore qualitatively homogeneous (contrasting, in this respect, to mythic time) may lead, in practice, to a paradox. This is well brought out in Finley's account of the Greek approach to history, particularly in his interpretation of Thucydides. Thucydides, as Finley says, recognized the principle that the historical significance of actions and events could only be understood through an exact account of their relations in time, and he therefore accepted the importance of narrating events in their actual sequence. However, the understanding to be gained by historical analysis, as Thucydides saw it, was of a timeless rather than a specifically temporal character. He sought to grasp the essence of politics and political behavior, which if he succeeded would be a "possession for ever," among other reasons because "human nature is a constant and therefore recurrence is the pattern. But if so, what is the point to a linear account over long periods of time? One can really only know one's own time, and that is sufficient anyway. The past can yield nothing more than paradigmatic support for the conclusions one has drawn from the present; the past, in other words, may still be treated in the timeless fashion of myth" (Finley 1965:301). Thus may a historical conception of the homogeneity of time and of social action in time lead back again to the dichotomization of mythic past and social present, that is, to the heterogeneity of mythic time.

History and historical consciousness need not, then, entail in practice an awareness of or concern with time as a homogeneous continuum, through which events in the relatively remote past are uniformly connected with the recent past and present. Such an awareness of time as "universal history" does appear outside the modern West, for example, among the Old Testament Hebrews. Auerbach's (1953:11–13, 16) famous contrast between the consciousness of time in Homer and in the Old Testament, where the Greek epic is seen as presenting every moment as equally important, equally *present*, and complete in itself, but only as framed within individual episodes or works (such as the Homeric epics), while the Hebrew stories are constructed of differently stressed moments and events, which are variously connected with the past and future in an ongoing, as yet incomplete universal history, prefigures in this respect the contrast between the attitude of the Greek historians as characterized by Finley and that of Hebrew sacred history. Here again, however, another variant of the paradox that we have encountered in Thucydides reappears. As Auerbach suggests, the Hebrew vision of the relevance of the whole continuum of historical time was based upon the idea that the successive moments of time were of varying and unequal significance. They were not only heterogeneous in terms of the social and human traits and potentialities realized in them but of unequal value in terms of the mythic order in which time as a whole was framed, of the covenant with Yahweh and the ambivalent, perpetually open and unfinished relation of the Hebrews to their god that flowed from it.

One point that emerges from this discussion of different notions of historical time is that myth and history are harder to separate in practice than in theory. This is obviously an important issue in the essays collected here, and I shall return to it in a moment. First, however, I want to raise the question of the social and cultural significance of the difference between the Greek and Hebrew attitudes toward historical time. The question is relevant because there are instances of both types among the essays in this volume, as well as elsewhere in the South American literature.

Greek historical consciousness, it is germane to recall, developed in conjunction with the polis. Greek poleis displayed a wide variety of institutional forms, but the Greeks thought of the polis as a general idea or set of ideas, of which any existing polis could be understood as a more or less adequate specific expression. The many poleis that made up the Greek world could thus be seen by Thucydides as comprehending the total range of fully developed human political forms (i.e., those forms fit for a Greek). However, Thucydides did not see these forms as sequential phases in the development of a single social entity (on the Old Testament model) but as synchronically coexisting totalities, each in its own way manifesting the common general principles of polis society and its possibilities. This generalized vision of the polis also served as the master schema of the Thucydidean historical vision, for which an account of any crisis that could reveal the workings of the generic principles upon which the political institutions and processes of the polis were based could ipso facto be counted as universal history.

The Kayapó as described in my essay may be said to have historical accounts of particular situations and events but no connected universal history. The Andean peoples of the preconquest period, if we can take as representative the great Huarochiri compendium of mythohistorical texts written down some fifty years after the conquest, afford, as we might expect, the best example of a Hebraic historical consciousness in the South American literature (Taylor 1980). It is instructive to compare the astonishingly biblical form and content of the Huarochiri manuscript, with its successive episodes of creation and conquest, divine covenants and deeds of local divinities, foundings of temples and sacred sites, mythic tales and historical references, all recounting the mythohistorical past of one of the subject peoples of the Inca Empire, with the truncated representations of historical events, such as the Spanish Conquest, contained in the ritual dance-dramas of present-day Andean communities (see, e.g., Wachtel 1971). The historical representations of these contemporary, isolated indigenous communities resemble far more closely the relatively simple, episodic Kayapó historical narratives than the scale, complexity, and temporal depth of the Huarochiri manuscript.

What accounts for the development of these different forms of historical consciousness? The "Greek" model of discontinuous but totalizing
history proceeds from a sense that society as presently constituted (i.e.,
as organized in mutually discrete, autonomous political and social
units, the poleis) embodies the sum total of human possibilities. An
understanding of any one global episode, like an understanding of any
one polis, may stand for all. By contrast, the Hebrew vision of continuous historical time seems to proceed from a situation in which society is
at all moments perceived to be relatively incomplete or contingent
because it is part of a larger imperial or other form of interethnic
political system that transcends the boundaries of the ethnicity or
society in question. This was the common situation of Andean peoples
in the Inca period and probably long before; it certainly corresponded to
the situation of the Yauyos, the people from whom the Huarochirí
corpus was derived. Leach (1966) argues that this was as true of Hebrew
social consciousness at the time of the Solomonic kingdom as in the
stateless periods of Hebrew Old Testament history. Under such circumstances, political society as it exists at any given historical moment is
not seen as embodying in any total or universal sense the fundamental
principles, powers, or potential forms of social existence as laid down in
the cultural tradition of any given ethnic or social group.

Hebrew society as represented in the Old Testament takes a number of
different forms, no one of which is taken to be the total realization of its
range of social possibilities, nor a full realization of its essential character.
Hebrew social identity had constantly to be asserted in situations of
contact with non-Hebrew peoples, sometimes in a dominant and sometimes in a subordinate role. In the former case, the problem was how
to dominate without absorbing; in the latter, how to accommodate to
subordination without being absorbed. The ability of Hebrew society to
reproduce itself as a distinct entity under these drastically shifting
political circumstances derived from a set of ritual, social, and political
forms of a sufficiently nonspecific character to survive and subsume the
successive permutations in the structure of the Hebrew polity, yet
sufficiently concrete and socially specific to preserve a focus of social
unity and political continuity.

All of this corresponds closely to the historical experience of the
Andean societies, such as the ethnic kingdoms of the Yauyos, Charcas,
Lupaqa, Killaka, and others absorbed within the Inca Empire. With
them as with the Hebrews of the Old Testament, the ability to subsume
a series of variations in the form of political society, imposed by the
dominant society in the situation of contact, under the continuity of a
ritualized form of communal leadership that could guarantee the repro-

duction of the essential components of society, resulted in a powerfully developed historical consciousness of the relativity and continuity-in-change of sociopolitical forms.

Contemporary Andean peoples such as those described by Dillon and Abercrombie or by Rasnake possess social and ritual mechanisms that allow them to "internalize" the relation of domination through which they are subordinated to the dominant state. They are thus able to identify themselves (however vicariously) with the social totality constituted by the situation of contact of which they are a part. Many lowland peoples, on the other hand, have succeeded in representing the local Western society, and thus the situation of contact as a whole, as a transformation (in effect, as we shall see later, an "externalization") of their own internal processes of social reproduction. This allows them, although in a rather different way from the Andeans, to conceive of their societies as complete matrices of social possibilities, so that the contact situation as it currently exists becomes merely a realization (albeit in alienated form) of powers or principles latent in themselves.

In this way, many lowlanders and Andeans succeed in representing the harsh realities of their dependence within the contact situation in terms of an image of social totality that exhausts the possible modes of social being. Insofar as they generate historical attitudes at all, these therefore tend to take a relatively Greek form, in the sense of seeing particular historical events as embodying paradigmatic relations valid for events in general. A case in point is the Kayapó (Central Brazilian Gê) story of the fission of the ancestral village of Gorotire, included in my essay. As I suggest, this historical narrative is primarily of interest to the Kayapó, not because of its preservation of details of the past as such, but because it presents one of the central structural tensions of contemporary Kayapó society and shows the consequences to which it can lead if allowed to get out of control. What I am suggesting is that many native South American societies have managed to envision themselves, in the context of their relation to the dominant society to which they are bound in struggle within the situation of contact, as similarly comprehending the totality of social possibilities, and for this reason, like the Greeks, they find history in the Hebrew sense, but not the Greek, to be irrelevant.

The complementary relationship of myth and history. The preceding discussion has touched repeatedly on a general issue I mentioned earlier and to which I now return, namely, that history and myth, far from being contradictory modes associated with different evolutionary stages of social development, are not merely compatible but complementary forms of consciousness, and that this relation continues to hold in complex societies with secular historical traditions (including our own). This general contention is reinforced by the theoretical and ethnographic arguments of Pocock, Lederman, and Cohn adduced earlier for the coexistence of a plurality of pasts within the same society, which bear equally on the coexistence of *historical* and *mythic* pasts in the same society as on that of different *historical* pasts. Finley (1965) makes the point that the rise of history in Greece did not mean the demise of myth. On the contrary, despite history's roots in Ionian skepticism about the truth of myth, the relationship between myth and history remained essentially one of complementarity rather than contradiction.

Myth, as Finley points out, functioned in Greece as the basis for history by virtue of its role in identifying significant aspects of social experience and thus providing the criteria for the selection of appropriate subjects for historical inquiry. Myth, in other words, continued to provide the general framework of meaning within which history oriented its skeptical accounts of self-determining acts and contingent events. Leach (1969:114, n.7), in his study of Hebraic myth and history in the Book of Kings, cites Finley on this point in support of his contention that, "It may not be inconsistent to affirm that an historical record has mythical characteristics and functions."

Cohn (1961) makes a similar point. In the South Asian village in question, as he explains, the "traditional" or "mythological" past serves as the basis of religious life, legitimizes social positions, and orients general cultural consciousness, while the "historic" past serves to orient action within the local social system in such matters as political and property disputes. The mythic past thus provides the highest-level, all-embracing framework of social life, while the historic past is "not only a unifying factor but carries a divisive component as well" (faithfully representing, in this respect, that sphere of social existence in which the villagers experience their own activities as making a difference in the determination of the form and content of their lives; 1961:242).

The general implication of these arguments and instances is that the coexistence of mythic and historical accounts within the same society is not an anomaly but, on the contrary, a general condition. Myth and history do not in practice appear as contradictory modes of consciousness because they are essentially forms of understanding related to different levels of questions. Myth is an attempt to formulate the *essential* properties of social experience in terms of a series of "generic events," at a level transcending any particular context of historical relations or events; history, by contrast, is concerned precisely with the level of particular relations among particular events.

This distinction is widely recognized in indigenous classifications of narrative genres. Ireland gives a good example of this from the Waurá of the upper Xingu. The Waurá distinguish between stories relating events in another, qualitatively different, mythic time and those relating personal experiences in this-worldly time. The events recounted in tales of the former sort and the patterns they form are conceived as persisting in present time as latent or potential principles that embody the inner essence of everyday relations in contemporary time. The same distinction is certainly recognized among the Kayapó, and it appears to be common, if not universal. To return once more to the Greeks, it is similar in many ways to Aristotle's distinction between poetry and history (Aristotle, it will be recalled, preferred poetry as the vehicle of essential and universal truths, to history, which merely trafficked in contingent, specific, unique, in a word, superficial facts).

There is no reason why these two levels should not be combined in the same process of thought, act of discourse, or mode of historical or mythic representation. Roe gives several good examples of this in his essay. The "heroic histories" of the Andean ethnic kingdoms, which we have just considered, and the messianic myths of the Wakuénai, to be considered later, are further cases in point. From a Marxian point of view, this combination of mythic and historical perspectives is precisely what one would expect. Myth, as the domain of the fetish, is always lurking at the boundaries of objective social (i.e., historical) consciousness (for an analysis of a lowland South American myth in these terms, see Turner 1985). I shall return to this Marxian point in my conclusions.

Major and minor levels of historical consciousness. An important distinction remains to be drawn between the level of awareness of historical events as merely replicating the same essential pattern of human or social nature, that is, varying within the limits of the received social structure, and the conception of historical events and processes as bringing about changes in the sociocultural structure itself. These two levels or modes of awareness might be designated the "minor" and "major" modes of historical consciousness, respectively. Both are consistent with an awareness of events and actions as contingent and undetermined *at some level* by structure.

It is important to bear in mind that, even in the case of what I have called "minor" historical consciousness, this level may be very important to informants in their own cultural terms. Accounts of how villages split up in the past, for example, are very important to Kayapó informants precisely because the causes of the fission, and the form of the new villages founded as a result, are seen as conforming to contemporary structural stereotypes.

Major historical consciousness is that which formulates the existing social order as a whole, or some significant aspect of it, as a contingent product of an ongoing stream of action, events and forces that, just as they gave rise to it, can and will also transform it. This is obviously a more powerfully reflexive mode of historical awareness and is much rarer than the minor mode. It is nonetheless found in many traditional and tribal societies, especially but not invariably in connection with their attempts to come to terms with the effects of contact with Western society. Examples in this volume are the speech of the Kayapó chief recounted in my essay and the oratory of the Indian representatives at the Brazilian pan-Indian conference reported by Ramos.

Major historical consciousness clearly presupposes the homogeneous conception of time outlined in the general definition of historical consciousness offered earlier; it may nevertheless formulate its interpretation of historical changes within that time in relation to "essential" truths or patterns defined by myth, considered as underlying constraints upon the overt sequence of events. However, minor historical explanations of particular events within the general framework of the basic sociocultural order are in practice directly compatible with a bifurcated notion of time continuous with that of myth, in which the events leading to the foundation of the existing order are treated as a qualitatively different level or mode of time than those constituting the historical sequences of events that transpire within that order. We thus return by a different route to the same point raised in the previous section, to wit, that historical and mythic frames of reference, however contradictory in the logical abstract, are in practice complementary and contextually compatible. This complementarity, as I have suggested, tends to take different forms in the cases of the two levels of historical consciousness in question.

It is, in sum, impossible to assume for purposes of cross-cultural comparison that history is a homogeneous category that entails, in all its manifestations, uniform attitudes toward time, structure, and contingency, or a uniform relation to myth. On the contrary, history as a generic mode of social consciousness comprehends significant variations in the construction of time and the relation of social structure to temporal process.

Varieties of Myth

Myth and anti-myth. It is not enough, then, to speak of indigenous cultural formulations of the nature of Western society in terms of a simple contrast between myth and history. Myth is not a unitary category at this level of discourse, any more than history is. Like the latter, myth includes alternative modalities that are directly correlated with different types of native societies and situations of contact. The general definition suggested above of mythic consciousness as an alienated awareness of the creative (productive) and reproductive processes of the sociocultural order, framed within a specific mode of time, is consistent with profoundly different conceptions of social order in general and the relation between native and Western societies in particular.

A case in point was perceived and defined some years ago by Da Matta (1970) in an article that in many ways anticipated the concerns of this volume. Entitled "Myth and Anti-Myth among the Timbira," it is a study of representations of the relation between native and Western society among the Gê-speaking Timbira of East-Central Brazil. Da Matta's main point is that the structure of the Timbira myth of the origin of the Brazilians is a systematic inversion of the structure of the main Gê myth of cultural origins, the well-known story of the bird-nester and the fire of the jaguar. The hero of the latter story leaves his family (human society) for a sojourn in the wilderness, where he becomes identified successively with fledgling macaws and jaguars, receives the bow, roast meat, and cooking fire from the latter, and returns with them to society, which thereupon reorganizes itself around the process of reproducing the fire. Society thus defines itself by internalizing, on a general basis, the cooking fire and the other, heretofore alien "natural" powers and possessions of the Jaguar (who thereby loses them). (For an analysis of the Kayapó variant of this myth, which develops a number of the same ideas, see Turner 1985.)

In the myth of Auke, which accounts for the origin of Brazilians, everything proceeds in reverse. A boy is born to an unmarried girl of the sexually promiscuous, prostitute-like category that Nimuendajú (1946), the ethnographer, called "wantons." The mother attempts to kill the boy at birth (which would be the normal means for her to keep her single, "wanton" status rather than settle down to married life with the father). She first learns she is pregnant when he calls to her with the cry of a guinea pig, while she is bathing in the river outside the village. He is saved and raised by the mother of the girl but grows up as a monster, capable of transforming himself into animal forms, his preference being that of Jaguar. The Indians repeatedly try to kill him, but he always returns to life. In the final attempt, they burn his body and flee the village, founding a new village elsewhere. Auke, meanwhile, returns to life as the first Brazilian (in fact, the nineteenth-century emperor of Brazil, Dom Pedro Segundo), builds a splendid palace on the old village site, and creates black slaves, horses, and cattle for himself. He is found in this state by two Indians sent at his mother's behest to bring back his ashes, and through them he bids his mother (but no other Indian) to come to live with him.

Auke's trajectory is thus from a prenatal debut as an animal-like being outside the village, through a sojourn in society as an antisocial, animal (and especially Jaguar)-associated figure, to extrusion from society by passage through the cremation fire to his final place outside Timbira society. As a corollary of this final step, he transforms his ashes, the result of the futile attempt of native society to protect itself against him via its most fundamental and powerful instrument of cultural and social self-reproduction, the fire, into the power to control and reproduce the alien possessions of Brazilian society in a way that remains inaccessible to the Indians.

Da Matta calls the myth of Auke an anti-myth, because, while remaining a myth in the fundamental sense of the definition given earlier, it nevertheless inverts the structure of the transformations of nature into (Indian) culture set out in the Timbira myths of cultural origin. This inversion becomes the basis of an opposite kind of statement about the nature of Indian society to that made in the culture-origin myths. In the anti-myth, Indian society is confronted with a "natural," antisocial force it cannot contain, co-opt, or reproduce within its own structure. The antisocial character of this force is manifested in the form of the were-jaguar, which mocks the figure of the culture-mediating jaguar in the main culture-origin myth, which recounts how the jaguar gave the cooking fire to humans, who acquired culture through the process of reproducing it. Society's futile attempts to destroy this force culminate in the burning of Auke. This is itself an inversion of the triumphant symbol of the success of Indian society in co-opting and reproducing natural powers in the standard cultural origin myth, viz., the use of cooking fire to transform nature into social form and, above all, to reproduce itself as a reflexively self-generating cultural pattern. The failed attempt to use fire to destroy Auke, by contrast, results in *his* self-reproduction and acquisition of powers and possessions outside of Indian society. The source of the alien and exponentially greater reproductive powers of Brazilian society (the myth makes clear that the reproduction of both human population and commodities is at issue) is thus defined as an alienation of the analogous powers of native society.

If myth in its standard form (as represented by the Timbira myths of the origin of their own society and culture) defines the essence of human culture as the reproduction, on a generalized basis, of the basic processes through which it transforms nature (i.e., its basic processes of production, including the production of social persons), then anti-myth defines the essence of the dominant, alien Brazilian society as the alienation of this power of reproduction, as the consequence of the failure of the basic cultural instruments of productive transformation of asocial nature. This failure is the measure of the strength of the alien, asocial forces in question. Myth (as exemplified by the basic myths of cultural origin) explains the possibility and the essential nature of native society; anti-myth explains its limits and inferiority in relation to Brazilian society.

I have taken a few liberties with the details of Da Matta's interpretation, but my recensions of his basic categories of myth and anti-myth are, I believe, faithful to the spirit of his argument. Da Matta stresses that while anti-myth defines the limits, and in this special sense the "end" of Indian society and its system of myth, and as such represents the first step in the opening of native culture toward the possibility of ideological and historical interpretations of its relation to the dominant national society, it is not yet, in itself, such an interpretation. Anti-myth remains essentially myth, consistent with the structural principles of Timbira mythology as a whole. While the native society fails to neutralize or transform the contradiction represented by Auke within its own structure, and the awareness of insurmountable contradiction marks a new and important step, perhaps the ultimate possible step, in the development of mythic thought as such, the anti-myth nevertheless ends with the contradictory element extruded from the native society proper, albeit as the fulcrum of its incorporation in a new and alien order. The native order thus survives *internally* unchanged. What begins as an internal contradiction is projected onto the alien society, and the latter is defined, in egocentric terms, as an alienated manifestation of the dynamics of the native society, rather than as an independent historical entity in its own right (Da Matta 1970:103–5).

The relevance of Da Matta's formulation to the present collection of essays is obvious. The mode of anti-myth he identified among the Timbira applies more widely to other South American peoples' mythic representations of Western society and the situation of intercultural contact. In my essay on the closely related Kayapó, I analyze the Kayapó variant of the Auke story as well as a number of other Kayapó myths of the origin of Brazilians and other alien peoples, and I show that they conform to the anti-myth pattern.

Recursive anti-myth in the Andes. The anti-myth form is not confined to the Central Brazilian Gê but is common in the Andes (with an interesting additional twist), as the Bolivian examples analyzed by Dillon and Abercrombie and also Rasnake attest. It is instructive to ask why this should be so.

The indigenous societies of Central Brazil and the Andes, in spite of their many differences, have certain important traits in common, both with respect to their internal social structures and to the typical forms of their situations of contact. Both are well known for their complex institutional superstructures, comprising moieties, elaborate ceremonial organizations, and forms of age-grading that identify the social stages of the human life cycle with the reproduction of the basic segments of the social order (extended families or endogamous clusters of families forming localized kindreds, respectively). These superstructures can be shown in both cases to comprise the collectively standardized forms of the reproduction of the segmentary groups and thus of the social order as a whole (Turner 1979, 1984). The most important difference is that the Andean systems are structurally adapted for inclusion, as subordinate enclaves, within imperial or colonial states dominated by alien elites.

The contact situations of both sets of societies, like the societies themselves, have important structural similarities. In both cases the dominance of the national society is exercised, as it were, at a sufficient social, political, and religious distance to permit the continuity of native communal existence on its own social and ritual terms (more or less modified, to be sure, to accommodate the exigencies of the contact situation). In spite of great population losses following contact and various forms of oppression by colonial and national regimes, the native societies of both areas, at the village level of organization, have achieved a relatively stable modus vivendi with the local Western society that allows them to maintain their communal integrity and to exercise considerable internal social and ritual autonomy. The antimyth, I suggest, provides at once an appropriate ideological representation and an apt program for accommodation to this type of contact situation for this type of native society, inasmuch as it remains able to define the alien encompassing society in terms of its own internal schemata of social reproduction.

That the two cases treated by Rasnake and by Dillon and Abercrombie should be similar is not surprising, since they come from neighboring societies, but the pattern they reveal is in fact widespread in the Andes. Rasnake's example is the more complete at the level of mythic narrative. It consists in essence of an origin myth that recounts the simultaneous creation of contemporary Indian and Spanish (colonial) societies, and thus the structure of the contact situation, as a corollary of the succession of distinct epochs or "worlds": a former stage inhabited by a people called Chullpas and the actual one peopled by Indians and Spaniards. The transition is effected by a creator-god variously identified with the sun and with Jesus Christ. The latter first eliminates the Chullpas, who inhabit a sunless world and require darkness and cold, by burning or drying them out with his heat and light. An important aspect of the demise of the Chullpas is that they are driven inside of mountain caves, mines, or "houses" (the prehistoric tombs, also called *chullpas,* in which their dessicated remains can still be seen and which are believed to be stocked, like archaeological analogues of mines, with gold and silver treasure). The Chullpas are thus associated with *below* and *inside* in relation to the sun/creator-god, who is relatively *above* and *outside.* The Chullpas, in other words, are autochthone connected with the earth and the places in it of which they were the original inhabitants. The sun god is by contrast a sky-dwelling outsider, a foreign conqueror. After the Chullpas have been effectively finished off (a few survive as the latter-day ethnic group of Urus) the sun god, in Rasnake's myth, makes the Indians but also brings, or at least presides over the coming of, the Spanish.

God is an Indian and remains to a degree identified with the Indians; but as conqueror and ruler he is also identified with the Spanish. In Rasnake's story, God is identified with the "King Inca"; and in revenge for his murder in that form by the Spanish, he hides all the gold and silver (which before the Spanish came, had lain on the surface of the ground) deep *inside* the mountains and *under* the earth. This is why it must now be mined; and it is also why the Spanish subordinate the Indians, to make them mine it for them. The Indians thus become identified with the *below* and *inside* of the treasure-bearing earth, whose *upper* and *outward* surface they inhabited before the Spaniards arrived as conquering foreigners with armor flashing like the sun. In this respect they share the fate of the treasure with which they, like the Chullpas before them, have become identified.

The relation of Indian to Spaniard is thus analogous to that of Chullpa to sun god in the previous episode of the myth. The Indians, however, are not identified with the Chullpas. Rather, they are identified with the sun/Christ in contrast to the Chullpas, but the sun god/Christ then becomes (somewhat more ambiguously) identified with the Spanish in relation to them. The measure of ambiguity is derived from the Indians' identification with the god relative to the Chullpas, as manifested in the identification of God with Inca in opposition to the Spanish at the time of the latters' first arrival. With the successful conquest and killing of the Inca by the Spanish, God becomes effectively identified with the latter. This transference, however, can be accomplished only by destroying the previous identity of God with the Indians, an act of *lèse majesté* that entails a retribution, the form of which amounts to a vicarious participation by the Indians in their own subordination to the Spanish, represented simultaneously as their revenge.

The relation of Indian to Spaniard in the situation of contact is accounted for in Rasnake's myth as a transformation of the divine, but Indian-identified, powers of the process by which Indian society was created (as the successor of the Chullpas). The result is a recursive, or reflexively redoubled, form of anti-myth in which the two successive episodes not only replicate the same internal structure but stand to each other in the same structural relation. This characteristically Andean twist adds a further level of structure to the simpler Central Brazilian form, transforming it into a hierarchical system in which the Indians are able to participate in the structure of domination *as dominators* at a lower level, while accepting domination, at a higher level, in terms of the same structure. The full significance of this convoluted arrangement as a fundamental principle of Andean social organization is brought out by Dillon and Abercrombie.

Dillon and Abercrombie show that in their community, where the final episode of Rasnake's story (the hiding of the gold in revenge for the murder of the Inca) was not told, the same structure is embodied in communal ritual and the symbolism of the moieties. The latter, designated (as everywhere in the Andes) "upper" and "lower," and respectively associated with dominant and subordinate status and roles, embody a relational model of a situation of inequality and domination identical with that encoded in Rasnake's myths. This model is ritually perpetuated as the structure (in fact, the form of reproduction) of Indian society, as embodied in its moiety organization; but in a broader perspective it represents the structure of the contact situation as a whole, with its central principle of inequality and domination of Indian society by the Spanish conquerors and their descendants. Note that the implication of this identification is that the dominance of the Spanish (or contemporary Western state) over Indian society is itself a transformation of the basic process of reproduction of the latter, as embodied in its most inclusive level of institutional structure (the moiety system). The rituals that enact and reproduce the moiety system thereby not only identify the native society with this situation but place the Indians in the role of its reproducers.

The Indians, in reproducing the structure of their own social totality, thus become, by the same token, the vicarious authors of their own subordination within the situation of contact as a whole. However, the terms of this subordination limit its effects and preserve a sphere of internal autonomy for the community itself: on the one hand, by presupposing the separation of the dominant and subordinate societies as complementary and coexisting spheres, on the model of the complementary segments of the native society with which they are respectively identified (central plaza and peripheral residential zones, upper moiety and lower moiety); and, on the other, by identifying the Indians as the original agents and reproducers of their own subordination, thus asserting a measure of control over their situation. This same complex pattern of acquiescence in subordination and identification with the dominant power, coupled with the assertion of a separate sphere of continuing autonomy, is elegantly brought out in Silverblatt's analysis of the Indians' construction of the figure of Santiago as a transformation of their own thunder and mountain deities (Illapa and Wamanis).

Silverblatt's data are drawn principally from Central Peru, which attests to the generality of this pattern among Quechua as well as Aymara speakers in the Andean region as a whole. Her powerful and admirably concise analysis stands as an excellent example of the way in which the best of the new Andean ethnohistorical scholarship is supplanting the old notions of syncretism and the persistence of an essentially unchanged Andean substratum beneath the outwardly Iberian forms of political, ritual, and civil hierarchy with a critical understanding of the way in which Andean and Spanish political, ritual, and ideological forms became suspended within an ambivalent synthesis in which each transformed the other up to a point. The effect of this synthesis, and in particular of this limiting point, was to render submission and resistance simultaneously possible, on condition that neither be carried too far. Indian consent to Spanish rule could thus be defined as a part of a bargain, or at least of an interdependent relationship, that guaranteed a sphere of Indian autonomy within the colonial regime, protected by Andeanized versions of the conquerors' own pantheon.

Messianic myths as "anti-anti-myths." The anti-myth is clearly not the only mythological form in which South American native peoples have framed their experience of contact and struggle with Western society. Another mythic mode that has been important for both the Andean and lowland areas of the continent is the messianic myth or myth cycle, which has sometimes been associated with overt resistance against Western conquest or oppression, sometimes with "cargo"-type ideas, and sometimes with other-worldly notions of collective death and rebirth. Examples of these modalities of messianic myth are respectively provided by Hill and Wright's study of the myth and historical resistance movement of Venancio Christu from an Arawakan group of the Northwest Amazon, Chernela's Arapaço (Tukanoan) myth of the anaconda-ancestor who transformed himself into a cargo-bearing submarine from the same area, and Roe's briefly noted example of the Shipibo "new fire" movement, which was led by shamanesses utilizing a symbolic transformation of the main culture-origin myth. The Northwest Amazon, as Hill and Wright recount in their historical introduction, has been an area of violent conflict between indigenous peoples and slave raiders, rubber gatherers, and government troops since the seventeenth century. Fighting with and abuse of the natives became intense again in the late nineteenth century, the time of the historical resistance movement led by Venancio. (It is a pity that no Andean examples of messianic myths could be included, for example, the stories of Inkarri. See Ortiz Rescaniere 1973.)

Messianic myths differ most obviously from anti-myths in that they posit the inversion of the unequal relationship between the native and Western society in the existing situation of contact. This may take the overt form of a triumph of native over Western exemplars in some magical or military contest, or of the direct integration of native society into Western society on equal terms, or of the integration of Western goods and technology as cargo into native society. Messianic myths, on the other hand, resemble anti-myths in that the specific aspect of the native society that serves as the medium or instrument of the victorious transformation is a manifestation of its basic relation(s) or principle(s) of social reproduction. This principle or relation is either directly embodied by the native messiah or culture hero or contained in some instrument or magical procedure he wields or controls. The destructive Western social forms or forces arrayed against the hero usually turn out to be negative transformations of this native power or principle of social reproduction.

The terms of this discussion apply equally to messianic movements as to messianic myths; the two are obviously inseparable. In this connection, the main points of this analysis of the character of messianic myths and movements as inversions of anti-myths have been brilliantly anticipated by Carneiro da Cunha (1973) in her study of the 1963 messianic movement of the Ramkokamekra-Canela. The Ramkokamekra movement is particularly relevant to the present discussion because it was conceived and acted out as a point-for-point inversion of the anti-myth of Auke, Da Matta's study of which provided the paradigm for the general characterization of anti-myths in the preceding section. The charismatic leader of the Ramkokamekra was a pregnant woman who prophesied that she would give birth to the sister of Auke, who would immediately restore to the Indians all of the riches and powers alienated to the Brazilians by Auke, starting with the cattle of the surrounding ranchers. As Carneiro da Cunha emphasizes, the woman presented herself as a good mother who had refrained from intercourse with her husband (the opposite of Auke's mother, an unmarried public woman who neglected her maternal duties). In sum, the Ramkokamekra messianic leader presented herself as the embodiment of the principle of social reproduction, the negation of which by Auke's mother had led directly to the alienation of an inverted form of this power by Auke (further transformations turned out to be required when the woman gave birth to a stillborn boy instead of the promised live girl).

Essentially the same points are made by Hill and Wright in their analysis of messianism in the Northwest Amazon. The leaders of the native resistance movements in this area have tended to be shamans, who have a recognized role in the societies of the area as mediators on behalf of society as a whole, not only in relation to external social entities (traditionally either affines or less ambiguously hostile native groups), but also with the ancestral cosmic sphere that is the source of the forms and powers of social creation and renewal. Contact with this sphere is the focus of collective ritual, which is in turn the focus of articulation of the system of descent and affinal relations, which links the individual longhouse groups into a wider, collectively self-reproducing structure of clans and interclan alliances. The shaman embodies the creative power of the ancestral spirits that is manifested and preserved by the ritual and social renewal of this structure; and he channels this power outward against indigenous and Western foes who would destroy the ancestral system. Messianism is the historical form that this socially integrated variety of shamanic power assumed in the context of the violent struggle of the Arawakan and Tukanoan peoples of the Northwest Amazon against Western slavers and exploiters.

In the Wakuénai (Arawakan) story of Venancio Christu, for example, the evil governor and rubber baron tries to kill Venancio Christu by having him nailed in a coffin and thrown into the river. The coffin, as Hill and Wright point out, is an obvious transformation of the tree-trunk container of the trickster-creator figure and also of the womb from which Kuwái, the primordial human being, was born. The transformation of life-giving, society-creating container to death-giving coffin represents the attempt of local Western society, as represented by the murdering and enslaving rubber collectors, to destroy the native society and subsume its members as slaves or corpses in its own productive project. The coffin is also a *manufactured product* of Western society, and as such it is an instance of the contradictory productive principle (from the Indian point of view) that society embodies. Venancio Christu triumphs by retransforming the coffin into a womb, and emerging from his submersion in it as an anaconda, the form of the original creator-ancestor of native society. He thus asserts the superior power of the reproductive principle of native society and its ability to prevail over the inversion of that principle by Western society into a principle of social destruction.

Chernela's Arapaço cycle is based on a similar set of transformations. The anaconda-ancestor, swimming in the river, first encounters a native house on the riverbank, seduces the woman (who brews manioc beer), is killed and pushed back into the river by her husband (who is armed with blowgun darts), but is then reborn from the woman's mouth. In the second episode, the Anaconda, swimming in the river, sees a house by the shore with a white man sitting before it. The man has a shotgun (a transformation of the native blowgun and darts) and whiskey (a transformation of native manioc beer), and he kills the Anaconda when the latter approaches to procure these things and leaves the body in the river. In the third episode, the Anaconda transports himself to Brasilia, where he assumes the human form of a worker named Honorato. He amasses great stores of merchandise, transforms himself into a submarine, and in this form transports his cargo back up the river, stopping to found a great underwater city, a counterpart of Brasilia, at the ancestral landing place where the first anaconda-ancestor had founded the first native village.

In the second episode of this story, the properties of native society as depicted in the first (the house, the husband's weapons, the manioc beer brewed by the wife) are transformed into lethal opposites. The womanless whiskey-drinking white man who embodies Western society occupies a hut on the riverbank identical with that of the Indian woman in the first episode, which is the setting for the reproduction of the anaconda-ancestor himself. The encounter between the Anaconda, who embodies the basic male creative principle of native society, and the white man, with his commodities embodying the reproductive principle of white society, ends apparently in the death of the Anaconda without the reproduction that accompanied his death at the hands of the husband of the Indian woman in the first episode. In the third episode, however, we discover that the Anaconda has, after all, *reproduced himself* and, moreover, has appropriated the reproductive power of Brazilian capitalist society, taking the form of a Brazilian worker in order to amass a cargo of trade goods to bring back to the Indians. He thus reasserts the fundamental native principle of social creation and reproduction embodied in his relation to a native woman attached in marriage to a riverside longhouse over the power of the inverse (destructive) transformation of that principle embodied in his contact with the white man.

This victorious reassertion enables the Anaconda to control the productive powers of Brazilian society, to the extent of possessing himself of bountiful supplies of Western goods such as those disposed of in such an exclusive and antisocial manner by the white man of the house on the riverbank. The supreme manifestation of this control is the Anaconda's co-option of the Western form of the cargo-carrying submarine, transforming it into an avatar of the anaconda-ancestors who carried the first people within their bodies to the primal riverbank village sites. He thus ends by subsuming all of white civilization (the "city" of cargo he builds under the river) within the native form of social reproduction. As in the tale of Venancio Christu, the fundamental principle of the creation and reproduction of native society, represented as a life-giving container or anaconda-vessel, triumphantly reasserts itself over the attempt of Western society (again represented as a lethal transformation of native social forms) to destroy it.

Western society in these two myths is presented essentially as an antithetical transformation of the fundamental reproductive powers of native society. In both the Wakuénai and Arapaço cases, Western society, as embodied either in its human representatives or its products, is directly presented as such. In the anti-myth, the antithetical transformation of native social powers represented by Western society is seen both as inaccessible to and irreversibly dominant over the native society yet also as removed from it in a way that allows it to continue relatively untransformed. An unequal coexistence thus remains possible. In the messianic myth, the Western transformation of the native principle of social reproduction is seen as directly and totally destructive of it. The two societies, however, are also seen as directly interpenetrating rather than separate from each other, as in the anti-myth. Separate coexistence is thus impossible.

This very interpenetration, however, is seen in the messianic myth as rendering Western society accessible and therefore vulnerable to counterattack and manipulation by the native society. Through the latter's manipulation of its ultimately more potent principle of reproduction, Western society may either be transformed back into the life-giving native form by native messianic or creator figures or else native society, through an opposite process of collective death and rebirth, may transform itself into the Western form. The basic structure of the messianic myth can thus be understood as a simple transformation of the structure of the anti-myth: messianic myths, in other words, are in effect "anti-anti-myths."

Mythological individualism and myths of original inequality. There is a third, simpler form of mythic account of the origin of Europeans and other alien peoples that is relatively common in South America. This takes the form of a story of the simultaneous creation of the alien and the native peoples in terms that prefigure their subsequent relationship of inequality in the situation of contact. The creation itself very often takes the form of, or is accompanied by, the creation of artifacts that remain characteristic of the native and alien groups. A further common feature of stories of this type is that the creator and his/her creations take the form of individuals rather than of social groups; also, that collective social action plays no part in the narrative. These stories, in other words, evince a certain "mythological individualism," a primitive ideological counterpart of contemporary "methodological individualism," which plays an analogous role in the origin myths of Western social science. There is an underlying connection between these apparently unrelated features which appears when their social referents are analyzed in the context of the situations of contact of the groups from which the myths are drawn.

The most obvious difference between myths of original inequality and the other two types of myth, anti-myth and messianic myths, is the absence of social dynamics. There is no intimation that the contact situation, with its unequal relation between the native and Western societies, is the product of action by either toward the other, much less of a transformation of the former into the latter, nor does any opening seem to be left for the transformation of this relation by messianic or other forms of action on the part of the natives. This lack of dynamics is paralleled at an even more fundamental level by the lack of any notion of internal *social* process or transformation as an aspect of the creation of indigenous society itself (as is found, for example, in the myths of social origin, in contrast to which anti-myths are typically defined, or in the anti-myths themselves). Instead, both native and Western societies are created (in the form of individuals rather than societies or social relations per se) by an external creator figure whose act of creation does not become the model for an internal process of social reproduction. Such myths may, however, be supplemented within the same society by other myths of different types (e.g., anti-myths), and in such cases it is the latter that appear to become the basis of political or messianic resistance to domination by national societies.

There are two examples of myths of original inequality in the collected essays that show how they function within different social situations and mythic traditions in the ways just discussed. One is the Waurá origin myth given by Ireland (it is actually common to the upper Xingu tribes; see Villas Boas and Villas Boas 1972 and Agostinho 1974), in which the creator gives the Xinguano Indian, the "wild" (i.e., Kayapó or Suya) Indian, and the whiteman their choice of weapons and of nourishment. The Xinguano (Waurá) gets to choose first each time, the "wild" Indian second, and the whiteman last. The Waurá chooses the bow over the rifle but then selects the civilized food of manioc gruel over the cup of blood, which is greedily slurped down by the "wild" Indian and the whiteman. The "wild" Indian also chooses the bow, leaving the whiteman to take the gun. This simple story creates a two-dimensional Guttman scale upon which the three groups are differentiated on a continuum from civil and militarily ineffective to savage and militarily potent, thus accounting for the whiteman as simultaneously more powerful and less human, or at least less socialized, than the Waurá. These two dimensions provide a minimal but adequate account of the main features of the contact situation as seen by the Waurá—one of the valuable points Ireland develops about the functions of myth in Waurá society—in terms that emphasize that this situation, including the subordinate position of the Waurá in it, is the creation and responsibility of the Waurá (who had first choice and refused the gun). In short, the Waurá are given a measure of vicarious responsibility for the conditions of their own subordination.

A second example of this type of myth is the Shipibo tale related by Roe. In this story, the creator (not conceived as Shipibo but rather as "the Good Inca") makes three ancestral humans out of fired clay: one is underdone and becomes the whiteman; one is overdone and becomes the blackman; and one is *au point* and becomes the Indian. Here there is no question of participation by the Indian figure, hence no effect of vicarious control over the resulting situation. However, the inequality produced by the creator-Inca's action is in the Indians' favor: the whites and blacks emerge as relatively inferior, incomplete, or unbalanced beings, while the Indians embody the fullness of humanity. Taken by itself, this myth would neither account for the reality of the situation of interethnic friction between the Shipibo and the national society as the Shipibo experience it nor for the terms of their attitude toward Westerners, which, as Roe characterizes it, is one of ambivalence, similar to the Waurá. The Shipibo, on the one hand, view Westerners (including whites, blacks, and mestizos) with condescension, as Failed Proto-Humans; on the other hand, they envy the whiteman's vast wealth and respect his power.

It thus comes as no surprise to find that the Shipibo have another myth that accounts for the superior powers of the Westerners they both fear and admire. Interestingly enough, this turns out to be an anti-myth formulated as an inversion of the creation myth just cited. In the latter, as we have seen, the role of creator-spirit is played by the "Good Inca." In the anti-myth, the whiteman receives his superior powers (above all, the secrets of manufacturing "machines, factories, and airplanes") from the "Bad Inca," the negative doppelgänger of the "Good Inca." The "Bad Inca" had taken over the Indians' world and inflicted a series of catastrophies on them, after the "Good Inca" had done his work of creation and "ascended into heaven" (as Roe points out, he is assimilated here as elsewhere with Christ). The "Good Inca" eventually returns to earth and kills the "Bad Inca" to save his creatures, the Indians, but the soul of the "Bad Inca" flies off to gringo-land and, from his new headquarters in a palatial bunker beneath the White House, imparts to the whites their superior powers of commodity production. The latter are thus accounted for as projections of a dynamic originally internal to Indian society, defined as including its two alien, but still Indian, "Inca" demiurges. The powers of the Westerners are thus accounted for as the alienated, antisocial powers of an Indian creator-spirit, and the alienation of these powers is explained as the result of the success of the creator of Indian society in expelling them from within the Indian world.

The Shipibo, according to Roe, insist on the historicity of their anti-mythic explanation of the productive powers of Western society as alienated powers of the "good" and "bad" Indian culture-creators because of the hope this gives them that the dominance of the Western national society guaranteed by those powers will be reversed in future historical time. As in numerous other instances from across the continent, historical hopes nourished by anti-myths (and in this case also by a myth of original inequality in the Indians' favor, that is, of original superiority) have led to the birth of at least one messianic movement. A revitalistic cult in the 1950s, led by female shamans, claimed to usher in a new age in which the whiteman would be overthrown. The key symbol of the movement appears to have been a "blue" cooking fire. As Roe suggests, this represented a manipulation of the symbolism of the basic culture-origin myth, which like its Gê counterpart centers upon the acquisition of cooking fire. The shamanesses' "new" cooking fire was presented as a fresh Promethean acquisition that would usher in a new and higher human culture, from which the whiteman would be excluded as the animals had been from the original human culture started by the first theft of cooking fire.

The historical experience of contact and interaction with Western society has been very different for the Waurá and the Shipibo. As Roe says, the contemporary Shipibo have been "insulated" by the interposition of other tribes from direct pressure from Peruvian settlers or exploiters, and in this sense they may be said to resemble the Waurá situation to some extent. It was not always so, however. During the rubber boom at the beginning of this century, the Shipibo were decimated by disease and exploitation, forced to disperse their larger communities and move to more remote areas. With the dissolution of large communities, their main communal ritual complex, the female initiation, lapsed. Their present relatively amorphous social organization is thus in considerable part the product of a catastrophic historical experience, which as Roe suggests parallels the catastrophes of the reign of the "Bad Inca" recounted in their anti-myth of white domination.

The Waurá, by contrast, have led a sheltered existence on the upper Xingu, which even before its designation as a national park was never penetrated by hostile or exploitative elements of the national society. They thus lack both the experience and the consciousness of overt conflict, slaughter, enslavement, and exploitation that has been the lot of the native peoples of the Shipibo area in the times of the rubber boom and, to a lesser extent, thereafter. The Waurá have never had to submit, flee, or resist, merely to maintain their distance and their separate autonomy.

For the Shipibo, in short, involvement in the situation of contact meant a fundamental transformation of their social order. For the Waurá, it has taken the form of an ambivalent relation of dependence on the national society for certain commodities, coupled with a maintenance of distance motivated by a fearful awareness of the power and capricious malevolence of local representatives of the national society. These aspects of the contact situation (the superior technology and manufactured goods of the whiteman, together with his threatening, barbaric hostility) are well represented in the Waurá myth of the origin of whites and Indians reported by Ireland. Significantly, the Waurá appear to have no counterpart of the Shipibo anti-myth recounted by Roe, and they have never had a messianic movement of resistance like that of the Shipibo.

The historical experience of contact of the Waurá and other upper Xinguano societies, on the one hand, and the Shipibo and similar societies of the montaña and marginal sub-Andean lowlands, on the other hand, have been very different. For all their historical differences, however, they share certain fundamental features of social organization that differentiate them from societies of the types so far considered. Perhaps the most important of these is the lack of any prescriptive form for constituting the basic segmentary units of society (in both cases, extended family households). Household composition in both cases is flexible, consisting of collaterals and affines of both genders clustered around a core of dominant individuals (often a sibling group, sometimes a married couple). In the Waurá case, as in other Xinguano societies, the village as a whole, made up of several such households, is symbolically clustered in an analogous way around a line of "chiefly" individuals of both genders, and the relations among the different tribal villages of the regional system are defined through a series of intervillage rituals focusing on the celebration of each group's chiefly ancestors (the *quarup* ceremony).

For both Shipibo and Waurá, then, social organization is essentially individualistic. Among the Shipibo, the predominant ritual forms (shamanism and, in certain of its aspects, pottery making) are overtly individualistic. Even where a communal structure with collectively ritualized relations exists, as among the Waurá, it remains formulated in terms of core "individuals" (e.g., chiefly ancestors) who serve as foci of attachment for the individual members of society at large. There is, in other words, no social or ritual reproduction of a collectively standardized form of social organization.

Finally, the Shipibo and Waurá have in common their participation in intertribal or interethnic systems of relations defined in terms of exchanges of specialized products—in this case, in their respective regional systems, both have specialized in pottery (and, for the Shipibo, other decorated artifacts). The manufacture and exchange of specialized products, above all ceramics, is thus for both groups the principal basis of the definition of a distinctive social identity in relation to the other groups of their respective regions. This is, again, essentially an individual process. In the Shipibo myth, in which the creator (an individual) makes and differentiates the Shipibo, whites, and blacks as different qualities of pottery, the production of the distinctive Shipibo craft product directly becomes the metaphor for social production. In the Waurá case, the creator separates the Waurá, "wild Indian," and whiteman by giving each of them distinctive artifacts and different drinks (the drinking of manioc gruel from pottery vessels, the distinctive choice of the Waurá ancestor, being identified with the Waurá craft specialty).

The distinctive tokens of social identity thus become invested in individuals through a process identical with that by which the groups in question assert their distinctive identities vis-à-vis the more or less alien groups with which they interact in their respective contact situations. These tokens, their unequal values, and the asymmetrical relationship that follows from these values are at the same time defined as attributes of individuals rather than as overtly social products. The individualistic basis of social organization in the societies in question means that the individual is in effect prior to society rather than the other way around, a principle epitomized by the Waurá cult of chiefly ancestors, the ultimate "prior individuals" upon whom all subsequent society has depended. Mythological individualism and the mythic chartering of the unequal relations comprising the contact situation in terms of original inequality defined at the moment of social creation are thus deeply connected, given that society is self-defined in terms of attachment to individuals embodying to the fullest extent the attributes of valued social identity.

Tales of the dumb gringo: Limitations of white effectiveness as guarantees of Indian separateness. Reeve and Roe both give examples of narratives that deal with the failure of members of the local dominant society in some characteristically Western project (i.e., one involving economic greed) through an inept attempt to utilize some aspect of Indian knowledge or cultural technique. These stories are neither so ambitious nor so culture specific as the other types of narrative with which we have been concerned. They resemble tales more than myths or histories, even though they contain elements proper to both. Found in the highlands and the lowlands, they do not account for the origin or nature of the contact situation as such but merely affirm the separation of Indian and Westerner within it. Their main point is the juxtaposition of the ineptitude of the gringos in exploiting some technique or form of Indian cultural efficacy with the affirmation of its continuing potency from the Indian point of view, thus reinforcing the security and inviolability of the Indian sphere. The effect is to assert the limits of the ability of members of the dominant society to exploit the Indians or encroach upon their social or cultural sphere for the satisfaction of those goals that typically lead them to try to do so. There is no attempt to explain the existence or the nature of the dominant society or its relation to the Indians as such. The Indian technique, instrument, or effective principle in question is not a basic principle of social reproduction. We are not dealing here with anti-myth in reverse. Tales of this kind presuppose no specific type of indigenous society. Their contextual reference is simply to the most generic and nonspecific features of the structure of the contact situation (the inequality and separateness of the two societies). They are therefore to be found among widely differing societies.

Genre, Modality, and Narrative Structure

Genre and Context

It is particularly important in dealing with aliterate cultures to be aware of the possibility that different aspects and levels of social consciousness may be expressed in different genres and contexts. Ramos makes a valuable distinction between modes of discourse intended for internal communication within native societies (in which she includes both myth and historical narratives) and discourse intended for external communication with representatives of Western society. Such political discourse, she suggests, is characterized by its own modality of time (the "progressive present"). Her distinction is explicitly based on *dialogic contexts* and *intended uses* of the modes of discourse in question, but it is implicitly also a distinction of genre (narrative forms in the case of myth and history, oratory in the case of political discourse). Ramos thus points to an important consideration in the analysis of modes of social consciousness and their contents, namely, the interdependence of genre and context. In my essay on the Kayapó, I make the same argument, contrasting myths and historical narratives designed for internal consumption with an oration directed at a delegation of Brazilian officials and an Anglo-American television crew.

In terms of the categories I have adopted in this discussion, Ramos's political discourse is a case of what I have defined as historical consciousness, and her progressive present corresponds to the form of temporal and social consciousness that I have argued is in fact the origin and basis of historical awareness. The terminological issue is not important. What is significant, it seems to me, is that the conclusions at which we arrive (above all, the presence of different modalities of social consciousness, associated with different contexts and genres, and the rejection of the characterization of indigenous societies as "totemic," that is, exclusively mythic and ahistorical) are the same.

There is, I suggest, an important relation between myth and history as different modes of social consciousness (as this concept was defined earlier) and the narrative genres in which they are typically encoded. Myth is prototypically identified with culturally defined genres that may be collectively denominated "narratives of fixed form." Most cultures possess at least one such genre. This is not, of course, the only sort of genre in which myth can be expressed. Not every story related in such a genre is a myth, and many cultures possess distinct genres of "tales of fixed form," only one of which may be a vehicle for myth or several of which may be the vehicles of culturally differentiated genres of myth. After all of these qualifications have been duly registered, however, the fact remains that myth, as it has been defined here, tends in most if not all cultures to be conveyed primarily through the medium of narratives of a more or less standardized form. By "standardized form" I mean that there is a normative or ideal sequential order to the story, at the level of what the Russian Formalists called the *fabula*, which is collectively known and accepted as the standard version. Individual performances or tellings of the story (or *syujet*, in Formalist terms) may vary more or less widely from this standard, but it remains the *background* against which they are *foregrounded* (to use yet another pair of Formalist categories).

Tales of collectively standardized form are thus culturally defined as independent, at the level of essential form or *fabula*, of the context of performance, or the variations of actual performances (*syujet*). They exist as abstract ideas and as such are apt vehicles for attempts to define the essential features of social phenomena in abstraction from their concrete manifestations in particular contexts, actions, or events. Just the opposite could be said about the genre affinities of historical thought. As the consciousness of the interdependence of particular actions and circumstances juxtaposed in concrete contexts or events, historical thought might be expected to express itself by preference in more flexible and context-sensitive genres (prose or its cultural equivalents). Oratory is one such genre. It is well developed in most lowland as well as highland cultures, and, as I report in my essay on the Kayapó, it is the genre of choice for most historical and political discourse in that society. These genre differences, I have suggested, are associated with the subject matter of the narrative in question and the level at which it is being formulated and explained. These are not differences on the order of the contrast between cultures as wholes or their associated levels of social development. Different levels of definition and explanation appropriate to different contexts are to be found within any society or even within the same narrative.

The point is that such differences in what is talked about and how it is said convey important cultural information quite apart from the question of whether the different forms in question share the same symbol system, which Roe, in dismissing the importance of genre distinctions, asserts is the only significant consideration. The essential cultural information coded in different genres of narrative expression, to repeat, relates to different levels or modes of social consciousness, history and myth among them. Relatively free narrative forms, in which speakers can extemporize, create particular variations or invent unique combinations of narrative elements (which may be thought of as the preliterate counterparts of prose), may be preferred as forms of discourse about history for reasons related to the cultural conception of history as such. Conversely, relatively rigid, standardized forms of narrative, drama, or ritual may be preferred as the vehicles of mythic tales, with their relatively abstract, essential, and invariant patterns.

All I am saying is that in talking about historical or mythic modes of social consciousness in indigenous cultures, we must be careful not to bias our sample by considering only one genre of expression when other genres may be employed in the societies in question to express different modes of consciousness. To base one's entire analysis of social consciousness in a lowland society on one or a few traditional rituals and narratives, and then to conclude that the culture as a whole is in the mythic phase, lacking a concept of history, may reflect a lack in the investigative procedure more than a lack in the culture. Some studies of South American cultures leave one wishing that the authors would have paid a little more attention to all that shouting that was going on out in the plaza while they were struggling to transcribe their myth tapes.

The Narrative Dimension

Narrative structure, ritual organization, and choreographic form in the Andes. Both myth and history are primarily narrative forms. They consist of sequences of actions and events arranged so as to constitute an intelligible pattern. Just as myth and history (and the subvarieties into which they can be classified) constitute different modes of consciousness of the relationship between time (in the material form of action and causal orders of events) and the structure of the existing social order, so also the narratives through which they are expressed tend to be constructed in different ways. As Dillon and Abercrombie argue, the conceptual form of the perspective on historical time or mythic creation conveyed in a story tends to be encoded in the structure of its plot (by which they mean *fabula* rather than *syujet*, to retain the Formalist terms, although in their case the latter conforms closely to the former).

Dillon and Abercrombie's analysis provides an elegant paradigmatic model for their argument. In their essay they identify two main aspects of the structure of a K'ulta (highland Bolivian) narrative. First, the structure of the plot, as a system of relations in space and time, takes the form of a progression from simple polarity through the disintegration and mediation of the constituent features of the opposition to a synthesis in which the opposing elements are reconciled in the form of alternating complementarities. Second, there is a transformation of the protagonists' subjective attitudes, identities, and capacities for action that is correlated with the transformation of the spatiotemporal structure of the world in which they interact. In both respects the structure of the narrative effects and embodies a *cumulative* change in the nature of its constituent oppositions and the relations among them. This change takes the form of the construction of a *higher level of structure* (more inclusive and comprising more complex relationships than the situation at the beginning of the story).

It is this cumulative, hierarchically ordered pattern of transformations, rather than the simple linear order of events, that constitutes the *structure* of the narrative, and what Dillon and Abercrombie proceed to show is that this structural pattern is identical with the pattern of relations that comprises the message content or meaning of the myth. Their elegant analysis suggests how narrative structures themselves may serve as the instruments for formulating the modalities of temporal and social consciousness they represent and convey, at the level of social action as well as of cultural performance.

Narrative structure in the origin myths and anti-myths of Central Brazil and the Andes. The selection of one or another narrative order (i.e., one or another form of cumulative pattern in the sense just defined) is directly related to the conceptual content of the narrative in question. This is as true of mythic as it is of historical narratives. To speak, as I have done, of different modalities of myth as alternative structural possibilities within the generic category of mythic narratives is to emphasize the importance of variations in narrative structure in conveying crucial dimensions of meaning.

Myth and anti-myth, for instance, are not merely distinct at the level of message but at the level of narrative form itself. In the standard creation myth (represented for Da Matta by the Gê culture-origin myth of the fire of the Jaguar), the structure of the narrative is cumulatively self-transforming. It constructs a hierarchically ordered, reflexively self-replicating system of relations (concretely embodied by the infinitely self-reproducing cooking fire). The specific devices through which this is achieved include the progressive embedding of its constituent relations, the transformation of their structural features into more abstract and general forms, and the controlled reversal of the temporal and spatial dimensions of the action (for a full account of these structural devices and transformations see Turner [1985]). The message of the myth is that this sort of structure is what culture essentially is; the important point in this context is that this message is concretely encoded in the structure of the narrative itself.

In anti-myth, by contrast, the structure of relations fails to embed itself and become reflexively self-regenerating. Instead, it becomes self-decomposing. The transformation of the key "natural" element and its relations to the other (social) elements takes the opposite form to that which it assumes in the culture-origin myth and strengthens rather than destroys the natural entity in question. Instead of an integral, self-embedding, self-reproducing system of transformations, one is left with a cleavage between mutually exclusive and external processes of replication (those located in Auke as the representative of the new Brazilian society, on the one hand, and those of the original native system, on the other, with its fire, clubs, and bows and arrows). In form, the narrative consists of an irreversible externalization, as contrasted with the reversible self-embedding or internalization, of a process of productive transformation. Different narrative structures thus formulate different narrative meanings, and they constitute those meanings in different modalities of social time and space. These in turn are correlated with different forms of social agency and different patterns of relationship between social actors and processes. They form, in short, different "chronotopes" (Bakhtin 1981). (Similar points can be made about the recursive structure of the more complex Andean forms of anti-myth analyzed earlier and, mutatis mutandis, about the other forms of myth, historical narrative, and ritual dance that have been discussed.)

Conclusions

The working hypothesis with which this commentary began was that a society defines its relationship to others by reference to the same internal processes by which it reproduces (and thus pragmatically defines) itself. This is necessarily so, since "defining itself" in this context means reproducing not only its internal structure but also its pattern of accommodation to the situation of contact between it and the other societies in question. Such reproductive processes comprise forms of consciousness, patterns of interaction, and material social activities: in sum, a system of collective action that is at once social and cultural. Representations of other societies and their relations to one's own society form an integral part of this process of collective self-definition. Yet such representations, precisely because they form integral parts of the processes and situations under discussion, cannot be regarded as constituting a purely cultural, much less a purely mythic order.

The modalities of mythic and historical representations defined in the course of this commentary are obviously of a tentative and heuristic character; others will doubtless be found to be appropriate to different questions and data, and in any case the list is certainly not exhaustive as a typology of native South American ethno-ethnohistorical representations. The heuristic value of this exercise lies in the convergence of the various types of mythic and historical representations that have been defined with the modes of self-reproductive processes and contact situations of the societies from which the narratives and allied symbolic forms are drawn. This convergence, I would argue, is of a sort that tends to confirm the working hypothesis.

These collective forms of consciousness and group activity distribute themselves into a simple, hierarchically ordered pattern. At the lowest level are societies like the Shipibo or Waurá, which lack prescriptive forms of segmentary structure and therefore also lack institutions that directly regulate or impose collective social forms, up to and including the structure of the community as a whole. The reproduction of segmentary groupings, such as extended family households, and of larger social agglomerations, where such exist, is accomplished in these societies as the aggregate result of ad hoc associations among individuals and elementary families, which thus constitute their basic structural units.

The next level consists of societies like those of Central Brazil or the Northwest Amazon, which possess a level of collective institutional structure that serves to guide the reproduction of the segmentary units of society (longhouses, extended family households) in a standardized form. This institutional structure reflexively becomes a form through which the members of society can directly participate in the reproduction of the structure of their communities as totalities. At the next level, represented by the Andeans, are communities that possess collective institutions of the Central Brazilian type modified so as to model, and thus symbolically introject, their relation of subordination to the dominant state structure within which they are embedded. Through this additional layer of structural complexity these communities vicariously reproduce, and thus participate in, their subordination within the contact situation, as an aspect of their own internal structures.

The classification of subtypes of myth that has emerged from this analysis turns out to correspond to this rough scale of degrees of social complexity. The myths associated with groups of the first level (myths of original inequality) represent the situation of contact in terms of a simple relation of difference and distance, articulated at the level of social individuals. Those associated with societies of the next level (simple anti-myths) formulate the contact relation as one of complementary contrast arising from the failure of the indigenous society's powers of reproduction to transform the founder-figure of Western society, who then retransforms the products of the failed native transformations into the more powerful productive transformations of Western society.

The Andean societies comprising the next level have a more complex variant of the basic anti-myth pattern (i.e., the recursive anti-myth). In this variant of the pattern the myth is formulated as two consecutive stories that repeat the same structure, associated with successive ages (timpus, pacha) of the world. These two stories are themselves related in terms of the same structure that serves as the internal structure of each. This relatively complex, hierarchical structure elegantly embodies the basic structure through which Andean communities relate themselves to the dominant state, while continuing the basic formula of the anti-myth, viz., that the power of the dominant (Western) member of the situation of contact is a transformation of the power or principle through which the native society is created and reproduced.

The final type of myth, comprising the messianic and cargo examples, analytically was shown to be a further transformation of the anti-myth structure. If the transformation of the native principle of social reproduction into the Western society's principle of domination over it, which forms the endpoint of the anti-myth, can be described in dialectical terms as a negation, then the messianic myth posits a reversal of that transformation and thus constitutes itself as a "negation of the negation." The myths of this category constitute the most powerful and complex structures among all the types and subtypes identified here. They arise as conceptual forms of organized efforts by native societies to transform the structure of the situation of contact so as to reverse the relation of domination upon which it is founded.

A society's collective capacity for regulating its own production, in conjunction with its situation of contact, not only conditions the form of its mythic representations but conditions its capacity for historical consciousness, as well as the form of that consciousness. The boundary between the mythic and historical levels of social self-awareness is a function of the degree to which the indigenous society has managed to achieve a form of collective self-determination powerful enough to survive and subsume the disruptions and transformations of its cultural structures and social organization entailed in the situation of contact. This is illustrated by the contrasting historical attitudes of Ancient Hebrews and the Inca (or, more specifically, the Yauyos of Huarochirí), on the one hand, and the Greeks and the Kayapó, on the other. Where the transformations in question take the diachronic form of successive changes externally forced by the actions of dominant societies in the contact situation, as among the Hebrews or the peoples of the Inca Empire, the historical representation of the society tends to take the form of a universal history, that is, a continuous temporal succession of relatively unstable and incomplete social forms linking the present to the beginning of historical time. Where it takes the form of a synchronic copresence of alternative social possibilities, simultaneously embraced as actual or potential courses of action within a universal present, as among the Greeks or the Kayapó, it tends to take the form of a discontinuous set of bounded episodes, each embodying the potential totality of social forms as a background of the realization of only one or a few of them at a time.

I have obviously stretched my classical parallels to the breaking point (or beyond), but my argument does not really depend upon making the identification of the Kayapó and the Greeks stick. My general point is simply that history and myth are both primarily to be understood as modes of consciousness of the social present, expressed in terms of the relation of that present to its past (and future). As such, they form part of the sociocultural structures through which the present is produced, which always means in large part *reproduced,* as an instance of a pattern of the past. Social consciousness, in both its mythic and historical modes, is thus formed as an integral part of the process of social reproduction through which a society reflexively defines itself.

It should be clear that this is not a question of society determining culture or vice versa. The notion of social action that serves as the point of departure of this analysis, and of which social reproduction is only a special, reflexive form, presupposes the pragmatic synthesis of social forms of action and cultural forms of consciousness. The implications of this conception, and of the analysis I have attempted to develop from it, may be summed up in two general theses. First, cultural structure itself is constructed as an aspect of the general process of producing and reproducing the structures, not merely the isolated actions or events, of the sociohistorical context. It is therefore internally related to those structures and is in fact an aspect of them rather than an externally related, theoretically autonomous order of structure. Second, as this implies, cultural structure consists not merely of paradigmatic relations in a Saussurian sense, an abstract langue whose social roots are cut, but of a complex syntagmatic structure for the construction of events and processes in social action. Such structures include the basic internal processes of social production and reproduction as well as the patterns of interaction with other societies involved in situations of contact. These structures of action and interaction are culturally encoded, as the essays in this collection richly attest, in the structures of mythic and historical narratives, danced out in patterns of ritual choreography, and declaimed in the rhetoric of orators.

It is complex social and cultural structures at this level, rather than decontextualized structures in the Saussurian sense, that reflexively become the primary cultural instruments for interpreting and integrating new events into the sociocultural structure. The point is that at both levels, as structures and as events, they are as much social as cultural. The more we shift away from the archaic Saussurian model of cultural structure as langue (and its continuation in structuralism), toward a more generative and dynamic conception of both cultural and social structure—in other words, the more the equally archaic theoretical dichotomy between culture and society breaks down—the more obvious it becomes that it makes no sense to try to speak of the relation between structure and event in terms of the relation between culture and history (or society).

What I have tried to suggest, in sum, is the utility of replacing the culture/society contrast, along with the positivist and idealist traditions of social thought from which it derives, with a focus on the relationship between a sociocultural system and the reflexive structures through which it reproduces itself. This reflexive relationship is not only the crucible within which social consciousness is formed but also the channel through which it in turn shapes social action.

A society's capacity to determine its own form of reproduction also constitutes the basis of its capacity to shape its social and political-economic relationship to another society in a situation of contact. The structure of the native society, meaning in particular its mode of social reproduction, and the structure of the situation of contact in which it participates are not independent variables. Andean and Central Brazilian societies, for example, with their complex systems of collective institutions, are far better adapted to sustain a relation of integration and intensive interaction with local Western society while maintaining a separate, internally autonomous collective identity than are simple societies like the Shipibo, Aguaruna, or Waurá. The types of contact situations in which the former are found to be engaged, combining interdependence, resistance, and the maintenance of a separate social identity in the midst of intensive contact, differ from those of the latter, with their emphasis on insulation, distance, and sporadic contact. These differences, as we have seen, are faithfully evoked in the characteristic mythic and historical representations of contact of the two groups. But they are also translated into action, and in this process myth and history become integral components of the concrete social processes that shape the contexts they represent.

The same points have been made in connection with Northwest Amazonian societies. The structures of these societies have been shown to be directly related to the ways in which they shaped their respective situations of contact through forms of direct resistance. In all of these cases historical action, mode of social consciousness, and the social relation of the native society to the contact situation and to itself through its internal processes of reproduction have to be understood in relation to one another as parts of a single process. This process is at once social and cultural, historical and ethno-ethnohistorical: at this level of totalization, an anthropological conception of history becomes indistinguishable from a historically conceived anthropology.

Commentary

Historical and Mythic Evocations of Chthonic Power in South America

Norman E. Whitten, Jr.

> ... such highly structured symbolic forms as myth and ritual
> cannot be viewed as conservative forces, preserving some origi-
> nal "precontact" cultural logic. Rather, they provide the active
> locus for the simultaneous distillation and recreation of the
> values (now presupposing the conquest and colonial dom-
> ination) that motivate social action.
> —Mary Dillon and Thomas Abercrombie

This volume marks a significant advance in the ethnography and ethnology of native South American peoples and signals the demise of the pervasive anthropological polarity between cultural-ecological evolutionism, as manifested especially by the late Julian H. Steward, and structuralism, as championed by Claude Lévi-Strauss. Whether or not the reuniting of anthropology, history, and native new-world cosmography that it portends ever crystallizes as a "theory of practice" —revealed so tortuously by Bourdieu (1977) and Giddens (1981), reviewed by Ortner (1984) and Karp (1986), and suggested by Hill in his excellent introduction to this volume—remains to be seen. My own sense is that we would do well to re-examine history since Marx and Weber, as do Boon (1982) and Worsley (1984), before we accept without reservation recent post-Weberian sociology and interpretive anthropology (see, e.g., the confrontation between Geertz [1973b, 1983, 1984] and Spiro [1986]). At a time when even Worsley (1984:37) speaks of proponents of "new marxisms" who seek to understand culture as being "closet Weberians," caution with regard to prelabeled anthropological theory is urged, together with sustained, contemporary, creative, interpretive ethnography based on continuous, rigorous empirical field research. The latter is clearly represented in this volume, providing apt refutation of the absurd interpretive/empiricist polarity currently favored in some quarters.

Rethinking History and Myth is about narratives that reveal structures of time, structures of imagery, and the processes of domination and hegemony as they cohere in native South American cultures from various, diverse, and contrasting ecological and topographical regions. What comes to the fore—what literally jumps out of most of these essays—is a sense of the power of cultural constructions and constitutions, a very special chthonic power, that is both time binder and release mechanism. "Chthonic" pertains to the underworld, and in Greek mythology, of course, the underworld was in specific contrast to the heavenly world. But in native South American cosmology, chthonic qualities are inner ones, and the contrasts made emphasize the penumbra. Chthonic power in native thought is linked to that which is within water and that which contains water, and water itself is both a container of earth—that which is "here" and "ours"—and a vehicle to another place where "we" go to "others" and "they" come to "us." Chthonic power, then, is inner but universal. We are, in a sense, contained by our own essence.

This commentary seeks to draw together some of the dimensions of the sense and reference systems of chthonic power that motivate history, myth, and the transmission of the structure of conquest wherein native cultures came to exist as they do, to resist, to be contained, yet to release their own powers to reconstitute and reproduce not only themselves but also the system of domination and their dynamic, forceful, resistant place within it. Because this volume is especially concerned with time and space in indigenous thought, I begin with these concepts and then move to other facets of commonality in the essays (and in native societies of South America), returning to an illustration of the ideas in a specific setting to eventually compare ideas about the duality of power patterning and the specificity of chthonic power in indigenous cosmography.

The Structure of Time-Space

Reeve, Hill and Wright, Rasnake, Roe, and Chernela draw upon data from Upper Amazonian Canelos Quichua, Orinocan Arawakan, South-Central Andean Quechua, Upper Amazonian Shipibo-Conibo, and Northwest Amazon Arapaço peoples to demonstrate the complex processing of time-space imagery in native cultures. Reeve, for example, shows that recent and traumatic historical episodes among the Curaray Runa are tied inextricably to place and that the evocation of place provides the indexical power to retrieve, in mythic and legendary telling, the historical event linking the Andes and Amazonia within the structure of old-world domination, which thereby is rejected by the contemporary people. I return shortly to this issue, using the Curaray Runa to demonstrate how such evocations are stored in graphic imagery imparted to ceramics, and to the disposition of such objectifications. But first let us be sure of our own English usage of such critical concepts as *time-space.*

According to Webster, *time* refers primarily to the parting or dividing up of something, as in an interval, "the period between two events or during which something exists, happens, or acts; measured or measurable intervals." *Space,* too, is conceived of in intervals, in one sense as an "interval or length of time." Western philosophers such as Newton-Smith (1980) speak of the *topology of time,* an apt depiction from Western philosophy of local-knowledge systems of South American native thought. One supposes that Einstein's theory of relativity springs from the mind of a genius but is rooted nonetheless in Western thought. In anthropology, Leach (1982), following Lévi-Strauss to build a school of British structuralism, deals with time topographically, in well-known ways: quotidian time and space are continuous, but time and space of culture are discontinuous; it is in the segmentation of social time that distinct spaces are created and in the segmentation of space that time is created (e.g., p. 86; see also Firth 1951). Such universal time-space is *cultural,* wherein events, persons, intervals, all sorts of discontinuities and altered social relations (including ritual and dominance, resistance and hegemony) constitute marking mechanisms that provide indexical and evocative systems through which humans conceptualize historicity— something that almost every essay in this volume touches on. Victor Turner (1974) undertook a topography of ritual and politics in his multiple discussions of passages, margins, limens, and so on, by which collective, historical consciousness is constructed, deconstructed, and periodically reinforced and transformed. In short, the English language and anthropology as a discipline are no strangers to the thought patterns of the Canelos Quichua, Arawak, Aymara, Shipibo, Andean Quechua, or Portuguese- and Tucano-speaking Arapaço. We should be well prepared to understand more fully just how time-space structures may configure through elicited narrative as we undertake sustained Native American cosmography.

The original symposium succeeded, and this volume clearly succeeds, in revealing realms wherein South American thought and enactment systems are teased out of universal time-space to show us exquisitely particular dimensions of the intersections of indigenous creativity and the mythic-historical framing mechanisms for such creativity. The chapters in this volume give us a firm basis for future comparison, and in their particularism they build toward generalizations that should allow us to rethink cherished polarities of our forebears and join colleagues working with Asian, European, and African systems to develop appropriate theories of culture applicable to our professional concerns, as well as to understand the religious and cosmological underpinnings of radical change throughout this hemisphere. Where the symposium failed was in the insistence, in some quarters, that to conjoin time and space as a conceptual unit fundamental to indigenous historicity was to discover "the Andean system" as something that contrasts totally with what Westerners "know" to be the distinctions between times and spaces. It is to the credit of the authors of these fine essays that the initial symposium biases toward Andean discovery have been set aside.

Ñucanchij callarirucugunata cuti yachashpa, unaimandata cuti yachashpa ("Learning again from our mythic time-space, we are knowing once more our beginning times-places"). This phrase, from Canelos Quichua of the Bobonaza drainage of Amazonian Ecuador, is underscored by slightly different terminology in Reeve's excellent account of the Curaray Runa, and it also comes through strongly in most of the other essays on indigenous South American cultures. I suspect that Roe has heard something very close to it, in Quechua, on the Ucayali River and its tributaries. Significantly, it could come forth just as easily from an Afro-American setting, as demonstrated convincingly by Richard Price (1983a:5):

> All history is thus: a radical selection from the immensely rich swirl of past human activity . . . the selection that is made by those people who gather together at this shrine. [Here think of the mythohistorical plaza and fire described by Reeve for the Curaray Runa or of the ancient Inca village of the Shipibo described by Roe.] . . . [The book *First-Time*] is about those distant people and those long-ago events that Saramakas today choose to think about, talk about, and act upon; but it is also about the ways that Saramakas transform the general past (everything that happened) into the significant past, their history.

It is again to the credit of the symposium, and to many of the articles in this volume, including the Introduction, that reference is made not only to indigenous systems but to Afro-American ones. As noted elsewhere (Whitten 1986:94), "Throughout the New World, ethnohistory of indigenous and black people swirls and spirals through reinforcing general events relegated to palpable time-space periods that may (or must) be resurrected and entered during times of collective crisis." These essays, especially when conjoined with Price (1983a) on Suriname, Drummond (1981) on Guyana, Gudeman (1986) on Panama, and Taussig (1987) on Colombia, for example, continue to contribute to a deeper

understanding of more general features of the particularities of indigenous and black existence, dialogic as they are with regard to various
shades of white conquest culture and what Taussig (1987:5ff.) argues is
an inborn "culture of terror and space of death."

A Particular, Graphic Representation of the Power of Evoked Time-Space

To understand the evocative and indexical character of framed time-
space in indigenous cultures, let us turn to the people described by the
lead essay—to the Curaray Runa of Canelos Quichua culture who live
on the very edge of Waorani territory. Until recently the Curaray Runa
and Waorani hated, feared, and sometimes killed one another. The
Canelos called the Waorani *auca,* and the Waorani tagged the Canelos
cohouri. Each thought the other was prone to cannibalism.

Reeve convincingly demonstrates how the concept *cauchu uras*
(rubber-boom time-space) bundles the knowledge of conflict and resistance that "is . . . a source of autochthonous power, forming a counterdiscourse through which a system of political and economic domination
by foreigners is apprehended" (see also Price 1983a; Taussig 1980, 1987;
Whitten 1985). During 1971–74, a petroleum boom hit the Curaray
Runa (Whitten 1976), converting their territory into a major staging
area for foreign oil exploration and exploitation. Some years later, while
oilmen were still occasionally coming and going on the Curaray River
in their motorized canoes, signaling the possibility of the return to
secular chaos, Alegría Canelos constructed an interesting and, at first
glance, whimsical effigy pot (Figure 1) for the upcoming Easter festival
to be held in the Josephine Mission–controlled plaza. To anyone who
knows Canelos Quichua imagery, this pot represents two utterly distinct but inextricably conjoined worlds—the secular, international political economy of escalating domination in all parts of Ecuador and the
sacred, indigenous way of life based upon the relationships among
spirit-masters of the hydrosphere, rain forest, and garden soil and pottery clay.

Looking first at the upper segment of the pot (Figure 2) we see an oil
boss riding in a motor-driven canoe, holding onto his hat—once a
common sight on the Curaray, where anyone will tell you that when
this man opens his mouth, orders that no one understands are shouted
to native workers. The oil boss represents, in animal form, the *machin
runa,* a monkey person. In spirit form he is the forest master of other

Figure 1. Entire effigy pot.

Figure 2. Upper segment of pot.

people, other people's Amasanga, the fearsome Jurijuri spirit that coughs like a jaguar. Alegría Canelos decorated this monkeylike spirit-person from the world of political-economic domination with anaconda spots, with head and neck rearing out of the water. When a human being swims underwater and encounters an anaconda, enormous danger exists. When the human surfaces, the anaconda surfaces too; and the instant the human head breaks the surface, the anaconda strikes. This is what all Canelos Quichua say, and this is what the Jacques Cousteau camera-man learned when videotaping an anaconda sequence for the four-hour television documentary *The Amazon*.

Looking at the bottom of the pot (Figure 3) we see that the monkey-man in the canoe rests on a turtle seat of power, with anaconda spots on the base. The turtle is *charapa*, Amazonian water turtle. As a reptile its eggs are an important source of food for humans. As a spirit force the *charapa* is the seat of power, *bancu*, of Sungui, the first shaman and ultimate source of shamanic power, who himself appears to human shamans as the anaconda, to some humans as a naked, bearded white man standing on a riverbank, to vision-seekers and dreamers as a shimmering spirit-person (usually female) dressed in rainbow colors, and to all as a rainbow, or pair of them, in the hydrosphere that contains all of the earth. Looking more closely at the canoe motif, we see that the anaconda design encapsulates Christian cross symbols. Such graphic encapsulation evokes knowledge of the historical process of containment and replication of the dominant political economy, itself reproducing antinomy and ordering chaotic relationships (Whitten 1985; Whitten and Whitten 1988; for a different but complementary view see Taussig 1987). But the graphic imagery of the cross within the anaconda motif reverses the substance of history by asserting an ultimate, indigenous, chthonic power as dominant.

The Canelos Quichua annually enact this very process, in a cere-mony that expands the universe to include all spirits, souls, beings, and people. The encapsulation process, in other words, contains a space to structure time, and in the annual ceremony—described elsewhere as an *ayllu* ceremony (Whitten 1976, 1978, 1985; Whitten and Whitten 1988; Reeve 1985)—this time-space includes all of the senses of myth, legend, and history discussed by Reeve, Rasnake, Roe, Hill and Wright, Chernela, and others in this volume. There is a profound duality of patterning to this festive ceremonial event and especially to its climactic set of termi-nal performances.

The *ayllu* ceremony is about the historical experience of external social domination and about the inner world of Canelos Quichua power. The Runa refer to the final events of the *ayllu* ceremony as

Figure 3. Lower segment of pot.

dominario, from the Spanish *dominar*, "to control." Always, as the Runa begin the activities signaling the *dominario*, the local or visiting *cura* begins to ring the chapel bell. To the Runa this bell-ringing signals the beginning of a sacred mass to celebrate Western cannibalism and the resurrection of the crucified, bearded Christ, whom they see as representing ancient Spanish domination. To many, the raucous bell-ringing congers an imagery of the imminence of a devouring external force. On the other side, the indigenous/Western polarity is heightened to its extreme, for the Runa move toward a release of the awesome power of the mighty, chthonic anaconda. As containment of Runa souls by the Catholic chapel begins to crumble in the very processes of ritual enactment of political-economic dominance structuring, the Runa bring forth the heretofore contained chthonic power. The symbols of this event not only conjoin an effigy jar with ceremonial enactment of a given people but, mutatis mutandis, exemplify the narrative substance of "rethinking history and myth" described repeatedly in this volume.

As the *dominario* begins, an indigenous outsider, downriver (*uraimanda*) powerful shaman gently plays a combination of flute and drum associated with Andean masked ceremonies. The melody itself is a skillful blend of his private Amazonian shaman's song (*taquina*) and a public Andean motif. With the sound of this special melody and rhythm, the indigenous world expands into the continental container of the Western power signaled by the *cura*'s pumping, two-armed assault through his chapel bell on the Runa's ears and into their very psyches. Four men, each representing the mighty black jaguar (corporeal representative of forest spirit-master Amasanga), go to the river and remove from it a bamboo pole, into which four copal fires are placed (recall Chernela's and Roe's essays). As the pole with the four fires within is brought into the plaza, everyone's breathing becomes labored, for they all know that the anaconda is no longer in the water. Its crushing power is now on land. When the anaconda is on land, it is there only to hunt people, to crush them, and then to put the crushed person into that mighty, expanded mouth to swallow and swallow and then vomit noisily, to allow the crushed ones to putrify, to again swallow and vomit, until at last that which was human flesh and bone is within the anaconda, the body of which is now terribly swollen. The giant anaconda then returns to its chthonic lair within mud within water to lie more or less dormant for up to half a year, digesting its meal and growing stronger, increasing its size and power for its next sojourn through water and onto land. This is the sort of thinking—as a network of palpable images—that the emergence of the ceremonial pole with glowing fires inside instantly evokes.

As the four men come forth bearing the pole, festival participants dance through palm-frond arches constructed for the Catholic mission. Then the great transformation, called *tucuna,* begins. The pole, as *amarun* (anaconda), Sungui's corporeal form, is carried in a lurching, going-out-of-control manner, which almost instantly becomes destructive. The bearers and the pole crash right into and through the bamboo walls of the church, slamming, falling, rising again, running, frightening everyone, going completely out of control while still in a cultural domain characterized by Catholic mission control, or domination. The church is symbolically being penetrated and crushed by a mighty constrictor, itself homologous with the indigenous *ayllu* (kinship) system (Whitten 1985:66–69ff.), and the people themselves are being symbolically devoured by the manifestation of the release of their own contained power.

Acting against domination, within a domain of domination, the festival reaches a crescendo that is, quite literally and quite obviously, terrifying to the participants. Women dance with their hair flying to and fro, their sideways motion being the feminine analogue of the male-performed two-tone hum of shamanic chanting that evokes the imagery of mythic time-space (*unai*). Men beat snare drums, circling and circling while producing a resonating pulse-tremolo signifying Amasanga's rumble of approaching thunder and the buzz of approaching spirit-bees as shamanic helpers. All souls and spirits and beings are indiscriminately summoned as all containment dissolves into a mighty tropical storm that surrounds the entire earth-world. Escalating chaos reigns as nightfall rapidly approaches, and the church is said to be destroyed in one great transformation of the world of forest and garden and earth and mire into an encompassing, rushing, surging, eastward-flowing sea. When performing this ritual the Canelos Quichua say that they fear *tucurina,* ending everything (which derives from *tucuna,* transformation). The concept *tucurina* is one of the most powerful ones in Canelos Quichua thought, particularly when applied reflexively to one's own family, group, or people. *Tucurina* means, in this sense, that to truly destroy the hegemonic authority of the church by the invocation of the ultimate power of Sungui, here portrayed as the crushing, devouring anaconda, the Canelos Quichua may also destroy themselves, embedded, however resistantly, as they are—in a revelatory manner through the vehicle of this ritual—in that very domination.

By expressing in a profound manner the contradiction of indigenous resurgence and national-international domination of indigenous existence, and by moving to the brink of ending everything, the Canelos Quichua structure the processes of domination that bear down upon them while repelling hegemony. They also forge anew a ritual link that easily traverses Bolivian Quechua ceremony, as described by Rasnake, Arapaço and Arawak narratives of the Amazon, as described by Chernela and by Hill and Wright, respectively, right back to Central Andean enactments and narrations, as described by Silverblatt and by Dillon and Abercrombie, and the Upper Amazonian "Inca tales" of the Shipibo, as described by Roe. Indeed, given the correspondences (some transformed, some not) from culture to culture across these vastly different topographical zones, the Andean/lowland argument (see, e.g., Roe) dissolves. Quite clearly, we seem to be dealing with expressive tropes that reflect transformations of a new-world cosmology as manifest in indigenous narrative, enactment patterns, and art styles across contrasting geophysical and time-space topologies.

Chthonic Power

There are three great hydraulic systems at work in the areas of South America that are covered in these essays. The first is the Andean system of uplift of seawater thousands upon thousands of feet (see, e.g., Bastien 1985); the second is the mighty Amazon and its tributaries; and the third, perhaps less familiar to many, is the rain-forest system itself (see, e.g., Myer 1984). These systems serve as major reference configurations through which indigenous narrative in South America makes sense of history and cosmologically constructs interpretable historicity.

"Reference" and "sense" are used here in the manner described by Tambiah (1985:4, 5; see also 1–13): "By 'reference' I mean the things in the world out there that the terms of classification or cosmology 'name'; or 'designate'." "By the 'sense' of a term in a classificatory scheme I mean its place in a system of relationships with other component terms." He goes on to say, "This way of looking at the matter necessarily sets up a dialectic between the sense and referential axes of a classification scheme. . . ." This very dialectic is most apparent in the majority of chapters in this volume. Its salience is underscored in Roe's extended discussion of Shipibo history, legend, and sets of contrasts as a dual set of Venn diagrams with revelatory penumbrae (Proto-culture and Supernature) of Shipibo/other humans, Shipibo/other beings, Shipibo/ spirit relationships, and how these relationships shift in four different regions of time-space (Ancient, Incaic, Grandfathers, and Now). It is also significant that Roe places the dialectic in a prehistoric, archaeological context that takes us back 1,000 years or more and upriver to a village that the contemporary Shipibo, who contrast themselves with the Inca, say the Inca founded with their (Shipibo) unique custom of female clitoridectomy and its ritual trappings before the village rose and moved downriver to the Ucayali. The upriver-downriver flow of the Shipibo/Inca contrast and unity, as the village itself remains stable, is a theme reflected, one way or another, in all of the essays dealing with lifeways east of the mighty Andes, as well as in the literature relevant to these essays.

The iconic reference to chthonic power in the Andes and Amazonia (including, in the latter, the Orinocan drainage and adjacent regions) is to the anaconda (*amaru*, in Quechua) and/or its most striking properties, such as the ability to crush, the transformation of living beings of flesh and bone into vomit fit to eat, its lair within mud and mire within water, its dormant nature after it has fed, its ability to swell tremendously upon eating, its dual penises, its underwater explosive noises, its violently entangling sexuality, or its vestigial hind limbs. The anaconda, in turn, signals the hydraulic power of the Andes upwelling or waterfall, of Amazonian water flow, or of rain-forest hydrology. Reference and sense may come very close together in some settings, such as those of the Canelos Quichua, the Shipibo, the Arapaço, and the Wakuénai. Elsewhere, as in most of the Andes, perhaps everywhere there, sense may be derived more clearly by reference to the fusion of hydrosphere symbolism with transforming violence of contact and subsequent dominance of Spanish colonial society. Rasnake writes:

> Four hundred fifty years have passed since the Spaniards first invaded [the southern Bolivian] highlands. Yet that key historical event remains a basis for understanding the present. The sequence of stories that recount the changes brought about by the Spanish invasion endows that event, by association, with a world-creating power, a power that is not used, at least at present, as a legitimation for struggles within the group but is called upon as a means to comprehend, and to confront, the realities of what we might call "national powerlessness," of class subordination in the wider social context. At the same time, this pivotal event provides an affirmation of another kind of power, the Yura perception of what I call their "chthonic power."

Hill and Wright say virtually the same thing, though their metaphor, as one expects from an Amazonian society, is explicit:

> Venancio [Camico, a messianic hero of the late nineteenth century] symbolically reverses the processes of constriction and alienation [of national power wielders] by replacing an image of alien power, the coffin, with one of a more powerful but equally dangerous autochthonous power [the anaconda]. . . . The appearance of an enormous anaconda inside Venancio's

coffin expresses a similar theme: the anaconda is stuck inside the container, whereas Venancio . . . has escaped unharmed. At the same time, the anaconda as an indigenous symbol of dangerous sexual power is used to create an image of the autodestruction of the white's power structure through military rebellion.

Enter *tupaj amaru*. *Tupaj* in Quechua is the possessive form of the verb *tupana*, which means "to encounter." The current term comes to Quechua from the Spanish verb *topar*, which means "to collide with, to run into or against." It presumably also derives from the Incaic Quechua noun *tupa* (*topa*), meaning "head" or "leader." *Amaru* (or *amarun*, as I shall use it hereafter) means "giant constrictor" in Amazonian and Andean Quechua, in specific contrast to *machacui*, which means "snake." All boas are *amarun*, but the two anacondas—the multicolored, spotted one and the black one—are the prototype of *amarun*; tree boa constrictors, too, are *amarun*. The practice about to be described applies to all boas, but the primary symbolism is that of the multicolored giant anaconda.

In various parts of Amazonian Ecuador there are strikingly similar practices (not just narratives) engaged in by the strikingly different peoples speaking unrelated languages. One of these practices has to do with an anaconda (the following description comes from Canelos Quichua practices). When found on land, the anaconda is bludgeoned on its head with a pole until it can be approached with a machete. The human hunter, always male, severs the anaconda's head from its body. If he so chooses, he takes some of the stomach, lungs, and heart (which beats for hours after death)—these organs constitute the anaconda's will (*shungu*)—some of its body fat (which, mythically, is a human penis; see Whitten 1985:66–67 and for cognate symbolism see Goldman n.d.), and then carefully buries the entire body in earth, not water. The anaconda is not sent home to its chthonic mire within water; instead it is buried in the ground, and it is hoped that the anaconda stays buried there. The head is taken home where its jaw, skull fragments, and other special bones are removed to be cleaned and polished and eventually put into a special, small palm-nut container. The rest of the head is buried far away from the body, and a pole (representing a lance) is driven into the head from above the ground.

Danger now exists in the space between the body and the head of the dead anaconda, for it is said that the body will begin to grow toward the head. Part of the head—often the jaw, skull, and brain—together with the will of the anaconda and its body fat are now in a foreign domain, that of a human family. If the anaconda is ever to live and see again, it must be led by one who is fully human. The body begins to grow toward the head, and, if successful, native people say that a phenomenon they (the Canelos Quichua) call *tupaj amarun* occurs. *Tupaj amarun* symbolizes the ultimate danger of resurrection of the slain constrictor, for when the body of the anaconda meets up with, or confronts, its head—altered as that head is by the knowledge and culture of a killer human—terrible upheaval occurs. Earth and forest and garden are torn asunder by an enormous, underearth (chthonic) surge of energy that creates mountains, causes thunder and lightning to radiate, and initiates volcanic activity in the Andes and floods to the east. That is what people say who live east of the Andes, where the large constrictors also live.

Socially, in many Andean rebellions, Tupaj Amaru, whether regarded as an indigenous or a mestizo revolutionary, draws on his past indigenous existence to do the same thing. Stories such as this (but with reference to human or spirit heroes, not the anaconda) abound in the Andes following the Spanish conquest, especially in the Inkarri myths (see, e.g., Ossio 1973a). It is as though the restless, socially interred body of indigenous peoples, crushed first by Incaic expansion and then by Spanish hierarchy, dominance, and oppression, "connected" with a new knowledge system of the outside (white) world and with that system also brought the outside world into a sustained set of clashing antinomies. Tupaj Amaru seems to suggest the spirit of change into "other" to find that the "other" is now the head and mind of "us." But the growth toward rebellion has long been going on throughout indigenous society, just as the movement of the anaconda's body through dangerous, underearth space has long transpired in indigenous mythology.

Chthonic power, then, in the sense revealed in many of these essays, reflects clearly the duality of two systems of power, one emanating from the national or international political economy and the other from indigenous systems of knowledge as revealed in postconquest myth, narrative, and other forms of historicity such as shamanic gnosis, ceremony, and art (Whitten and Whitten 1988). But, as the Andean specialists make so utterly clear, chthonic power, and its embodiment in native cultures, is not merely a carryover of segments of autochthonous lifeways; rather, it is part and parcel of the experiences of conquest. Herein, then, lies the duality of power patterning upon which most of the essays in this volume touch, some extensively, and which has been the implicit subject of recent work by Salomon (1981) and Taussig (1980a), as discussed by Silverblatt, and the explicit subject addressed elsewhere by Whitten (1981, 1985).

Duality of Power Patterning

Duality does not just refer to something having two sides or to a contradiction, antinomy, or division in half. It refers also to the ability of the human mind to take a minimal number of culturally patterned contrast sets and organize them variously and creatively by reference to a third-term construct (Whitten 1984) so as to engage in unending discourse on various subjects without losing the structured (paradigmatic and syntagmatic) nature of the contrasts, sets, and third-term references themselves. Duality is far more than a dialectic, for the contrasts crucial to duality do not necessarily form the reference points for a proposition ↔ counter proposition ↔ synthesis chain.

Dillon and Abercrombie critically discuss Taussig's and Salomon's work with regard to their many insights on Andean ritual within the structure of domination. I, too, wish to mention Salomon's important ethnography of the *yumbada* and my own observations on that celebratory ritual, which takes place in and near north Quito at the time of Corpus Christi. During this festival celebrants who, in their quotidian lives, would be *blanco* or *mestizo* by self-ascription and self-identification, become Quito Runa and, as such, take on contradictory roles as coastal blacks, monkeys, and "Yumbo" (see Figure 4). In this context *yumbo* refers to Amazonian native peoples who are neither fierce remnants of savage tribes nor migrating nationals. They are viewed as rural bumpkins who speak the language of the Inca and the Catholic evangelizing church—Quichua. They are not *infieles* but *incultos;* the processes of civilization have not made them *racional,* so they remain *indio.*

As the ceremony unfolds the *yumbos* dance with heavy palm lances as *aucas,* savages, and blacks perform more and more as aggressive *libres* rather than passive *bozales* (see Figure 5). The Quito Runa, in short, resurrect the colonial antinomies, bring the lowland and highland peoples from other times-spaces together, and enact a climactic clash (to be described shortly). Two features of the festival relate to duality of patterning. The first is that Quito evokes all senses of urbanity that are distinctly Ecuadorian, Andean, and Iberian. Runa belongs on the opposite side of a set of asymmetric contrasts described elsewhere (Stutzman 1981:45–94; Whitten 1981:776–97; 1985:217–52). According to such pernicious paradigms, one cannot "be" urban and "Indian" at the same time (see, e.g., Stutzman 1981; Salomon 1981; Fine 1986). Here is where the duality of patterning enters: by making the concept "Runa" central to the power to constitute, the groundswell of indigenousness of the Quito "cultural switchboard" between the Andes, Upper Amazonia,

Figure 4. *Yumbo* dancers near Panamerican highway, north of Quito.

Figure 5. An aggressive black *libre* in the same festival.

and the Coast (Salomon 1981:162–208) is evoked. The tertium quid that constitutes the pattern is that of the positive notion of *runa* as human, Andean, Amazonian, and other beings.

The second feature of the festival has to do with a small ritual enacted by native people ranging (at least) from the Yanomami of Orinocan Venezuela and Brazil (Lizot 1985) to the Waorani, Canelos Quichua, and Achuar of Ecuador. When hunting deep in the forest, peccary may be encountered, and it is important that, for such encounters, hunters are certain that they are fully human and their prey is fully animal and neither is a spirit-being. Soul substances of animal and spirit and human mediate these distinctions. The distinctions are forever maintained and blurred. The ritual begins when a hunter asks, "What person is passing by?" Hunters, like animals, sniff the air and decide that it is a peccary-person. Peccary and hunter are briefly, and rhetorically, the same being; neither is a spirit. Then one hunter says that he thinks this is meat for humans to eat, and the others agree that to take this peccary's life will show its soul respect, for its meat will be distributed to others upon the hunters' return, to be cooked by boiling by women. Then the peccary is killed by the hunters and immediately "smoked" (actually roasted) by them.

During the *yumbada,* in north urban Quito, the very same ritual of the forest hunters is enacted by the Quito Runa. One man is regarded to "be" the forest pig (*sacha cuchi*). The lance wielders, who represent both human hunters and the swaying forest, sniff and decide that this is, indeed, a wild forest pig–person, and they chase it and kill it. Later, as described so vividly by Salomon (1981:162–208; see also Fine 1986), the wild forest pig–person is resurrected by blowing *trago* (presumably produced by the black population, known to have restorative powers) on it(him), and he dances again as fully human Quito Runa Yumbo.

It is very apparent during the *yumbada* that the principal performers know something of the rain forest and its inhabitants and are able to bundle both hunting ritual and urban festival elements into sets of syntagmatic and paradigmatic chains and associations. As the international jets fly overhead in the warm, glittering, Andean sunshine, the idea of chthonic power brought from the deep, dark recesses of the jungle is set in all participants' minds. Indeed, under the hot poncho, nearly smothered by onlookers, the fallen wild forest pig–person does seem, in his own mind, to sink into sticky, sweaty mire and then to rise from an inferno into the cooling, rarefied air of the Andean masked dancers.

As I suggest elsewhere, the power of the enacted tropes is so strong, especially to one who knows the Andes and Amazonia, that one thinks of the nation as a body divided, which can be united only if the nature of the forest native is destroyed and then reconstituted: "Enduring ritual expression of massive contradictions is a theme which runs through the ceremonial enactment. On the one hand, the Oriente is 'marginal' to everything 'national'—it is full of savages smothered by the jungle, in vivid contrast to Quito, which is populated by citizens liberated by urban Christianity. On the other hand, the Oriente represents a potential resolution of nationalist problems, if only its oppositions to nationalist thought can be overcome (the *yumbo* killed) and its potential brought to life (the *yumbo* resurrected)" (Whitten 1981:24). It is as though the collective body of forest natives is growing toward the Quito head, itself transformed by conquest to something alien yet attainable.

To "be" Quito Runa during the *yumbada* is to play *yumbo*, to slay *yumbo*, and to resurrect *yumbo*. *Yumbo* as so constituted comes out of the depths, regarded not only as below Quito but within (*adentro, ucui*). To perform the *yumbada* is to engage in enacted rhetoric expressing the nature of stratified and interacting Spanish, highland Quichua, Amazonian savage, and black African, in all sorts of ways. To so perform (and audiences become performers, too, to some extent) is to create, re-create, and motivate the sense of being urban, human, indigenous, and savage. This cultural performance draws heavily on paradigms discussed by Whitten (1974, 1976, 1981, 1985), Stutzman (1981), Salomon (1981), Reeve (1985; this volume), Fine (1986), and Weismantel (1986). Such paradigms are nationalist constructions that reflect political-economic power to repress native and Afro-American peoples and their lifeways. But the way by which Quito Runa work with and on such paradigms takes the structure of domination and oppression into a realm of resurgence of indigenousness (and blackness) that, in its rhetorical dimensions, takes celebrants to the near brink of rebellion (see, e.g., V. Turner 1974 for a discussion of such activities in comparative perspective).

What makes the duality of power patterning and ethnic patterning so dynamic is the two sets of iconic reference systems available for symbolic predication. One of these is one or more of the hydraulic systems of Andean upwelling, the Amazonian system of rivers, and the rain-forest system of moisture circulation. The other reference system is the stratified political-economic system of domination. Chthonic power derives from the patterned conjunction of power from within that taps the hydraulic force of conceptualized nature-spirit against the dominance of felt hegemonic socioculture. I see themes such as these running through all of the essays in this volume.

Let us return here to the nature of time-space in culture. It seems reasonable to suggest that human life everywhere is precariously perched between a remembered past and an imagined future (see, e.g., Fernandez 1974, 1977; Gudeman 1986). The questing self of the inchoate and uncertain present, whether shaman, storyteller, festival participant, artist, or traveler, with others and/or alone, seeks to predicate his or her "being" by drawing from various domains of experience and knowledge. To do so evokes reference systems that take humans "within," to what is regarded as the essence of "us." By the criterion of contrast, universally used in paradigm construction, "others" are set outside. This process may be illustrated as a cone (Figure 6). Such setting out, however, draws upon an inherent contrast from "within," as when people distinguish between "us" and "others like us" (Figure 7). Examples of the latter include Runa *puralla*/Runa (Canelos Quichua), Yanomami/Shamatari (Yanoáma), contemporary Shipibo/past Inca (Shipibo-Conibo), and Waorani/Warani (Wao).

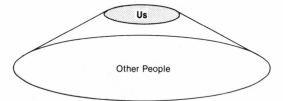

Figure 6. "Us"/"other" as "inside"/"outside."

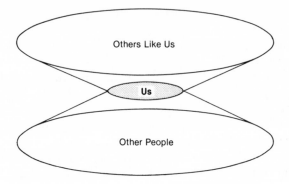

Figure 7. Double distinctions of "us"/"other."

The next remove, of course, is that of the "us"/"other" polarity with regard to humans/other beings. As Roe presents such material, the constant bucking up of the contemporary Shipibo "us" in the face of stronger and stronger "others" leads to varying compartmentalizations of the sphere of "them." Such is the case throughout South America, where the "we"/"they" ("us"/"them") contrast is transformed culturally to something that, looking up or down from within the cone, might look like Figure 8. The "us" in such a paradigm is clearly superior to the "other," but the boundary or threshold that marks the contrast is not clear; indeed, it is constantly in need of cultural construction. Often, perhaps universally, in native South American cultures the distant "other" is said to be sufficiently nonhuman as to be cannibalistic (see, e.g., Lizot 1985). Origin myths of human-animal-spirit intersection out of cannibal ancestors abound. When, as in festival activity, the container of "us" ("our" sets of contrasts and "our" sense of being and "our" system of reference to evoke networks of imagery of power) expands, "we" merge with the spirits, other people, others like us, and animals to achieve a transformed identity. But the power of "us" is still within, and when it is brought forth (externalized), as chthonic power, chaos reigns.

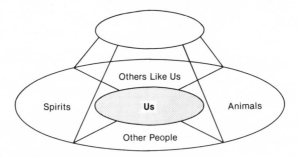

Figure 8. Further distinctions of "us"/"other."

Superiority of the cultural selfhood system is manifest positively by an insistence on being fully human and negatively by the denial of cannibalism.

But the reality of the world since 1492 cannot so delude native people or their black counterparts to think only about relatively egalitarian markers of shifting ethnicity. Accordingly, there are now, and have long been, significant, powerful "others" above—the power wielders who control "our" political economy, "our" lives—and "others" below—the known "other" people, such as the Cohouri to the Waorani, the Nabë to the Yanomami, and the Auca to Quechua speakers. To the extent to which such *known*, significant others constitute the boundaries of selfhood, the diagram must look more like Figure 9. Harking back to the Shipibo situation and the double intersection of Venn diagrams to reveal two penumbrae, we arrive at the point where the idea of reproduction of the dominant system's categories within the system of native culture emerges (see Figure 10). As we debundle the processes of such reproduction by use of native texts, we forge ethnological theory on the anvil of competent ethnography. When the narratives of time-space enter, concepts reflecting "where we are from" and "what we are to become" emerge as salient themes. The Inca tales of the Shipibo and the mythic heroes of Arapaço and Wakuénai illustrate this point. It seems to me that something like this is discussed by most, if not all, of the contributors to this volume.

Figure 9. Another version of "others like us"/"us"/"other."

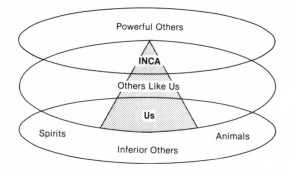

Figure 10: Reproduction of the dominant system's categories within the system of native culture.

The Rhetoric of Nationalism and Ethnic Bloc Formation

Although it is widely accepted that ethnically identifiable peoples within a nation (or colonial regime) tend toward either assimilation or enclave formation at a given time, most of the essays in this volume present critically important information to counter that notion (and some of them clearly counter it). If we assume the opposite, whether for colonial domination or for contemporary nationalism, that nationalist (or colonial) culture and ethnic bloc culture should be interpreted as complementary and mutually reinforcing systems of symbols sustained by dialogic discourse—and this certainly comes through in all of the essays—then we have more generalizations to make. The dialogic discourse seems to create synthetic symbolic units—erroneously portrayed by most social scientists as ethnic identity versus national identity—which, in their rhetorical conjunction, bring forth a predicative link that carries the double act of assertion and denial. This generalization should hold for the Kayapó described by Turner as well as for all of the Andean groups discussed, and it certainly applies to the Canelos Quichua, Shipibo-Conibo, Arapaço, and Wakuénai. In addition, most materials available on Upper, Central, and Northwest Amazonas support this generalization. Such symbolic units, in conjunction with one another through dialogic and other forms of patterned discourse, may develop rapidly into contrasting paradigms that shape a people's perceptions of "self" and "other" on both sides (or many sides) of the cultural opposition. Roe's essay represents the most sustained attempt here to deal with this phenomenon (but see also Whitten 1985; Reeve 1985; Fine 1986; Weismantel 1986).

I wish to bring this out here because all of us are working in settings where nationalist and ethnic bloc paradigms abound. Indeed, whether or not we realize it, such paradigms represent the starting point of our own discourse about "Indians and their narratives." In the Afterword to *Cultural Transformations and Ethnicity in Modern Ecuador* (1981), I discuss the sets of cultural opposition that exist within nationalist ideology and within the ideological paradigms of the native peoples of Upper Amazonia: "The 'national oppositions' available for paradigmatic construction are regularly set forth in the press, in popular magazines, over the radio, and in scholarly debate. The indigenous oppositions themselves emerge in contexts ranging from shamanic performances to indigenous-nonindigenous meetings and are communicated back and forth from indigenous to national settings. . . . This is a process of reproduction of oppositions with symbolic and pragmatic dimensions" (Whitten 1981:791).

From Weber (1964) to Geertz (1973b), Royce (1982), Herzfeld (1982, 1985), and Taussig (1987), among many others, note is made that diverse peoples within consolidating nation-states tend toward centralization and a shared common purpose, just as they move autonomously toward fragmentation as ethnic blocs in search of counternationalism. Nations and ethnic blocs (which often refer to themselves as nations) share two common features, which have been noted but not labeled throughout this volume: epochalism and essentialism. Epochalism is the international validation of a people's statehood. Essentialism is the affirmation of a common style, quality, and culture—the oneness of a people—that strives for a renewed sense of historical depth at each crucial moment of epochal emergence and consolidation.

For rhetorical convenience, following Graburn (1976), we could say that a third-world/fourth-world cultural paradox permeates the South American nation-states and native cultures under discussion in this volume. The authors of these essays, by interpreting the rhetorical and enactment systems expressing paradox, contradiction, and irony (among many other tropes) in many areas of Andean, Amazonian, and Central Brazilian settings, and by basing their interpretations on extensive experience bolstered by recent ethnography, should move the understanding of these processes to a new level. Perhaps, with more attention on the nationalist/ethnic rhetorical discourse itself, we would come to speak effectively about the smoldering symbolic debris and sparked paradigmatic clashes that ignite the dialogic rhetoric of diverse peoples within nation-states to seek and enact not only strategies to their liking but also those opposite to their original intentions.

Materials in this volume, when combined with programmatic works such as those of Sapir (1977:3–32) and Crocker (1977:33–66), suggest strongly that national (third-world) paradigms and indigenous (fourth-world) paradigms are conjoined in their very differences by sets of analogies that themselves depend on the internal and external pairing of oppositions. A key to understanding such contradictory mutuality lies in the fact that oppositions endure within nationalist ideology and within indigenous and black cosmologies. At times, under circumstances that are yet to be specified adequately to allow us to illustrate such complex processes in South America (but see Fernandez 1982 for a West African system), the nationalist ideological oppositions may be mapped onto the native cosmological oppositions, and vice versa. In this volume Chernela, Rasnake, and Hill and Wright come closest to doing this, though Roe's analysis of the position of "Inca" in Shipibo ideology and cosmology is also quite germane. When such mapping occurs, opposition A/B in the nationalist system (e.g., capitalism versus socialism) is juxtaposed to opposition C/D in the indigenous or black systems (e.g., asymmetric accumulation of goods and capital by a shaman or political leader versus egalitarian exchange of goods and redistribution of power and prestige). By focusing on patterned oppositions and the polarization of symbols in paired metonymic chains linked by metaphoric prediction, remarkable, dynamic syncretisms may be seen to occur. These essays are full of such focusing and provide a splendid basis for considering anew actual relationships between nationalist and ethnic bloc conjunctions, paradigms, synthetic symbolic units, and actual alliances that are occurring all over South and Central

America. Such syncretisms are especially salient in political-economic movements of selfhood and identity currently manifest in indigenous federations and black alliances throughout the hemisphere.

These syncretisms are equally salient when one examines the ways by which the rhetoric of identification and selfhood bound to "being black" and "being indigenous" imbue and shape the processes of production of narrative and myth within paradigms of native historicity. As such historicity is packaged for national and international consumption, as is currently the case with at least some of the peoples discussed in this volume, the reproduction of oppositions intensifies symbolic processing to create a heightened sense of national identity and ethnic bloc identity, at one and the same time. By understanding the ongoing construction and deconstruction of syncretic formations, and by acknowledging that people can and do move their identity paradigms in and out of opposing formations, the cultural dynamics of nationalism and ethnic bloc formation should become clear.

NOTE

I appreciate the critical comments offered by Jonathan Hill, Enrique Mayer, Helaine Silverman, and Sibby Whitten on various drafts of this essay.

References Cited

Abercrombie, Thomas
1986 "The Politics of Sacrifice: An Aymara Cosmology in Action." Ph.D. dissertation, University of Chicago.

Agostinho, Pedro
1974 *Mitos e Outras Narrativas Kamayurá.* Salvador: Universidad Federal da Bahia.

Allen, Catherine J. (see also Wagner, Catherine Allen)
1982 "Body and Soul in Quechua Thought." *Journal of Latin American Lore* 8(2): 179–96.

1983 "Of Bear-Men and He-Men: Bear Metaphors and Male Self-Perception in a Peruvian Community." *Latin American Indian Literatures* 7(1): 38–51.

1984 "Time in Quichua Narrative." Paper presented at the 83rd Annual Meeting of the American Anthropological Association, Denver.

Appadurai, Arjun
1981 "The Past as a Scarce Resource." *Man* (n.s.) 16:201–19.

Arguedas, Jose-Maria
1956 "Puquio, una Cultura en Proceso de Cambio." *Revista del Museo Nacional* (Lima) 25:184–232.

1973 "Mitos Quechuas Post-Hispanicos." In *Ideología Mesianica del Mundo Andino.* ed. Juan Ossio. Lima: Ignacio Prado Pastor, pp. 377–92.

Arriaga, Father Pablo Joseph de
1968 *The Extirpation of Idolatry in Peru.* trans. L. Clark Keating. Lexington: University of Kentucky Press (first published in 1621).

Auerbach, Erich
1953 *Mimesis: The Representation of Reality in Western Literature.* trans. Willard Trask. Princeton: Princeton University Press.

Avila, Francisco de
1966 *Dioses y Hombres de Huarochiri.* trans. Jose-Maria Arguedas. Lima: El Museo Nacional de Historia y el Instituto de Estudios Peruanos.

Azevedo, Soares de
1933 *Pélo Río Mar.* Rio de Janeiro: C. Mendes Junior.

Bakhtin, M. M.
   1981   *The Dialogical Imagination*. trans. C. Emerson and M. Holquist.
          Austin: University of Texas Press.
Balandier, Georges
   1955   *Sociologie Actuelle de l'Afrique Noire: Dynamique des Changements
          Sociaux en Afrique Centrale*. Paris: PUF.
Banner, Horace
   1957   "Mitos dos Indios Kayapó." *Revista de Antropologia* (n.s.; Sao Paulo)
          5:37–66.
Bardales, Rodriguez Cesar
   1979   *Quimisha Incabo Ini Yoia: Leyendas de los Shipibo-Conibo sobre los
          Tres Incas*. Pucallpa, Peru: Instituto Linguistico de Verano, Yarinacocha.
Barthes, Roland
   1984   *Empire of Signs*. trans. Richard Howard. New York: Farrar, Straus and
          Giroux.
Basso, Ellen B.
   1985   *A Musical View of the Universe: Kalapalo Myth and Ritual Per-
          formances*. Philadelphia: University of Pennsylvania Press.
   1987   *In Favor of Deceit: A Study of Tricksters in an Amazonian Society*.
          Tucson: University of Arizona Press.
Basso, Keith
   1979   *Portraits of "the Whiteman": Linguistic Play and Cultural Symbols
          among the Western Apache*. New York: Cambridge University Press.
Bastide, Roger
   1960   *Les Religions Africaines au Bresil: Vers une Sociologie des Interpenetra-
          tions de Civilizations*. Paris: Presses Universitaires de France.
Bastien, Joseph
   1985   "Qollahuaya-Andean Body Concepts: A Topographical-Hydraulic Model
          of Physiology." *American Anthropologist* 87:595–611.
Beidelman, Tom O.
   1980   "The Moral Imagination of the Kaguru: Some Thoughts on Tricksters,
          Translation and Comparative Analysis." *American Ethnologist* 7:27–42.
Beksta, Padre Casimiro
   n.d.   "Origem e Divisão das Tribos." Unpublished ms.
Bertonio, Ludovico
   1612   *Vocabulario de la Lengua Aymara*. Cochabamba, Bolivia: CERES and
          the Museo Nacional de Etnografia y Folklore, and the Instituto Frances
          de Estudios Andinos (1984 facsimile edition).
Bloch, Maurice
   1983   *Marxism and Anthropology*. Oxford: Clarendon Press.
Boon, James A.
   1982   *Other Tribes, Other Scribes: Symbolic Anthropology in the Compara-
          tive Study of Cultures, Histories, Religions, and Texts*. New York:
          Cambridge University Press.

Bourdieu, Pierre
1977   *Outline of a Theory of Practice.* New York: Cambridge University Press.

Braudel, Fernand
1980   *On History.* Chicago: University of Chicago Press.

Bravo, Vincente H.
1907   "Viaje al Oriente." *Boletin de la Sociedad Geografica de Lima* 21(1): 48–67.

Brown, Michael F.
1985   *Tsewa's Gift: Magic and Meaning in an Amazonian Society.* Smithsonian Series in Ethnographic Inquiry. Washington, D.C.: Smithsonian Institution Press.

Bruzzi, Alcionilio Bruzzi Alves da Silva
1977   *A Civilização Indigena Uaupés.* Sao Paulo: Centro de Pesquisas Iauareté.

Bucher, Bernadette
1985   "An Interview with Claude Lévi-Strauss, 30 June 1982." *American Ethnologist* 12:360–68.

Burns, E. Bradford
1980   *A History of Brazil.* New York: Columbia University Press.

Cardoso de Oliveira, Roberto
1964   *O Indio e o Mundo dos Brancos.* Sao Paulo: Diffusão Europeia do Livro.
1974   "Indigenous Peoples and Sociocultural Change in the Amazon." In *Man in the Amazon.* ed. Charles Wagley. Gainesville: University of Florida Press, pp. 111–35.

Carneiro, Robert
1960   "Research on the Amahuaca of Peru." Field notes, Department of Anthropology, American Museum of Natural History, New York.

Carneiro da Cunha, Manuela
1973   "Logique du Mythe et de l'Action: Le Mouvement Messianique Canela de 1963." *L'Homme* 12(4): 5–37.

Casement, Roger
1912   *Correspondence Reflecting the Treatment of British Colonial Subjects and Native Indians Employed in the Collection of Rubber in the Putumayo District.* Miscellaneous Publication 8. London: Harrison and Sons.

Certeau, Michel de
1986   *Heterologies.* Minneapolis: University of Minnesota Press.

Chantre y Herrera, Jose
1901   *Historia de los Misiones de la Compania de Jesus en el Maranon Espanol, 1637–1767.* Madrid: Imprenta de A. Avrial.

Chernela, Janet
1983   "Hierarchy and Economy of the Uanano (Kotiria)-Speaking Peoples of the Middle Uaupés Basin." Ph.D. dissertation, Columbia University.
1984   "Why One Culture Stays Put: A Case of Resistance to Change in Authority and Economic Structure in an Indigenous Community in

the Northwest Amazon." In *Change in the Amazon Basin,* vol. 11. ed. John Hemming. Manchester: Manchester University Press, pp. 228–36.

1988 "Some Considerations of Myth and Gender in a Northwest Amazon Society." In *The Dialectics of Gender: Papers in Honor of Robert F. and Yolanda Murphy.* ed. Richard Randolph, David Schneider, and May Diaz. Boulder: Westview Press, pp. 67–79.

Choy, Emilio

1979 "De Santiago Matamoros a Santiago Mata-indios." In *Antropología e Historia.* ed. E. Choy. Lima: Universidad Nacional Mayor de San Marcos, pp. 333–437.

Cobo, Bernabe

1964 *Historia del Nuevo Mundo.* 2 vols. Madrid: Biblioteca de Autores Espanoles (first published in 1653).

Cohen, Abner

1979 "Political Symbolism." *Annual Review of Anthropology* 8:87–113.

Cohn, Bernard

1961 "The Pasts of an Indian Village." *Comparative Studies in Society and History* 3(3): 241–49.

1980 "History and Anthropology: The State of Play." *Comparative Studies in Society and History* 22(2): 198–221.

1981 "Anthropology and History in the 1980s." *Journal of Interdisciplinary History* 12(2): 227–52.

Colby, Benjamin, James Fernandez, and David Kronenfeld

1981 "Toward a Convergence of Cognitive and Symbolic Anthropology." *American Ethnologist* 8:422–50.

Collier, Richard

1968 *The River That God Forgot: The Story of the Amazon Rubber Boom.* New York: Dutton.

Comaroff, Jean

1985 *Body of Power, Spirit of Resistance.* Chicago: University of Chicago Press.

Comissão Pro-Indio

1982 *Indios: Direitos Historicos.* Cadernos da Comissão Pro-Indio No 3. Sao Paulo.

Cotari, Daniel, Daniel Meja, and Victor Carrasco

1978 *Diccionario Aymara-Castellano, Castellano-Aymara.* Cochabamba: Instituto de Idiomas de los Padres de Maryknoll.

Coudreau, Henri

1887 *La France Equinoxiale.* Vol. 2: *Voyage a Travers les Guyanes et l'Amazonie.* Paris: Challamel Ainé.

Crocker, J. Christopher

1977 "The Social Functions of Rhetorical Forms." In *The Social Use of Metaphor: Essays on the Anthropology of Rhetoric.* ed. J. David Sapir and J. Christopher Crocker. Philadelphia: University of Pennsylvania Press, pp. 33–66.

Crocker, William

1983 "Ultimate Reality and Meaning for the Ramkomekra-Canela, Eastern

Timbira, Brazil: A Triadic Dualistic Cognitive Pattern." *Journal of Ultimate Reality and Meaning* 6(2): 84–111.

Crummey, Donald (ed.)
1986   *Banditry, Rebellion and Social Protest in Africa.* London: James Currey.

Cuentas Ormachea, Enrique
1982   "La Danza 'Choquela' y su Contenido Magico-religioso." *Boletin de Lima* 4(19): 54–70.

Da Matta, Roberto
1970   "Mito e Antimito entre os Timbira." In *Mito e Linguagem Social.* ed. Claude Lévi-Strauss, Roberto Cardoso de Oliveira, Julio Cezar Melatti, Roberto da Matta, and Roque de Barros Laraia. Rio de Janeiro: Tempo Brasileiro, pp. 77–106.

DeBoer, Warren R.
1981   "The Machete and the Cross: Conibo Trade in the Late Seventeenth Century." In *Networks of the Past: Regional Interaction in Archaeology.* ed. Peter D. Francis, F. J. Xense, and P. G. Duke. Calgary, Canada: Archaeological Association of the University of Calgary, pp. 31–47.

Derrida, Jacques
1970   "Structure, Sign, and Play in the Discourse of Human Sciences." In *The Languages of Criticism and the Sciences of Man.* ed. Richard Macksey and Eugenio Donato. Baltimore: Johns Hopkins University Press, pp. 247–65.

Dixon, R. M. W.
1983   *Where Have All the Adjectives Gone?* New York: Mouton.

Dolgin, Janet L., David S. Kemnitzer, and David M. Schneider
1977   "As People Express Their Lives, So They Are . . . " In *Symbolic Anthropology: A Reader in the Study of Symbols and Their Meanings.* ed. J. Dolgin, D. Kemnitzer, and D. Schneider. New York: Columbia University Press, pp. 3–4.

Drummond, Lee
1981   "The Serpent's Children: Semiotics of Cultural Genesis in Arawak and Trobriand Myth." *American Ethnologist* 8:633–60.

Dumont, Jean-Paul
1976   *Under the Rainbow: Nature and Supernature among the Panare Indians.* Austin: University of Texas Press.

Duviols, Pierre
1971   *La Lutte contre les Religions Autochtones dans Perou Colonial: L'Extirpation de l'Idolatrie entre 1532 et 1660.* Lima and Paris: Institut Français d'Études Andines.

1974   "Une Petite Chronique Retrouvée: Errores, Ritos, Supersticiones y Ceremonias de los Yndios de la Provincia de Chinchaycocha y Otras del Piru." *Journal de la Société des Américanistes* (Paris) 63:275–97.

1980   "Periodización y Politica: La Historia Prehispanica del Peru Segun Guaman Poma de Ayala." *Bulletin de l'Institut Français d'Études Andines* 3/4:1–18.

Eakin, Lucille, Erwin Lauriault, and Harry Boonstra
    1980   *Bosquejo Etnografico de los Shipibo-Conibo del Ucayali.* trans. Marlene
            Ballena Davila. Lima: Ignacio Prado Pastor.
Earls, John
    1973   "La Organización del Poder en la Mitologia Quechua." In *Ideología
            Mesianica del Mundo Andino.* ed. Juan Ossio. Lima: Ignacio Prado
            Pastor, pp. 393–414.
Eliade, Mircea
    1959   *The Sacred and the Profane: The Nature of Religion.* trans. William R.
            Trask. New York: Harcourt, Brace and World.
Esquivel y Navia, Diego de
    1901   *Anales de Cusco (1601–1749).* Lima: Imprenta de El Estado.
Fabian, Johannes
    1983   *Time and the Other: How Anthropology Makes Its Object.* New York:
            Columbia University Press.
Farabee, William C.
    1922   *Indian Tribes of Eastern Peru.* Peabody Museum of American Archaeol-
            ogy and Ethnology, Papers 10. Cambridge, Mass.
Farriss, Nancy
    1984   *Maya Society under Colonial Rule: The Collective Enterprise of Survival.*
            Princeton: Princeton University Press.
Feely-Harnik, Gillian
    1978   "Divine Kingship and the Meaning of History among the Sakalava of
            Madagascar." *Man* (n.s.) 13:402–17.
Fernandez, James W.
    1974   "The Mission of Metaphor in Expressive Culture." *Current Anthropol-
            ogy* 15(2): 119–45.
    1977   "The Performance of Ritual Metaphors." In *The Social Use of Metaphor:
            Essays on the Anthropology of Rhetoric.* ed. J. David Sapir and J.
            Christopher Crocker. Philadelphia: University of Pennsylvania Press,
            pp. 100–131.
    1982   *Bwiti: An Ethnography of the Religious Imagination in Africa.* Princeton:
            Princeton University Press.
Figueiredo Tenreiro Aranha, Bentode
    1907   *Archivo do Amazonas.* vol. 1, no. 3. Amazonas.
Fine, Kathleen
    1986   "Ideology, History, and Action in Cotocollao: A Barrio of Quito, Ecuador."
            Ph.D. dissertation, University of Illinois at Urbana-Champaign.
Finley, M. I.
    1965   "Myth, Memory, and History." *History and Theory* 4(3): 281–302.
Firth, Raymond
    1951   *Elements of Social Organization.* London: Watts and Company.
Flores Ochoa, Jorge A.
    1978   "Classification et Denomination des Camelides Sud-Americaines."
            Annales E.S.C. 33(5–6): 1006–16.

Fortes, Meyer
  1978   "An Anthropologist's Apprenticeship." *Annual Review of Anthropology* 7:1–30.
Frank, Andre Gunder
  1967   *Capitalism and Underdevelopment in Latin America.* New York: Monthly Review Press.
Fuenzalida, Fernando
  1968   "Santiago y el Wamani: Aspectos de un Culto Pagano." *Cuadernos Antropológicos* 5:118–65.
Gadamer, Hans-Georg
  1975   *Truth and Method.* New York: Crossroad.
Galeano, Eduardo
  1981   *As Veias Abertas da America Latina.* Rio de Janeiro: Paz e Terra.
Galvao, Eduardo
  1959   "Aculturação Indígena no Río Negro." *Boletin do Museu Paraense Emilio Goeldi, Anthropología* 7:1–60.
Gebhart-Sayer, Angelika
  1985a "Some Reasons Why the Shipibo-Conibo (Eastern Peru) Retain Their Art." Paper presented at the 45th International Congress of Americanists, Bogota.
  1985b "The Geometric Designs of the Shipibo-Conibo in Ritual Context." *Journal of Latin American Lore* 11:143–75.
  1986a "Inca Tales of the Shipibo-Conibo." Ms. Voelkerkundliches Institut. Tuebingen: University of Tuebingen.
  1986b "Rabe Incabo: The Two Incas." Ms. Voelkerkundliches Institut. Teubingen: University of Tuebingen.
Geertz, Clifford
  1973a "The Cerebral Savage: On the Work of Claude Lévi-Strauss." In *The Interpretation of Cultures: Selected Essays.* New York: Basic Books, pp. 345–59.
  1973b *The Interpretation of Cultures: Selected Essays.* New York: Basic Books.
  1983   *Local Knowledge.* New York: Basic Books.
  1984   "Anti Anti-Relativism." *American Anthropologist* 86:263–78.
Genovese, Eugene D.
  1974   *Roll Jordan Roll: The World the Slaves Made.* New York: Vintage.
  1981   *From Rebellion to Revolution: Afro-American Slave Revolts in the Making of the New World.* New York: Vintage.
Giacone, Antonio
  1949   *Os Tucanos e Outras Tribus do Rio Uaupés Afluente do Negro-Amazonas, Notas Etnográficas e Folclóricas de um Missionario Salesiano.* Sao Paulo: Imprenta Oficial do Estado.
Giddens, Anthony
  1979   *Central Problems in Social Theory: Action, Structure, and Contradiction in Social Analysis.* Cambridge: Cambridge University Press.
  1981   *A Contemporary Critique of Historical Materialism.* Vol. 1: *Power, Property and the State.* Berkeley: University of California Press.

Gisbert, Teresa
  1980 *Iconografía y Mitos Indígenas en el Arte.* La Paz: Editorial Gisbert y Cia.
Gluckman, Max
  1942 *Analysis of a Social Situation in Modern Zululand.* Manchester: Manchester University Press.
Godelier, Maurice
  1978 "Economy and Religion: An Evolutionary Optical Illusion." In *The Evolution of Social Systems.* ed. J. Friedman and M. Rowland. Pittsburgh: University of Pittsburgh Press, pp. 5–11.
Goldman, Irving
  1979 *The Cubeo: Indians of the Northwest Amazon.* Urbana: University of Illinois Press (first published in 1963).
  n.d. "Creation and Emergence." In *Cubeo Religion and Society.* Unpublished book ms.
Goldstein, Kenneth
  1976 *Historical Knowing.* Austin: University of Texas Press.
Goody, Jack
  1968 (ed.) *Literacy in Traditional Societies.* Cambridge: Cambridge University Press.
  1977 *The Domestication of the Savage Mind.* Cambridge: Cambridge University Press.
Gow, David
  1976 "The Gods and Socal Change in the High Andes." Ph.D. dissertation, University of Wisconsin.
  1980 "The Roles of Christ and Inkarri in Andean Religion." *Journal of Latin American Lore* 6:279–98.
Graburn, Nelson H. H.
  1976 *Ethnic and Tourist Arts: Cultural Expressions from the Fourth World.* Berkeley: University of California Press.
Gramsci, Antonio
  1973 *Selections from the Prison Notebooks of Antonio Gramsci.* ed. and trans. Q. Hoare and G. N. Smith. New York: International Publishers.
Gregor, Thomas
  1981a "A Content Analysis of Mehinaku Dreams." *Ethos* 9(4): 353–90.
  1981b " 'Far, Far Away My Shadow Wandered . . .': Dream Symbolism and Dream Theories of the Mehinaku Indians of Brazil." *American Ethnologist* 8:709–20.
  1983 "Dark Dreams about the Whiteman." *Natural History* 92(1): 8–14.
  1984 "O Branco dos Meus Sonhos." *Anuario Antropológico* 82: 53–68.
Grohs, Waltraud
  1974 *Los Indios de Alto Amazonas del Siglo XVI al XVIII: Poblaciones y Migraciones en la Antigua Provincia de Maynas.* BAS 2 (Estudios Americanistas de Bonn), Bonn.

Guaman Poma de Ayala, Felipe
   1936   *El Primer Nueva Cronica y Buen Gobierno.* Paris: Institut d'Ethnologie.
   1956   *La Nueva Cronica y Buen Gobierno.* ed. Luis Bustíos Gálvez. 3 vols.
          Lima: Editorial Cultura, Ministerio de Educación Pública del Perú.
Gudeman, Stephen
   1986   *Economics as Culture: Models and Metaphors of Livelihood.* London:
          Routledge and Kegan Paul.
Guss, David
   1986   "Keeping It Oral: A Yekuama Ethnology." *American Ethnologist* 13:
          413–29.
Hardman, Martha J.
   n.d.   "Gentiles in Jaqi: An Example of Contact Literature." Unpublished ms.
Harman, Inge Maria
   1987   "Collective Labor and Rituals of Reciprocity in the Southern Bolivian
          Andes." Ph.D. dissertation, Cornell University.
Harner, Michael
   1974   "Waiting for Inca God." Paper presented at the 73rd Annual Meeting of
          the American Anthropological Association, Mexico City, November
          19–24.
   1980   *The Way of the Shaman.* New York: Harper and Row.
Harris, Olivia
   1982   "The Dead and Devils among the Bolivian Laymi." In *Death and the
          Regeneration of Life.* ed. Maurice Bloch and Jonathan Parry. Cambridge:
          Cambridge University Press, pp. 45–73.
Harwood, Frances
   1976   "Myth, Memory, and Oral Tradition: Cicero in the Trobriands." *American
          Anthropologist* 78:783–97.
Havranek, Bohuslav
   1964   "The Functional Differentiation of the Standard Language." In *A
          Prague School Reader on Esthetics, Literary Structure and Style.* ed.
          and trans., Paul L. Garvin. Washington, D.C.: Georgetown University
          Press, pp. 3–16.
Hernandez Principe, Rodrigo
   1923   "Mitologia Andina." *Inca* 1:24–68 (first published in 1621).
Herzfeld, Michael
   1982   *Ours Once More: Folklore, Ideology, and the Making of Modern Greece.*
          Austin: University of Texas Press.
   1985   "Lévi-Strauss and the Nation-State." *Journal of American Folklore*
          98:191–208.
Hill, Jonathan
   1983   "Wakuénai Society: A Processual-Structural Analysis of Indigenous
          Cultural Life in the Upper Río Negro Basin, Venezuela." Ph.D.
          dissertation, Indiana University.
   1984a "Agnatic Sibling Relations and Rank in Northern Arawakan Myth

and Social Life." In *Working Papers on South American Indians*, no. 7. ed. J. Shapiro. Bennington, VT: Bennington College, pp. 25–33.

1984b   "Los Misioneros y las Fronteras." *America Indígena* 44(1): 183–90.

1984c   "Los Arawacos del Río Negro." In *Sistemas Ambientales Venezolanos, Region Guayana*. Vol. 1: *T. F. Amazonas*. Caracas: Ministerio de Ambiente y Recursos Naturales Renovables, pp. 290–307.

1984d   "Social Equality and Ritual Hierarchy: The Arawakan Wakuénai of Venezuela." *American Ethnologist* 11:528–44.

1985   "Myth, Spirit-Naming, and the Art of Microtonal Rising: Childbirth Rituals of the Arawakan Wakuénai." *Latin American Music Review* 6(1): 1–30.

Hohlfeldt, Antonio, and Assis Hoffmann

1982   *O Gravador do Juruna*. Serie Depoimentos 2. Porto Alegre: Mercado Aberto Editora e Propaganda Ltda.

Hugh-Jones, Stephen

1985   "Review of *The Cosmic Zygote* by Peter G. Roe." *Archaeoastronomy* 7:154–59.

Hyslop, John

1976   "An Archaeological Investigation of the Lupaca Kingdom and Its Origins." Ph.D. dissertation, Columbia University.

Illius, Bruno

1982   "Some Observations on Shipibo-Conibo Shamanism." Paper presented at the 44th International Congress of Americanists, Manchester.

Isbell, Billie Jean

1978   *To Defend Ourselves: Ecology and Ritual in an Andean Village*. Latin American Monographs 47. Austin: Institute of Latin American Studies, University of Texas.

1985   *To Defend Ourselves: Ecology and Ritual in an Andean Village*, 2d ed. Prospect Heights, Ill.: Waveland Press.

Jackson, Jean E.

1974   "Language Identity of the Colombia Vaupés Indians." In *Explorations in the Ethnography of Speaking*. ed. R. Bauman and J. Sherzer. New York: Cambridge University Press, pp. 50–64.

1983   *The Fish People: Linguistic Exogamy and Tukanoan Identity in Northwest Amazonia*. New York: Cambridge University Press.

Jaskol, Lisa

1983   " 'Ideology' in *The Devil and Commodity Fetishism* in South America." Paper presented at the meeting of the Central States Anthropological Society, Cleveland.

Jay, Martin

1984   *Adorno*. Cambridge: Harvard University Press.

Jouanen, Jose

1941   *Historia de la Compania de Jesus en la Antigua Provincia de Quito*. Vol. 1: *1570–1696*. Quito: Editorial Ecuatoriana.

1943   *Historia de la Compania de Jesus en la Antigua Provincia de Quito*. Vol. 2: *1696–1773*. Quito: Editorial Ecuatoriana.

Journet, Nicolas
1981 "Los Curripaco del Río Isana: Economia y Sociedad." *Revista Colombiana de Antropología* 23:127–82.

Kaplan, Joanne
1981 "Amazonian Anthropology." *Journal of Latin American Studies* 13(1): 151–64.

Karp, Ivan
1986 "Agency and Social Theory: A Review of Anthony Giddens." *American Ethnologist* 13:131–37.

Karp, Ivan, and Martha Kendall
1981 "Reflexivity in Fieldwork." In *Concepts in the Human Sciences.* ed. P. Secord. Oxford: Blackwell, pp. 249–73.

Kensinger, Kenneth
1975 "Studying the Cashinahua." In *The Cashinahua of Eastern Peru,* ed. Jane P. Dwyer. Bristol, R.I.: Haffenreffer Museum of Anthropology, Brown University, pp. 9–85.

King, Georgiana Goddard
1980 *The Way of St. James.* New York: AMS Press.

Koch-Gruenberg, Theodor
1909 *Zwei Jahre unter den Indianern: Reisen in Nordwest Brasilien, 1903–5.* Stuttgart: Strecker and Shroder.

Lanning, Edward P.
1967 *Peru before the Incas.* Englewood Cliffs, NJ: Prentice-Hall.

Larson, Brooke
1983 "Shifting Views of Colonialism and Resistance." *Radical History Review* 27:3–20.

Lathrap, Donald W.
1970 *The Upper Amazon.* Ancient Peoples and Places series, 70. New York: Praeger.
1973 "The Antiquity and Importance of Long Distance Trade Relationships in the Moist Tropics of Pre-Columbian South America." *World Archaeology* 5:170–86.
1976 "Shipibo Tourist Art." In *Ethnic and Tourist Arts: Cultural Expressions from the Fourth World.* ed. Nelson H. Graburn. Berkeley: University of California Press, pp. 197–207.

Lathrap, Donald W., Angelika Gebhart-Sayer, and Ann M. Mester
1985 "The Roots of the Shipibo Art Style: Three Waves on Imariacocha or There Were 'Incas' before the Incas." *Journal of Latin American Lore* 11(1): 31–119.

Lavallee, Danielle
1973 "Estructura y Organización del Habitat en los Andes Centrales durante el Período Intermedio Tardio." *Revista del Museo Nacional* 39:91–116.

Lea, Vanessa
n.d. "Txukarramae Myths." Unpublished ms.

Leach, Edmund
1954 *Political Systems of Highland Burma.* Boston: Beacon Press.

1966 "The Legitimacy of Solomon." *European Journal of Sociology* 7:58–101.

1969 *Genesis as Myth.* London: Grossman, Cape Editions.

1982 *Social Anthropology.* New York: Oxford University Press.

Lears, T. J. Jackson

1985 "The Concept of Cultural Hegemony: Problems and Possibilities." *American Historical Review* 90:567–93.

Lederman, Rena

1986 "Changing Times in Mendi: Notes towards Writing Highland New Guinea History." *Ethnohistory* 33(1): 1–30.

Lefebvre, Henri

1977 "Ideology and the Sociology of Knowledge." In *Symbolic Anthropology.* ed. J. Dolgin, D. Kemnitzer, and D. Schneider. New York: Columbia University Press, pp. 254–69.

Lévi-Strauss, Claude

1955 "The Structural Study of Myth." In *Myth: A Symposium.* ed. T. Sebeok. Bloomington: Indiana University Press, pp. 81–106.

1963a *Structural Anthropology,* 1. trans. Claire Jacobson and Brooke Grundfest Schoepf. New York: Basic Books.

1963b *Totemism.* trans. R. Needham. Boston: Beacon Press.

1964 *Le Cru et le Cuit.* Paris: Plon.

1966a *Du Miel aux Cendres.* Paris: Plon.

1966b *The Savage Mind.* Chicago: University of Chicago Press.

1968 *L'origine de Manieres de Table.* Paris: Plon.

1969 *The Raw and the Cooked.* trans. John and Doreen Weightman. Introduction to a Science of Mythology, 1. New York: Harper and Row.

1971 *L'Homme Nu.* Paris: Plon.

1973a *From Honey to Ashes.* trans. John and Doreen Weightman. New York: Harper and Row.

1973b *Tristes Tropiques.* New York: Atheneum. (NW)

1978 *The Origin of Table Manners.* trans. John and Doreen Weightman. Introduction to a Science of Mythology, 3. New York: Harper & Row.

1979 *Myth and Meaning.* New York: Schocken Books.

1981 *The Naked Man.* trans. John and Doreen Weightman. Introduction to a Science of Mythology, 4. New York: Harper & Row.

Levy, Carlos Daniel

n.d. "Histrionics in Culture." Unpublished ms.

Lifton, Robert Jay

1967 *Death in Life: Survivors of Hiroshima.* New York: Random House.

Lizot, Jacques

1985 *Tales of the Yanomami: Daily Life in the Venezuelan Forest.* New York: Cambridge University Press. (PR,

Lopes de Sousa, Marechal Boanerges

1959 *Do Rio Negro ao Orenoco.* Rio de Janeiro: Ministerio da Agricultura, Conselho Nacional de Proteção aos Indios.

MacCormack, Sabine
  1985a "The Heart Has Its Reasons: Predicaments of Missionary Christianity in Early Colonial Peru." *Hispanic American Historical Review* 65(3): 443–66.
  1985b "Pachakuti: Miracle and Last Judgement." Paper presented at the meeting of the American Society for Ethnohistory, Chicago.
Magalli, Jose Maria
  1890 *Collección de Cartas sobre las Misiones Dominicanas del Oriente.* 2d ed. Quito: Imprenta de Juan Pablo Sanz.
Magaña, Edmundo
  1982 "Note on Ethnoanthropological Notions of the Guiana Indians." *Antropológica* 24:215–33.
Malinowski, Bronislaw
  1955a *Magic, Science and Religion.* New York: Doubleday.
  1955b "Myth in Primitive Psychology." In *Magic, Science and Religion.* New York: Doubleday, pp. 93–148.
Martinez, Gabriel
  1976 "El Sistema de los Uywiris en Isluga." In *Homenaje al Dr. Gustavo Le Paige.* Antofagasta, Chile: Universidad del Norte, pp. 255–327.
  1983 "Toponimos de Chuani." *Antropológica* 1:51–86.
Marx, Karl
  1977 *Capital,* vol. 1. trans. B. Fowkes. New York: Vintage Books.
Maxwell, Nicole
  1975 *Witch Doctor's Apprentice.* New York: Collier.
Maybury-Lewis, David
  1969 "Review of *Mythologiques: Du Miel aux Cendres,* by Claude Lévi-Strauss." *American Anthropologist* 71:114–21.
Medick, Hans
  1987 " 'Missionaries in the Row Boat'? Ethnological Ways of Knowing as a Challenge to Social History." *Comparative Studies in Society and History* 29:76–98.
Miller, Joseph
  1976 *Kings and Kinship.* Oxford: Clarendon Press.
  1980 (ed.) *The African Past Speaks.* Hamden, CT: Archon.
Molina, Cristobal de
  1943 "Relación de las Fabulas y Ritos de los Incas." In *Los Pequeños Grandes Libros de Historia Americana.* ed. Francisco Loayza. Serie 1, vol. 4. Lima: D. Miranda, pp. 1–253 (essay first published in 1573).
Moore, Sally F.
  1976 "Epilogue." In *Symbol and Politics in Communal Ideology.* ed. Sally F. Moore and B. Meyerhoff. Ithaca: Cornell University Press, pp. 230–38.
Mukarovsky, Jan
  1964 "Standard Language and Poetic Language." In *A Prague School Reader on Esthetics, Literary Structure and Style.* ed. and trans. Paul L. Garvin. Washington, DC: Georgetown University Press, pp. 17–30.

Muller, Thomas, and Helga Muller
1984 "Mito de Inkarri-Qollari." *Allpanchis* 23:125–44.

Murphy, Robert
1960 *Headhunter's Heritage.* Berkeley: University of California Press.
1971 *The Dialectics of Social Life.* New York: Basic Books.

Murphy, Yolanda, and Robert Murphy
1974 *Women of the Forest.* New York: Columbia University Press.

Murra, John V.
1964 "Una Apreciación Etnológica de la Visita." In *Visita Hecha a la Provincia de Chucuito . . . en el Año 1567.* ed. Garci Diez de San Miguel. Lima: Casa de la Cultura, pp. 421–42.
1967 "La Visita de los Chupachu como Fuente Etnologica." In *Visita de la provincia de Leon de Huanuco (1562),* vol. 1. ed. Inigo Ortiz de Zuniga. Huanuco, Peru: Universidad Hermillo Valdizan, pp. 383–406.
1968 "An Aymara Kingdom in 1567." *Ethnohistory* 14:115–51.
1978 *La Organización Económica del Estado Inca.* Mexico, DF: Siglo XXI.
1984 "Andean Societies before 1532." In *The Cambridge History of Latin America.* Vol. 1: *Colonial Latin America.* ed. Leslie Bethell. Cambridge: Cambridge University Press, pp. 59–90.

Myer, Norman
1984 *The Primary Source: Tropical Forests and Our Future.* New York: W. W. Norton.

Myers, Thomas P.
1974 "Spanish Contacts and Social Change on the Ucayali River, Peru." *Ethnohistory* 21:135–57.

Nash, June
1979 *We Eat the Mines and the Mines Eat Us.* New York: Columbia University Press.

Newton-Smith, William H.
1980 *The Structure of Time.* London: Routledge and Kegan Paul.

Nimuendajú, Curt
1946 *The Eastern Timbira.* Berkeley: University of California Press.
1952 "Os Gorotire. Relatorio Apresentado ao Serviço de Proteção aos Indios, em 18 Abril de 1940." *Revista do Museu Paulista* (n.s.) 6: 427–53.
n.d. "Notes on the Pau d'Arco Band of the Northern Kayapó." trans. Robert H. Lowie. Unpublished ms.

Oliveira, Adelia E., and Eduardo Galvão
1973 "A Situação Atual dos Baniwa (Alto Rio Negro), 1971." In *O Museu Goeldi no Ano do Sesquicentario.* Publicações Avulsas, 20. Belem, Para, Brazil: Museu Emilio Goeldi, pp. 27–40.

Ong, Walter
1982 *Orality and Literacy: The Technologizing of the Word.* London: Methuen.

Ordem dos Advogados do Brasil
1981 *O Indio e o Direito.* Rio de Janeiro: OAB.

Ortiz Rescaniere, Alexandro
1973 *De Adaneva a Inkarri: Una Visión Indígena del Peru.* Lima: Retablo de Papel.

Ortner, Sherry
  1984   "Theory in Anthropology since the 1960s." *Comparative Studies in Society and History* 26(1): 126–66.
Ossio, Juan
  1973a (ed.) *Ideología Mesiánica del Mundo Andino.* Lima: Ignacio Prado Pastor.
  1973b "Guaman Poma: Nueva Corónica o Carta al Rey: Un Intento de Aproximación a las Categorias del Pensamiento del Mundo Andino." In *Ideología Mesiánica del Mundo Andino.* ed. J. Ossio. Lima: Ignacio Prado Pastor.
  1978   "Las Cinco Edades del Mundo segun Felipe Guaman Poma de Ayala." *Revista de la Universidad Católica* 2: 43–58.
Pagden, Anthony
  1983   *The Fall of Natural Man.* Cambridge: Cambridge University Press.
Pease, Franklin
  1973   *El Dios Creador Andino.* Lima: Mosca Azul.
  1974   "Un Movimiento Mesianico, Huancavelica (1811)." *Revista del Museo Nacional* 40:221–52.
  1978   *Del Tawantinsuyu a la Historia del Peru.* Lima: Instituto de Estudios Peruanos.
Platt, Tristan
  1978   "Symetries en Miroir: Le Concept de Yanantin chez les Macha de Bolivie." *Annales E.S.C.* 33(5–6): 1091–1107.
  1983   "Identidad Andina y Conciencia Proletaria: Qhuyaruna y Ayllu en Norte de Potosí." *HISLA Revista Latinoamericana de Historia Economica y Social* (Lima) 2:47–73.
Pocock, J. G. A.
  1962   "The Origins of the Study of the Past: A Comparative Approach." *Comparative Studies in Society and History* 4:209–46.
Polo de Ondegardo, Juan
  1916   "Errores y supersticiones. . . . " In *Coleccion de Libros y Documentos Referentes a la Historia del Peru.* ed. H. Urteaga and C. A. Romero. Serie 1, no. 3. Lima: Sanmarti y Ca, pp. 1–44.
Porras, Pedro
  1979   "The Discovery in Rome of an Anonymous Document on the Quijo Indians of the Upper Napo, Eastern Ecuador." In *Peasants, Primitives and Proletariats: The Struggle for Identity in South America.* ed. D. Browman and R. Schwarz. New York and The Hague: Mouton, pp. 13–47.
Price, Richard
  1983a *First Time: The Historical Vision of an Afro-American People.* Baltimore: Johns Hopkins University Press.
  1983b *To Slay the Hydra: Dutch Colonial Perspectives on the Saramaka Wars.* Ann Arbor, MI: Karoma.

Radcliffe-Brown, A. R.
1952   *Structure and Function in Primitive Society.* New York: Free Press.

Rappaport, Joanne
1985   "History, Myth, and the Dynamics of Territorial Maintenance in Tierradentro, Colombia." *American Ethnologist* 12:27–45.

Rasnake, Roger
1982   "The Kurahkuna of Yura: Indigenous Authorities of Colonial Charcas and Contemporary Bolivia." Ph.D. dissertation, Cornell University.
1986   "Carnaval in Yura: Ritual Reflections on *Ayllu* and State Relations." *American Ethnologist* 13:662–80.

Raymond, J. Scott, Warren R. DeBoer, and Peter G. Roe
1975   *Cumancaya: A Peruvian Ceramic Tradition.* Occasional Papers, 2. Calgary, Canada: Department of Archaeology, University of Calgary.

Reeve, Mary-Elizabeth
1985   "Identity as Process: The Meaning of Runapura for Quichua Speakers of the Curaray River, Eastern Ecuador." Ph.D. dissertation, University of Illinois at Urbana-Champaign.

Ribeiro, Darcy
1970   *Os Indios e a Civilização.* Rio de Janeiro: Civilização Brasileira.

Ricoeur, Paul
1978   *O Conflito das Interpretações.* Rio de Janeiro: Imago.

Roe, Peter G.
1973   "Cumancaya: Archaeological Excavations and Ethnographic Analogy in the Peruvian Montana." Ph.D. dissertation, University of Illinois at Urbana-Champaign.
1976   "Archaism, Form and Decoration: An Ethnographic and Archaeological Case Study from the Peruvian Montana." *Ñawpa Pacha* 14:73–94, plates 26–29.
1980   "Art and Residence among the Shipibo Indians of Peru: A Study in Microacculturation." *American Anthropologist* 82:42–71.
1982a *The Cosmic Zygote: Cosmology in the Amazon Basin.* New Brunswick: Rutgers University Press.
1982b "Ethnoaesthetics and Design Grammars: Shipibo Perceptions of Cognate Styles." Paper presented at the 81st Annual Meeting of the American Anthropological Association, Washington, DC.
1983a "Mythic Substitution and the Stars: Aspects of Shipibo and Quechua Ethnoastronomy Compared." Paper presented at the 1st International Conference on Ethnoastronomy, Washington, DC.
1983b "The Effect of Age and Sex of Narrator on Shipibo Mythic Imagery." Paper presented at the 1st Annual Meeting of the Latin American Indian Literatures Association, Pittsburgh.
1984   "Pano Huetsa Nete: A Shipibo Version of the Canoe Voyage of the Sun and the Moon." Paper presented at the 2d Annual Meeting of the Latin American Indian Literatures Association, Washington, D.C.

Roe, Peter G., and Peter E. Siegel
    1982 "The Life History of a Shipibo Compound: Ethnoarchaeology in the Peruvian Montaña." *Archaeology and Anthropology* 5(1, 2):94–118.

Rosaldo, Renato
    1980 *Ilongot Headhunting, 1883–1974: A Study in Society and History.* Stanford: Stanford University Press.

Rostworowski de Diez Canseco, Maria
    1977 *Etnia y sociedad: Ensayos sobre la Costa Central Pre-Hispanica.* Lima: Instituto de Estudios Peruanos.
    1978 *Senores Indígenas de Lima y Canta.* Lima: Instituto de Estudios Peruanos.

Rowe, Ann P.
    1977 *Warp Patterned Weaves of the Andes.* Washington, D.C.: Textile Museum.

Royce, Anya P.
    1982 *Ethnic Identity: Strategies and Diversity.* Bloomington: Indiana University Press.

Sahlins, Marshall
    1976 *Culture and Practical Reason.* Chicago: University of Chicago Press.
    1981 *Historical Metaphors and Mythical Realties.* Ann Arbor: University of Michigan Press.
    1983 "Other Times, Other Customs: The Anthropology of History." *American Anthropologist* 85:517–44.
    1985 *Islands of History.* Chicago: University of Chicago Press.

Said, Edward
    1979 *Orientalism.* New York: Vintage Books.

Salomon, Frank
    1981 "Killing the Yumbo." In *Cultural Transformations and Ethnicity in Modern Ecuador.* ed. Norman E. Whitten, Jr. Urbana: University of Illinois Press, pp. 162–208.
    1982 "Chronicles of the Impossible: Notes on Three Peruvian Indigenous Historians." In *From Oral to Written Expression.* ed. R. Adorno. Syracuse, NY: Maxwell School, pp. 9–39.
    1986 *Native Lords of Quito in the Age of the Incas.* Cambridge: Cambridge University Press.

Sapir, J. David
    1977 "The Anatomy of Metaphor." In *The Social Use of Metaphor: Essays on the Anthropology of Rhetoric.* ed. J. David Sapir and J. Christopher Crocker. Philadelphia: University of Pennsylvania Press, pp. 3–32.

Sapir, J. David, and J. Christopher Crocker (eds.)
    1977 *The Social Use of Metaphor: Essays on the Anthropology of Rhetoric.* Philadelphia: University of Pennsylvania Press.

Schneider, Jane
    1978 "Peacocks and Penguins: The Political Economy of European Cloth and Colors." *American Ethnologist* 5:413–47.

Scott, James

1985 *Weapons of the Weak: Everyday Forms of Peasant Resistance.* New Haven: Yale University Press.

1986 "Everyday Forms of Peasant Resistance." *Journal of Peasant Studies* 13:5–35.

Siegel, Peter E., and Peter G. Roe

1986 "Shipibo Archaeo-ethnography: Site Formation Processes and Archaeological Interpretation." *World Archaeology* 18:96–115.

Silverblatt, Irene

1987 *Moon, Sun, and, Witches: Gender Ideologies and Class in Inca and Colonial Peru.* Princeton: Princeton University Press.

1988 "Imperial Dilemmas, the Politics of Kinship, and Inca Reconstructions of History." *Comparative Studies in Society and History* 30(1): 83–102.

Simson, Alfred

1886 *Travels in the Wilds of Ecuador and the Exploration of the Putumayo River.* London: Sampson, Low, Marston, Seale and Rivington.

Spalding, Karen

1970 "Social Climbers: Changing Patterns of Mobility among the Indians of Colonial Peru." *Hispanic American Historical Review* 50:645–54.

1973 "Kurakas and Commerce: A Chapter in the Evolution of Andean Society." *Hispanic American Historical Review* 54:581–99.

1984 *Huarochiri: An Andean Society under Inca and Spanish Rule.* Stanford: Stanford University Press.

Spiro, Melford

1986 "Cultural Relativism and the Future of Anthropology." *Cultural Anthropology* 1(3): 259–86.

Stastny, Francisco

1979 *Las Artes Populares del Perú.* Madrid: Ediciones Edubanco.

Stein, William

1961 *Hualcan: Life in the Highlands of Peru.* Ithaca: Cornell University Press.

Steinen, Karl von den

1886 *Durch Zentral-Brasilien.* Leipzig: F. A. Brockhaus.

1894 *Unter den Naturvolkern Zentral-Brasiliens.* Berlin: D. Reimer (Hoefer and Vohsen).

Stern, Steve J.

1982 *Peru's Indian Peoples and the Challenge of Spanish Conquest.* Madison: University of Wisconsin Press.

1983 "The Struggle for Solidarity: Class, Culture, and Community in Highland Indian America." *Radical History Review* 27:21–45.

Steward, Julian H.

1955 *Theory of Culture Change.* Urbana: University of Illinois Press.

Stutzman, Ronald

1981 "*El Mestizaje:* An All-Inclusive Ideology of Exclusion." In *Cultural Transformations and Ethnicity in Modern Ecuador.* ed. Norman E. Whitten, Jr. Urbana: University of Illinois Press, pp. 45–94.

Swartz, Marc, Victor Turner, and Arthur Tuden
   1966   "Introduction." In *Political Anthropology*. ed. M. Swartz, V. Turner, and A. Tuden. Chicago: Aldine, pp. 1–41.

Sweet, David G.
   1974   "A Rich Realm of Nature Destroyed: The Middle Amazon Valley, 1640–1750." Ph.D. dissertation, University of Wisconsin.

Tambiah, Stanley
   1985   *Culture, Thought, and Social Action: An Anthropological Perspective*. Cambridge: Harvard University Press.

Taussig, Michael
   1980a   *The Devil and Commodity Fetishism in South America*. Chapel Hill: University of North Carolina Press.
   1980b   "Folk Healing and the Structure of Conquest in the Southwest Colombian Andes." *Journal of Latin American Lore* 6:217–78.
   1984a   "Culture of Terror, Space of Death: Roger Casement's Putumayo Report and the Explanation of Torture." *Comparative Studies in Society and History* 26(3): 467–97.
   1984b   "History as Sorcery." *Representations* 7:87–109.
   1987   *Shamanism, Colonialism, and the Wild Man: A Study in Terror and Healing*. Chicago: University of Chicago Press.

Tavera Acosta, B.
   1927   *Río Negro: Reseña Etnografica, Historica y Geographica*. Maracay, Venezuela: Imprenta del Estado.

Taylor, Gerald
   1980a   *Rites et Traditions de Huarochiri*. Paris: L'Harmattan.
   1980b   "Supay." *Amerindia* (Paris) 5:47–63.

Tessman, Gunter
   1928   *Menschen ohne Gott: Ein Besuch bei den Indianern des Ucayali*. Veroffentlichung der Harvey-Bassler-Stiftung Volkerkunde, 1. Stuttgart: Verlag von Strecker und Schroder.

Thompson, Edward P.
   1974   "Patrician Society, Plebeian Culture." *Journal of Social History* 8:382–405.
   1978a   "Eighteenth-Century English Society: Class Struggle without Class?" *Social History* 3(1): 133–65.
   1978b   *The Poverty of Theory and Other Essays*. New York: Monthly Review Press.

Tschopik, Harry
   1948   "Aymara Texts: Lupaca Dialect." *International Journal of American Linguistics* 14(2): 107–14.
   1951   *The Aymara of Chucuito, Peru*. Anthropological Papers of the American Museum of Natural History, vol. 44, no. 2. New York.

Turner, Terence
   1969   "Oedipus: Time and Structure in Narrative Form." In *Forms of Symbolic Action*. ed. Robert Spencer. Seattle: University of Washington Press, pp. 26–68.

1977   "Transformation, Hierarchy, and Transcendence: A Reformulation of Van Gennep's Model of the Structure of Rites de Passage." In *Secular Ritual*. ed. Sally F. Moore and Barbara Meyerhoff. Assen: Van Gorcum, pp. 53–69.

1979   "The Gê and Bororo Societies as Dialectical Systems." In *Dialectical Societies*. ed. David Maybury-Lewis. Cambridge: Harvard University Press, pp. 147–78.

1983   "Moiety Systems, Social Space, and Political Structure in Central Brazil and the Andes." Paper presented at the 82nd Annual Meetings of the American Anthropological Association. Chicago.

1984   "Dual Opposition, Hierarchy and Value: Moiety Structure and Symbolic Polarity in Central Brazil and Elsewhere." In *Differences, Valeurs, Hierarchie: Textes Offerts a Louis Dumont et Reunis par Jean-Claude Galey*. ed. Jean-Claude Galey. Paris: Editions de l'Ecole des Hautes Etudes en Sciences Sociales, pp. 335–70.

1985   "Animal Symbolism, Totemism, and the Structure of Myth." In *Animal Myths and Metaphors in South America*. ed. Gary Urton. Salt Lake City: University of Utah Press, pp. 49–106.

1986   "Production, Exploitation, and Social Consciousness in the Peripheral Situation." *Social Analysis* 19:179–217.

n.d.   "The Fire of the Jaguar: Myth and Social Organization among the Northern Kayapó of Central Brazil." Unpublished ms.

Turner, Victor W.
1957   *Schism and Continuity in an African Society*. Manchester: Manchester University Press.

1974   *Dramas, Fields, and Metaphors: Symbolic Action in Human Society*. Ithaca: Cornell University Press.

Urban, Greg
1985   "The Semiotics of Two Speech Styles in Shokleng." In *Semiotic Mediation: Sociocultural and Psychological Perspectives*. ed. Elizabeth Mertz and Richard J. Parmentier. New York: Academic Press, pp. 311–29.

Urbano, Henrique
1980   "Dios Yaya, Dios Churi, Dios Espiritu." *Journal of Latin American Lore* 6:111–28.

1981a   "Del Sexo, Incesto y los Ancestros de Inkarri: Mito, Utopia e Historia en las Sociedades Andinas." *Allpanchis* 17/18:77–103.

1981b   *Wiracocha y Ayar: Heroes y Funciones en las Sociedades Andinas*. Cuzco: Centro de Estudios Rurales Andinos "Barolome de Las Casas."

Urioste, George L. (ed.)
1983   *Hijos de Pariya Qaqa: La Tradición Oral de Waru Chiri: Mitología, Ritual y Costumbres*. Syracuse, N.Y.: Maxwell School of Citizenship and Public Affairs.

Urton, Gary
1981   *At the Crossroads of the Earth and the Sky: An Andean Cosmology*. Austin: University of Texas Press.

Valderrama, F., and C. Escalante
1978 "Mitos y Leyendas de los Quechuas del Sur del Peru." *Antropología* (Lima) 2:125–35.

Valladares, Alvaro
1912 *Cartas sobre las Misiones Dominicanas en la Region Oriental del Ecuador.* Quito: Imprenta de Santo Domingo.

Vidal, Lux
1977 *Morte e Vida de uma Sociedade Indígena Brasileira: Os Kayapó-Xikrin do Río Cateté.* Sao Paulo: Editora Hucitec, Editora da Universidade de São Paulo.

Villas Boas, Orlando, and Claudio Villas Boas
1972 *Xingu: Os Indios, Seus Mitos.* Rio de Janeiro: Zahar.

Wachtel, Nathan
1971 *La Vision des Vaincus: Les Indiens du Perou devant la conquete espagnole, 1530–70.* Paris: Gallimard.
1973 *Sociedad e Ideología.* Lima: Instituto de Estudios Peruanos.
1977 *The Vision of the Vanquished.* New York: B & N Imports.
1978 "Hommes d'Eau: Le Probleme Uru (XVIe–XVIIe Siecle)." *Annales E.S.C.* 33(5–6): 1127–59.

Wagner, Catherine Allen
1978 "Coca, Chica and Trago: Private and Communal Rituals in a Quechua Community." Ph.D. dissertation, University of Illinois at Urbana-Champaign.

Wagner, Roy
1972 *Habu: The Innovation of Meaning in Daribi Religion.* Chicago: University of Chicago Press.
1975 *The Invention of Culture.* Chicago: University of Chicago Press.

Waisbard, Simone-Roger
1958–59 "Les Indiens Shamas de L'Ucayali et du Tamaya." *L'Ethnographie* (n.s.) 53:19–74.

Wallerstein, Emmanuel
1976 *The Modern World System.* New York: Academic Press.

Warren, Kay Barbara
1978 *The Symbolism of Subordination: Indian Identity in a Guatemalan Town.* Austin: University of Texas Press.
1985 "Creation Narratives and the Moral Order: Implications of Multiple Models in Highland Guatemala." In *Cosmogony and Ethical Order: New Studies in Comparative Ethics.* ed. Robin Lovin and Frank Reynolds. Chicago: University of Chicago Press, pp. 251–76.

Wasserstrom, Robert
1983 *Ethnic Relations in Central Chiapas, 1528–1975.* Berkeley: University of California Press.

Weber, Max
1964 *The Theory of Social and Economic Organization.* ed. and with an introduction by Talcott Parsons. New York: Free Press.

Weismantel, Mary
  1986   "Zumbagua Cooking: Structure, Discourse, and Practice." Ph.D. dis-
         sertation, University of Illinois at Urbana-Champaign.
Whitten, Dorothea
  1981   "Ancient Tradition in a Contemporary Context: Canelos Quichua
         Ceramics and Symbolism." In *Cultural Transformations and Ethnicity
         in Modern Ecuador.* ed. Norman E. Whitten, Jr. Urbana: University of
         Illinois Press, pp. 749–75.
Whitten, Dorothea, and Norman E. Whitten, Jr.
  1988   *From Myth to Creation: Art from Amazonian Ecuador.* Urbana: Uni-
         versity of Illinois Press.
Whitten, Norman E., Jr.
  1974   *Black Frontiersmen: Afro-Hispanic Culture from Ecuador and Colombia.*
         Prospect Heights, Ill.: Waveland Press.
  1976   *Sacha Runa: Ethnicity and Adaptation of Ecuadorian Jungle Quichua.*
         Urbana: University of Illinois Press.
  1978   "Ecological Imagery and Cultural Adaptability: The Canelos Quichua
         of Eastern Ecuador." *American Anthropologist* 80:836–59.
  1981   (ed.) *Cultural Transformations and Ethnicity in Modern Ecuador.*
         Urbana: University of Illinois Press.
  1984   "Introduction" to the special issue on "Social Structure and Social
         Relations." *American Ethnologist* 11:635–41.
  1985   *Sicuanga Runa: the Other Side of Development in Amazonian Ecuador.*
         Urbana: University of Illinois Press.
  1986   "Review of *First-Time: The Historical Vision of an Afro-American
         People* and *To Slay the Hydra: Dutch Colonial Perspectives on the
         Saramaka Wars,* by Richard Price." *Ethnohistory* 33:91–94.
Wilbert, Johannes
  1978   *The Folk Literature of the Gê Indians,* vol. 1. Los Angeles: University
         of California Press.
  1984   *The Folk Literature of the Gê Indians,* vol. 2. Los Angeles: University
         of California Press.
Williams, Raymond
  1977   *Marxism and Literature.* Oxford: Oxford University Press.
Wolf, Eric
  1982   *Europe and the People without History.* Berkeley: University of Califor-
         nia Press.
Worsley, Peter
  1984   *The Three Worlds: Culture and World Development.* Chicago: Univer-
         sity of Chicago Press.
Wright, Robin
  1981   "History and Religion of the Baniwa Peoples of the Upper Río Negro
         Valley." Ph.D. dissertation, Stanford University.
  1983   "Lucha y Supervivencia en el Noroeste de la Amazonia." *America
         Indígena* 43(3): 537–54.

Wright, Robin, and Jonathan Hill
 1986 "History, Ritual, and Myth: Nineteenth-Century Millenarian Movements in the Northwest Amazon." *Ethnohistory* 33: 31–54.

Wright, Robin, and Sally Swenson, eds.
 1982 *The New Tribes Mission in Amazonia.* ARC Bulletin 9. Boston: Anthropology Resource Center.

Zuidema, R. Tom
 1964 *The Ceque System of Cuzco: The Social Organization of the Capital of the Inca.* Leiden: E. J. Brill.
 1973 "Kinship and Ancestor Cult in Three Peruvian Communities: Hernandez Principe's Account of 1622." *Bulletin de l'Institut Français d'Etudes Andines* 2(1):16–33.
 1982 "Myth and History in Ancient Peru." In *The Logic of Culture: Advances in Structural Theory and Methods.* ed. Ino Rossi. South Hadley, Mass.: Bergin and Garvey, pp. 150–75.

Notes on Contributors

THOMAS ABERCROMBIE has a Ph.D. in anthropology from the University of Chicago (1986) and has taught at Cornell University and the Universidad Técnica de Oruro. His fieldwork in Bolivia has focused on kinship, religion, and ritual-political institutions, and he has researched the ethnohistory of the region in Bolivian, Argentine, and Spanish archives. More recent archival work concerns the transformation of Andean societies as well as colonial and republican forms of resistance, rebellion, and ethnogenesis. His current interests include expressions of class and ethnicity and the forging of a national identity in the dance-dramas of Oruro's Carnaval.

JANET CHERNELA is assistant professor of anthropology at Florida International University and has conducted field research with the Arapaço, Uanano, and other Tukanoan peoples of the Northwest Amazon region in Brazil. She specializes in the study of social, political, and economic organization, ritual discourse, and gender. Her publications include essays in *Cultural Survival Quarterly, Interciencia, Anuario Antropologico,* and *Journal of Latin American Lore.*

MARY DILLON has studied anthropology and linguistics at the University of Chicago and has carried out anthropological and linguistic fieldwork with the Aymara speakers of Ayllu K'ulta in Bolivia. During 1988 she taught ethnolinguistics at the Universidad Técnica de Oruro while investigating Aymara narrative and verbal art.

JONATHAN D. HILL is assistant professor of anthropology at Southern Illinois University at Carbondale and contributing editor for the *Handbook of Latin American Studies,* Library of Congress. He has conducted fieldwork among the Arawak-speaking peoples of southernmost Venezuela and specializes in interpretive anthropology, ethnohistory, ethnomusicology, and ecological anthropology. His publications include essays in *Ethnomusicology, American Ethnologist, America Indígena, Latin American Music Review, Ethnohistory,* and other journals and books.

EMILIENNE IRELAND has done research among the Waurá of Central Brazil, focusing upon political organization and customary law. Recent works include essays on political gossip and the uses of misinformation, covert leadership in witchcraft executions, and decision making in infanticide cases. She is currently completing her dissertation at Yale University and preparing works on the public display of silence in "informal" legal decisions and ritually sanctioned violence.

ALCIDA RAMOS, professor of anthropology at the Universidade de Brasília, has conducted fieldwork among the Yanoama of Brazil and specializes in the study of social organization, ethnic identity, and Indian-white relations. She is the author (with Bruce Albert and Kenneth Taylor) of The Yanoama of Brazil, Hierarquia e Simbiose: Relações Intertribais no Brasil, and Sociedades Indígenas, and has published in American Ethnologist, Ethnology, Cultural Anthropology, and other professional journals and books.

ROGER RASNAKE, staff anthropologist at the Program for Alternative Development of Cochabamba, in Bolivia, taught anthropology at Goucher College, in Baltimore, from 1983 to 1987. His principal fieldwork was carried out in Yura, Potosí, between 1977 and 1979, and he has returned to the area regularly since that time. He is the author of Domination and Cultural Resistance: Power and Authority among an Andean People and has published in American Ethnologist and other professional journals.

MARY-ELIZABETH REEVE, a research associate with the Department of Anthropology at the University of Illinois at Urbana-Champaign, is currently carrying out ethnohistorical research on the missionization of eastern Ecuador and northeast Peru through Mellon Foundation and American Philosophical Society grants. Her publications include Historia y Acción: El Concepto de Runapura para los Quichua del Río Curaray en la Amazonia Ecuatoriana.

PETER G. ROE, associate professor of anthropology at the University of Delaware and curator of the Centro de Investigaciones Indígenas de Puerto Rico y el Caribe, specializes in aesthetic anthropology, formal analysis, material cultural analysis, cosmology, and ethnoastronomy. His areal specialties include late prehistoric archaeology of the Peruvian montaña, early prehistoric archaeology of the Peruvian west coast and highlands as well as the Greater Antilles, and ethnology of the Shipibo of Peru and the Waiwai of Guayana. He is the author of The Cosmic Zygote: Cosmology in the Amazon Basin and has published essays in American Anthropologist, World Archaeology, and other professional journals.

IRENE SILVERBLATT, assistant professor of anthropology at the University of Connecticut, has conducted research in the Central Andes on culture, gender, and power. She is the author of Moon, Sun, and Witches: Gender Ideologies and Class in Inca and Colonial Peru and essays in Comparative Studies in Society and History, Feminist Anthropology, and other professional journals and books.

Terence Turner, professor of anthropology at the University of Chicago, has conducted field research among the Kayapó of southeast Pará, Brazil, over the past twenty-five years. He is author of *Os Kayapó do Suleste de Pará* and essays in *Social Analysis, Revista de Antropologia,* and numerous other journals and books. He has recently completed work on the film "Disappearing Worlds: The Kayapó," directed by Michael Beckham for Granada Television, Manchester, England.

Norman E. Whitten, Jr., professor of anthropology and Latin American Studies at the University of Illinois at Urbana-Champaign, has conducted research in coastal, Andean, and Amazonian Ecuador since 1961 on topics ranging from ecology, political economy, and ethnicity to art, cosmology, and ideology. He is author of *Sacha Runa: Ethnicity and Adaptation of Ecuadorian Jungle Quichua, Sicuanga Runa: The Other Side of Development in Amazonian Ecuador,* and (with Dorothea S. Whitten) *From Myth to Creation: Art from Amazonian Ecuador,* as well as the editor of *Cultural Transformations and Ethnicity in Modern Ecuador.* Past editor of the *American Ethnologist,* he has published in that journal, in the *American Anthropologist,* and in many others. He is currently working on subjects pertaining to cultural endurance in systems of radical change focusing on South and Central American peoples.

Robin M. Wright is professor of anthropology at the Universidade Estadual de Campinas, in Brazil, and staff member of the Ecumenical Center for Documentation and Information (CEDI), in São Paulo. He has conducted research in the Brazilian Northwest Amazon since 1976 on the history, religion, and current political situation of the upper Río Negro Indians. More broadly, his research interests include indigenous history, ethnography of lowland South American Indians, and anthropology and indigenous advocacy. He is the author (with Jose Barreiro) of *Native Peoples in Struggle* and has published in *Ethnohistory, Revista de Antropologia,* and *Annual Review of Anthropology.* He is currently organizing a volume on the Indians of the Northwest Amazon, as part of the CEDI project "Indigenous Peoples of Brazil."

Index

Affinal relations, mythic representations of, 85, 126–27, 201–3
Afterlife: beliefs in, 203; spirits of the dead, 62–64
Agency, 2, 6–7, 65. *See also* Consciousness, historical
Alcoholic beverages, 31, 43, 141, 209–10, 232
Ambivalence, toward whites and *mestizos*, 141, 159–60
Anaconda: as metaphor for ethnic resurgence, 11, 98; in myth, sexual intercourse with humans, 17n.5, 41–42, 44–45, 98, 206, 264; as mythic ancestor, 11–12, 36–37, 40–42, 265; as symbol of power, 17n.5, 98
Ancestral tombs, 57, 64. *See also* *Chullpas*
Anti-myth, 14, 202–4, 256–61, 265–69, 277–78
Arapaço, 10–12, 35–49, 262, 264–65
Autonomy, political: and *ayllu*, 150; narrative images of, 48
Aymara, 4–5, 50–77. *See also* K'ulta

Beidelman, Thomas O., 109
Betrayal, as theme of myth, 11, 45
Blacks, origins in myth, 129
Borders, international, 84–85

Canelos Quichua, 18–34, 286–92; historical origins and geographical location, 19; mythic and historical time-space, 8; rituals of resistance to external domination, 16n.3, 289–92
Cannibalism, mythic images of, 85, 127
Cattle ranchers, 209–11, 216–17
Center of world, in myth, 85
Ceramic vessels, 27, 106–7, 286–89

Chiefs, Andean, 178–83
Christian beliefs: adoption of, in Andes, 4–5, 13, 71–72, 150–51, 175–76, 184–92, 260–61; adoption of, in lowlands, 99–100. *See also* Missionaries; Mission settlements
Chthonic power, 70, 98, 142, 149–50, 283, 293–96
Chullpa: as Aymara social category, 55–65, 70–72, 74nn.5, 7, 10, 11, 12, 76n.29; in narratives, 56, 143
Chullpas, as tombs in Andes, 59, 76n.29. *See also* Afterlife
Church records, on marriage and birth patterns, 31
Civilization: and adoption of urban lifestyle, 68; as cultural category, 29–30, 65; and domestication of animals, 57–58, 65
Classification, in ritual language, 88–89
Cold societies, critique of, 3–5, 79–80, 89–92, 102, 175, 195–98, 235–39
Colonization, by Inca, 122–23
Conquest, Inca, 178, 188
Conquest, Spanish: as extirpation of Andean religions, 66–68; narrative representations of, 7, 12–13, 55, 66–67, 124–25, 143–46
Consciousness, historical: analytic definitions of, 2, 6–7, 244; complementarity with mythic consciousness, 237, 251–53; major and minor levels of, 253–54; merging with mythic consciousness, 7–10; among Northern Kayapó, 210–13; among Old Testament Hebrews, 250–51; in pan-Indian movements, 229–30; rise of, in ancient Greece, 245–46, 249–50;